CREATIVE RESOURCES

FOR

Elementary Classrooms and School-Age Programs

CREATIVE RESOURCES

F O R

Elementary Classrooms and School-Age Programs

Ron Wheeler
The College of William and Mary

Delmar Publishers

an International Thomson Publishing company I(T)P®

Albany • Bonn • Boston • Cincinnati • Detroit • London • Madrid
Melbourne • Mexico City • New York • Pacific Grove • Paris • San Francisco
Singapore • Tokyo • Toronto • Washington

NOTICE TO THE READER

Cover Design: The Drawing Board

Delmar Staff
Publisher: William Brottmiller
Senior Editor: Jay Whitney
Associate Editor: Erin O'Connor Traylor
Production Editor: Marah Bellegarde
Editorial Assistant: Glenna Stanfield

COPYRIGHT © 1997
By Delmar Publishers
a division of International Thomson Publishing Inc.

I(T)P® The ITP logo is a trademark under license.

Printed in the United States of America

For more information, contact:

Delmar Publishers
3 Columbia Circle, Box 15015
Albany, New York 12212-5015

International Thomson Publishing Europe
Berkshire House
168-173 High Holborn
London, WC1V 7AA
England

Thomas Nelson Australia
102 Dodds Street
South Melbourne, 3205
Victoria, Australia

Nelson Canada
1120 Birchmount Road
Scarborough, Ontario
Canada, M1K 5G4

International Thomson Editores
Campos Eliseos 385, Piso 7
Col Polanco
11560 Mexico D F Mexico

International Thomson Publishing GmbH
Konigswinterer Strasse 418
53227 Bonn
Germany

International Thomson Publishing Asia
221 Henderson Road
#05-10 Henderson Building
Singapore 0315

International Thomson Publishing–Japan
Hirakawacho Kyowa Building, 3F
2-2-1 Hirakawacho
Chiyoda-ku, Tokyo 102
Japan

1 2 3 4 5 6 7 8 9 10 XXX 03 02 01 00 99 98 97

Library of Congress Cataloging-in-Publication Data

Wheeler, Ronald Charles.
    Creative resources for elementary classrooms and school-age programs / Ronald Wheeler.
      p. cm.
    ISBN 0-8273-7281-7
    1. Education, Elementary—United States—Curricula.
    2. Interdisciplinary approach in education—United States.
    3. Education, Elementary—Activity programs—United States.
  I. Title.
LB1570.W572 1997   96-35881
   372.19—dc20   CIP

Contents

Table of Contents by Subject

MOVEMENT

MUSIC

SCIENCE

Preface

Every Child Is Unique

Each child who enters school for the first time differs from every other child in knowledge of—and the ability to learn—scientific, mathematical, social, and language concepts. As a teacher, your job is not to reduce differences, but to help each child actualize his or her full learning potential. One barrier to learning in the curriculum is the artificial separation of subjects at the expense of wholeness. Another obstacle is the overemphasis of a few subjects at the expense of others. Nourishing further intellectual development requires integration of various content areas into an overall program.

The Thematic Approach

Research and firsthand experience suggest that learning can be enhanced by implementing an approach that includes the following elements:

- Interdisciplinary connections
- Student involvement
- Critical thinking

Theme-based learning is an excellent way to provide opportunities for your students to do all three of the above. As children explore high-interest themes, they will experience subject matter connections across the curriculum, establish concrete referents that make learning meaningful, and develop a common basis for oral and written communication.

Organization

This book contains instructional ideas and activities for fifty themes. Each of the fifty mini-units includes the following components: a "web," which displays critical attributes or characteristics of the theme; a list of theme goals, concepts, and key vocabulary; a parent letter; an instructional bulletin board; an introductory activity called "Linking Up"; activity suggestions from multiple content areas; and a list of theme-related book and software resources.

Developmental Guidelines

While the themes presented here were chosen because of their appeal for this age group and their popularity with elementary teachers, they are not the only ones—nor are they all necessarily the "best" ones—for your purposes. To achieve maximum success with theme-based instruction, consider the specific needs and interests of your students. Based upon your assessment of personal and developmental data, you may want to add, drop, and modify activities, or create entirely different thematic units. In determining the developmental appropriateness of themes and activities in this book, developmental psychologist Jean Piaget's ideas about how children learn can serve as a useful framework.

According to Piaget, knowledge acquisition is a process whereby each person constructs meaning for himself or herself through direct interaction with the immediate environment. Piaget formulated age-related stages of cognitive development through which children typically progress. Every child new to a field of knowledge, such as language arts, social studies, science, or mathematics, goes through developmental stages that begin with simple concrete actions and proceed to complex abstract operations. Consult the developmental chart on the inside covers for descriptions of behaviors at different stages for science, social studies, mathematics, and language arts. The chart provides guidelines for learning the fields of knowledge typically found in the elementary school curriculum.

Tips for Effective Theme-Based Learning

With fifty themes and over 800 activities, this book gives you a comprehensive guide for implementing theme-based learning. For example, the unit on "Media" includes many dynamic and exciting opportunities for children to experience the theme, such as the following: identifying the sections of a newspaper, using the newspaper, producing a class newspaper, conducting surveys, analyzing and designing media advertisements, compiling oral histories, creating comics, taking a field trip, measuring ad space, creating jingles, drawing posters, testing products, producing TV weather reports, finding information on the Internet, and using math in the media.

Yet, even with an abundance of activities, theme-based learning can falter in the absence of a supportive environment that makes the topics come alive. For the unit topics to be meaningful, they should connect to students' prior experiences, provide depth as well as breadth, affect emotions, excite the imagination, and allow children to experience success.

The "Linking Up" section that introduces each theme provides initial activities designed to make student-content connections. But to maximize involvement, make linkages between the children's lives and content at every opportunity. Students' "ownership" of particular themes can be enhanced by encouraging them to identify and investigate their own problems and questions related to the themes. Another very powerful way to grab students' attention, both emotionally and cognitively, is to incorporate good children's literature and visual media into the unit. To facilitate this, each of the book's fifty units concludes with a list of theme-related book and software resources. Since deep understanding is more important than superficial recall of facts, use this book selectively. To start out, choose a few themes that you know your students will enjoy. Then, research the topics thoroughly. The more interested and knowledgeable you are, the more enthusiastic and authoritative a facilitator of learning you will be. To further increase student motivation, let individuals make special contributions to the study of the theme that draw on their unique talents and skills.

Theme-based learning lends itself to authentic assessment. Use a variety of strategies to evaluate student progress, including collections of the students' work and visual records of their performance and projects (using still and video cameras). The assessment could include something as simple as a sketch done by a single child, or as complex as a videotape documenting the class's preparation and performance of William Shakespeare's *A Midsummer Night's Dream*.

To Summarize

To be effective, curriculum has to be tailored to meet the needs of every child. The thematic approach offers an exciting and rewarding way for children to experience the joy of personalized learning. By integrating content and connecting it to children's lives, you are taking a big step toward helping each student believe he or she can be successful.

Acknowledgements

Janine Kucik was especially helpful to the author in the preparation of this book.

Ron Wheeler

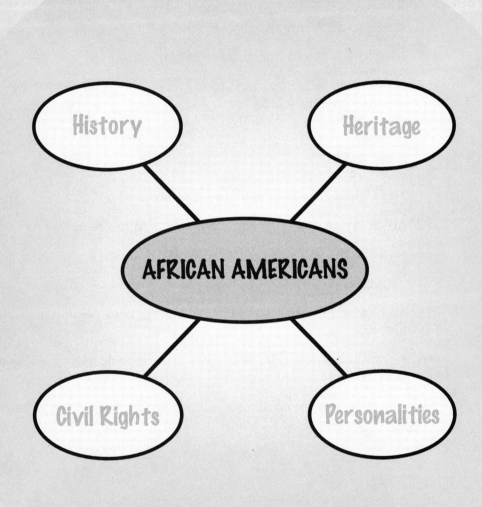

Theme Goals:

Students will:

1. learn about prominent African Americans from the local community.

2. locate important geographic features of Africa.

3. study selected African cultures.

4. examine the history of Africa's ancient black empires.

5. learn about the black experience in early American history.

6. celebrate an African American holiday.

7. study the life of Martin Luther King, Jr.

8. explore the influence of African Americans on different aspects of contemporary society.

Theme Concepts:

1. The United States is a multiracial society.

2. Africa is one of the largest land masses in the world.

3. Africa is the home of over 800 ethnic groups.

4. Africa's ancient black empires were rich and powerful.

5. African Americans have played an important role in American history.

6. Martin Luther King, Jr., and other civil rights leaders worked to overcome racial injustice.

7. African Americans continue to influence American society in many significant ways.

Vocabulary:

1. empire

2. plateau

3. civilization

4. fugitive

5. slavery

6. Kwanzaa

7. freedom rides

8. civil rights

Instructional Bulletin Board

The purpose of this bulletin board is to help students develop a historical perspective regarding some of the significant events in the African American experience. Students can match the event to the year it happened by hanging the event card on a pushpin located on the appropriate spot on the time line. Provide a covered answer key so students can check their answers. The event cards (each with a small hole, punched at the top center, for hanging) can be kept in a large envelope attached to the board. Print each of the events on a separate card. Have students draw pictures of the events and attach them to the appropriate point along the time line. (Note: To be meaningful to students, the events on the time line must receive in-depth treatment during the unit's implementation in the classroom.)

Event Cards for bulletin board: First blacks brought to American colonies (1619); Crispus Attucks killed in Boston Massacre (1770); Peter Salem fought in the Battle of Bunker Hill (1775); Nat Turner led slave revolt (1831); Frederick Douglass started abolitionist newspaper (1847); The 13th Amendment abolished slavery (1865); *Brown v. the Board of Education* (1954); Rosa Parks arrested for refusing to give up her seat on bus to white person (1955); Rev. Martin Luther King, Jr., gave his "I Have a Dream" speech to over 200,000 spectators at March on Washington (1963); Civil Rights Act passed (1964); General Colin Powell became first black Chairman of the Joint Chiefs of Staff (1989); and Carol Moseley-Braun became first black woman elected to U.S. Senate (1992).

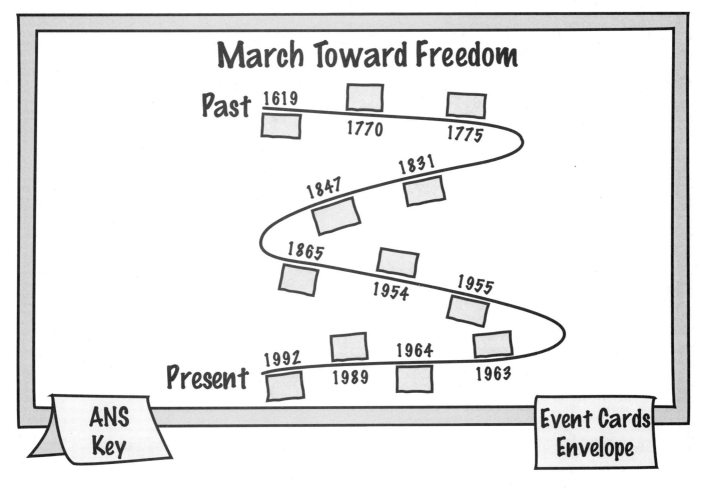

3

Parent Letter

Dear Parents:

We are beginning our study of America's African heritage. The United States is a multiracial society, and our future depends on the ability of all Americans, regardless of their ethnic backgrounds, to cooperate and work together. Studying the richness and diversity of our society should help give our children a greater appreciation for humanity.

In School:

We will engage in many interesting activities, including the following:

- Working with globes and maps to learn about Africa's land and people
- Studying a few of the over 800 African ethnic groups
- Making a diorama of an ancient African empire
- Dramatizing historical events in which African Americans played a significant role
- Investigating the contributions of African Americans past and present

At Home:

As a part of your child's normal development, she is forming increasingly sophisticated concepts about individuals and groups. To help your child better understand others, gently ask questions that encourage her/him to see the world from another person's perspective, such as "How do you think the other person might feel?" or "What would you do if you were that person?" If you would like to contribute in any way to our study of our African heritage, please contact us. We welcome your support.

Linking Up:

Unfortunately, many labels and stereotypes have been placed on ethnic minorities in the United States. In addition, when it comes to the subject of Africa, children's concepts of both the people and the country are often distorted and shallow. By studying the richness and diversity of our society's African American heritage, we can help children form accurate concepts and combat myths. Write the word "Africa" on the chalkboard. Ask students to tell you what comes to mind when they think about Africa and Africans (this activity will probably reveal students' misinformation and stereotypes). Ask students to think of ways to gain a more accurate image of Africa; then incorporate some of their better suggestions into the theme. Make two lists on the chalkboard: one column labeled "Things we think we know about Africa and Africans" and the other labeled "Things we need to learn about Africa and Africans." During the theme, you can encourage students to take the social perspective of others by asking questions such as "How do you think that person might feel?" or "What would you do if you were that person?"

Social Studies:

1. Local Connections

Invite prominent African Americans from the community into the classroom to discuss their experiences growing up in America. What were their aspirations? What obstacles did they have to overcome to achieve success? What careers did they eventually choose? Have your students formulate questions to ask the guest speakers. Remember to ask the speakers to keep in mind the age and maturity level of the audience as they prepare their remarks. Encourage speakers to bring pictures of the workplace and objects used in their jobs to share with the class.

2. The Geography of Africa

Brief Background. Africa is a tremendously diverse continent. Africa is the second largest continent and covers almost 21 percent of the world's total surface area.

Point out the location of Africa on a globe and world map. Have students note its size relative to other regions of the world. Provide students with individual maps of Africa. Let them trace Africa's relatively smooth coastline with their fingers. Then, have them trace the irregular coastline—consisting of numerous bays and peninsulas—of Europe with their fingers. Point out that although Africa is almost three times larger than Europe, Europe's coastline is more than twice as long as Africa's. Tell students that Africa is an immense plateau; a cross-section of Africa's landscape from coast to coast would look like an upside-down plate. Using their maps, students can trace with their fingers the following major rivers in Africa: Nile (the world's longest at 4,145 miles), Zaire, Niger, Zambezi, and Limpopo. To further familiarize your students with Africa's geography, you can:

- Encourage students to find Africa and places in Africa on the globe (Figure 1-1).
- Provide a three-dimensional relief map of Africa and let students *feel* physical features like mountains, valleys, plains, and plateaus.
- Let students construct salt and flour or papier-mache relief maps of Africa.
- Provide individual plastic-coated maps of Africa and let students use the compass rose, map scales, and map symbols to locate places (mountains, rivers, deserts, countries, cities, etc.) with felt-tip pens.
- Use the game format of "Twenty Questions" to encourage students' application of mapping skills. For example, you might say, "I'm thinking of a river in Africa." Students then ask questions, which can be answered by "yes" or "no," as they try to locate and name the river on their maps.

3. African Diversity

Brief Background. The African heritage of black Americans is rich and varied. Africa is the home of over 800 different ethnic groups, each with its own language and cultural traditions. The groups include the Egyptian, Berber, and Arab of northern Africa; the Asanti, Yoruba, and Hausa of eastern Africa; the Ethiopian, Massi, and Kikuyu of western Africa; the Pygmy, Tusi, and Hutu of central Africa; and the Bushman, Zulu, and Bergdama of southern Africa.

Assign students the task of gathering information about one of these groups. To stimulate interest in these groups' lifestyles, show students examples (using illustrations found in books and

Africa

FIGURE 1-1

other resources in the school and community library) of African art, architecture, food, clothing, sports, and customs. Gather an assortment of children's books on Africa and display them in a special area of the classroom that has been decorated with African maps and pictures (include brochures and posters donated by travel agencies). Place some comfortable chairs nearby and invite students to browse and read.

4. Ancient Civilizations

Brief Background. Africa is the home of some of the world's earliest civilizations. For thou-

sands of years, Egypt was one of the most powerful and advanced civilizations in the ancient world. Black people occupied important positions in the land of the Pharaohs. One of them, a Nubian who called himself Ra Nahesi, even claimed rights to the throne of Egypt. Three great ancient black civilizations in Africa were the Empire of Ghana (c.1000), the Empire of Mali (c. 1350), and the Songhay Empire (c. 1520). The Ghanaians ruled much of western Africa. They farmed, mined gold, and were among the first people to smelt iron ore. Their iron weapons helped them conquer other groups and expand their empire.

Show students pictures of ancient African artifacts found in oversized museum books. Read to your students some accounts of these early African civilizations and encourage them to bring up any questions they might have. After students have been given sufficient background information, they can construct a miniature model or diorama of the ancient empire (Figure 1-2).

5. Slavery

Brief Background. European colonization and exploitation of Africa began in the 1400s (and lasted until the 1960s, when most African colonies had gained their independence). The Portuguese came first in the late 1400s, and other European nations arrived shortly thereafter. They came to Africa is search of gold and slaves. There is evidence that some black slaves traveled with Columbus on his first epic voyage of discovery in 1492. Hundreds of African slaves accompanied Spanish expeditions to the Americas. During the search for the fabled "Seven Cities of Gold," a black slave named Estavancio led Spanish explorers to what is now Arizona. Estavancio is still remembered in Indian legends as the black "Mexican." It is esti-

mated that over 10 million Africans were taken to the Americas and forced into slavery.

The life of a slave was never good, and it was often harsh and cruel. To give students a deeper sense of compassion for the plight of slaves, read aloud selections from the following books: *The Captive*, a novel by Joyce Hansen (Scholastic, 1994), that chronicles the life of an Asanti boy who is brought to America in boundage and eventually gains his freedom; *A Picture Book of Sojourner Truth*, a biography by David A. Alder (Holiday House, 1994) of a woman born into slavery who goes on to fight injustice; and *Our Song, Our Toil: The Story of American Slavery as Told by Slaves*, edited by Michele Stepto (Ticknor & Fields, 1994). Ask students to talk about how they might think and feel if they had to do the folowing:

- Work from dawn to dusk in the fields.
- Go barefoot in cold weather.
- Sleep on dirt floors.
- Be separated permanently from family and friends.
- Suffer whippings and beatings.
- Be sold like an animal.
- Go without schooling and an education.

Ancient City of Timbuktu (Mali)

FIGURE 1-2

6. Significant Historical Happenings

As students learn about the black experience in early American history, they might want to recreate some of the events that involved blacks in significant ways. Events students can act out include:

- Crispus Attucks' role in the Boston Massacre. In 1770, Crispus Attucks and several other colonists were shot when they challenged the authority of British troops. The event helped ignite the movement for independence.
- The Battle of Bunker Hill. Another black hero of the fight for independence was Peter Salem, who fought gallantly at the Battle of Bunker Hill.
- Harriet Tubman's role in the underground railroad and Civil War. This brave black woman risked her life to go south and lead slaves north to freedom. During the Civil War, she served both as a nurse and spy for the Union.
- The life of Frederick A. Douglass. Douglass was a fugitive slave who escaped to New England. He spent much of his life traveling around the North denouncing slavery. Douglass endured the contempt of many Northerners and was once beaten severely by a mob for his views, but he refused to stop speaking out until slavery was eliminated.

7. An African American Celebration

Introduce students to *Kwanzaa*, an African American holiday that begins on December 26 and lasts seven days. *Kwanzaa* (KWAHN zuh) means "first fruits" in Swahili. Based on a traditional African harvest festival, Kwanzaa devotes each day to one of the following seven principles of black culture: *Umoja* (unity), *Kujichhagulia* (self-determination), *Ujima* (collective work and responsibility), *Ujamaa* (cooperative economics), *Nia* (purpose), *Kuumba* (creativity), and *Imani* (faith). For background on this festival, read aloud selections from *Kwanzaa: A Family Affair* by Mildred Pitts Walter (Lothrop, 1995). For recipes for preparing a Kwanzaa feast, consult *Kwanzaa Karamu: Cooking and Crafts for a Kwanzaa Feast* by April A. Brady (Carolrhoda, 1995). An important Kwanzaa ceremony is the lighting of seven candles (each candle stands for one of the seven principles, and one candle is lighted each day). To construct a *Kinara*, or candle stand, you'll need to mark off and saw a length of 2-by 4-inch wood into four pieces 13, 10, 7, and 4 inches long. Center the 10-inch piece over the 13-inch piece and nail. Then center and nail the 7- and 4-inch pieces. Nail down bottle caps in which to insert the candles as shown. Place three green candles on one side of the kinara, and three red candles on the other side. Place a black candle at the top of the kinara (Figure 1-3).

8. Rev. Martin Luther King, Jr., and Other Civil Rights Champions

Read aloud to your students selections from one of the many Martin Luther King, Jr., biographies written for children, such as *Martin Luther King* by Rosemary L. Bray (Greenwillow, 1995). During the reading, pause at appropriate points to check for understanding and to encourage students to ask their own questions about him. To help students visualize and remember King's life, you might want to dramatize his prominent role in the black boycott of Montgomery's (AL) buses, the marches and freedom rides, or the March on Washington in 1963. At the March on Washington, King gave one of his most stirring and eloquent speeches to a throng of over 200,000 civil rights demonstrators in front of the Lincoln Memorial. Encourage students to memorize and recite the famous address, which is presented below.

When we let freedom ring, when we let it ring from every village and every hamlet, from every state and every city, we will be able to speed up that day when all of God's children, black men and white men, Jews and Gentiles, Protestants and Catholics, will be able to join hands and sing in the words of the old Negro spiritual, "Free at last! Free at last! Thank God Almighty, we are free at last!"

In addition to Rev. Martin Luther King, Jr., some other civil rights leaders whom students can investigate include Ralph Abernathy, W.E.B. Du Bois, Thurgood Marshall, Jesse Jackson, Malcom X, Rosa Parks, A. Philip Randolph, Bayard Rustin, Mary C. Terrell, and Roy Wilkins.

FIGURE 1-3

Kinara

Language Arts:

1. African Storytellers

The storyteller was one of the most important people in an African village. In West Africa, villagers loved to sit in a circle around the storyteller and listen to the adventures of one particularly mischievous animal—Spider. Your students will also enjoy the many Spider folk tales. To find out how Spider got a thin waist and a bald head, why it lives in ceilings and dark corners, and how the world got wisdom, read to the children *The Adventures of Spider* by Joyce Cooper Arkhurst (Little, Brown and Co., 1964). After the children have listened to these stories, encourage them to make up and illustrate their own tales about Spider.

2. Honored Guest

Tell students to imagine that they can invite any African American past or present, to visit their school. Have them write or dictate a letter of invitation in which they describe what they most admire about him or her.

Math:

1. Population Percentages

Find out what part of the United States population is African American (use fraction or decimals).

2. Pie Graphs

Make pie graphs showing the percentage represented by African Americans in the total United States population.

3. Recipes for Maps

Have students follow this recipe for making salt and flour three-dimensional relief maps of Africa.

3 cups flour
3 cups salt
3 tablespoons alum
Use a spoon to combine the three ingredients and slowly add water until the mixture thickens. Continue mixing by hand until it has the feel of clay.

Science:

1. Contributions to Science

Brief Background. Among the many African Americans who made significant contributions to science, the first was Benjamin Banneker. He was an inventor, mathematician, astronomer, and essayist. He is credited with making the first clock ever made in America. Besides Banneker, other important black scientists include George Washington Carver, who created hundreds of products from soybeans, peanuts, and the sweet potato; Charles Drew, who did pioneering work in blood plasma research; Theodore Lawless, who was one of the world's leading skin specialists; and Daniel Hale Williams, who performed the world's first successful open-heart operation.

Have interested students make drawings that illustrate the accomplishments of famous black scientists. The illustrators can display their drawings and describe them to the class.

Music:

1. Musical Influences

The history of black music takes us from spirituals to ragtime, from blues to jazz, and from rock to rap. To introduce students to the rich variety of music influenced by Africans and African Americans, bring some to class for the children to sample. African songs by Ladysmith Black Mambazo and reggae songs from the Caribbean are available in most community libraries and music stores.

Current Events:

1. Famous African Americans Today

Give students a list of prominent contemporary African Americans, and let each student select one of them to study in depth. The list can in-

Dashiki

FIGURE 1-4

clude political leaders, athletes and sports figures, civil rights leaders, educators and scholars, musicians and singers, entertainers, military figures, scientists, and writers. Encourage them to read (or have read to them) a biography or article about the person.

Art:

1. African Attire

Make paper outlines of African dashikis (shirts) to decorate. Each child will need a 3-foot square of white paper. Cut the paper so that it resembles the pattern shown. To give students ideas about authentic designs, show them pictures of African dashikis found in library books and other sources. After students paint the designs, display the dashikis on the wall (Figure 1-4).

Books:

1. Paulson, Timothy. (1994). *Days of Sorrow, Years of Glory, 1831–1850: From the Nat Turner Revolt to the Fugitive Slave Law*. New York: Chelsea House. Intermediate, Advanced.

2. Weisbrot, Robert. (1994). *Marching Toward Freedom, 1957–1965: From the Founding of the Southern Christian Leadership Conference to the Assassination of Malcom X*. New York: Chelsea House. Intermediate, Advanced.

3. Collier, James & Collier, Christopher. (1994). *With Every Drop of Blood*. New York: Delacorte Press. Intermediate, Advanced.

4. Pinkey, Andrea Davis. (1994). *Dear Benjamin Banneker*. San Diego: Harcourt Brace & Co. Primary, Intermediate.

5. Young, Richard, & Dockrey, Judy. (1994). *African American Folktales for Young Readers: Including Favorite Stories from African and African American Storytellers*. New York: Dutton Children's Books. Intermediate, Advanced.

6. Dorothy, Strickland, & Strickland, Michael. (1994). *Families: Poems Celebrating the African American Experience*. Honesdale, PA: Boyds Mill Press. Primary, Intermediate.

7. Bray, Rosemary L. (1995). *Martin Luther King*. New York: Greenwillow. Intermediate, Advanced.

8. Adoff, Arnold. (1994). *My Black Me: A Beginning Book of Black Poetry*. New York: Dutton Children's Books. Advanced.

9. Davol, Marguerite. (1993). *Black, White, Just Right!* Morton Grove, IL: Whitman, Albert & Co. Primary.

10. Young, Ronder Thomas. (1993). *Learning by Heart*. New York: Puffin Books. Intermediate.

11. Walter, Mildred Pitts. (1995). *Kwanzaa: A Family Affair*. New York: Lothrop. Advanced.

12. Brady, April A. (1995). *Kwanzaa Karamu: Cooking and Crafts for a Kwanzaa Feast*. Minneapolis: Carolrhoda. Primary, Intermediate, Advanced.

13. Adler, David A. (1994). *A Picture Book of Sojourner Truth*. New York: Holiday House. Primary, Intermediate.

14. Hansen, Joyce. (1994). *The Captive*. New York: Scholastic. Advanced.

15. Stepto, Michele, ed. (1994). *Our Song, Our Toil: The Story of American Slavery as Told by Slaves*. New York: Ticknor & Fields. Advanced.

Software:

1. *Struggles for Justice* [Mac Laserdisc]. New York: Scholastic. Advanced

2. *Famous Black Americans* [VHS]. Chicago: Clearvue/eav. Intermediate, Advanced

3. *Africa Trail* [Mac Windows CD-ROM]. Minneapolis: MECC. Intermediate, Advanced

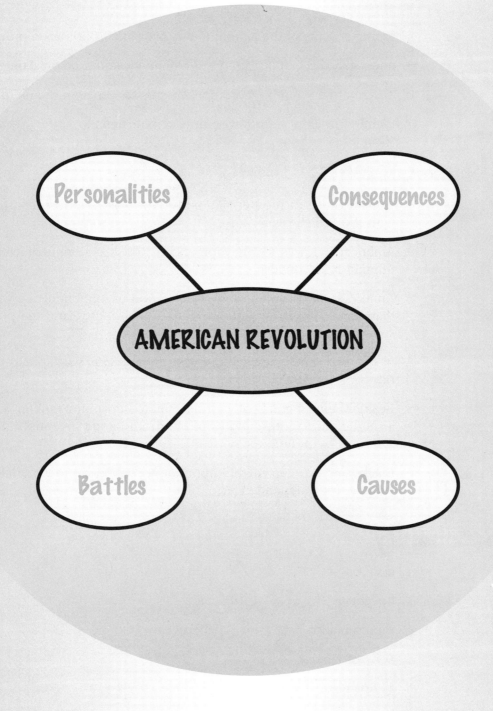

Theme Goals:

Students will:

1. identify causes of the American Revolution.

2. describe actions taken by colonists to protest British actions.

3. know some important principles found in the Declaration of Independence.

4. arrange events of the Revolutionary War in chronological order.

5. understand how information was communicated in colonial times.

6. describe the scientific accomplishments of Benjamin Franklin.

7. identify the important Revolutionary War figures.

Theme Concepts:

1. A main cause of the Revolutionary War was American conflict with the British over taxes.

2. American patriots strongly protested British actions that were thought to be unfair.

3. An important principle of the Declaration of Independence was that people have the natural rights of life, liberty, and the pursuit of happiness.

4. In colonial times, news about important events was spread by riders on horseback.

5. Besides being a great colonial statesman, Benjamin Franklin was a self-taught scientist, and some of his important inventions are still used by people today.

6. Blacks and women made important contributions to America's struggle for independence.

Vocabulary:

1. taxation
2. boycott
3. representation
4. Sons of Liberty
5. sympathizer
6. redcoats
7. correspondence
8. independence
9. liberty
10. colony
11. Liberty Tree

Instructional Bulletin Board

The purpose of this bulletin board is to give students practice locating the thirteen American colonies. Display a large map of colonial America on the bulletin board as shown. Attach a Velcro patch to each colony. Make a label card for each colony and attach a Velcro patch to the backside. Attach a large envelope to the lower right corner of the bulletin board for storage of the label cards. Attach an answer key to the lower left corner of the board. (Note: To give students a larger geographical perspective, attach a small map of the United States with the portion shown in the colonial map highlighted.)

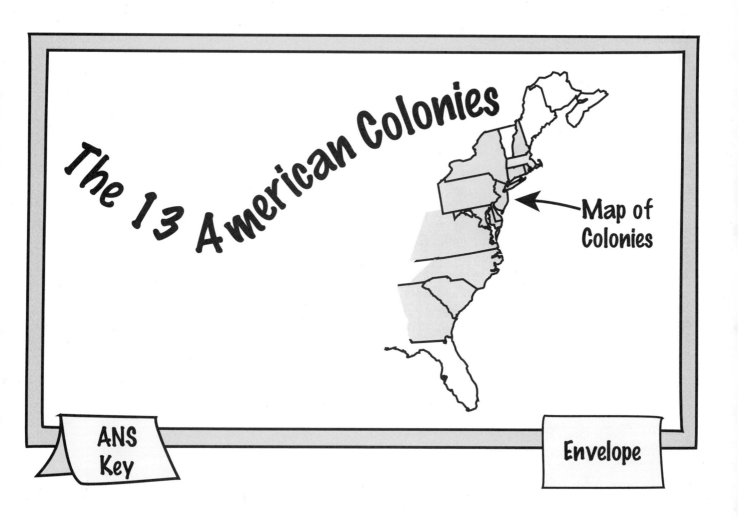

The 13 American Colonies

Map of Colonies

ANS Key

Envelope

Parent Letter

Dear Parents:

How did thirteen small, often quarreling American colonies defeat the most powerful nation in the world and gain their independence? We will travel back to the time of the American Revolution. The children will study the patriots and the significant events that led to war. The students will also consider what America's freedom means to them.

At School:

Some of the special activities planned include:

- Staging a taxpayers' revolt
- Making a Liberty Tree
- Mapping the British march to Lexington and Concord
- Applying principles of the Declaration of Independence to today's world
- Role-playing the spread of colonial news
- Listening to patriotic music
- Painting revolutionary murals

At Home:

Now would be a great time to do one or more of the following with your child:

- Read a book about a colonial patriot.
- Visit a museum, art gallery, or historical society that focuses on the Revolutionary War period.
- Talk about Revolutionary War events you studied as a child.
- Reveal what America's freedom means to you personally

Linking Up:

To dramatize some sources of contention between the American colonists and the British, involve students in the following simulation. Tell students that, as productive members of the class, they are each entitled to receive a salary. Give each of them ten play $1 bills (use the copier to make your own colonial "money" supply). Explain that they can buy treats with their cash, but first they must pay a $1 tax on their use of each of the following items or services provided by the school: desk, chair, pencil sharpener, water fountain, lunch, library books, computer time, bus transportation, and teacher. After you collect the taxes, students will discover that they are each left with only $1 to spend. At this point, some students may be upset with the taxes and feel they are unfair. Drawing on the simulation, lead students in a discussion of the following question: Who should decide whether or not someone can be taxed? Relate their ideas to the situation confronting the American colonists, when they had to pay taxes for such things as newspapers, tea, and glass. Introduce the patriotic slogan, "No taxation without representation!" Ask students what they would do if items they wanted and needed were taxed unfairly. Write the word "boycott" on the chalkboard. Explain how the colonists banned together and refused to buy English goods as a way to protest the hated taxes. The boycott proved very effective, and all the taxes were repealed by the British Parliament except for the one on tea. To conclude the activity, give the students a treat for their good thinking. As a follow-up, ask students to find out what kinds of taxes they and their parents pay. Do we need taxes today? Why, or why not?

Social Studies:

1. Rebellious Acts

Brief Background. Many of the events leading up to the Revolution unfolded in Boston. The Sons of Liberty were involved in most of them. Members of this fiery political organization harassed British officials and supporters and stirred up public outrage against the Crown. The Sons of Liberty sometimes took British tax collectors and sympathizers to the Liberty Tree in Boston. Here, the Sons forced the sympathizers to explain their conduct. When their answers failed to satisfy the pa-

triots, the sympathizers were sometimes subjected to greater humiliations, such as being tarred and feathered. It was also members of the Sons of Liberty who organized and participated in the Boston Tea Party. Enraged by the Tea Act of 1773, which placed a tax on tea sold to the colonies, a group of them, dressed as Indians, slipped aboard a British ship anchored in Boston Harbor and dumped the cargo of tea overboard. John Hancock and Samuel Adams were two important leaders of the patriots' revolt in Boston.

To give students a "feel" for the scene in pre-Revolutionary Boston, as viewed from the perspective of a 14-year-old boy apprenticed to a silversmith, read aloud sections of Esther Forbes' novel, *Johnny Tremain* (Houghton Mifflin, 1971). After students have received background information about the activities of the Sons of Liberty, help them make their own Liberty Tree. You can use a dead tree limb and anchor the base of the limb in a large pot of soil (or use a Christmas tree stand). Students can make a paper banner for each of the British policies that threatened the American colonists' liberty. After the banners are completed, let students hang them on the branches of their Liberty Tree. Some students might also want to reenact the Boston Tea Party, complete with homemade costumes and appropriate props (Figure 2-1).

2. "The British Are Coming!"

Read aloud Henry Wodsworth Longfellow's well-known poem, "Paul Revere's Ride" (Dutton Children's Books, 1990). On his famous ride to Lexington, Paul Revere warned the colonial militia that the "redcoats," or British troops, were on the march. To focus students' attention on these exciting events in American history, move around the classroom shouting "The British are coming! The British are coming!" Ask students: From where are the British coming? and To where are they going? Provide students with maps showing the routes from Boston to Lexington and Concord of Revere and fellow patriots William Dawes and Samuel Prescott. Read aloud sections of *The Story of Lexington and Concord* by R. Conrad Stein (Childrens Press, 1983), or some other appropriate children's book. Help students find places on the map that are mentioned in the reading. After students have heard about the Battle of Lexington, check for understanding by asking such questions as the following: Why did the British

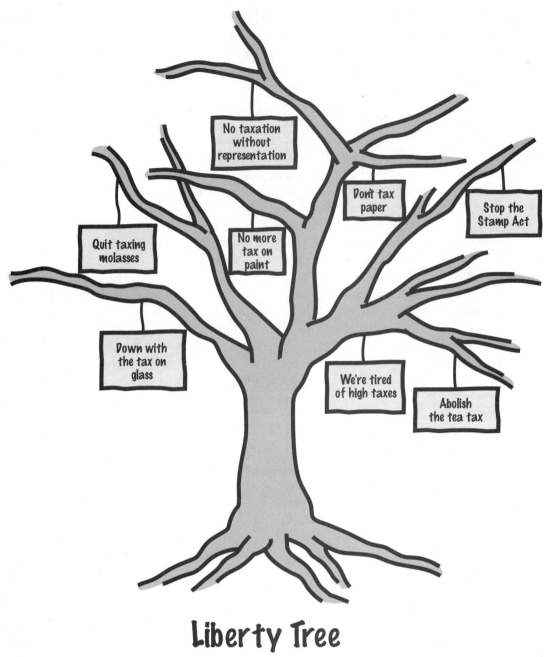

Liberty Tree

FIGURE 2-1

troops march to Lexington and Concord? Who fired the first shots? Were the British successful? and What effects did those events have on other American colonists (Figure 2-2)?

3. Declaration of Independence

Brief Background. Written mainly by Thomas Jefferson, the Declaration of Independence was a justification for revolution. A great principle of the declaration was that people have the natural rights of life, liberty, and pursuit of happiness.

Give students some concrete examples of these natural rights. Then provide well-illustrated magazines, scissors, and paste, and let them cut out pictures and sort them into the following three groups: things in life that people value, things in life that people are free to do, things in life that bring people happiness. Students can paste their pictures on large sheets of paper to illustrate each principle. This activity should help students realize that, although Thomas Jefferson wrote the Declaration of Independence more than 200 years ago, the natural rights of people do not change; they remain the same,

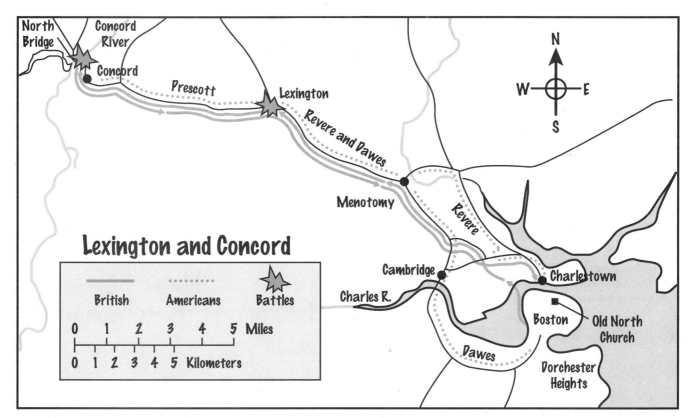

The Routes from Boston to Lexington and Concord
FIGURE 2-2

from the beginning through all future time. Can students think of ways our rights are protected by our government?

4. Revolutionary War Time Lines

Gather and make available in the classroom appropriate books on the Revolutionary War (see list at the end of this unit). Read aloud selections that highlight the following events: Sugar Act (1764), Stamp Act (1765), Townshend Acts (1767), Tea Act (1773), Boston Tea Party (1773), First Continental Congress (1774), Battles of Lexington and Concord (1775), Declaration of Independence (1776), Battle of Saratoga (1777), Surrender of British at Yorktown (1781) and Treaty of Paris (1783). Provide small groups of students with drawing paper, tape, scissors, and drawing materials, and let each group create an event card that includes the following elements: Show what happened (draw a picture); Tell what happened (write/dictate a paragraph); and Tell when it happened (list the year). After they complete their event cards, they can attach them in chronological order to a long string, and give

brief oral reports of their events to the class (Figure 2-3).

Language Arts:

1. Ads for American Patriots

Some important American patriots are listed below, together with some brief information about them. Have each student select a figure for in-depth research. When their research is completed, each student can write a newspaper advertisement for the figure's services. What qualities and experiences does each colonial figure have to offer?

- George Washington—surveyor, general, statesman
- Benjamin Franklin—printer, author, statesman
- Thomas Jefferson—lawyer, author, architect, statesman
- Patrick Henry—lawyer, orator, statesman
- John Adams—teacher, lawyer, statesman

19

Thomas Jefferson wrote the Declaration of Independence. It stated that colonies had a right to be independent. It also listed many complaints against the king. Fifty-six colonists signed the Declaration of Independence.

1776

Event Card

FIGURE 2-3

- Samuel Adams—writer, businessperson, leader of Boston patriots
- Crispus Attucks—runaway slave, killed by British soldiers in Boston Massacre
- Marquis de Lafayette—French military leader who served as general in colonial army
- Thomas Paine—writer, journalist, author of *Common Sense* (a pamplet that urged colonial rebellion)
- Molly Pitcher—water carrier to soldiers (she picked up rifle of fallen soldier and took his place in the battle)
- Betsy Ross—seamstress, upholsterer, maker of first American flag
- Peter Salem—former slave, soldier at Battle of Bunker Hill
- Deborah Sampson—woman who fought in Revolutionary War disguised as a man

2. Spreading the News

Brief Background. In colonial times, most news was disseminated by weekly newspapers, and important political information was carried from place to place by riders on horseback. To facilitate com-munication within and among the thirteen colonies, Committees of Correspondence were established. Through such activities as spreading patriotic pro-paganda and circulating petitions, Committees of Correspondence helped unite the colonies in a common cause. The Declaration of Independence was adopted on July 4, 1776, in Philadelphia. It took around two weeks for news of that famous event to reach Williamsburg, Virginia.

Write the word "correspondence" on the chalk-board. Provide dictionaries, and have students find the definition. Ask students how they would communicate with people in other towns and states if there were no cars, trains, planes, tele-phones, radios, televisions, or computers. Have students recreate the spread of the important news of the Declaration of Independence throughout the colonies. Take the class outside to a large open area for this activity and assign most of the students to small groups; students in each group will represent patriots in an impor-tant colonial city. Arrange the "cities" on the open area in a way that reflects their proper spatial re-lationship to one another. Have some students act out the signing of the Declaration of Independence in Philadelphia. Other small groups of students can represent colonists in Boston (MA), Newport (RI), New York (NY), Williamsburg (VA), Wilmington (NC), and Savannah (GA). Let other students role-play riders. They can carry copies of the Declaration of Independence from city to city. Ask a "colonist" in each "city" to read aloud, or play an audiotape of, the following excerpt from the Declaration of Independence:

We, therefore,. . . declare that these United Colonies are, and of right ought to be, free and independent states, that they are absolved from all allegiance to the British Crown, and that all political connection between them and the State of Great Britain is, and ought to be, totally dissolved. . . .

3. Patriotic Propaganda Posters

After students have studied the events leading up to the Revolutionary War, provide them with poster paper, markers, and crayons, and let them create patriotic messages on posters that promote liberty and independence.

Math:

1. Travel Time Then and Now

Most colonists did not venture very far from home, but when they did, they usually traveled overland on horseback or in wagons and coaches. Have students calculate how long it would take colonists to go the following distances on a horse traveling at fifteen miles an hour. Then, have students calculate how long it would take them to go the same distances in a car traveling at 55 miles an hour.

	By horse	By car
3 miles	_____	_____
7 miles	_____	_____
10 miles	_____	_____
15 miles	_____	_____

2. Taxing Problems

Give students play money, and then have them calculate their taxes at different rates—such as 10 percent, 27 percent, 40 percent, and so on.

3. Colonial Distances

Provide highway maps of the eastern United States, and let students use measuring instruments and the maps' scale to calculate distances between the following colonial towns: Boston, MA; Newport, RI; New York, NY; Philadelphia, PA; Annapolis, MD; Williamsburg, VA; Wilmington, NC; and Savannah, GA.

Science:

1. America's Scientific Founding Father

Brief Background. Benjamin Franklin's interests and abilities had no bounds. As one of the Founding Fathers, he was a mover and shaper of American independence. Besides being a great colonial statesman and diplomat, he found time to establish libraries, a fire department, a newspaper, and a college. Franklin also had a keen scientific mind. He was the creator of some remarkable and very practical inventions, such as the Franklin stove, which was more fuel efficient than other stoves. With his famous kite experiment, Franklin proved that lightning is electricity, which led to the invention of the lightning rod, a device still used today. People today are also indebted to Franklin for another practical invention, bifocal eyeglasses, which combined lenses for distant and up-close viewing within a single frame.

Read aloud sections of Milton Miltzer's *Benjamin Franklin: The New American* (Franklin Watts, 1988), or another appropriate children's book that describes Franklin's scientific accomplishments. Have interested students research Franklin's inventions in depth and draw pictures of them. Challenge students to design their own inventions. They can draw diagrams or make models of the inventions, and then share them with the class.

Art:

1. Murals of Revolution

Have students use colored chalk to make murals of Revolutionary War scenes on butcher paper. Some scenes that might be depicted include the Boston Massacre, the Boston Tea Party, the signing of the Declaration of Independence, the Battles of Lexington and Concord, the Battle of Bunker Hill, the colonial army at Valley Forge, the Battle of Saratoga, Washington crossing the Delaware River, and the British surrender at Yorktown.

Music:

1. Patriotic Music

Brief Background. Today, "Yankee Doodle" is one of America's most popular patriotic tunes. Back in colonial times, however, the song was played by Tories and British fifers and drummers when they wanted to insult American patriots, or Yankees. Read aloud or sing "Yankee Doodle."

> Yankee Doodle came to town,
>
> Riding on a pony,
>
> Stuck a feather in his cap
>
> And called it Macaroni.

Let students listen to fife and drums tunes that were performed at the time of the Revolutionary War (such as "Marching Out of Time," music performed by the Fifes and Drums of Colonial Williamsburg, available on cassette or CD from The Colonial Williamsburg Foundation, Williamsburg, VA 23187-1776).

Books:

1. Longfellow, Henry Wadsworth. (1990). *Paul Revere's Ride*. New York: Dutton Children's Books. Primary, Intermediate.

2. Meltzer, Milton, ed. (1987). *The American Revolutionaries: A History in Their Own Words 1750–1800*. New York: Crowell. Advanced.

3. Rappaport, Doreen. (1988). *The Boston Coffee Party*. New York: Harper and Row. Primary.

4. Siegel, Beatrice. (1985). *Sam Ellis's Island*. New York: Four Winds Press. Advanced.

5. Brown, Drollene. (1985). *Sybil Rides for Independence*. Niles, IL: A. Whitman. Intermediate, Advanced.

6. Griffin, Judith Berry. (1977). *Phoebe and the General*. New York: Coward, McCann & Geoghegan. Intermediate, Advanced.

7. Alderman, Clifford. (1974). *The War We Could Have Lost: The American Revolution*. New York: Four Winds Press. Advanced.

8. Benchley, Nathaniel. (1987). *Sam the Minuteman*. New York: HarperCollins. Intermediate.

9. Reische, Diana. (1987). *Patrick Henry*. New York: Franklin Watts. Advanced.

10. Stein, R. Conrad. (1983). *The Story of Lexington and Concord*. Chicago: Childrens Press. Intermediate, Advanced.

11. Davis, Burke. (1976). *Black Heroes of the American Revolution*. New York: Harcourt Brace Jovanovich. Advanced.

12. Miltzer, Milton. (1988). *Benjamin Franklin: The New American*. New York: Franklin Watts. Advanced.

13. Forbes, Esther. (1971). *Johnny Tremain*. Boston: Houghton Mifflin. Advanced.

Software:

1. *The American Revolution* [Mac IBM Windows CD-ROM]. Fairfield, CT: Queue. Advanced.

2. *The American Revolution: Declaration of Independence and the War* [Laserdisc VHS]. Chatsworth, CA: AIMS. Advanced.

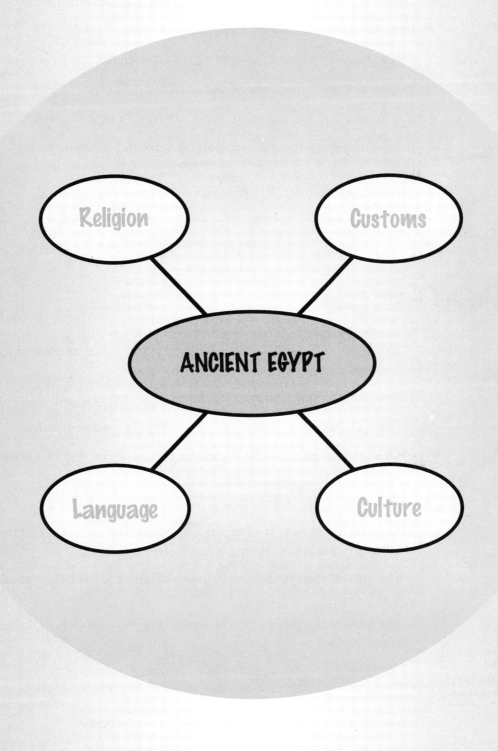

Theme Goals:

Students will:

1. recognize the contribution of the Nile River to the development of the ancient Egyptian civilization.

2. identify important aspects of the religion of ancient Egypt.

3. make inferences about a culture from data.

4. discuss the values of ancient Egyptian society.

5. map important features of ancient Egypt.

6. compare ancient Egyptian and modern American lifestyles.

7. trace the connections between ancient and modern technologies.

8. construct a model of a pyramid.

9. dramatize aspects of the ancient Egyptian way of life.

10. create picture symbols for their names.

Theme Concepts:

1. In the midst of a great desert, the Nile River provided ancient Egypt with drinking water, a transportation route, and water for irrigation.

2. Ancient Egyptians believed in many gods and in life after death.

3. Some dead rulers of ancient Egypt were buried in pyramids.

4. Objects buried with the pharaohs tell us about life in ancient Egypt.

5. The ancient Egyptians valued people of good character.

6. Ancient Egypt was a complex, highly developed, agriculture-based civilization.

7. The ancient Egyptians used a system of barter to exchange goods and services.

8. The ancient Egyptian writing consisted of picture symbols, called hieroglyphics.

Vocabulary:

1. pharoah	4. hieroglyphics	7. scribe
2. irrigation	5. pyramid	8. cartouche
3. barter	6. archaeologist	9. barter

Instructional Bulletin Board

The purpose of this bulletin board is to let students demonstrate their knowledge of ancient Egyptian beliefs and values by making pictures of the types of objects that might have been placed in King Tutankhamen's tomb. The following statement, completed by the student, should be written along the bottom of each picture: I believe this _____ would be placed in King Tut's tomb because _____. After you have checked the plausibility of pictures and the accompanying statements, attach them to the bulletin board.

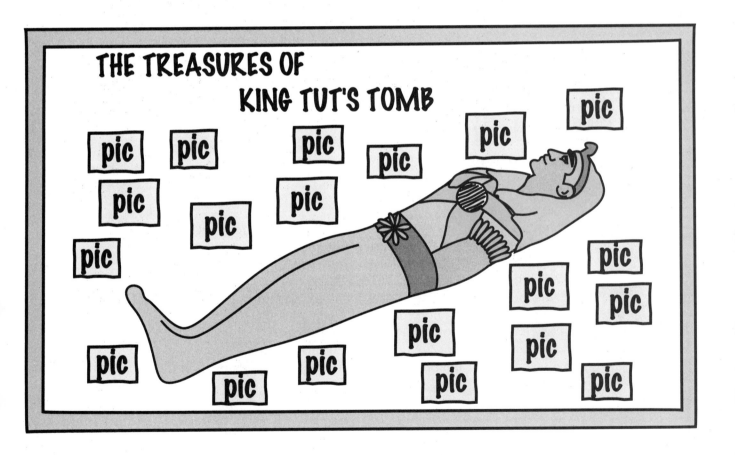

Parent Letter

Dear Parents:

The Egyptian civilization arose along the banks of the Nile River more than 4,000 years ago. Today, people still marvel at the achievements of this ancient culture. When most people think of Egypt, they picture the massive temples and monuments, including the giant pyramids that still stand majestically in the desert. Other accomplishments, although less spectacular, are just as impressive. Egypt was one the first societies in the world to develop complex systems of writing, religion, government, and trade. Your child will be learning about the ancient Egyptians. Some of the activities planned for the unit are highlighted below.

At School:

During our study of Ancient Egypt, your child will be involved in the following activities:

- Exploring King Tut's treasures
- Making statues of Egyptian gods and goddesses
- Comparing the lives of ancient Egyptians with today's Americans
- Connecting ancient and new technologies
- Surveying the many uses of cotton
- Constructing model pyramids
- Creating picture symbols

At Home:

You can reinforce the concepts about ancient Egypt studied at school by doing one or more of the following things with your child:

- Help your child make a list of clothing items made of cotton.
- Check the public library for books, especially picture books, about ancient Egypt, and pick one or more to read aloud.
- Ask your child to tell you all about ancient Egypt.
- Share facts about ancient Egyptian that fascinate you.
- Share a tasty ancient Egyptian snack of bread, honey, dates, and figs.

Linking Up:

Show students a picture of the pyramids of Egypt. Ask students to tell you what they know about these colossal ancient structures. Discuss their responses. Make a list of student-generated questions about the pyramids and the ancient Egyptians. Tell students you will help them find answers to their questions.

Social Studies:

1. The Source of a Civilization

Brief Background. Egypt produced one of the ancient world's greatest civilizations. But this great civilization would never have arisen along the edge of a desert without the Nile. The Nile River was the source of life-giving water. It provided drinking water for humans and domesticated animals,

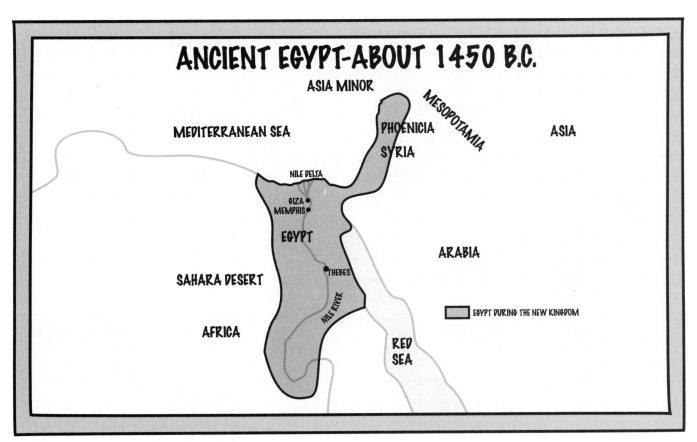

FIGURE 3-1

as well as water for irrigation. The annual flooding of the Nile left behind a cover of silt that enriched the soil and increased its productivity. The river was also the main transportation route, connecting one end of the kingdom to the other.

Provide globes and physical maps, and help students locate the Nile River and deserts in Egypt. Ask students to discuss how a river might contribute to the establishment of a large settlement. What conditions are necessary for settlements to develop anywhere? Make a list of the students' responses (Figure 3-1).

2. The Treasures of King Tut

Brief Background. King Tutankhamen ("King Tut") was a ruler of Egypt over 3,000 years ago. Unfortunately, the tombs of most ancient Egyptian rulers were robbed of their treasures long before archaeologists could get to them. King Tut's tomb, however, escaped detection until 1922, when it was opened for the first time. Inside King Tut's burial chambers, archaeologists found more than 5,000 objects, including jewels and priceless treasures of gold. As valuable as the objects themselves was the information they provided about King Tut's life and times. The objects buried with the young king were for his use in the *afterlife*, or his life after death.

Below is a list of some of the objects found in King Tut's tomb. List the objects on the chalkboard, and then ask students what the objects tell them about life in ancient Egypt. For example, the swords, daggers, shields, and bows and arrows are evidence that the ancient Egyptians might have had armies and enaged in warfare. Have students write their inferences down in their notebooks. They can check them for accuracy later using books and other resources (Figure 3-2).

chests	clothing	shields
thrones	necklaces	trumpets
linens	bracelets	statues of the king
beds	rings	
fans	earrings	statues of Egyptian gods
chariots	swords	figures of animals
bows and arrows	daggers	games
	toys	
models of ships		

3. Create a Culture

Let pairs of students create their own imaginary cultures. Provide each pair with a small box, and direct the pairs to fill their boxes with im-

Items Found in King Tut's Tomb

FIGURE 3-2

30

portant objects (represented by pictures from magazines, drawings, models, etc.) from their imagined cultures. Have the pairs also list some important characteristics of their imaginary cultures that are represented or suggested by the objects. Then, let pairs exchange boxes and make inferences, or educated guesses, about each others' cultures based upon their analyses of the objects. After the pairs have completed their analyses, discuss whether each pair's guesses matched the other pair's list of cultural characteristics.

4. The Gods of Ancient Egyptians

Brief Background. The ancient Egyptians had many gods and goddesses, which were believed to control society and nature. The gods were often the focus of Egyptian art: Their likenesses are found in paintings inside the tombs and in jewelry and sculpture.

Below is a list of some of the main gods, along with their major areas of influence. Show students pictures of the various gods (found in illustrated art and history books), and describe each one briefly. Assign small groups of students the task of researching one of the gods. They can consult various library sources for information about each one. After they have completed their research, each group can make a papier-mache statue of its deity, and then present a skit or an oral report that explains why the god was important (Figure 3-3).

God or Goddess	Role, Purpose, or Influence
Ra or Amon-Re	Sun god; provider of a good harvest
Isis	Moon goddess; devoted mother and wife
Osiris	God of the Nile and lord of the dead
Horus	Head of a falcon; god of the sky; Egyptian kings, or *pharaohs*, were believed to be the god Horus in human form
Thoth	God of wisdom and writing
Ptah	God of Memphis

Horus
FIGURE 3-3

5. Living a Good Life

Brief Background. The ancient Egyptians were one of the world's first people to believe in life after death. They believed that the afterlife would be filled with happiness and joy. But before the soul could enter the afterlife, it had to first prove that the person had lived a good and virtuous life on Earth. Each soul had to take an oath before the god Osiris that it had not engaged in dishonorable behavior.

Discuss the importance of having a good character and living a good life. Are these values shared by people today? Have students list some personal qualities for which people—at any time and anywhere—should strive.

6. Mapping Ancient Egypt

Using maps in atlases and encyclopedias as a guide, have students make relief maps of ancient Egypt from salt and flour, papier-mache, and other materials that show the Nile River, Nile Valley, Nile Delta, desert areas, and seas. Let them design symbols for their maps to represent major pyramids (such as Giza and Saqqarah), cities (including the capitals of Memphis and Thebes), and temples or monuments (such as the Valley of the Kings, Karnak, and Abu Simbel).

7. Ordinary People

The chart below shows characteristics of the life of the ancient Egyptian people. Have students complete the chart by describing the life of people in America today. In what ways were the lives of ancient Egyptians similar to the lives of modern Americans? In what ways were they different?

Science:

1. Ancient Egyptian Technology

Brief Background. Objects and paintings found in tombs reveal that ancient Egypt was an agriculture-based society that engaged in complex, economic activities including mining, manufacturing, and trade, as well as the practice of various skilled crafts and professions. Farmers used wooden plows to till the soil and built canals to irrigate crops. Many ancient Egyptians were part of a highly skilled and specialized labor force that included miners of gold, copper, and tin; manufacturers of linen clothing and textiles, papyrus writing material, pottery, bricks, weapons, glass, jewelry, perfume, rope, and ships; and traders for ivory, iron, and spices. The ancient Egyptians invented the first paper-like writing material (papyrus sheets) and the first sailboats.

Have students discuss contemporary objects (e.g., paper, computer monitor, yacht, windsurfboard) and activities (e.g., writing, word processing, yachting, windsurfing) that are connected in structure and/or function to ancient Egyptian objects, such as papyrus and sailboats.

2. Cotton

Brief Background. Although it may have originated in India, cotton was an important crop in ancient Egypt. The cotton plant thrived in the climate and soil of the Nile Valley. Ancient Egyptians wove the cotton into cloth and wore cotton garments. Today, cotton clothing is popular throughout the world, and Egypt continues to be an important producer of this cool and comfortable fiber.

	Ancient Egypt	Modern America
People	Father head of the family; children played with dolls, games	
Pets	Cats, dogs, monkeys, baboons, birds	
Schooling	Most children did not go to school	
Occupations	Mainly farmers; also pottery making, carpentry, and other crafts	
Food	Bread, vegetables, meat fruits, milk, cheese, butter, duck, and goose	
Fashion	Dressed in linen and cotton garments; both men and women wore makeup and jewelry	
Shelter	One-, two-, or three-bedroom house made from brick	
Recreation	Hunting, fishing, swimming, board games	

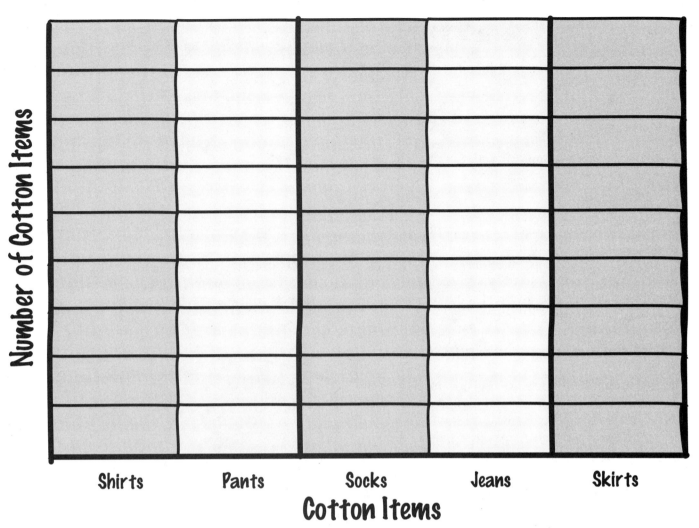

FIGURE 3-4

As a homework assignment, students, and their parents can check the labels on the family's clothing, and then make a list of the items made of cotton. Students can use these data to make a graph for the whole class that shows the quantity of different types of clothing (shirts, pants, jeans, pajamas, underwear, socks, etc.) made entirely or mostly of cotton. What does the graph tell the class about students' use of cotton? Encourage interested students to research the history of cotton and the steps in the production of cotton fabric (Figure 3-4).

3. Weather: Here and There

The climate of ancient Egypt was about like it is today. Weather data for Cairo, Egypt, are presented on page 34. How do Cairo's temperatures and precipitation compare with conditions locally?

Math:

1. Marvels of Antiquity and Geometry

Brief Background. Constructed over 4,000 years ago to protect the bodies and souls of dead pharaohs, the giant pyramids of Egypt are considered a wonder of the ancient world. Without a solid understanding of mathematics, especially geometry, these great structures could never have been built. Many people were needed to build the pyramids. It took more than 100,000 workers to build the pyramid of Khufu, which contains 2 million stone blocks, each weighing around 2 tons. Despite their massive size, grave robbers managed to reach the burial chambers and make off with their priceless contents. The design of the pyramid is elegantly simple. It has a square base and four triangular-shaped walls that meet in a point at the top.

COMPARATIVE TEMPERATURES

	January Temp		July Temp		Annual Rain
	High	Low	High	Low	
Cairo, Egypt	65° F	47° F	96° F	70° F	1.1 inches
Your community					

Provide students with cardboard, tape, scissors, and rulers, and let them make squares and triangles to use to construct their own pyramids. Students can make dioramas, complete with real sand on the ground and realistic backgrounds, in which to display their pyramids.

2. Bartering for Goods and Services

Brief Background. Instead of using money as a medium of exchange, ancient Egyptians would *barter*, or exchange one thing or service for another. Egyptian workers were often paid in wheat or barley. Egyptian traders exchanged wheat, barley, gold, and papyrus sheets for many goods from other lands.

Ask students to provide examples of the barter system as it is practiced today. Have they ever exchanged books, comics, toys, cards, or other items with their friends? How much are certain items worth in exchange for other items? Have students ever been paid in goods or services? If money did not exist, could they and their families meet their needs for food, clothing, and shelter by bartering? Let students bring items to class and engage in a mock barter session.

3. Measuring Things

Brief Background. The ancient Egyptians measured length and width in cubits. A *cubit* was about 18 inches, which was based on the length of the forearm from the elbow to the tip of the middle finger.

Provide measuring instruments, and let pairs of students measure each others' forearms from elbow to finger tip. Find the average "cubit" length for the class. For comparison, let students measure adults from elbow to finger tip. What is the average "cubit" length for adults? What is the difference in inches between the two averages?

Which average, the students' or the adults', is closer to 18 inches? As a follow-up, have students use their forearms to measure the lengths and widths of rooms, hallways, and various large objects in the school in cubits.

Cartouche

FIGURE 3-5

Language Arts:

1. Dramatizing Ancient Egypt

Assign small groups of students the task of dramatizing some aspect of the ancient Egyptian way of life (such as building the pyramids, bartering at the marketplace, collecting taxes from the farmers, writing hieroglyphics on a temple wall, honoring one of the gods or goddesses, or eating a typical family meal). To provide background, read aloud selections of *Ancient Egypt* by George Hart (Knopf, 1990), or some other appropriate children's book, that describes the lives of the ancient Egyptians. After groups have researched their topics, they can create costumes and write scripts for their dramatic enactments of Egyptian life. Allow sufficient time for students to rehearse their parts. Groups can take turns presenting their dramas.

Art:

1. Words in Pictures

Brief Background. The ancient Egyptian writing consisted of picture symbols, called *hieroglyphics*. For example, a circle was used to represent the sun god Ra and a shepherd's staff stood for ruler. The ancient Egyptians developed more than 8,000 symbols to represent sounds, ideas, actions, and objects. Only a few highly trained Egyptians, called *scribes*, could write hieroglyphics. Scribes enclosed the names of individuals inside a *cartouche*, which is pictured.

After you show students examples of Egyptian hieroglyphics (found in library books and other sources), provide large, individual copies of the cartouche and an assortment of felt-tipped pens, and let them create colorful picture symbols for their names. Display the students' work on the wall (Figure 3-5).

Books:

1. Odijk, Pamela. (1989). *The Egyptians*. Englewood Cliffs, NJ: Silver Burdett Press. Intermediate, Advanced.

2. Unstead, R.J. (1986). *See Inside an Egyptian Town*. New York: Warwick Press. Intermediate, Advanced.

3. David, Rosalie. (1994). *Growing Up in Ancient Egypt*. Mahwah, NJ: Troll Associates. Primary.

4. Langley, Andrew. (1986). *Cleopatra and the Egyptians*. New York: The Bookwright Press. Intermediate, Advanced.

5. Perl, Lila. (1987). *Mummies, Tombs, and Treasure: Secrets of Ancient Egypt*. New York: Clarion Books. Intermediate, Advanced.

6. Aliki. (1979). *Mummies Made in Egypt*. New York: Thomas Y. Crowell. Primary.

7. Hart, George. (1990). *Ancient Egypt*. New York: Knopf. Intermediate.

Software:

1. *Sphinx's Secret: A Perimeter, Area, and Volume Game* [Apple II IBM]. Big Springs, TX: Gamco. Advanced.

2. *Nile: Passage to Egypt* [Mac MPC CD-ROM]. Bethesda, MD: Discovery Channel. Advanced.

3. *Annabel's Dream of Ancient Egypt* [Mac Windows CD-ROM]. Austin, TX: Texas Caviar. Primary, Intermediate, Advanced.

4. *Secrets of the Pyramids* [Mac MPC CD-ROM]. Novato, CA: Mindscape/Ednovation. Intermediate, Advanced.

5. *King Tut: The Face of Tutankhamen* [Laserdisc]. Denver, CO: Lumivison. Advanced.

6. *DigIt: Egyptians* [IBM]. Cambridge, MA: Terrapin. Intermediate, Advanced.

7. *Everyday Life in Ancient Times* [Mac MPC CD-ROM]. Chicago: Clearvue/eav. Advanced.

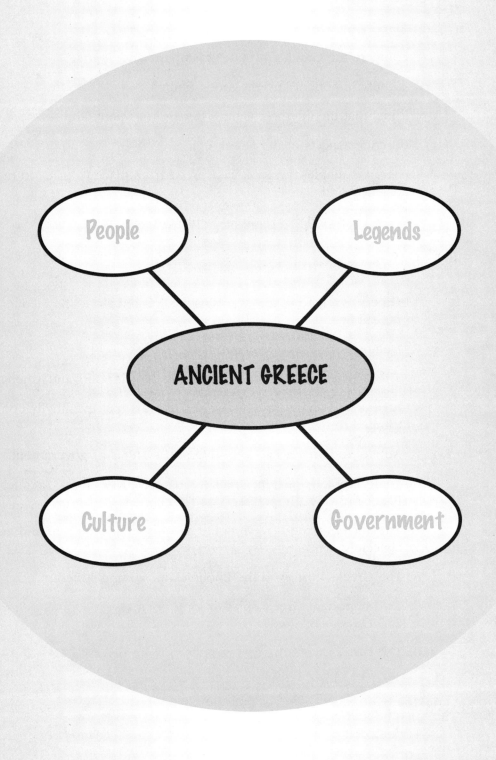

People

Legends

ANCIENT GREECE

Culture

Government

Theme Goals:

Students will:

1. know that democracy began in ancient Greece.

2. describe the shape of Greece and find Greece on a map.

3. identify the Greek gods.

4. compare the Greek city-states of Athens and Sparta.

5. identify important ancient Greek figures.

6. know that the Olympic Games began in ancient Greece.

7. describe aspects of the Greek epics.

8. cite an example of how ideas spread from place to place in the ancient world.

9. know characteristics of Greek sculpture and architecture.

Theme Concepts:

1. Greece is a land of many peninsulas located along the Mediterranean Sea.

2. Democracy began in ancient Greece.

3. The Greeks had many gods, including Zeus, Apollo, and Athena.

4. Athens and Sparta fought a series of wars that eventually contributed to the decline of Greece.

5. Athens and Sparta had very different systems of government.

6. Some important ancient Greek figures were Herodotus, Socrates, Plato, Aristotle, Hippocrates, and Archimedes.

7. The ancient Greeks were noted for their fine sculpture and architecture.

8. The Greeks borrowed the Phoenicians' writing system.

9. Two important Greek epics or long poems were Homer's *Iliad* and *Odyssey*.

10. The Greeks were the first people to write plays.

Vocabulary:

1. democracy	5. tragedy	9. gears
2. peninsula	6. comedy	10. compound pulley
3. historian	7. diffusion	11. cogged wheels
4. epic poem	8. Hippocratic oath	

Instructional Bulletin Board

The purpose of this bulletin board is to give students practice matching famous Greek figures with their notable characteristics. On the left side of the board, use Velcro patches to attach name cards of famous Greek figures. Next to the names, attach pictures of the figures, if available. On the right side of the bulletin board attach a flip chart for each figure. Use manila folders for the flip charts. On the outside cover of the flip chart write the notable characteristic, and inside, write the name of the figure it describes. Attach a Velcro patch at the bottom of each flip chart. Students can remove the name cards from the left side, then try to match them with the correct characteristics by attaching the name cards to the Velcro patches under the flip charts. After a student tries to match names and characteristics, she can check the answers by flipping the covers up to reveal the correct names. Among the famous Greek characters to highlight are the following: Athena (Greek goddess; protector of Athens), Socrates (a teacher and lover of wisdom), Plato (a Greek philosopher who believed that high ideals could be discovered by reflection), Aristotle (a scientific thinker who collected and analyzed facts), Hippocrates (the father of modern medicine), Archimedes (a scientist who invented machines), and Alexander the Great (Greek ruler who conquered the Persian Empire).

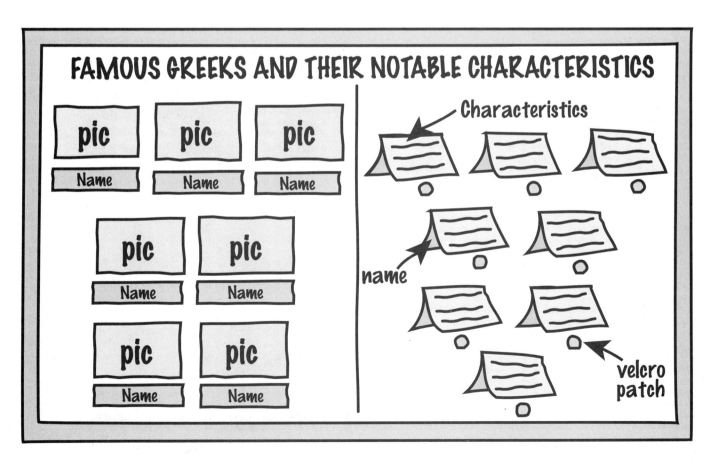

Parent Letter

Dear Parents:

We are going to explore one of the greatest civilizations in history—the ancient Greeks. Over 2,000 years ago, the ancient Greeks invented *democracy*, a form of government that many nations, including the U.S., have embraced today. The Greeks believed in the full development of both mind and body, and they held the first Olympic Games in 776 B.C. The Greeks can also be credited with developing precise procedures for analyzing facts from different bodies of knowledge, such as history, zoology, and medicine.

At School:

Some of the exciting activities that we will be doing include:

- Experiencing democracy in action
- Mapping Greece and the ancient world
- Learning about Greek gods
- Examining the differences between Athens and Sparta
- Researching famous Greek personalities
- Recreating Greek epics
- Comparing the English and Greek alphabets
- Making miniature Greek temples

At Home:

This would be a great time to check out some books about ancient Greece to read to your child. One title to consider is *Aesop's Fables*, of which a copy can be found in almost any library. In brief stories such as "The Tortoise and the Hare" and "The Ant and the Grasshopper," this collection of ancient fables offers useful advice in language children can understand. Some of the familiar proverbs we tell our children, like "Slow and steady wins the race," come from *Aesop's Fables*.

Linking Up:

Help students identify and research school-related issues, such as classroom rules and responsibilities, and community-based issues, such as traffic, curfew, and building regulations. Then, debate some of the issues and put them to a vote. Let students make graphs to display the results. Have the class follow up with letters to school officials and politicians and community leaders that express the students' stand on the issues. Relate the students' debate and vote to the concept of *democracy*, or rule by the people. Tell students that before the invention of democracy, the power to rule was in the hands of only a few people and most people had no say in government. Over time, democracy has expanded across the globe, and today, most of the world's countries, including the United States, have embraced democracy as the preferred kind of government. Tell students to ask their parents and other adults about how citizens participate in government by voting. Tell students they

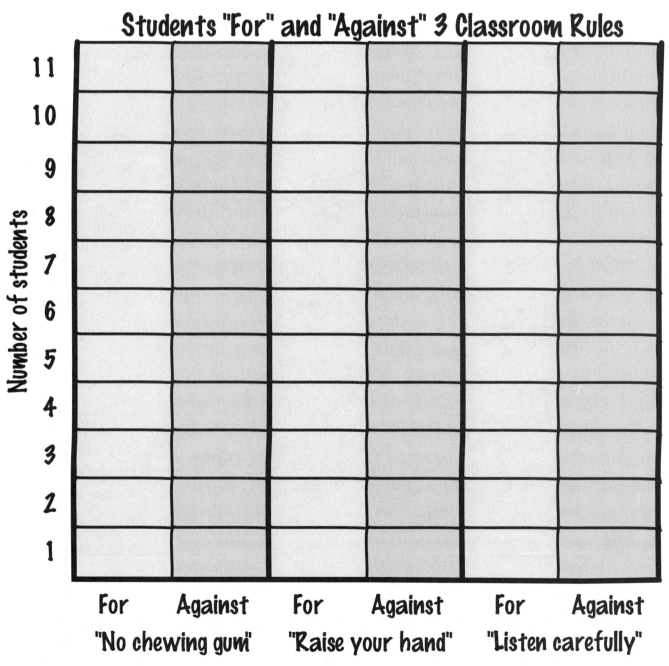

FIGURE 4-1

are going to study the place where democracy was born—ancient Greece (Figure 4-1).

Social Studies:

1. Center of the Ancient World

Show students maps of the Mediterranean Sea and the surrounding land area, which can be found in atlases. Help them identify the mainland of Greece. Introduce or review the definition of *peninsula*, which is a land area surrounded on three sides by water. Have students use the definition to locate peninsulas, both large and small, that extend into the Mediterranean Sea (Greece is part of the Balkan Peninsula; two other major peninsulas are the Italian and Iberian). Provide students with paper plates and art materials, and let them make maps of the Greek view of the world, which consisted of the ancient Mediterranean Region with Greece at its center (Figure 4-2).

2. Greek Gods

Brief Background. The ancient Greeks believed that their many gods lived on Mount Olympus. The Greeks endowed their gods with supernatural powers, yet they also had human forms and feelings.

Show students pictures and read aloud selections in *Ancient Greece* edited by John D. Clare (Gulliver, 1994), or other appropriate children's books, that describe Greek gods and their human qualities. Do the gods and their associated

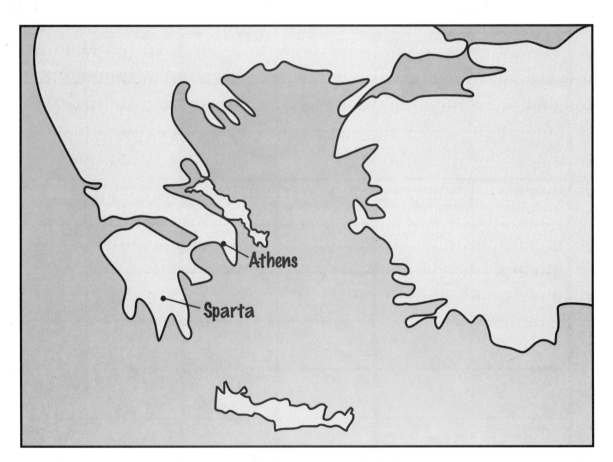

Map of Ancient Greece and Mediterranean Sea

FIGURE 4-2

qualities reveal anything about the values of the ancient Greeks (Figure 4-3)?

Gods	Function
Zeus	The most powerful god and lord of the sky
Apollo	God of music and poetry
Athena	Protector of Athens
Aphrodite	Goddess of love and beauty
Poseidon	God of the sea
Hermes	Messenger of the gods
Demeter	Goddess of agriculture

3. Athens and Sparta

Brief Background. A series of wars—called the Peloponnesian Wars—were fought between ancient Greece's two most powerful city-states, Sparta and Athens. The conflicting values and beliefs of these city-states contributed to the outbreak of war. While Sparta emerged the eventual victor, the wars so weakened all of the Greek city-states that they were eventually unable to defend themselves from external enemies.

On the next page, there is a chart that contrasts the two city-states. Highlight the differences, and provide students with other information about the two city-states. Then, assign small groups of students the task of recreating a scene that reflects some important aspect of one of the city-states.

4. The Invention of History

The father of history was a Greek named Herodotus. He was the first person to carefully record past events for posterity. To give your students the flavor of historical procedures, briefly show them a still picture of some scene or event (or, to add complexity, a video segment) then remove the picture and ask them to answer yes or no questions about what they saw. Have students write their answers down so that you have a record of their individual responses. Do students agree or disagree about the right answers to the questions? Ask students

Zeus   Athena

Greek Gods

FIGURE 4-3

Sparta

Sparta was led by a small group of rulers; the rest of the people had no rights.

The education of boys centered on military training.

The Spartans believed they had to forfeit their freedom to serve the government.

Spartans believed the development of a strong body—fit for military service—was more important than the development of the mind.

All Spartan men were required to spend 40 years in the military.

Athens

Athens had a democratic form of government. All Athenian citizens (men only) had a say in their government.

Boys studied the three Rs, a musical instrument called the lyre, and gymnastics.

Athenian citizens had maximum freedom.

Athenians believed that the development of the mind was as important as physical fitness.

Young men were required to complete two years in the military.

---

how they can determine whose observations are accurate and whose observations are not. Point out that historians try to find out what really happened in the past by carefully checking many different sources of information, rather than relying on only a few sources, which could be wrong.

5. Ancient Greek Personalities

Ancient Greece was the home of some very famous historical figures. Encourage students to select one of the four listed personalities to recreate. They can consult pictures of ancient Greece found in library resources to get ideas for props and costumes.

Personality	Profile
Socrates	A teacher and lover of wisdom, he believed that people should think for themselves.
Plato	He believed that high ideals regarding government, justice, virtue, and other topics resided inside the mind and could be discovered by reflection.
Aristotle	He was a scientific thinker. He collected and analyzed facts from different bodies of knowledge, including botany, zoology, and anatomy.
Alexander the Great	He conquered the Persian Empire and brought it under his rule.

Math:

1. The Olympics

Brief Background. The Olympic Games were begun in ancient Greece in 776 B.C. They were held every four years in honor of the god Zeus, and they included the following events: running, jumping, discus throwing, javelin throwing, boxing, and wrestling.

To involve your students in the spirit of Olympic competition, recreate the games in your classroom. Select some fun but safe indoor events, such as a beanbag toss, bowling with plastic pins and balls, and board games, for your classroom Olympiad. Be certain to include appropriate games and activities for any physically disabled students. Give everyone a chance to participate in associated math activities; students can measure times and distances, keep score, and graph the results. So that everyone can feel like an Olympic winner, fashion "olive leaf" wreaths (made from artificial ivy leaves) for the students to wear upon completion of the games. As a follow-up activity, let interested students report on modern-day Olympic sports heroes and records.

Language Arts:

1. Ancient Epics

Brief Background. The Ancient Greeks developed epics or long poems about their past that were chock-full of heroic people, terrible monsters, and meddlesome gods. Two of the most famous epics were Homer's *The Iliad* and *Odyssey*. The *Iliad* describes the last year of the Trojan War. The *Odyssey* is about a courageous and clever king, Odysseus, and his long voyage home after fighting in the Trojan War. During the trip, Odysseus and his crew are involved in many dangerous adventures that include encounters with one-eyed giants called Cyclopes, ghosts of old Trojan War heroes, and birdlike women called Sirens whose singing could lure seamen to their death.

Read aloud selections from the the *Iliad* and *Odyssey*. Encourage students to recreate scenes from the epics, and/or create their own epic poems about Ancient Greece.

2. Greek Tragedies and Comedies

Brief Background. The Greeks were the first people to write plays, and wealthy Greeks enjoyed going to the theater. The actors in Greek plays wore masks to indicate emotions.

Provide paper plates, art materials, scissors, and string, and have students make comic and tragic masks patterned after the two shown below. Then, encourage students to use the masks in brief dramatic skits of situations drawn from children's literature or everyday life (Figure 4-4).

3. The Spread of Language

Brief Background. Cultural diffusion refers to the spreading of cultural ideas from one place to another. When trade was first established between the Phoenicians and the Greeks (around 750 B.C.), the Greeks had no written language. But as a result of this cultural contact, the Greeks borrowed and adapted aspects of the Phoenicians' writing system. Over time, this adapted system evolved into classical Greek.

Write the Greek alphabet on the chalkboard, and let students discuss the similarities and differences between the Greek and English alphabets. Does it appear that any English letters may have been borrowed from the Greek alphabet? Let students compose a message to a friend using letters "borrowed" from the Greek alphabet (Figure 4-5).

Greek Comedy & Tragedy Masks

FIGURE 4-4

	Cap	Lower case
Alpha	A	α
Beta	B	β
Chi	X	χ
Delta	Δ	δ
Epsilon	E	ε
Eta	H	η
Gamma	Γ	γ
Iota	I	ι
Kappa	K	κ
Lambda	Λ	λ
Mu	M	μ
Nu	N	ν
Omicron	O	ο
Omega	Ω	ω
Phi	Φ	φ
Pi	Π	π
Psi	Ψ	ψ
Rho	P	ρ
Sigma	Σ	σ
Tau	T	τ
Theta	Θ	θ
Upsilon	Y	υ
Xi	Ξ	ξ
Zeta	Z	ζ

Greek Alphabet

FIGURE 4-5

Science:

1. Hippocrates' Rx for Medicine

Brief Background. An ancient Greek by the name of Hippocrates is called the father of modern medicine. Hippocrates believed there was a relationship between good health and a proper diet. He also taught that sickness was the result of natural causes, not magic or witchcraft. Hippocrates' high standards for the medical profession are exemplified by the Hippocratic oath, which physicians still take today.

Invite a physician or health worker to class to talk about the Hippocratic oath, as well as about good health and proper nutrition. Help students create a healthful and nutritious lunch menu. If feasible, involve students in the preparation of the lunch, and invite parents to attend the luncheon.

2. Archimedes

Brief Background. Archimedes was the greatest scientist of ancient Greece. He used the lever to build machines and invented both the compound pulley and gears using cogged wheels.

Have students identify and make drawings of machines that incorporate the principle of the lever, the compound pulley, and cogged wheels in their structure and function (Figure 4-6).

Art:

1. Greek Art

Brief Background. Greek sculpture and architecture are noted for their graceful and balanced proportions. The Greeks' great admiration for the beauty of the human body is reflected in the statues of athletes and gods. The ruins of ancient Greek structures can be seen today in Greece and the Mediterranean region. The most magnificent of them is the Parthenon, a white marble temple built in honor of the goddess Athena. The architectural style of the ancient Greeks has been admired and imitated by other cultures down through the ages.

Show students pictures of the Parthenon and other examples of Greek architecture as well as pictures of Greek statues. Also show students

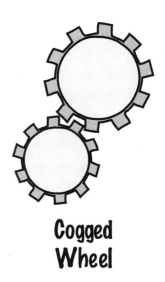

Cogged Wheel

Compound Pulley

Archimedes' Machines

FIGURE 4-6

photographs of buildings, monuments, and museums in our nation's capital, such as the Supreme Court Building and the Lincoln Memorial, that resemble ancient Greek temples. Give each student a Lincoln penny and a hand lens, and let the class observe the depiction of the Lincoln Memorial on the reverse side of the coin. Provide clay and let students make models of Greek temples and sculpture, which can be placed inside appropriately decorated dioramas.

Books:

1. Clare, John D., ed. (1994). *Ancient Greece*. San Diego: Harcourt, Brace & Co. is an imprint of Gulliver. Intermediate, Advanced.

2. Rutland, Jonathan. (1986). *An Ancient Greek Town*. New York: Warwick Press. Advanced.

3. Pluckrose, Henry. (1982). *Ancient Greeks*. New York: Gloucester Press. Primary.

4. Lafferty, Peter. (1991). *Archimedes*. New York: The Bookwright Press. Intermediate.

5. Descamps-Lequime, Sophie. (1992). *The Ancient Greeks*. Brookfield, CT: The Millbrook Press, Inc. Intermediate, Advanced.

6. Dawson, Imogen. (1995). *Food and Feasts in Ancient Greece*. Parsippany, NJ: New Discovery Books. Intermediate, Advanced.

7. Peris, Carme, and Verges, Gloria & Oriol. (1988). *The Greek and Roman Eras*. New York: Barron's Educational Series. Primary, Intermediate.

8. Williams, Susan. (1993). *The Greeks*. New York: Thomas Learning. Intermediate.

9. Lasky, Kathryn. (1994). *The Librarian Who Measured the Earth*. Boston: Little, Brown, & Co. Primary, Intermediate.

10. Poulton, Michael. (1993). *Life in the Time of Pericles and the Ancient Greeks*. New York: Mirabel Books, Ltd. Advanced.

11. *Aesop's Fables* retold by: Barner-Murphy, Frances (1994). NY: Lothrop, Lee & Shepard Books.

Software:

1. *Ancient Civilizations* [Mac Windows CD-ROM]. Victoria, British Columbia: Entrex. Intermediate.

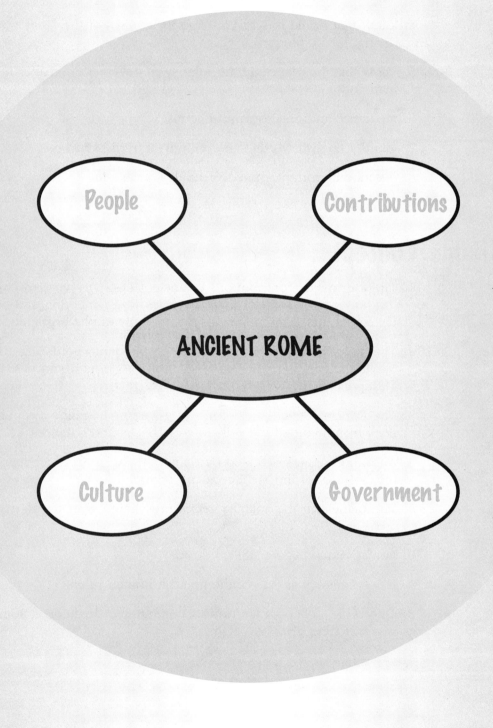

Theme Goals:

Students will:

1. identify the Roman contributions to western civilization.

2. locate Rome and the Roman Empire on a map.

3. describe the key elements of Roman government.

4. know that Rome fought Carthage for control of the lands bordering the Mediterranean Sea.

5. know that the planets in the solar system were named after Roman gods.

6. recognize and use Roman numerals.

7. identify English words that are derived from Latin.

8. describe important aspects of Julius Caesar's life.

9. describe the life of a gladiator.

Theme Concepts:

1. The four major contributions of ancient Rome to western civilization were a code of law, advances in engineering and architecture, the Latin language, and the spread of Christianity.

2. The Roman Empire included all of the land bordering the Mediterranean Sea, and extended north to Britain and east to Mesopotamia.

3. The Romans developed a form of government called a republic, which included the principle of checks and balances.

4. After the Romans defeated Carthage, they were free to expand their control of the Mediterranean region.

5. The planets in the solar system were named after the Roman gods.

6. Roman numerals are still used today.

7. Julius Caesar was one of the greatest Roman rulers.

8. One of the most popular forms of entertainment in ancient Rome was watching gladiators fight.

Vocabulary:

1. Justinian Code
2. arch
3. vault
4. republic
5. consul
6. tribunes
7. senate
8. dictator
9. separation of powers
10. checks and balances
11. veto
13. toga
14. amphitheater
15. aqueduct

Instructional Bulletin Board

The purpose of this bulletin board is to let students practice matching the names of lands in the Roman Empire with their locations on a map of the Mediterranean region. Draw a large political outline map of the Roman Empire on a sheet of large white paper, as shown below. Make name cards for the lands (they are identified below), and let students attach each name card to its correct location on the map. Use Velcro patches to attach name cards to the map. Attach an envelope for storage of the name cards to the lower right corner of the bulletin board. Attach a covered answer key to the lower left corner of the bulletin board.

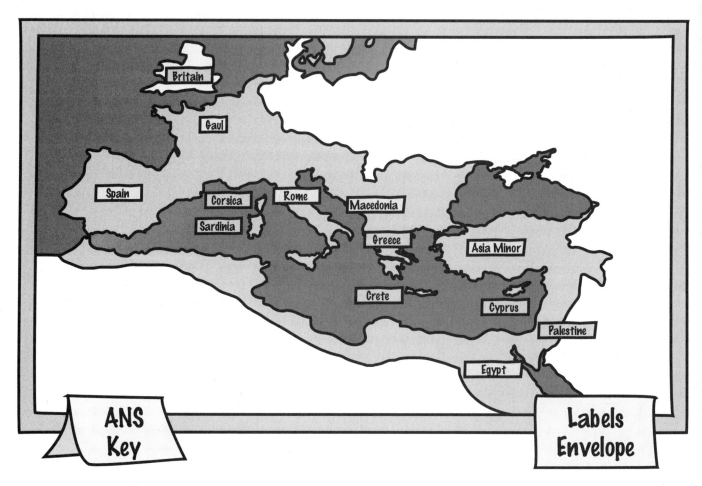

Map of the Roman Empire

Parent Letter

Dear Parents:

The class will be exploring the ancient Roman Empire. The Romans made many important contributions to western civilization. The legal principles of "equal rights under the law" and "a person is innocent until proven guilty" were originated by the Romans. About half of all English words came from Latin, the language of the Romans. Students will be learning these and other interesting facts about the Romans as they participate in a variety of hands-on activities, such as those listed below.

At School:

Students will be engaged in:

- Experiencing the ancient Romans' "gifts" to us
- Mapping the lands in and around the Roman Empire
- Taking the roles of consuls, tribunes, and senators to learn about Roman government
- Traveling with Hannibal as he crosses the Alps and tries to defeat Rome
- Using Roman numerals
- Identifying English words of Latin origin
- Tracing the life and times of Julius Caesar
- Looking at the dangerous life of a gladiator in ancient Rome

At Home:

Now would be a fine time to check out a children's book on ancient Rome from the local library and read it with your child. Stories about the rise and fall of Rome make good reading because they are filled with action, intrigue, and human drama. Also, you can look for evidence of our Roman heritage locally. Can you find examples of Roman numerals being used? Are there any local examples of Roman-style architecture?

Linking Up:

Ask students to tell you about their classroom rules. Do students believe the rules are applied fairly? Explain that the idea for fair and just rules came from the ancient Romans. Encourage students to talk about their ideas and images of the Romans. What were the sources of their prior information (television, film, books, magazines, etc.)? How adequate and accurate is their knowledge?

Social Studies:

1. Roman Contributions

Brief Background. Some important contributions of the ancient Romans to western civilization were as follows: establishing legal principles (Justinian Code), developing engineering and architectural forms, and advancing the spread of ideas through oratory, writing, drama, the use of Latin (which influenced many modern languages), and the adoption of Christianity.

To introduce students to ancient Rome, show the class the following items: (1) a copy of the school rules, the U.S. Constitution, and the Bill of Rights; (2) a picture of Monticello, Thomas Jefferson's famous home in Virginia; (3) a list of English words based on Latin (such as aquarium, feminine, frigid, manual, moveable, cent, quart, and videotape); and (4) a cross. Encourage students to speculate about what all of these items have in common. Then, explain that all of these items tell us about important Roman contributions to our modern world.

1. The Romans collected and organized a book of laws, which came to be known as the *Justinian Code*. Some of these laws, such as "All people have equal rights under the law" and "A person is innocent until proven guilty," were incorporated into our justice system. Dramatize some classroom situations that demonstrate the importance of these laws in everyday life.
2. Influenced by the Greeks, the Romans made many contributions in the areas of engineering, architecture, writing, and drama. The Roman use of the arch and vault made it possible to construct buildings with vast interior spaces. Thomas Jefferson was an ad-

mirer of ancient Roman buildings. He used some Roman architectural ideas—mainly the dome—in the design of his famous home, Monticello.
3. As the Roman Empire expanded, so, too, did the Latin language. Even after the fall of Rome, Latin remained the language of educated people throughout Europe. About half of all English words are derived from Latin.
4. By the end of the fourth century A.D., Christianity had been adopted as the official religion of the Roman Empire. This hastened the religion's spread throughout Europe. Today, Christianity is both the world's and the United States's most practiced religion.

2. The Roman Empire

Provide students with maps of Italy and the Mediterranean Region. Ask students to describe Italy's bootlike shape. Help them find Rome on the map. At the height of their power, the Romans controlled all of the land bordering the Mediterranean Sea, and their empire extended north to Britain, west to Spain, east to Mesopotamia, and south to Egypt. Students can create salt and flour and/or papier-mache maps of the Roman Empire.

3. Roman Government

Brief Background. The Romans developed a government called a *republic*, in which voters elected their leaders. Different government powers and duties were assigned to different groups, with each group serving as a check and balance on the others. Citizen assemblies elected two *consuls*, who ran the government and who had veto power over each other, and ten *tribunes*, who could veto government actions. The *senate*, comprised of 300 members of Rome's wealthiest families, controlled finances and foreign policy. If the consuls agreed, the senate could select a *dictator*, with absolute power, to run the government for up to six months. The Roman idea of separation of government powers and duties among different groups was intended to ensure that no one person or group held all of the power. The principles of *separation of powers* and *checks and balances*, along with the *veto power*, have been adopted by many modern nations, including the United States.

Have students assume the roles of Roman consuls, tribunes, and senators, and let them discuss an issue of current interest to them. To make the simulation more authentic, let students wear togas. A toga was a loose outer garment that was worn in public in ancient Rome. To fashion the toga, drape a white sheet around the body and over one shoulder as shown (Figure 5-1).

3. Rome vs. Carthage: And the Winner was. . . .

Brief Background. Rome's chief rival for control of the Mediterranean region was Carthage, a city-state located on the coast of North Africa (in present-day Tunisia). Long before Rome was a force

Toga

FIGURE 5-1

in the region, Carthage was an important trading center and naval power. Carthage also ruled part of Spain, an area that the Romans wanted to control. The two rivals fought each other off and on for over a hundred years in a series of conflicts called the Punic Wars. In an effort to defeat Rome once and for all, Carthage's great general, Hannibal, led his army and 50 war elephants eastward from Spain across present-day southern France. His plan was to cross the Alps Mountains into Italy and then attack the Roman army, but freezing snow and landslides in the Alps interfered. During the crossing, over half the army and most of the elephants died. Despite the losses, Hannibal was still able to win some important battles against the Romans, but his greatly outnumbered forces weren't strong enough to win the war. When Rome launched an invasion of Carthage, Hannibal was called back home. His army was eventually defeated by the Romans, and in 146 B.C., the Romans destroyed Carthage. With the defeat of Carthage, Rome was free to expand its control of the lands around the Mediterranean Sea.

To bring these exciting times from history to life, students can participate in one or more of the following projects:

1. Make oral reports, dressed in costume, on Hannibal's life and times,
2. Draw battle maps of the Punic Wars (military maps of ancient battles can be found in historical atlases),
3. Recreate Hannibal's crossing of the Alps,
4. Design a diorama to depict the Roman invasion of Carthage, and
5. Draw two maps of the Mediterranean region, one to show land under Roman control before the defeat of Carthage (146 B.C.), and the other to show the Roman Empire at the height of its expansion in 120 A.D.

Science:

1. Roman Gods and the Planets

Brief Background. The planets in the solar system have been named after Roman gods as follows: Mercury (winged messenger of the gods); Venus (goddess of love); Earth (called Gaia, the mother of all gods); Mars (god of war); Jupiter (king of the gods); Saturn (god of the harvest); Uranus (god of the heavens); Neptune (god of the sea); and Pluto (god of the dead).

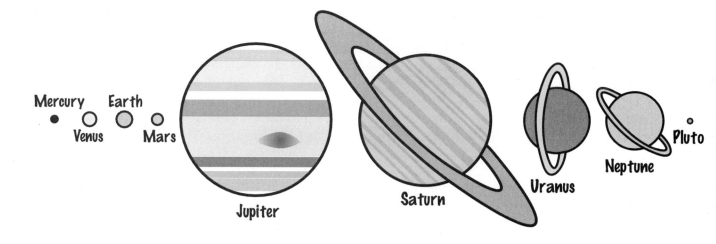

Planets Drawn to Scale

FIGURE 5-2

Let each student research one of the Roman gods and make a brief illustrated presentation to the class. Students can make a model of the solar system to show the relative distance of each planet from the sun (Figure 5-2).

Math:

1. Roman Numerals

Brief Background. Roman numerals are still used today for outlines, chapter titles, and copyright dates. There are only seven Roman numerals: I = 1, V = 5, X = 10, L = 50, C = 100, D = 500, and M = 1000. All of the other numerals are formed in either of two ways: by adding to a numeral one or more numerals of equal or smaller value after it, such as VI = 6, or by subtracting from a numeral by placing a smaller number before it, such as IV = 4.

I = 1	XI = 11
II = 2	XII = 12
III = 3	XIII = 13
IV = 4	XIV = 14
V = 5	XV = 15
VI = 6	XVI = 16
VII = 7	XVII = 17
VIII = 8	XVIII = 18
IX = 9	IXX = 19
X = 10	XX = 20

FIGURE 5-3

Review or teach the Roman numerals, such as the numeral 1997 = MCMXCVII, where M = 1000, CM = 900, XC = 90, and VII = 7. Challenge students to find examples of Roman numerals in use (in books, on clock faces, on buildings and monuments, etc.) Let students practice their Roman numerals by translating numbers found in newspapers—such as prices in ads, weather page temperatures, sports page box scores, and stock market quotes in the business section—into Roman numerals (Figure 5-3).

Language Arts:

1. Roman Adventure

Encourage students to imagine they are citizens of ancient Rome, and have them write about their life.

2. Latin Trackdown

Have students use dictionaries to identify English words that are derived from Latin. Show students some examples of how words develop and change, such as the word "equestrian" derived from the Latin word *equis*, which means "horse," and "aquatic" derived from the Latin word *aquae*, which means "water."

3. Biographical Sketch

Let students write biographical sketches about ancient Rome's most famous personality, Julius

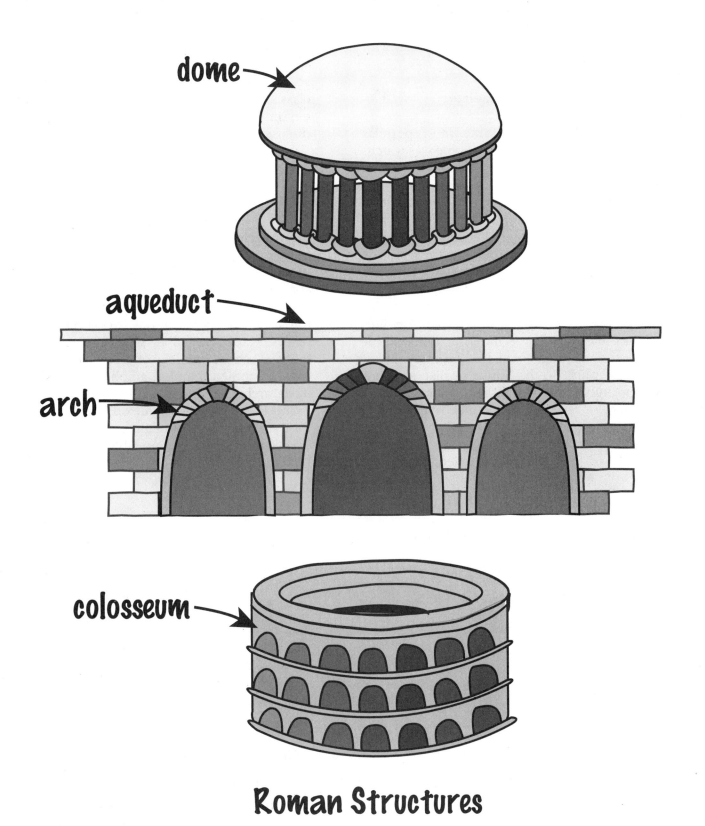

dome

aqueduct

arch

colosseum

Roman Structures

FIGURE 5-4

Caesar. Gather books on Caesar and make them available to students. To stimulate interest in his life, read aloud selections from *Julius Caesar* by Rupert Matthews (Bookwright, 1989), or other appropriate children's books. Make certain students investigate the following aspects of Caesar's life: (1) military accomplishments as commander of the Roman army; (2) rise to absolute power and selection as dictator; (3) accomplishments while dictator of Rome; (4) decision of senators to murder Caesar; and (5) effects of Caesar's death on Rome. Encourage students to illustrate their biographies with scenes from Caesar's life.

4. A Day in the Life of a Gladiator

Brief Background. One of the most popular forms of entertainment in ancient Rome was watching gladiators fight each other. These fights, which took place in outdoor, oval-shaped arenas, attracted thousands of spectators. The gladiators were usually slaves or criminals who were trained to fight. Most gladiators wore helmets and carried shields for protection. They fought with swords or daggers, or with spears and nets. Two gladiators would fight until one of them was killed or too wounded to continue. If able, a wounded gladiator would appeal to the crowd to spare his life. Sometimes the crowd was merciful, especially if the gladiator had fought well, but more often, they signaled for his death. Some gladiators were trained to hunt lions, bears, and other wild animals that were set loose inside the arena.

Have interested students report on the life of gladiators. Their fighting was a fierce and cruel sport. Do students think there are any modern sports that could be called deadly and cruel? If so, should these sports be banned? Have the class survey other students' attitudes about cruelty in sports. They can graph the results and discuss their implications.

Art:

1. Engineering Marvels

Provide students with an assortment of art and construction materials—paint, brushes, colored markers, modeling clay, construction paper, Styrofoam blocks, pins, stones, wood blocks and pieces, cardboard, tape, glue—and challenge them to create models of Roman structures, such as domed temples, amphitheaters, aqueducts, archways, and roads (Figure 5-4). If small groups of students can agree on a standard scale for their models, they might want to pool their efforts and jointly create a tabletop model of a Roman city.

Books:

1. Macaulay, David. (1974). *City: A Story of Roman Planning and Construction*. Boston: Houghton Mifflin Company. Advanced.

2. Corbishley, Mike. (1994). *Growing Up in Ancient Rome*. Troll Associates. Primary, Intermediate.

3. Matthews, Rupert. (1989). *Julius Caesar*. New York: Bookwright Press. Primary, Intermediate.

4. Bombarde, Odile, and Moatti, Claude. (1986). *Living in Ancient Rome*. Ossining, NY: Young Discovery Library. Primary.

5. Ballard, Robert D. (1990). *The Lost Wreck of the Isis*. New York: Odyssey Corporation. Intermediate, Advanced.

6. The World Heritage. (1993). *The Roman Empire*. Chicago: Children's Press. Intermediate, Advanced.

7. Howarth, Sarah. (1993). *Roman People*. Brookfield, CT: The Millbrook Press. Intermediate, Advanced.

8. Howarth, Sarah. (1993). *Roman Places*. Brookfield, CT: The Millbrook Press. Intermediate, Advanced.

9. Caselli, Giovanni. (1986). *A Roman Soldier*. New York: Peter Bedrick Books. Intermediate.

10. Pluckrose, Henry. (1982). *Romans*. New York: Gloucester Press. Primary.

11. Dineen, Jaqueline. (1992). *The Romans*. New York: New Discovery Books. Advanced.

12. Corbishley, Mike. (1991). *What Do We Know about the Romans?* New York: Peter Bedrick Books. Intermediate.

Software:

1. *Hannibel's Heroes* [Mac Windows CD-ROM]. Victoria, British Columbia: Entrex. Advanced.

2. *Ancient Civilizations* [MPC CD-ROM]. London: Flag Tower. Advanced.

4. *Everyday Life in Ancient Times* [Mac MPC CD-ROM]. Chicago: Clearvue/eav. Advanced.

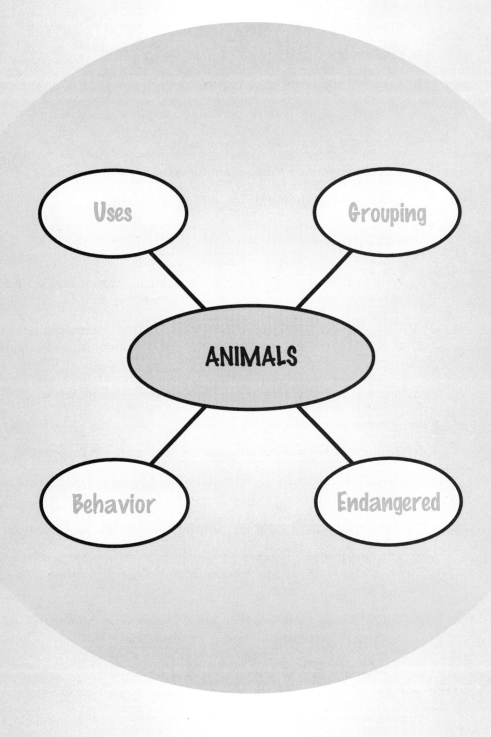

Uses

Grouping

ANIMALS

Behavior

Endangered

Theme Goals:

Students will:

1. categorize animals according to certain criteria.

2. know that animals have adapted to their environment in many ways.

3. observe the behavior of live animals.

4. take a survey of pets.

5. calculate the costs of caring for a pet.

6. know that animals have benefited people in many ways.

7. locate the seven major animal habitats.

8. examine common misconceptions about some animals.

9. trace the growth and development of animals.

Theme Concepts:

1. Based on their physical structure, animals can be divided into two main groups—vertebrates and invertebrates.

2. Based on the their food consumption behavior, animals can be divided into three groups—herbivores, carnivores, and omnivorous.

3. Animals are well adapted to their natural environments.

4. Animals can be studied scientifically.

5. Because of human actions, some animals are endangered.

6. Certain animals that frighten some people are actually harmless and help control pests.

7. It is important for people to know how to care for their pets.

8. The seven major habitats in which animals live are mountain, polar region, grassland, temperate forest, tropical forest, desert, and ocean.

9. Animals assist people in their work and provide them with food, clothing, transportation, and companionship.

Vocabulary:

1. herbivores	5. polar region	9. invertebrates
2. omnivores	6. temperate forest	10. domesticated
3. carnivores	7. tropical forest	
4. adaptation	8. vertebrates	

Instructional Bulletin Board

The purpose of this bulletin board is to help students identify the names of the following ten endangered animals (habitats are in parentheses): green seas turtle (warm oceans), orangutan (Indonesia), giant panda (China), tiger (India), black rhinoceros (Africa), California condor (California), blue whale (oceans), Indian elephant (India), and American crocodile (Florida). Cover the bulletin board with a large sheet of white paper and attach pictures of the animals. Place one Velcro patch under each animal, positioning the patch so that a name card can be attached. Make name cards for the animals and place a Velcro patch on the back of each card. Put the name cards in a large envelope attached to the lower right corner of the bulletin board. Attach a covered answer key to the lower left corner.

ENDANGERED ANIMALS

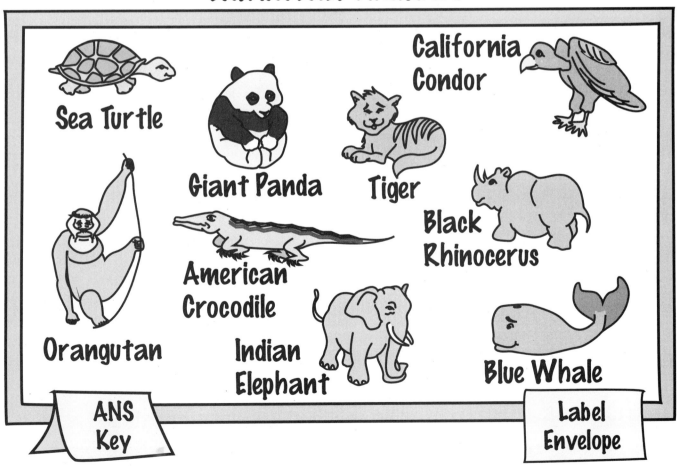

Sea Turtle

California Condor

Giant Panda

Tiger

Black Rhinocerus

Orangutan

American Crocodile

Indian Elephant

Blue Whale

ANS Key

Label Envelope

Parent Letter

Dear Parents:

We are beginning our study of animals. Since prehistoric times, animals have helped humans in many ways. Today, many animals are endangered because of human actions. This theme will help children realize that humans have a responsibility as guardians of the planet to preserve and protect animals and their habitats.

In School:

Some of the interesting things we will be doing include:

- Exploring how animals are alike and different
- Learning how animals adapt to their environment
- Observing live animals in the classroom
- Conducting animal research
- Measuring the biggest, fastest, and heaviest animals
- Finding the places where animals live
- Studying how animals grow and develop
- Looking for animal tracks and making animal masks

At Home:

Here are some ways you can reinforce the concepts your child is learning at school:

- Take your child to the zoo, aquarium, natural history museum, wildlife sanctuary, or nature center.
- Watch a TV documentary about animals together.
- If you have a pet, talk with your child about its care.
- Select an animal book at the library for your child.

Linking Up:

Ask students to name their favorite animals or pets. What do they like best about their favorite animals? What feeling do they have for them? What kind of care do their pets need?

Science:

1. The Chain of Life

Brief Background. Animals do not exist in isolation from one another or from plant life. They interact with their environment. Through the food chain, matter and energy are continuously interchanged. Plants are food for animals. Based on animals' food consumption behavior, biologists classify them into three groups. Many animals, such as rabbits, cows, and sheep, eat only plants (*herbivores*). Other animals eat both plants and animals (*omnivores*) or just animals (*carnivores*).

Have students name their main energy sources. Based on the sources listed, are most students herbivores, omnivorous, or carnivores? Then have students tell you where their main energy sources got their energy. Write *eaten* and *eater* on the chalkboard. Have students give names of living things to list under the two headings. What do the lists tell the students about the chain of life?

2. Animal Diversity

A trip to a zoo or aquarium can give students a sense of the great diversity among animals. Once a field trip is planned, have students list animals that might be seen. Assign each student the task of reporting on one zoo or aquarium animal. As an enrichment activity, let students conduct a panel discussion on the following topic: Should animals be kept in a zoo?

3. Adaptation

Brief Background. Animals are well adapted to their natural habitats, or places where they naturally live. A large chest, long legs, and streamlined body make the cheetah a fast runner, an adaptation that gives it an advantage over slower animals on the open plains. Similarly, a giraffe's long neck makes it ideally suited to eat the tender leaves from the upper branches of a tall tree.

Display drawings of various animals. As students observe a particular animal displayed, ask them to list its physical characteristics. Then, based on the list, have students predict the environmental characteristics of that animal's natural habitat. To check their predictions, show visuals (slides, computer images, videos) of the animals in their natural habitats.

4. Classroom Animals

If you haven't done so yet, now is the time to bring animals into your classroom. (Note: first check your school's policy regarding animal visits.) To create an instant aquarium, all you need is a clean, clear-plastic beverage bottle, water, sea salt, and brine shrimp (feed them yeast). A land habitat for a salamander can be fashioned almost as quickly. You need a large, clear plastic garment box (drill a few air holes in the top cover), decayed wood (2-inch layer to cover bottom of box), a few stones or small pieces of wood for hiding places, and a small container of water. Since a salamander's habitat requires high humidity, make certain the decayed wood is moist (the plastic cover will help retain moisture). Salamanders will eat almost any worm or insect small enough for them to swallow. Cages, bedding materials, and other equipment for gerbils, hamsters, guinea pigs, mice, and other small animals are available at most pet stores. Other animals that make great classroom pets include ant farms, guppies, goldfish, hermit crabs, snails, turtles, and frogs. Let students help you decide on the "best" animal for your classroom. They can research animals' habitats, what they eat, and how to care for them. Consult with the local pet store(s) for availability of particular animals and information about their care (also check a veterinary clinic). (Notes: For aquariums, use distilled water, or tap water that has been allowed to stand for 24 hours. Aquariums and terrariums should be placed near, but not in, direct sunlight.) (Figure 6-1).

5. Animal Research

To stimulate scientific inquiry, have students make systematic and careful observations of animals, such as brine shrimp and/or a hamster. As students observe brine shrimp eggs in a bottle of salty water, they can make drawings of

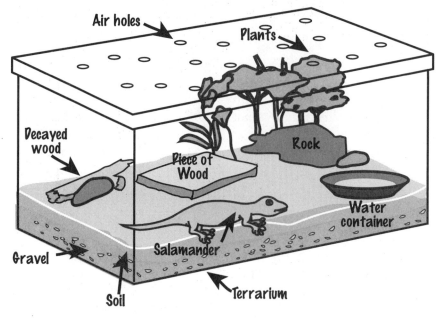

Salamander Habitat

FIGURE 6-1

what they see and jot down questions to investigate, such as What will happen to the eggs? and Why is the water salty? (To simulate the brine shrimp's natural habitat.) After the eggs hatch, students will want to use their observation and analysis skills to answer questions like these: What happened to the eggs? (They changed.) What are the new animals? (Larva.) From where did they come? (The eggs.) and What will happen them? (They will change into little shrimp.) A hamster can generate a different set of student questions, including the following: What foods does it like to eat? Which plants does it like best? How can we find out which plants it prefers? After students make predictions about the hamster's food preferences, they can put different kinds of plants, such as lettuce, celery, and carrots, in the cage and observe its feeding habits.

6. Animal Tracks

In a clearing near the school, place some food, such as seeds and nuts, in a small pile. Dust the area around the food with flour. Let students check the area the next day. Have students try to answer the following questions: Is any of the food gone? Are there any animal tracks in the flour? If there are tracks, what animal(s) left them (Figure 6-2)?

7. Classifying Creatures

Have students locate their bumpy backbones with their hands. Then, let them take turns feeling a sponge. Ask them to try to locate the sponge's backbone. Tell students that the animal kingdom can be divided into two groups—*vertebrates*, or animals with backbones, and *invertebrates*, or animals without backbones. In which group do they belong? How about sponges? Let students classify as many animals as they can into these two main groups. About which animals are they unsure? How can they check their ideas? Divide the students into small groups and let each group classify animals by one of the following criteria: big vs. little, fly-

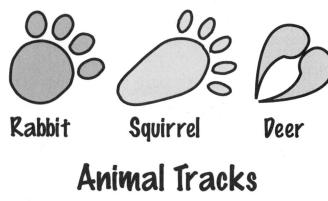

Rabbit   Squirrel   Deer

Animal Tracks

FIGURE 6-2

ing vs. nonflying, wild vs. domesticated, and water vs. land.

8. Twenty Questions

Divide the class into teams and let them take turns asking yes–no questions to gain knowledge about the identity of a particular animal.

Math:

1. Class Pets

Have students conduct a survey to determine the number and kinds of pets owned by students or their families. Help them graph and interpret the results of the survey (Figure 6-3).

2. Lengthy Animals

Have students check library resources to determine the greatest lengths obtained by various species of animals. Provide appropriate measurement instruments and challenge students to devise unique ways to visually represent the lengths. For example, the longest ant could be represented by a 1-inch long stick, and the longest whale by a 100-foot long rope. The school hallway would probably be a good place to display the measurements.

3. Measuring the Biggest and Fastest Animals

Students can construct bar graphs that show the relative weight and speed of the world's largest and fastest animals.

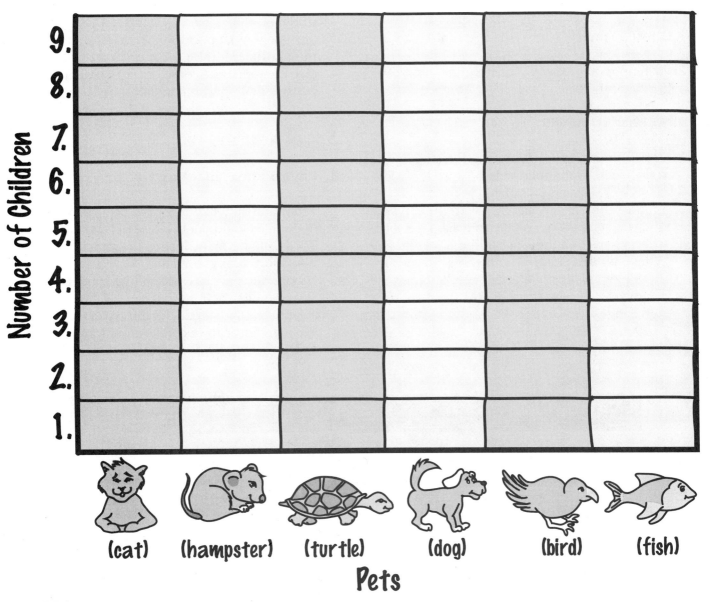

FIGURE 6-3

Biggest	Fastest
Blue whale (220 tons)	Golden eagle (120 mph)
American buffalo (3,000 pounds)	Cheetah (70 mph)
African elephant (14,500 pounds)	Canvasback duck (70 mph)
Brown bear (500 pounds)	Hummingbird (60 mph)
African lion (500 pounds)	Pronghorn antelope (62 mph)
White rhinoceros (3 1/2 tons)	Sailfish (65 mph)
Shire horse (2,300 pounds)	Dragonfly (50 mph)
River hippopotamus (5,800 pounds)	Peregrine falcon (120 mph)

4. Animal Arithmetic

Create animal math problems for students to solve, such as the following:

1. After students are familiar with the physical characteristics of certain animals, give them problems like this one: Add the legs of five insects, two spiders, and three horses. Divide by the shells of one clam. Subtract the tentacles of one octopus. (Answer: $6 + 6 + 6 + 6 + 6 + 8 + 8 + 4 + 4 + 4 = 58 \div 2 = 29 - 8 = 21$)

2. Fred has two cats. Each cat eats a can of food each day. How many cans of cat food will they eat in a week?
3. Mary has five kittens. Three are grey. The others are black. How many are black?
4. Arrange cut-outs of animals. Ask students to sort and count the animals.

5. Animal Cookies

Provide students with animal-shaped cookie cutters. They can apply measuring and arithmetic skills as they follow the recipe below to make animal cookies.

6. Pet Costs

Have each student research the cost of caring for a particular kind of pet, such as a dog, cat, horse, canary, turtle, or fish. Some of the costs students will need to consider include: food (cost per day); opportunity cost (amount of time per day that must be spent on care of pet); special equipment; license fees; veterinarian expenses; and special handling needs.

Social Studies:

1. Environment in a Box

Some animals, like the passenger pigeon and dodo, have died out because of human actions. Today, many animals are threatened with the possibility of extinction. Let each student choose an endangered animal, and then research human actions that caused the animal to become endangered. To illustrate the report, each student can decorate an empty box—us-

---

RECIPE

Ingredients:

1 package (14.5 ounces) gingerbread mix
1/4 cup milk
1/4 cup salad oil

Directions:

Mix ingredients and chill dough in refrigerator 1 hour. Roll dough until 1/4 inch thick. Cut cookies and bake approximately 12 minutes at 350°.

ing magic markers, colored tissue paper, construction paper, pipe cleaners, glue, modeling clay, sand, rocks, twigs, leaves, and other materials—to depict the animal in its natural environment. Some endangered animals to research include:

Green sea turtle	Black rhinoceros
Woolly spider monkey	Aye-aye
Whooping crane	Indian elephant
Orangutan	California condor
Giant panda	Blue whale
Tiger	Cheetah
	American crocodile

2. Animals and People

Read aloud sections of *Who Harnessed the Horse? A Story of Animal Domestication* by Margery Facklam (Little, Brown and Company, 1992), or another appropriate children's book that illustrates how animals have benefited humans since earliest times. They have provided food (meat), clothing (fur, wool, silk, and leather), and transportation (horses, camels, and llamas). Have students list animals that fall under the following categories: animals that provide transportation (horses, llamas, camels, oxen, etc.); animals that provide food (cattle, pigs, sheep, chickens, fish, etc.); animals that provide clothing (cattle, sheep, etc.); animals that help people work (sheep dogs; police dogs, draft horses, camels, etc.); animals that provide people with companionship (dogs, cats, etc.); and animals that perform special roles (seeing-eye dogs). Assign each student the task of researching the history of a particular animal used by humans.

3. Animal Rights

Lions in the wild have to kill to survive, but people do not need to eat animals for their own survival. Some people feel that animals should not be killed for research, food, or clothing. Have small groups of students take the perspective of particular animals. What "rights," if any, should humans guarantee to animals? What would happen if people stopped eating meat, and instead ate only fruits, vegetables, and grains? Have each group make an "animal rights" poster that expresses the group's position on the issue.

4. Habitat Displays

Animals can be grouped according to the type of place or habitat in which they live. Divide the class into seven small groups of students. Assign each group the task of creating a display for one of the following seven major types of habitats: (1) mountain, (2) polar region, (3) grassland, (4) temperate forest, (5) tropical forest, (6) desert, and (7) ocean. Provide each group with a 1-square yard piece of cardboard. Help students fold the cardboard into three equal 12" × 36" parts and tape the two ends together to form a three-sided display area as shown in Figure 6-4. After researching their assigned habitats, each group can mount each side of the cardboard with one of the following: (1) brief reports about the habitat written in script, (2) cut-out pictures of animals found in the habitat, and (3) pictures of the habitat. Place the displays on shelves or tables around the room, or if you prefer, hang them from the ceiling (Figure 6-4).

Language Arts:

1. My Favorite Animal

Let students write about their favorite animal. Encourage students to pick any animal they want, including stuffed animals and cartoon animals, as well as pets and other real animals. Students can illustrate their papers with photos or drawings of the chosen animals.

2. Animals in the News

Encourage students to look for news articles or information on TV about animals for show and tell. They can use the gathered information to write and perform their own radio and/or TV news reports.

3. Make Believe Animals

Let students create imaginary animals and give them names. To stimulate the students' imaginations, read aloud Dr. Seuss's *If I Ran the Zoo* (Random House, 1950).

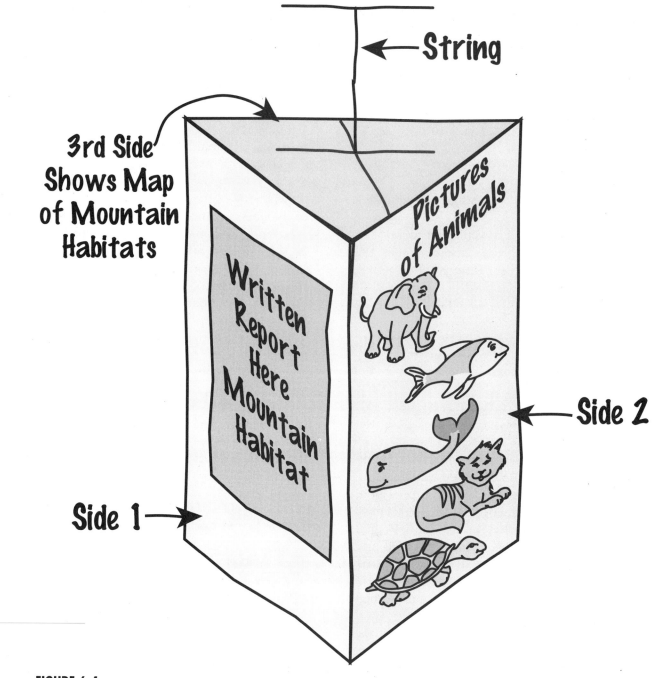

← String

3rd Side Shows Map of Mountain Habitats

Pictures of Animals

Written Report Here Mountain Habitat

← Side 2

Side 1 →

FIGURE 6-4

4. Misconceptions About Animals

Brief Background. While it is true that some animals are dangerous to people, it is also true that some very beneficial animals have been the subjects of many myths and superstitions. Many people fear snakes, bats, and spiders, for example, yet only a few kinds of these animals are harmful to humans and most are very helpful in controlling pests.

Have students discuss animals they fear. Provide them with books and other resources about the animals. What positive attributes can they discover about them? Does understanding more about the animals make students more or less fearful of them? Role-play a person who is afraid of a particular animal, and ask students to try to persuade you to change your attitude about it.

5. Animal Symbols

Brief Background. Animals, both real and mythical, are used as official and unofficial symbols for nations, states, sports teams, airlines, and cars and trucks. Some animals associated with nations include the bald eagle with the United States, the lion and the unicorn with Great Britain, the giant panda with China, the beaver with Canada, the garuda with Indonesia, the quetzal with Guatemala, and the koala bear with Australia.

Let interested students track down the names, histories, and locations of animal symbols, nicknames, and mascots. Have each student pick an animal to be the symbol for the classroom, and then write a persuasive letter giving reasons for the choice.

6. How Animals Develop

Brief Background. Animals grow and develop in many different ways. For example, sea turtles must take care of themselves from the day they are hatched. Kangaroos carry their babies in a pouch until they are mature enough to move around on their own. Lion cubs learn how to hunt for themselves by watching their parents.

Read sections of Cathryn Hilker's *A Cheetah Named Angel* (Franklin Watts, 1992), Russell Freedman's *Growing Up Wild, How Young Animals Survive* (Holiday House, 1975), or another appropriate children's book that traces the growth and development of animals from birth to independence. Have students pick an animal to study in depth. Let students make illustrated booklets on the growth and development of their animals, including diagrams that portray birth to the present. Have them make another diagram that traces their own development from birth to the present. Let students compare and contrast the two diagrams. Compared to the animals they studied, does it take humans more or less time to become independent?

7. Scientific Writing

Pick an animal species common to your locality as a class research and writing project. For example, the eastern cottontail rabbit is found over the entire eastern half of the United States. If your class picked that animal, you could encourage students to do field and library research to carefully answer the following questions: What do the rabbits look like? What do they eat? If you don't actually see rabbits in the field, how can you tell if they have been there before? How do rabbits care for their young? What link are rabbits in the food chain? After students answered these and other questions, they could then develop an accurate written profile of the cottontail.

Art:

1. Dog Drawing

Students can get plenty of tips on drawing dogs from *Draw Fifty Dogs* by Lee Ames (Doubleday, 1981).

2. Animal Cartoons

TV shows, comic strips, and books featuring animal characters are popular with most students. After students look at cartoons from newspapers that have animal characters, let them draw their own cartoon strips starring animals. Provide drawing and painting materials, and encourage them to be creative.

3. Animal Masks

Let students make masks of their favorite animals. Provide students with drawing materials, white paper plates, brown paper bags, construction paper, yarn, string, fabric, glue, and scissors. Students can wear their masks while making brief oral reports to the class on their favorite animals.

Music:

1. Music to the Ears

Play an audio recording of bird calls. Help students identify common birds by their calls. If it is possible, take students on a field trip to a bird sanctuary.

Books:

1. Hilker, Cathryn. (1992). *A Cheetah Named Angel*. New York: Franklin Watts. Primary, Intermediate.

2. Facklam, Margery. (1992). *Who Harnessed the Horse? A Story of Animal Domestication*. Boston: Little, Brown and Company. Advanced.

3. Smith, Elizabeth. (1986). *A Dolphin Goes to School*. New York: William Morrow and Company, Inc. Intermediate.

4. Pringle, Lawrence. (1972). *Pests and People: The Search for Sensible Pest Control*. New York: MacMillan Company. Intermediate.

5. Patent, Dorothy. (1987). *The Way of the Grizzly*. New York: Clarion Books. Primary, Intermediate.

6. Roy, Ron. (1986). *Big and Small, Short and Tall*. New York: Ticknor & Fields. Primary.

7. Greene, Carol. (1993). *The Peregrine Falcon*. Hillside, NJ: Enslow Publishers, Inc. Primary.

8. Freedman, Russell. (1975). *Growing Up Wild, How Young Animals Survive*. New York: Holiday House. Advanced.

9. Bare, Colleen Stanley. (1990). *Elephants on the Beach*. New York: Cobblehill Books/Dutton. Primary.

10. Cossi, Olga. (1991). *Harp Seals*. Minneapolis: Carolrhoda Books, Inc. Primary.

11. Ames, Lee. (1981). *Draw Fifty Dogs*. Garden City, NY: Doubleday. Intermediate.

12. Dr. Seuss. (1950). *If I Ran the Zoo*. NY: RandomHouse. Primary.

Software:

1. *Mammals: A Multimedia Encyclopedia* [Mac IBM CD-ROM]. Washington, DC: National Geographic. Primary, Intermediate, Advanced.

2. *How Animals Move* [Mac MPC CD-ROM]. Bethesda, MD: Discovery Channel. Primary, Intermediate, Advanced.

3. *The San Diego Zoo Presents: The Animals! 2.0* [Mac MPC CD-ROM]. Novato, CA: Mindscape Educational Software. Primary, Intermediate, Advanced.

4. *Scavenger Hunt Adventure Series: Africa* [Mac MPC CD-ROM]. Torrance, CA: Davidson/Swede. Intermediate, Advanced.

5. *Discovering Endangered Wildlife* [MPC CD-ROM]. Fairfield, CT: Queue. Advanced.

6. *The Multimedia Animal Encyclopedia* [Mac MPC CD-ROM]. West Chester, PA: RomTech, Inc. Primary, Intermediate, Advanced.

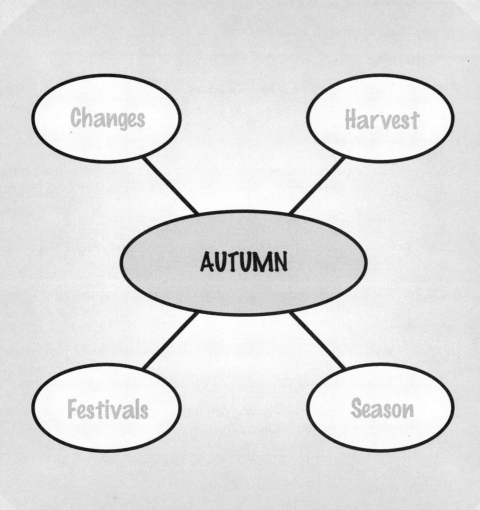

Theme Goals:

Students will:

1. explain how the seasons change.

2. gather, sort, and identify autumn leaves.

3. explain why leaves change color in autumn.

4. record the length of daylight during autumn.

5. record the daily temperature during autumn.

6. measure pumpkins.

7. participate in a harvest festival.

8. help write a story about Halloween.

9. incorporate leaves into art forms.

Theme Concepts:

1. The seasons change because places on the earth receive different amounts of light during the earth's journey around the sun.

2. Broadleaf tree leaves fall during autumn.

3. Factors that influence leaf color are leaf pigment, length of night, and weather.

4. The days get increasingly shorter during autumn.

5. The days get increasingly cooler during autumn.

6. Math skills can be applied in the measurement of pumpkins.

7. Nations around the world have different school schedules.

8. Harvest festivals have been an important tradition in many countries and cultures for centuries.

9. Students can pool their ideas to create an original story.

10. Leaves can be used to create art.

Vocabulary:

1. chlorophyll

2. carotenoid

3. anthocyanin

4. autumnal equinox

Instructional Bulletin Board

The purpose of this bulletin board is to give students practice sorting autumn leaves into different categories based on their color, or pigment. Cover the bulletin board with a large sheet of white paper. Using leaves students have collected and/or you have provided, let students pin leaves to the board within the correct color grouping. (Note: some kinds of trees, like oaks have leaves that turn a range of autumn colors.)

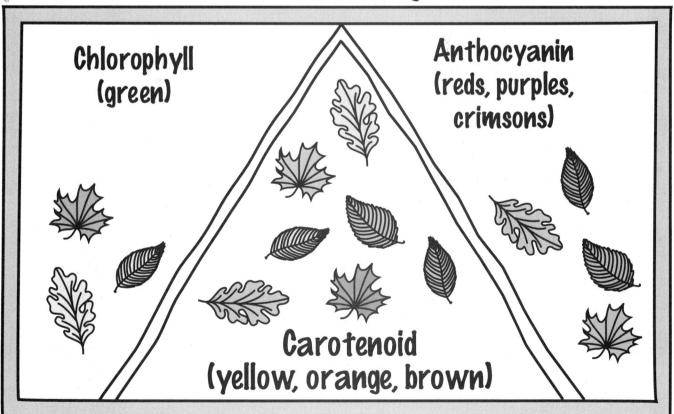

To Which Groups Do My Leaves Belong?

Chlorophyll (green)

Anthocyanin (reds, purples, crimsons)

Carotenoid (yellow, orange, brown)

Parent Letter

Dear Parents:

In most parts of the United States autumn means shorter days, crisper temperatures, and landscapes transformed into brilliant arrays of colors. Throughout America, autumn is the time when children start a new school year, and special holidays—Columbus Day, Veterans' Day, Halloween, Thanksgiving—are shared.

As we begin our study of autumn, we want to share some of the questions students will investigate.

- Why do the seasons change?
- Why do leaves change color?
- Where do the autumn colors come from?
- Why do leaves fall?
- Why do Americans celebrate Halloween Day and Thanksgiving Day?
- How do you measure a pumpkin?

At Home:

Autumn is a great season of the year to take a nature walk with your child, or perhaps rake the yard together. You can identify trees and collect fallen leaves. Remind your child that those fallen leaves that cover the ground have an important role to play in nature; decomposed leaves are food for both the soil and the organisms that live there.

Linking Up:

Ask students what they like best about autumn. Make a list of their responses and discuss them. Probe to check if students are aware of any seasonal changes that have occurred.

Science:

1. Changing Seasons

Brief Background. Seasons change because geographical areas receive different amounts of light during the Earth's revolution, or annual journey around the sun. Places receive different amounts of light because the Earth is tilted slightly more than 23 degrees on its axis. The diagram shows the relation of the Sun and Earth during the year. In the Northern Hemisphere, either September 22 or 23 (it depends on the year) is the first day of autumn. The first day of autumn is called the *autumnal equinox*. On that day, the Sun appears directly over the equator, giving places on Earth about 12 hours of daylight and 12 hours of darkness. During autumn, the days get increasing shorter until December 21 or 22, the day of fewest hours of daylight, which marks the arrival of winter.

Go over the diagram with the students, and then demonstrate the earth's revolution. Use a spotlight to represent the Sun and a globe to represent the Earth. Then, in a darkened room, walk the globe around the light (let a student

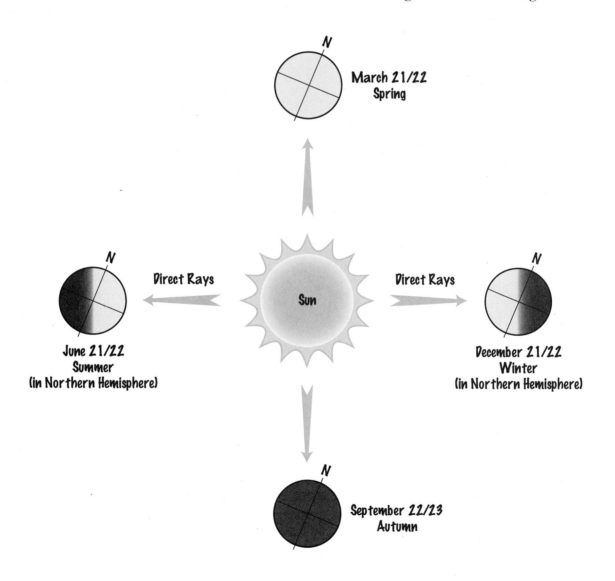

March 21/22
Spring

Direct Rays

Sun

Direct Rays

June 21/22
Summer
(in Northern Hemisphere)

December 21/22
Winter
(in Northern Hemisphere)

September 22/23
Autumn

Earth's Revolution Around Sun

FIGURE 7-1

hold and turn the light so that its beam stays on the globe) to simulate the Earth's revolution. Stop at each of the four points that show when one season changes to the next so that students can pay special attention to the slant of the Earth in relation to the Sun. Show and tell students that when the North Pole is tilted away from the Sun, the Northern Hemisphere has winter and when it's tilted toward the Sun, the Northern Hemisphere has summer. Provide small groups of students with flashlights and small spheres (about 3" or 4" in diameter; use Styrofoam, clay balls, or oranges). Stick a pencil all of the way through the center of each sphere to represent the Earth's imaginary axis. Have students in groups take turns walking their "earths" around the "sun." Make certain students hold their spheres so that they are tilted at a 23 degree angle in relation to the light (Figure 7-1).

2. Fall Fling

Brief Background. One of fall's most breathtaking sights is the color of autumn leaves in the temperate zones. In the United States, autumn color can be seen anywhere you find deciduous broadleaf trees, the ones that drop their leaves in autumn. Some areas famous for their spectacular autumn colors include New England and the Appalachian and Rocky Mountains. Among the trees that provide brilliant autumn color are oaks, maples, beeches, sweetgums, yellow-poplars, dogwoods, hickories, aspens, and larches.

If possible, take students on a walking tour of a park or woodlands during the autumn season. Provide leaf guides that describe and illustrate leaves and trees. Help them identify the names of trees and collect fallen leaves. Back in the classroom, let students use hand lenses for closeup observation of leaf specimens. Ask students to describe each leaf's shape and veins. For comparison, provide students with specimens of evergreen foliage—pines, spruces, firs, and so on. Ask students to speculate as to why broadleaf plants drop their leaves in the autumn while evergreens don't. Help the class make a chart, like the one below, that lists similarities and differences between the two types of trees. Attach specimens of both types on the chart. (Note: Besides their protective wax covering, evergreen needles also contain a fluid that is resistant to freezing.)

Broadleaf tree leaves	Evergreen tree needles
Broad and thin	Narrow and tough
No protective covering	Protective wax covering

3. Why Leaves Change Color

Brief Background. Three factors influence leaf color: leaf pigment, length of night, and weather. As days grow shorter and nights grow longer, biochemical activity in the leaf starts the change process. The three pigments that give leaves their autumn color are:

- *Chlorophyll*, which gives leaves their green color. During autumn, chlorophyll production slows down and then stops.
- *Carotenoid*, which produces yellow, orange, and browns.
- *Anthocyanin*, which produces reds, purples, and crimsons.

Certain colors are characteristic of particular kinds of trees. After students collect their autumn leaves, have them describe the color of each leaf in their own words. Then, provide the following information to help them identify the name of the tree. Have students use encyclopedias and other resources to find drawings that show the different leaf shapes (Figure 7-2).

Tree Name	Autumn Color
Oak	Red, brown, or russet
Hickories	Golden bronze
Dogwood	Purplish red
Beech	Light tan
Sourwood	Crimson
Black tupelo	Crimson
Red maple	Scarlet
Sugar maple	Orange-red
Black maple	Yellow

American Beech   White Oak

Paper Birch   Sugar Maple

FIGURE 7-2   Some leaf shapes

Math:

1. Keeping Track of the Days

This activity reinforces understandings developed in Science Activity #1. To help students relate the Earth's journey around the Sun to changes in the seasons, help students keep a weekly record of the length of the days from the beginning to the end of autumn. Once a week, assign students (on a rotating basis) the task of watching the evening sky so they can record the time at sunset. Some students might also be willing to get up early in the morning so they can check the time at sunrise. Students can also check the newspaper, which usually gives the exact times of sunrise and sunset. Have students use that information to calculate the length of the day in hours and minutes, and then record it on a chart. Over time, the chart will show that the days are gradually growing shorter.

2. Cooler Days Are Coming

During autumn, in most places in the United States, the days become cooler. Let students draw on prior experience to make predictions about changes in temperature during autumn for their community. To check the outside temperature, place a thermometer on or near a window so that it is visible to students inside the classroom. Have students check the thermometer at the same time each day, and then write the temperature next to that date on a large wall calendar. Periodically, students can graph the daily temperature data. If appropriate for your class, let students use the daily temperature data to calculate the average weekly and monthly temperatures for the season. Students can also compare their own measurements with those published in the local newspaper.

3. Pumpkin Measurement

Provide students with small individual pumpkins and measuring instruments (rulers, yardsticks, pieces of yarn, scale, and weights). Have pairs of students assist one another in the measurement of each pumpkin's circumference and weight. Follow up with charts and graphs to display class measurement data.

4. Sorting Leaves

Provide an assortment of autumn leaves in a variety of colors. Let pairs of students sort and label the leaves by color and shape.

Social Studies:

1. It's Time for School

Brief Background. For almost everyone in America, autumn means school time. Historically, the reason why American schools shut down in summer was so children could help their parents on farms during the growing season.

Let students consult farmer's almanacs and seed catalogues to identify the growing seasons for various plants. How does your school's summer vacation schedule compare with the traditional national pattern? Have students write or E-mail letters to the embassies of selected countries (addresses of embassies of nations of the world can be found in most almanacs) to find out if other nations follow the same school schedule as we do. Help students make charts to display the information received.

2. Harvest Festivals

Brief Background. Fall festivals have been an important part of many countries' and cultures' histories and traditions for centuries. Many fall festivals center around harvest. For rural people, autumn was a time of celebration. After months of toil in the fields, the bounty of the land was finally at hand. If the harvest was good, then farmers' storerooms, cellars, and pantries would be bulging with food—hopefully enough to last through an often harsh winter. The first harvest festival celebrated in America took place in 1621 in New England. To show their thanks for a good harvest, the Pilgrims held a three-day festival, which included the participation of many Native Americans.

For an engaging description of the Pilgrim's struggle to survive their "first" Thanksgiving and the development of that harvest festival into the holiday it is today, read aloud selections of Margaret Baldwin's *Thanksgiving* (Franklin Watts, 1983), or some other appropriate children's book. Help students plan and hold their own Thanksgiving celebration. They can create and dress in costumes of the period. Traditional foods that were probably served at the Pilgrim's Thanksgiving included duck, goose, deer, clams, fish, squash, beans, pumpkins, and cornbread. Have students list and discuss reasons why they are thankful.

Language Arts:

1. The Most Scary Halloween Ever!

Brief Background. Halloween, which is celebrated in the United States on October 31, is thought to have originated with the ancient Celts, a mysterious people who lived in Britain, Ireland, and northern France more than 2,000 years ago. Halloween celebrations did not become commonplace in America until the 1800s. Traditional American Halloween events include dressing in scary costumes, bobbing for apples, and carving jack-o-lanterns. The most popular Halloween activity for children is "trick or treating." However, instead of going door to door for treats, many neighborhoods and communities today provide an evening of special events for children to enjoy.

To get students into a Halloween mood, read aloud Tony Johnson's wild and creepy *The Ghost of Nicholas Greebe* (Dial, 1996), or another children's Halloween book. Then, lead the class in the development of its very own Halloween story, entitled "The Most Scary Halloween Ever!" Encourage individual students to contribute ideas—characters, setting, plot. As students volunteer ideas, write them down on a large wall chart. Make a storyboard to illustrate the sequence of events. After the story is finished, it can be dramatized with appropriate costumes and props.

Art:

1. Leafy Animals

Provide each student with white construction paper, glue, drawing materials, and a leaf. Have each student glue the leaf in the center of the construction paper and look at it carefully. Tell them to imagine that their leaf has magically changed into an animal. Ask them what animal their leaf looks like. Then, have them draw their animal, incorporating the leaf into the drawing. You may want to provide an example of your own leaf art drawing to serve as a model.

2. Leaf Rubbings

Provide each student with a piece of plain white typing paper, a crayon with covering removed, and a leaf. Direct students to place the paper over the leaf and use the crayon to make a rubbing of the leaf. Display the student's leaf rubbings on the wall.

Books:

1. Rosen, Mike. (1990). *Autumn Festivals*. New York: Bookwright Press. Intermediate.

2. Bauer, Caroline Feller, ed. (1994). *Thanksgiving Stories and Poems*. New York: HarperCollins Publishers. Intermediate, Advanced.

3. Maestro, Betsy. (1994). *Why Do Leaves Change Their Colors?* New York: HarperCollins Publishers. Primary.

4. Simon, Seymour. (1993). *Autumn Across America.* New York: Hyperion Books for Children. Primary, Intermediate.

5. Corwin, Judith Hoffman. (1995). *Harvest Festivals Around the World.* Parsippany, NJ: Silver Burdett. Intermediate, Advanced.

6. Johnson, Sylvia A. (1986). *How Leaves Change.* Minneapolis: Lerner Publications Co. Advanced.

7. Johnson, Tony. (1996). *The Ghost of Nicholas Greebe.* New York: Dial. Primary, Intermediate.

Software:

1. *Fall Brings Changes* [Laserdisc]. Van Nuys, CA: Churchill Media. Primary, Intermediate.

2. *Animals in Spring & Summer/Animals in Autumn & Winter* [Laserdisc]. Chicago, IL: Encyclopedia Britannica. Primary, Intermediate, Advanced.

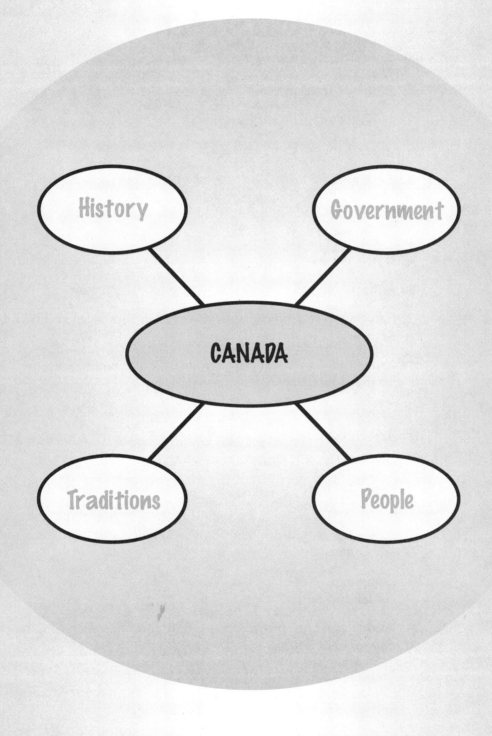

Theme Goals:

Students will:

1. make inferences from a Canadian coin.

2. identify and locate Canadian provinces and territories.

3. simulate political parties in parliament.

4. participate in a Canadian festival.

5. examine reasons for Canadian settlement patterns.

6. identify Canadian plants and animals.

7. identify Canadian products.

8. create a mural about Canada.

9. write about a Canadian province or territory.

10. construct a replica of a totem pole.

Theme Concepts:

1. Artifacts can tell us about a culture.

2. Canada is a federation comprised of ten provinces and two territories.

3. Canada has a parliamentary form of government patterned after the British.

4. Canada celebrates some of the same festivals as the United States.

5. Four important national holidays are Canada Day, Victoria Day, Labour Day, and Remembrance Day.

6. Canada's national police force is called the Royal Canadian Mounted Police.

7. Most of Canada's population lives in cities and towns in southern Canada.

8. Compared to much of the United States, Canada's climate is colder and harsher.

9. Particular plants and animals can be found in each of Canada's different environments.

10. Important Canadian raw materials and products include cars, foods, paper, chemicals, metals, petroleum, natural gas, gold, and copper.

11. Indians of Canada's Pacific coast are famous for their woodcarvings.

Vocabulary:

1. sovereign

2. parliament

3. tundra

Instructional Bulletin Board

The purpose of this bulletin board is to help students identify and locate the provinces and territories of Canada. Make a large unlabeled political map of Canada and attach it to the bulletin board. On 3" × 5" cards, print the names of the provinces and territories of Canada (*Alberta, British Columbia, Saskatchewan, Manitoba, Ontario, Quebec, Newfoundland, Nova Scotia, New Brunswick, Prince Edward Island, Yukon,* and *Northwest Territories*). Place the cards in a pocket. Students can take turns pinning the names on the appropriate locations. Provide an answer key.

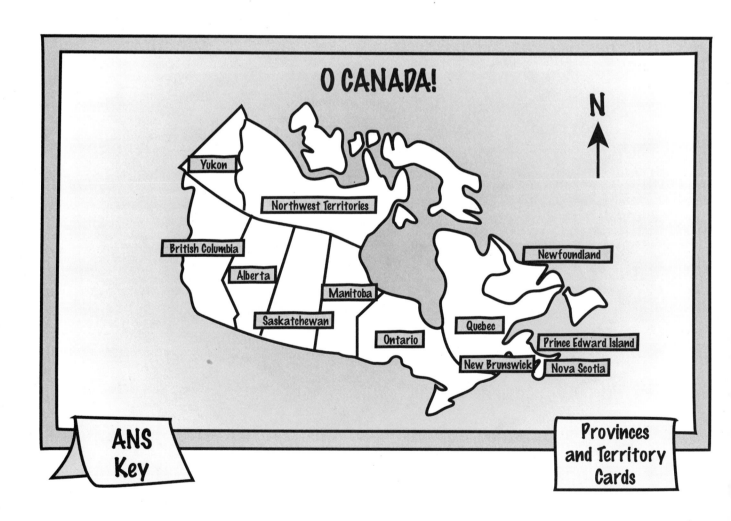

Parent Letter

Dear Parents:

The United States and Canada are important trading partners and long-time friends. We share the longest undefended border in the world, and Americans and Canadians constantly go back and forth between the two countries. Despite the fact that Canada is nearby, many American children often seem to know little about our neighbor to the north. This theme will highlight some of Canada's important characteristics.

At School:

Specifically, in this theme students will be:

- Making inferences about Canada based on analysis of a Canadian coin
- Comparing the U.S. form of government with Canada's
- Participating in a Canadian festival
- Mapping Canada's settlement patterns
- Investigating Canadian products
- Creating a mural about Canada
- Constructing a replica of a totem pole

At Home:

Check out a well-illustrated book on Canada from the community library, and read it aloud with your child. As you discuss the contents of the book, see if there is one area about Canada of special interest to your child, such as the Royal Canadian Mounted Police, Native Canadian cultures, or Canada's geography. If so, let us know so we can tailor our theme to your child's interests.

Linking Up:

Brief Background. Artifacts can provide information about the people who made and used them. As shown, the obverse side of a Canadian penny shows a likeness of Queen Elizabeth II, who is acknowledged by Canada as sovereign, and the reverse side depicts the maple leaf, which, along with the beaver, is a national symbol of Canada.

First, have students look carefully at a Lincoln penny. Ask students to tell you about the images on the coin. Review Lincoln's role in American history. Then, provide students with Canadian pennies. (Check with local supermarkets or other stores for Canadian pennies; if Canadian pennies are not available, enlarge and make a transparency of the illustration of a Canadian penny shown.) Have students write down or dictate what they think the pennies tell them about Canada and/or Canadians. Some possible inferences by students include: "Canada has a queen." "Canadians value women." "Canada has maple trees." and "Canadians think maple trees are important." Make a chart listing students' inferences, and emphasize that they can check them for accuracy later as they learn more about Canada in the unit (Figure 8-1).

Social Studies:

1. Mapping Canada

Brief Backgound. Canada is the world's second largest country. Located directly north of the United States, it covers the northern part of the continent of North America. Whereas the United States is divided into 50 political units called states, Canada is a federation comprised of 10 provinces and two territories.

Point out the locations of the Canadian provinces (Alberta, British Columbia, New Brunswick, Newfoundland, Nova Scotia, Manitoba, Ontario, Prince Edward Island, Saskatchewan, and Quebec) and territories (Northwest Territories and Yukon) on a globe and wall map. Assign each student the task of gathering an important geographic fact about one of the provinces or territories that helps describe its relative location, such as "Ontario is directly north of the Great Lakes" or "The western boundary of British Columbia is along the Pacific Ocean." To help students make place-name associations, guide them through the following activities:

1. Match the shapes of the provinces and territories (outlined on individual cards) with appropriate locations on a map of Canada;
2. Put together a map puzzle of cutouts of Canada's provinces and territories; and
3. Make papier-mache three-dimensional relief maps of Canada (Figure 8-2).

2. Canada's Government

Brief Background. Like the United States, Canada is a former British colony. Today, Canada is an independent nation with a parliamentary form of government patterned after the British. Canada continues to maintain close political ties with Great Britain, as evidenced by the fact that it recognizes the British monarch as sovereign. As in Britain, the

Canadian Penny

FIGURE 8-1

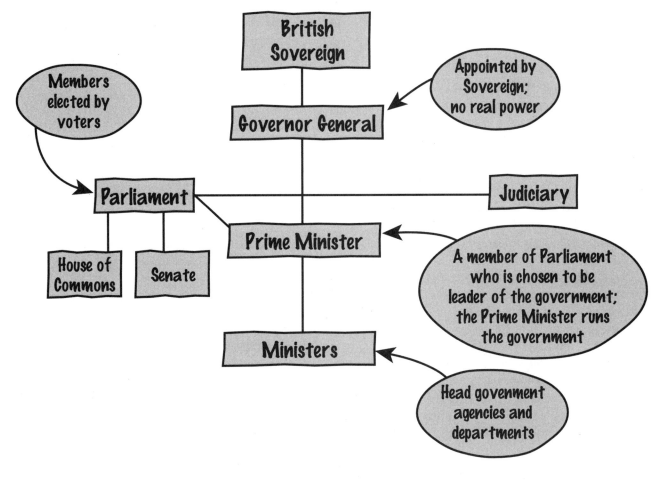

Government of Canada

FIGURE 8-2

role of the monarch is mainly ceremonial. Instead of a president, Canada has a prime minister to head its government. The prime minister is the leader of the major party or coalition in parliament. Canada has five major political parties, of which the largest have been the Liberals and Progressive Conservatives.

To help students understand the party system, explain that a political party consists of a large group of people who share many of the same views on important issues. Ask students to indicate their views on various school-related concerns, such as homework, cafeteria foods, and rules. Divide students into groups that share particular viewpoints. Students within interest groups can develop their position or stand on the issues and present their views to the class. Two major issues of concern to Canadians are

international trade policies—especially with its largest trade partner, the United States—and the possible secession of the French-speaking province of Quebec.

3. Major Canadian Events

Brief Background. Canada celebrates some of the same events as the United States. Most people in both countries participate in similar Christmas and Easter customs. Both nations also celebrate Mother's Day, Labour Day (spelled the British way in Canada), and Thanksgiving Day (Canada's Thanksgiving Day is held on the second Monday in October). Since Canada is a multicultural nation, the festivals of many different groups are celebrated across Canada, including powwows by Native groups, a harvest festival called Kwanzaa by African Canadians, and Fete Nationale (June 23) by French

Canadians in Quebec, as well as the observance of Passover by Jews. There are a variety of multicultural New Year celebrations in Canada that reflect Anglo, Native, Chinese, Japanese, Hindu, and Jewish traditions. As in the United States, it is customary for Canadians to sing "Auld Lang Syne," a Scottish song, at midnight on December 31 to welcome in the new year. In addition to Labour Day, three national holidays celebrated by Canadians are: Canada Day, on July 1, the country's birthday; Victoria Day, on the Monday before May 25, to celebrate the birthdays of Queen Victoria and the current British monarch (Quebec celebrates a holiday to honor a French Canadian hero on the same day); and Remembrance Day, at 11:00 A.M. on November 11, to remember the sacrifices made by Canadians during past wars. On Canada Day, many Canadians celebrate the occasion by eating birthday cake and watching fireworks.

Assign small groups of students the task of researching one of Canada's holidays. As a culminating activity, you can involve all of your students in a celebration of Canada Day. To experience this happy Canadian holiday, help them bake and decorate a big birthday cake with the inscription, "Happy Birthday Canada!" After everyone eats a slice of cake, have the class discuss how Canadians and Americans might feel on their nations' birthdays. To give students the flavor of various Canadian festivals, read aloud selections from Bobbie Kalman's *Canada Celebrates Multiculturalism* (Crabtree Publishing Company, 1993), or some other appropriate children's book.

4. Canada's Finest

Brief Background. The Royal Canadian Mounted Police, or Mounties, with their bright red jackets and wide-brimmed hats, are a famous symbol of Canada. During America's Wild West days when law and order were hard to find, the Mounties helped keep Canada's rugged western frontier peaceful. Although Mounties today usually wear brown uniforms and drive police cars, they have maintained a mounted unit that performs precision riding maneuvers at shows and on special occasions.

Show students pictures of Mounties, or better yet, show a video of Mounties doing modern police work and precision riding. Discuss the need for law and order, both now and in the past. What laws or rules must students obey? Who enforces the rules? Encourage students to create skits in which they can portray various aspects of the Mounties' work.

Science:

1. Predicting Population

Brief Background. Most of Canada's population lives in cities and towns in southern Canada along a border shared with the United States.

Provide students with Canadian maps that show physical features, vegetation, bodies of water, and climate. Then, give them blank maps of Canada, and let them predict where Canadian cities might be located by marking them on the maps. Probe to determine the students' reasoning behind their predictions. Have students find the actual locations of cities on a political map of Canada. Did the students' predictions match the actual locations? Ask students to give reasons why most Canadians live in southern Canada. (Some possible reasons include: warmer climate, nearness to lakes and rivers, and availability of fertile land for farming.)

2. Comparing Weather in Canada and the United States

Have students check temperatures and other weather data for major Canadian cities like Toronto, Quebec, Montreal, and Vancouver. Then let students compare Canadian weather data with those of major cities in the United States and the local area.

3. Canadian Plants and Animals

Brief Background. Much of Canada's natural environment remains unspoiled. In the far north lies the tundra. Because the sun is always low in the sky, the tundra receives little radiant energy at any time. Only hardy grasses, lichens, mosses, and a few woody plants can grow there. Among the few species of animals found on the tundra are caribou, ptarmigan, arctic foxes, and snowshoe hares. Vast coniferous, or needleleaf, forests lie south of the tundra. Mixed forests that include broadleaf trees, such as the maple tree (which is one of the national symbols), are also found in some parts of southern Canada. Animals found in coniferous and/or mixed forests include the squirrels, spotted owls, porcupines, moose, elk, wolves, deer, beavers, muskrats, otters, skunks, and downy woodpeckers. Prairies, or grasslands, cover much of the central part of southern Canada. Before hunters nearly wiped them out in the nineteenth century, millions of bison roamed these prairies. Also once found on the Canadian prairies in great numbers were pronghorns and prairie dogs. Now most of these animals have been replaced by wheat fields and cattle. Along the Pacific coast of Canada is a narrow band of rain forest filled with shrubs, ferns, mosses, and large conifers. Deer and elk feed on the shrubs. The cold, upper levels of the Rocky Mountain region of Canada look similar to the tundra environment of the far north.

Show students pictures, computer images, and/or videos of Canada's different environments. Assign the task of researching one of the environments to small groups of students. The groups can make maps of Canada that highlight the environments. They can also showcase the environments in museum displays. Let them use a cardboard box and art materials to create dioramas showing the plants and animals of particular Canadian environments.

4. Paper and Other Canadian Products

Brief Background. Canada has an abundance of valuable natural resources that are used to produce a variety of goods including cars, foods, paper, chemicals, metals, petroleum, natural gas, gold, and copper. Many U.S. newspapers are made from Canadian paper. In fact, Canada produces more newsprint than any other nation.

Contact your local newspaper company to see if its newsprint comes from Canada. Assign students the task of researching an important Canadian product. Each report should try to answer the following questions about the Canadian product: Where is the product made? What resources are used to make it? How is the product made? and Who buys the product?

Math:

1. Mural Design

Divide students into small groups. Provide each group with a large sheet of butcher paper. Explain that each group's task is to create a colorful and accurate mural about Canada. Each student in the group is to be responsible for a section of the mural. Have students measure the sheet of paper and then divide it into equal parts so that each student in the group has the same amount of surface area upon which to draw. After students plan their individual drawings, have students estimate the amount of art materials needed by the group to complete the mural. Provide the groups with the materials, and then let one or two students at a time work on the group's mural.

Language Arts:

1. Canada Words and Phrases

Challenge students to think of words or phrases that relate to Canada's geography, history, and culture. Each word or phrase should begin with one of the letters in the word "Canada." An example is shown below.

Cold weather

Awesome scenery

Natural beauty

Arctic circle

Dog sleds

Acres of fertile farmlands

2. Thumbnail Sketch

A thumbnail sketch is a brief written account or description. Assign each student the task of writing or dictating a thumbnail sketch of one of Canada's provinces or territories. Each sketch can be accompanied by an illustration. To give students an example of thumbnail sketches, read selections from Ted Harrison's *O Canada* (Ticknor & Fields, 1993), or some other appropriate children's book. To get students started, here are some facts about each of Canada's provinces and territories.

Newfoundland—Leif Ericsson was the first European to arrive here nearly a thousand years ago. Today, many Canadians who live on this easternmost province depend on the sea for their livelihood.

Nova Scotia—Almost entirely surrounded by the sea, this small province is noted for its apples, dairy products, coal mines, and manufacturing.

New Brunswick—This province has a varied landscape that includes forests, farms, and fishing villages.

Prince Edward Island—Sandy beaches and rich green mountains and valleys make this province a popular tourist destination.

Quebec—First settled by the French, this province differs from the rest of Canada because of its French culture.

Ontario—This wealthy province is Canada's main manufacturing area.

Manitoba—This fertile province is an important producer of wheat.

Saskatchewan—One of the world's largest deposits of potash (used to make fertilizers) is located in this province.

Alberta—Most of Canada's oil and coal comes from this province.

British Columbia—Forest products, fishing, and mining are big industries in this Pacific coast province.

Yukon Territory—Gold and other rich mineral deposits lure individuals and industries to this northern region.

Northwest Territories—When it comes to people, this vast land is practically empty. Most of the inhabitants are natives, called Inuit, who know how to survive in the harsh Arctic environment.

Art:

1. Native Wood Carving

Brief Background. The Indians of Canada's Pacific coast are famous for their woodcarvings. Some of their largest and most interesting carvings were in the form of totem poles. Totem poles are wooden poles carved and painted with a series of symbols, or totems (such as animals), representing family lineage. A totem pole was placed in front of the family's home.

Each student can make one section of a totem pole replica from an empty cylinder-shaped oatmeal container (or similarly shaped containers) by following these directions: Design a totem (the stylized face of an animal was often used, as suggested by the totem pole illustrated); use paper and other materials to make parts (such as ears, legs, or wings) to attach to the totem; decorate and paint the totem; stack seven or eight totems on top of each other; and secure with tape to create the totem pole (Figure 8-3).

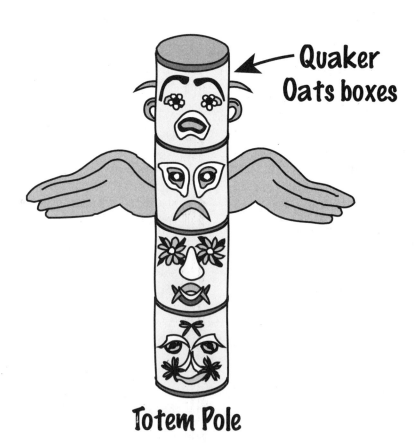

Quaker Oats boxes

FIGURE 8-3

Totem Pole

92

Books:

1. Kalman, Bobbie. (1993). *Canada Celebrates Multiculturalism*. New York: Crabtree Publishing Company. Late Elementary.

2. Harrison, Ted. (1993). *O Canada*. New York: Ticknor & Fields. Middle to Late Elementary.

3. Poulin, Stephane. (1986). *Have You Seen Josephine?* Montreal: Tundra Books. Early to Middle Elementary.

4. Greenwood, Barbara. (1995). *A Pioneer Sampler: The Daily Life of a Pioneer Family in 1840*. New York: Ticknor & Fields Books for Young Readers. Middle to Late Elementary.

5. Anderson, Joan. (1990). *Pioneer Settlers of New France*. New York: Lodestar Books. Late Elementary.

6. Bannatyne-Cugnet, Jo. (1992). *A Prairie Alphabet*. Montreal: Tundra Books. Early Elementary.

7. Andrews, Jan. (1986). *Very Last First Time*. New York: Antheneum. Early Elementary.

Software:

1. *Crosscountry Canada* [Apple II IBM]. Seattle, WA: Didatech. Intermediate, Advanced.

2. *ZipZapMap! Canada* [Mac IBM Windows]. Washington, DC: National Geographic. Intermediate, Advanced.

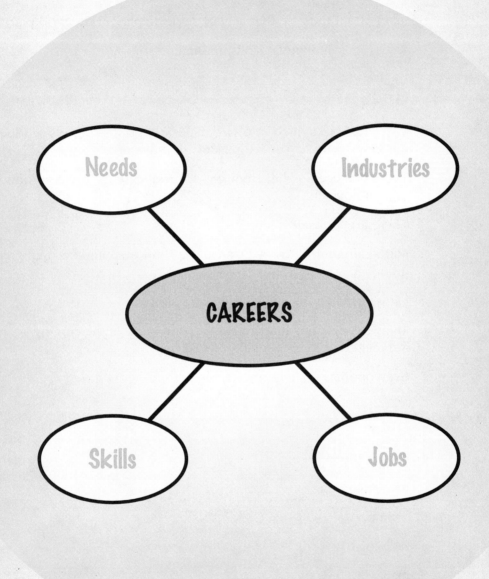

Theme Goals:

Students will:

1. interview adults about their occupations.

2. learn that work can be divided into different categories.

3. study 12 occupational groups.

4. learn about the shifting pattern of employment.

5. learn about the role that school subjects play in the workplace.

6. assess their individual skills and talents.

Theme Concepts:

1. Work can be divided into two major categories—goods-producing industries and service-producing industries.

2. There has been a shift from goods-producing to service-producing employment.

3. There are 12 basic occupational groups.

4. Many different kinds of jobs can be found in each occupational group.

5. Many occupations use mathematics skills.

6. Many occupations that are expected to grow in the coming years are related to various fields of science.

7. Everyone has abilities and talents.

Vocabulary:

1. qualifications

2. manufacturing

3. technician

4. radiologic

5. manager

6. pathologist

7. resume

8. therapist

Instructional Bulletin Board

The purpose of this bulletin board is to help students identify the characteristics of various occupations. To represent occupation groups (see Social Studies Activity #4 for listing), construct figures out of tagboard, and attach the figures to the bulletin board. Write label and clue cards for each of the figures. On each of the clue cards, write a statement that describes some aspect of one of the occupations. Punch a hole near the top center of each clue card, and put the cards in an envelope attached to the board. Students must match the statement with the occupation by hanging the clue card on a push pin next to the appropriate figure. For example, the clue card "I clean your teeth" would be hung on the pushpin next to the card labeled "Dentist." Provide an answer key for students to check their answers.

Parent Letter

Dear Parents:

We are just beginning a theme of study on careers. A sense of industry emerges within children during their elementary-school years. By sense of industry, we mean that during this period children want to know how things are made, how they work, and what they do. Your child will have an opportunity to answer such questions as we study the world of work.

At School:

Some of things we will be doing in the theme include:

- Interviewing an adult about his or her job
- Investigating a variety of occupational groups
- Role-playing workers in the community
- Identifying mathematics skills needed on the job
- Exploring some of the many science-related jobs
- Becoming more aware of our abilities and talents

At Home:

One of your child's tasks is to interview an adult about his or her occupation. If you would prefer to have your child interview someone other than yourself, please help with the contacts and arrangements. The interview format is attached. If the interview is tape-recorded, please have your child bring the audiotape to school.

This would be a great time to take your child to your workplace and show him or her what you do.

Linking Up:

According to developmental psychologist Erik Erikson, a sense of industry emerges within children during their elementary-school years. By sense of industry, he meant that during this period children develop a heightened concern for how things are made, how they work, and what they do. Thus, right now is an opportune time to introduce your students to the world of work. Ask students to speculate about what kinds of jobs they would like to have when they grow up. List and discuss their responses.

Social Studies:

1. Interviews with Different Workers

Have students collect information about the world of work by interviewing a parent or some other adult. Before students conduct the interviews, let them practice their interviewing skills in class. Students can either take notes or tape-record the interview. Have students brainstorm questions they want to ask. Some possibilitiies include the following:

What is the name of your job?

Why did you choose the job for a career?

How did you get the job?

What are the qualifications for the job?

What do you do on the job?

What do you like most about your job?

What do you like least about your job?

2. Guest Speakers

Invite workers from the community (including the interview respondents in Activity #1 above) to the classroom to describe their careers in detail. They can bring along special equipment and clothing and explain how they are used on the job. Try to include representatives of a variety of occupational groups.

3. Categories of Work

Work can be divided into two major categories, goods-producing industries and service-producing industries. Goods-producing industries include construction, manufacturing, farming, mining, forestry, and fisheries. Service-producing industries include transportation, communications, utilities, retail and wholesale trades, service occupations, government services, finance, and real estate. Have students bring to class pictures of people engaged in work. Let small groups of students sort the pictures into goods-producing and service-producing categories.

4. Occupational Groups

Discuss the following 12 occupational groups or clusters and give students some examples of specific jobs that fall under each category. Then provide an assortment of profusely illustrated magazines, and challenge students to identify examples of jobs that represent the different occupational groups. They can cut out the examples and paste them on large sheets of paper (provide 12 sheets; write the name of the occupational group at the top of each sheet). The 12 occupational groups with examples follow:

1. technicians (radiologic technician, medical records technician);
2. professional specialties (psychologist, schoolteacher);
3. service occupations (flight attendant, travel agent);
4. executives (head of a hospital, store manager);
5. sales workers (retail sales person, food service worker);
6. transportation and material-moving occupations (truck driver, taxi driver);
7. construction trades (carpenter, bulldozer operator);
8. mechanics, installers, and repairers (car mechanic, TV repair person);
9. clerical occupations (secretary, office clerk);
10. helpers and laborers (carpenter's helper, ditch digger);
11. agriculture, forestry, and fishing occupations (forest ranger, farmer); and
12. production occupations (steel worker, auto worker).

5. Create a Mock Workplace

After students have researched the different occupational groups, they should be ready to turn the classroom into a workplace. Have children set up mock stores, businesses, banks, factories, construction companies, and other enterprises commonly found in the larger community. They can create storefronts and signs for their places of work. Pictures, drawings, and other materials can be used as props. Ask some children to role-play the workers in occupations, and other children to role-play the customers, or consumers of the products and services. After an appropriate period of time, reverse the roles of the two groups.

6. Community Business Trends

For some years now, there has been a nation-wide shift from goods-producing to service-producing employment. Help students check the employment pattern in their community. The local Chamber of Commerce might have information on employment. If feasible, take a bus tour of the business and industrial sections of the community. Have students keep a record of the types of businesses and industries observed on the trip. Introduce or review the function of the Yellow Pages of the local phone book. After students are familiar with its organization, they can gather data about businesses from the Yellow Pages. What does their analysis tell the students about businesses and work in their community?

Math:

1. Workplace Skills

Social Studies Activity #5 above should provide an excellent opportunity for students to apply their addition, subtraction, multiplication, and division skills as they buy and sell products and services in their simulated workplace.

2. Showcase Math

Almost every occupation today uses mathematics. To help students become more aware of the importance of math in the workplace, showcase the role math plays in some specific careers. For example, you could explain that a construction worker must be able to measure areas, make scale drawings, decide on the size of things to be built, and estimate the amount of materials required. An airplane pilot must be able to read numerical gauges on the instrument panel, fly at correct altitudes, measure distance of flight on a map, compute the approximate flying time, and compute the approximate fuel consumption. Challenge students to identify mathematics skills needed in occupations in which they have an interest.

Science:

1. Graphic Maps

Among the occupations that are expected to grow in the coming years are many that are related to various fields of science. They include the following specializations: computer scientists, operations research analysts, registered nurses, respiratory therapists, speech-language pathologists, dental hygienists, nuclear medicine technicians, and radiologic technicians. But it is also probably fair to say that in the high-tech world of the future, a sound understanding of science will be essential for practically everyone. Help students construct on the chalkboard a graphic map of science-related occupations connected with a particular area of the world of work. For example, a "map" for "environment" might include the following science-related occupations: zoologists, biologists, chemists, veterinarians, physicians, geologists, engineers, industrial hygienists, anthropologists, city planners, sociologists, forest rangers, conservationists, entomologists, botanists, photographers, explorers, surveyors, and teachers (Figure 9-1).

2. Tools of the Trade

Bring an assortment of tools and machines to the classroom and let students try to figure out how they work and what they do.

3. Scientific Devices

Teach students how to use a scientific tool, such as a compass, microscope, telescope, thermometer, rain gauge, metal detector, or barometer.

FIGURE 9-1

4. On-Site Visits

Take a field trip to a water treatment plant, medical clinic, university or company laboratory, or any other appropriate site where scientific work is performed.

Language Arts:

1. Special Talents

To help students become more aware of their preferences, interests, and talents, have them write a paper on one of the following topics: a favorite subject; a hobby; or a special talent, ability, interest, or skill.

2. Oral Reports

Have students give oral reports about the people they interviewed (see Social Studies Activity #1).

3. Help Wanted

After students have researched an occupation, have them write a job advertisement for the position.

4. In the Newspaper

Provide classified sections of newspapers and let students record the types of occupations listed.

5. Career Profiles Booklet

Have each student write (or dictate) a brief article about an occupation he has investigated. The articles can be incorporated into a student-produced booklet profiling all of the careers. The booklet should include a title page, table of contents, and index. Students can also illustrate the booklet with drawings and photographs.

6. Applying for a Job

Create some classroom jobs, such as teacher's helper, chalkboard cleaner, goldfish feeder, desk and chair duster, and line leader. Then advertise for the positions. Have students write resumes describing their education and work experience to date. The resumes should also include brief statements that explain why they think they are qualified for particular jobs. Before they begin, show them examples of resumes and give them a format to follow. After

Name: John Doe
Address: 14 Summer Ln.
         Williamsburg, VA

Education:
    School: Redbud Elementary
    Grade level: 4th

Work Experience:
    Chores: wash dishes, clean
            room, feed pet

Special Skills:
    drawing
    singing

Hobbies:
    collecting stamps, play softball

FIGURE 9-2 Résumé

the students finish their resumes, conduct some mock interviews that focus on the students' job objectives (Figure 9-2).

Art:

1. Colorful Collage

Students can make a collage entitled "The World of Work" that shows people working in various fields. Attach a large piece of brown paper to a wall of the classroom. Have students collect colorful pictures of work activities from magazines and other sources to glue on the brown paper. Make certain they position the pictures so that all of the brown paper is covered completely.

2. Future Work

Encourage students to create drawings of jobs of the future. Have them consider the effects that new forms of transportation, communication, and technology might have on the world of work some ten, twenty, or more years into the future.

Books:

1. Bonner, Staci. (1994). *Sports*. Parsippany, NJ: Crestwood House, Silver Burdett Press. Advanced.

2. Crisfield, Deborah. (1994). *Travel*. Parsippany, NJ: Crestwood House, Silver Burdett Press. Advanced.

3. Marshall, MaryAnn. (1994). *Music*. Parsippany, NJ: Crestwood House, Silver Burdett Press. Advanced.

4. Vitkus-Weeks, Jessica. (1994). *Television*. Parsippany, NJ: Crestwood House, Silver Burdett Press. Advanced.

5. Horenstein, Henry. (1994). *My Mom's a Vet*. Cambridge, MA: Candlewick. Advanced.

6. Miller, Margaret. (1994). *Guess Who?* New York: Greenwillow Books. Primary.

7. Kuklin, Susan. (1993). *Fighting Fires*. New York: Bradbury Press. Primary.

8. Florian, Douglas. (1992). *A Chef*. New York: Greenwillow Books. Primary.

9. Florian, Douglas. (1991). *A Carpenter*. New York: Greenwillow Books. Primary.

Software:

1. *Jobs for Me!* [Mac IBM]. Ontario: Logicus. Advanced.

2. *Career-O-Ram-A* [Mac MPC CD-ROM]. Brunswick, ME: Wintergreen/Orchard House. Intermediate, Advanced.

3. *Job City Series* [Mac IBM Laserdisc]. Altamonte Springs, FL: Techware Corp. Intermediate, Advanced.

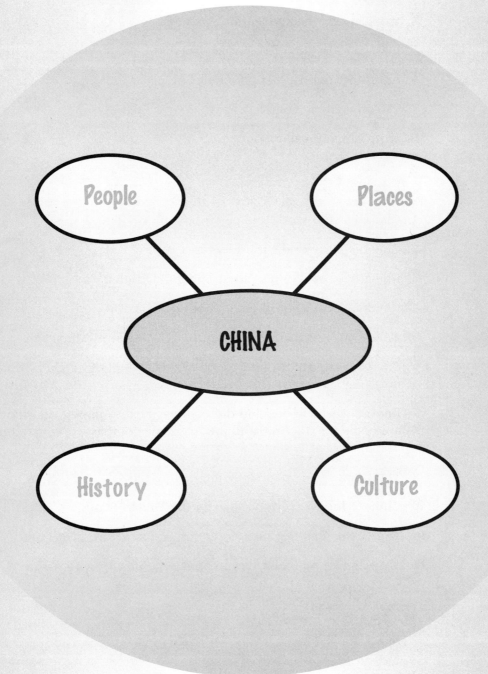

Theme Goals:

Students will:

1. locate and label important geographic features.

2. identify products made in China.

3. study the teachings of Confucius.

4. work in cooperative learning groups.

5. make a time line of China's history.

6. develop written descriptions of China.

7. use a magnetic compass.

8. write Chinese calligraphy.

Theme Concepts:

1. China has the world's largest population.

2. China is the world's third largest country.

3. China has the world's oldest living civilization.

4. China is located on the continent of Asia.

5. Americans use many products that are made in China.

6. The Chinese philosopher Confucius developed a code of conduct that still influences people today.

7. Important inventions and discoveries, such as paper, silk, movable type for printing, and the magnetic compass, originated in China.

8. The Chinese language is written using pictorial characters.

9. Chinese food is very popular in the United States.

10. The Great Wall of China is the longest structure ever built.

11. The Chinese valued a harmonious relationship with nature.

Vocabulary:

1. China

2. Asia

3. Huang He River

4. Confucius

5. Great Wall of China

6. Marco Polo

7. silk

8. magnetic compass

9. calligraphy

Instructional Bulletin Board

The purpose of this bulletin board is to let students practice their mapping skills. Construct a large outline map of China out of tagboard. Draw symbols for the following major geographic features on the map but do not include labels: rivers (Huang He and Yangtze), capital (Beijing), cities (Shanghai, Shenyang, Tianjin, and Wuhan), mountains (Himalayas and Kunlun), deserts (Taklimakan and Gobi), and the Great Wall of China. Attach the map to the bulletin board. Attach a pushpin next to each of these geographic features. Make label cards for each and punch a hole in the top center of each card. Put the label cards in a large envelope attached to the lower right corner of the board. Let individual students match place and name by hanging each label card on the appropriate pushpin. Attach a covered answer key that flips up to show a correctly labeled map of China.

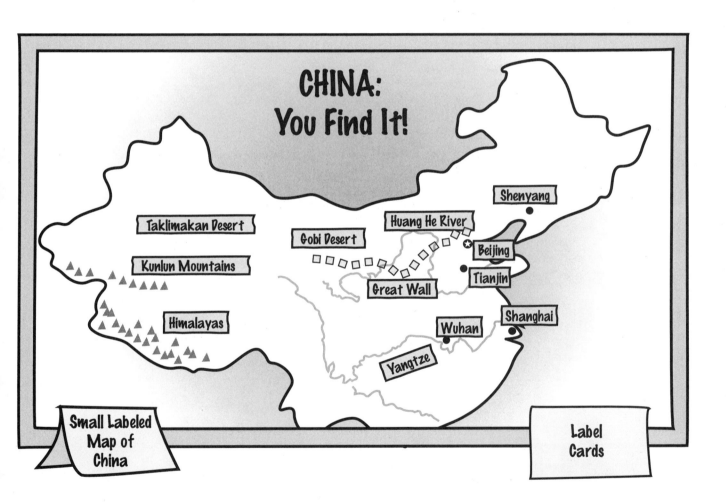

Parent Letter

Dear Parents:

We are going to explore the world's oldest living civilization—China. China is notable for other reasons as well: it has the world's largest population, and it is the world's third biggest country in land area.

At School:

Some of the exciting activities that we will be doing during our study of China include:

- Mapping the geographic features of China
- Searching for products made in China
- Studying the ancient teachings of Confucius
- Working in cooperative learning groups
- Making a time line of China's long history
- Writing about China
- Using a device that originated in China—the magnetic compass
- Writing Chinese calligraphy

At Home:

There are many activities you might want to do with your child to reinforce the concepts being taught at school. For instance, you might want to do one or more of the following:

- Eat at a Chinese restaurant—use your chopsticks!
- Read aloud a Chinese folk story.
- Talk about current events in China.
- Point out China-made products found in the home.

Linking Up:

Announce to students that they will be studying China. Have them close their eyes and imagine what they might find there. If you want to be more specific, ask questions like "What would the land in China look like?" and "What kind of things would the people be doing?" Keep a list of their predictions for retrieval later.

Social Studies:

1. Comparing Countries

Point to China and the United States on the globe. Let individuals find both places on the globe and wall map of the world. Compare and contrast the two countries. Which country appears bigger? (China is the world's third largest country and the United States is the fourth largest.) What ocean separates the United States and China? (Pacific) In what continents are China and the United States located? (Asia and North America, respectively) What are the two longest rivers in the United States and in what direction do they flow? (Mississippi and Missouri, north to south) What are China's two longest rivers and in what direction do they flow? (Huang He and Yangtze, west to east)

2. Chinese Products

Tell the class that a huge variety of Chinese manufactured items are transported to the United States and sold. Chances are good that some of your students are wearing shoes and clothing made in China and/or are carrying Chinese-made products in their book bags. Students can check their clothing labels and other personal items and note the China-made things found. Make a wall chart of the items found on a 3′ × 3′ piece of butcher paper.

3. Cities of China

Review the location of major population centers in the United States. What patterns can the students infer by analyzing their locations? (Many large cities in the United States are located near or alongside bodies of water.) Project an outline map of China on the chalkboard. Let students take turns predicting where China's cities are located by marking the spots with an "X" on the projected map. Provide atlases and let students check the accuracy of their predictions. What patterns can students infer by analyzing the locations of major Chinese cities?

4. Ancient Civilization

Brief Background. China has the world's oldest living civilization, which began in the Huang He Valley of North China.

Locate the Huang He Valley on a map of China (it is along the Huang He or Yellow River). Have students speculate about why the civilization began where it did. Ask students how conditions in the Huang He Valley might have allowed those who lived there to meet their basic needs. You should emphasize that they had a stable, constant water supply since the river never ran dry. There was plenty of rich farmland because flooding made the soil fertile. Let students make vegetation and climate maps of China. Have students compare maps of China that show population and vegetation. Do areas of lush vegetation also contain the largest concentrations of people?

5. Confucius' Code of Conduct

Brief Background. Around 500 B.C., the great philosopher Confucius developed a code of conduct for the Chinese people that still influences Chinese values today. One of Confucius' teachings was that people cannot be forced to learn good conduct. Instead, people learn correct conduct by example.

Discuss this teaching with your students. Can they name people who have modeled—and thereby taught—any of the following values or virtues: civility (politeness and respectfulness), honesty, fairness, courage, wisdom, kindness, and loyalty? Read sections of children's books (biographies, fiction, folk tales, etc.) that portray characters who demonstrate exemplary moral and ethical values. Have students collect examples of good conduct. Print the examples on cards and pin them to a corner of the bulletin board, which has been identified as "Confucius' Corner."

6. Group Work

Divide students into six cooperative learning groups and assign each group one of the following topics: (1) people (including ethnic groups, language, and customs); (2) family (including food, clothing, and homes); (3) places; (4) beliefs (including political and religious); (5) art, entertainment, and sports; and (6) work. Create a division of labor within each group by giving each student a specific task. For example, individual tasks for the cooperative group studying "places" might be to locate and describe one of the following: (1) major regions, (2) major mountains, (3) major rivers, (4) major population centers, (5) major farming areas, and (6) major buildings and monuments. Gather books and other resources, such as maps, filmstrips, and study prints, on China from the school and community libraries and make them available in the classroom. Provide ample opportunities for students to share information within groups (for example, after the information has been checked for accuracy, all students in the "places" group would be expected to learn the information about each of the six subtopics listed above). Culminate the cooperate group study of China with a "China Festival," at which time each of the groups would take turns sharing their topic with the class. To make the sharing time as enjoyable and memorable as possible, help each group communicate an important aspect of their topic through a hands-on activity (such as using chopsticks, mapping locations, or learning a Chinese game) that involves the whole class.

Math:

1. The Chinese Calendar

Brief Background. In the traditional Chinese way of marking time, each year of a 12-year cycle in the calendar is linked with a particular animal. The cycle is repeated over and over again. A person's character and future are linked to his or her birth year and the particular animal with which it is associated. The first animal in the cycle is the rat, followed in order by the ox, tiger, hare, dragon, snake, horse, sheep, monkey, rooster, dog, and pig.

Given that 1996 was the year of the rat, have students figure out the animal associated with their own birth years.

2. Measuring the Great Wall

Brief Background. The Great Wall of China is the longest structure ever built. Including all of its side branches, it extends approximately 4,000 miles in length. The main wall is 2,150 miles long and snakes from the east coast to deep within the interior of north-central China. In some places the wall is 35 feet high and 25 feet wide.

Let students make a line, measure its length, and then figure out how many such lines would fit along the length of the Great Wall. Students can also measure the school and figure out how many schools could be placed from end to end along the length of the wall. Have pairs of students use the map scale to calculate the length of the Great Wall. Then have students find equivalent distances on maps of other geographic regions. For example, if the Great Wall extended from the United States's east coast, where might it end up?

3. Time Line

China's long history—over 4,000 years—can be represented by a time line. Help students construct a time line that shows important events in China's history arranged in way that represents their proper time relationship to one another. Stretch a clothesline rope across the classroom and let each 1-foot segment represent a time span of 200 years. Students can use rulers to find the approximate points on the line that correspond to the correct chronological sequence for important events in Chinese history. Assign each student the task of identifying one important event in China's history. They can print each event and the year in which it occurred on an index card. After students have made the correct measurements, their completed event cards can be attached along the line with clothespins. Among the important events that might be displayed on the line are the following: 1766 B.C.—China's first dynasty, the Shang, began; 1122 B.C.—Zhou dynasty began; 500 B.C.—Confucius developed a code of conduct; 202 B.C.—Han dynasty began; 1275—Marco Polo arrived in China; 1644—Qing dynasty began; 1912—Republic of China established; 1949—The People's Republic of China established; and 1989—large numbers of people demonstrated in Beijing for more freedom.

4. Population Pie Graphs

Brief Background. China is the world's largest country in population, with about a fifth of the world's people.

Have students use up-to-date sources, like a current almanac, to check the latest estimates of the world's and China's populations. Then, let students use these figures to make a pie graph that shows the percentage of the world's population who are Chinese.

Language Arts:

1. Marco Polo: Tales of Travel

Brief Background. In 1275, a young man from Venice, Italy, arrived in China. He became the trusted friend of the great Chinese ruler Kublai Khan and spent almost 20 years traveling throughout the empire. When he returned to Italy, he described his adventures to a man named Rustichello, who wrote a very popular book about them. Most people in Europe had never heard of China, and they were amazed by Marco Polo's stories about this mysterious and faraway land. Marco Polo described incredible things that were unknown to most Europeans, such as drains under streets, movable type for printing, paper money, a postal system, the magnetic compass, and the use of coal for fuel.

Read to students some accounts of Marco Polo's adventures from a children's book available in the school or community library, such as Richard Humble's *The Travels of Marco Polo* (Watts, 1990). Ask students to imagine that they are travelers in China. Have them write and illustrate a brief account of their adventures there. What did they see and do?

2. The Route to China

Provide students with world atlases. Ask them to write a detailed, step-by-step set of directions telling how to get from the United States to China traveling east to west by land and sea. Through which countries would they travel? What mountains, deserts, and rivers would they cross? Over which bodies of water would they travel? After students have finished, they can exchange papers and trace each other's routes on a world map. Can a student reach China using another student's directions?

Science:

1. Using the Magnetic Compass

Brief Background. One very important ancient Chinese scientific instrument was the magnetic compass, which enabled traders and explorers to guide their ships. The needle on a magnetic compass aligns itself with the Earth's magnetic field and points north.

Ask your students to imagine that they are explorers far out at sea. Remind them that on the open sea there are no landmarks to guide them. Ask them how they could get to their intended destination. Introduce your students to the wonderful invention that can help take them there, the magnetic compass. Tell students that since they will soon be sailing their ships on the open sea, they will need to know how to read a compass. Provide students with individual pocket compasses. Teach or review the cardinal points of the compass. Show them the points and degrees on the compass that indicate direction. Show them how to line up the needle so that its ends are over the north and south marks. After some practice inside the classroom, take the students outside to a large open area. Ask them to walk in the direction of north, then walk in the direction of west, and so on. Tell them to imagine they are a fleet of ships. Give them simple directions to follow, and let them use their compasses to steer a steady course. For example, a set of directions might read as follows: Sail five paces north, then sail ten paces east, and then sail four paces south.

2. Chinese Inventions

Two Chinese originals are silk and paper. Bring some silk fabric and paper of various textures to class and attach them to the bulletin board along with this question: "Guess where we are from?" Challenge students to track down the answer to this question. Provide books and other resources that contain historical and scientific facts about these Chinese inventions. Knowledge about the technology of making silk and paper was kept a secret from the West for thousands of years. Let students investigate how knowledge of silk and paper spread to other places over time.

Art:

1. Chinese Calligraphy

Brief Background. Introduce students to Chinese calligraphy. The Chinese language is written using pictorial characters that stand for a word or part of a word. There are approximately 50,000 Chinese characters. To understand a typical Chinese newspaper, a person would need to know about 4,000 characters. The art of forming the characters is called calligraphy. Calligraphy and painting are closely connected in Chinese art.

Provide sharp-pointed brushes, drawing paper, and ink, and let interested students try their hands at calligraphy. Students can practice the Chinese characters below. Before they begin, ask students to study the characters carefully. Do any of them resemble the objects they represent?

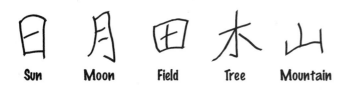

| Sun | Moon | Field | Tree | Mountain |

2. Interpreting Painting

Paintings can communicate much about the history and culture of a people. One important subject of traditional Chinese paintings is the expression of a harmonious relationship with nature. Show children examples of Chinese landscape paintings (found in large-sized art books and other sources) that depict some of these characteristic elements, such as mountains, trees, streams, rocks, bamboo, and the plum and orchid. What do such paintings tell the children about the values of the Chinese people?

Cooking:

1. Chinese Food Festival

Chinese food is very popular in the United States. Have students make lists of Chinese foods found in local supermarkets and specialty-food shops. Ask students to share with the class a favorite Chinese recipe from home. A great way to culminate the students' study of China is with an assortment of Chinese foods. Rice, noodles, cabbage and other vegetables, and *tofu* (soybean curd) served with small portions of meat or fish are some of the main ingredients of a Chinese meal. Egg rolls and dumplings filled with vegetables and bits of meat are also very popular foods in China. A large variety of heat-and-serve Chinese food snacks and dishes are available in most supermarkets. To make a Chinese food festival even more authentic, provide students with chopsticks and demonstrate their use.

Books:

1. James, Ian. (1989). *China*. New York: Franklin Watts. Intermediate, Advanced.

2. Mason, Sally. (1981). *Take a Trip to China*. New York: Franklin Watts. Primary.

3. Thomas, Peggy. (1991). *City Kids in China*. New York: HarperCollins. Advanced.

4. Stewart, Gail. (1990). *China*. New York: Crestwood House. Advanced.

5. Fyson, Nance, and Green, Richard. (1985). *A Family in China*. Minneapolis: Lerner Publishing Co. Intermediate, Advanced.

6. Odijk, Pamela. (1991). *The Chinese*. Englewood Cliffs, NJ: Silver Burdett Press. Advanced.

7. Stefoff, Rebecca. (1991). *China*. New York: Chelsea House. Intermediate.

8. Flint, David. (1994). *China*. Austin, TX: Raintree Steck-Vaughn. Primary.

9. Bradley, John. (1990). *China: A New Revolution?* New York: Gloucester Press. Intermediate.

10. Ashabranner, Brent. (1992). *Land of Yesterday, Land of Tomorrow: Discovering Chinese Central Asia*. New York: Cobblehill Books. Intermediate, Advanced.

11. Humble, Richard. (1990). *The Travels of Marco Polo*. Culver City, CA: Watts.

Software:

1. *Asia Alive* [MPC CD-ROM]. MediaAlive. Advanced.

2. *China: Home of the Dragon* [Mac Windows CD-ROM]. Orange Cherry/New Media Schoolhouse. Intermediate, Advanced.

THEME
11

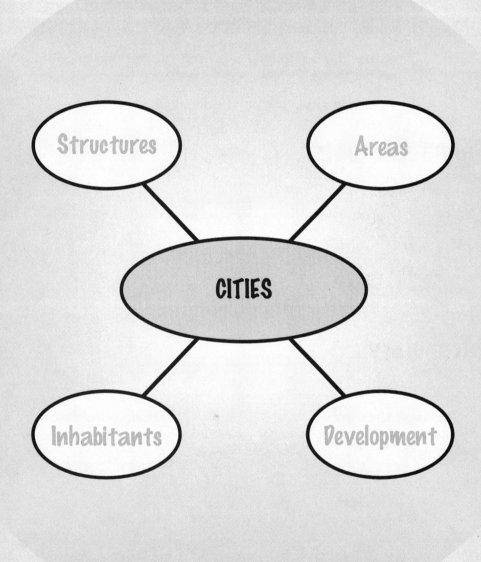

Structures

Areas

CITIES

Inhabitants

Development

Theme Goals:

Students will:

1. investigate life before the development of cities.

2. research famous ancient cities.

3. identify the different occupations and services found in cities.

4. plan their own cities.

5. explore population growth and ethnic diversity in cities.

6. calculate the areas of cities and graph population numbers.

7. discuss the opportunities offered to, and challenges faced by, people living in cities.

8. make clay models of city landmarks.

Theme Concepts:

1. Cities are crowded places.

2. A great variety of activities occur in cities.

3. Many cities are manufacturing centers.

4. A great variety of jobs are found in cities.

5. Planning can make cities better.

Vocabulary:

1. city planner

2. residential

3. business

4. industrial

5. homeless

Instructional Bulletin Board

This purpose of this bulletin board is to help students learn the names and locations of some of America's largest cities. Place a blank political outline map of the United States on the bulletin board. Use a felt-tip pen to mark the location of each of America's largest cities on the map with a dot. Print the name of each city on a card and laminate. Put the city label cards in an envelope and attach the envelope to one side of the bulletin board. The children can place the correct card next to the proper dot by using Velcro patches. Have an atlas or answer key available so students can check their own work.

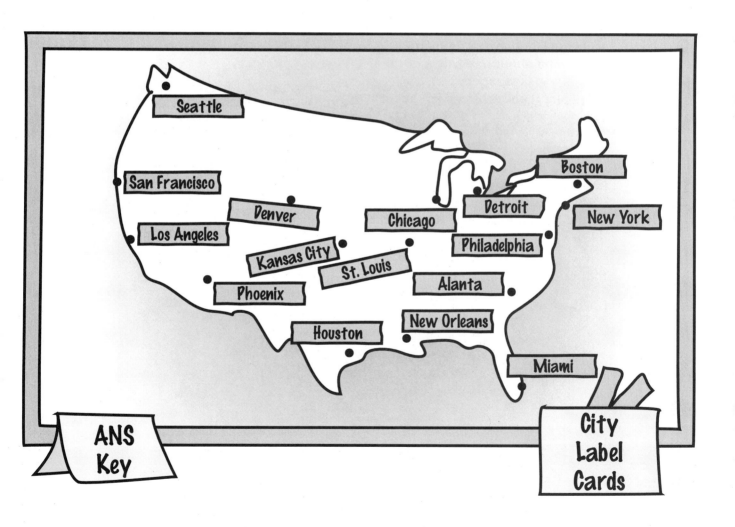

Parent Letter

Dear Parents:

Most Americans live in cities. Approximately 80 percent live in metropolitan areas, and over 50 percent live in areas with populations of at least one million. America's cities reflect our nation's diversity—they are the "hometowns" for a kaleidoscopic blend of cultures, lifestyles, and economic groups. Cities are also the places where America's Industrial Revolution began and flourished. During the up-coming study of cities, students will look at cities near and far, cities past and present, and cities of the future.

At School:

Some of the activities planned include:

- Planning model cities
- Investigating urban problems
- Learning about how cities developed
- Building skyscrapers
- Making replicas of city landmarks

At Home:

Please feel free to join us for any of these activities, or to share your own knowledge of cities with us. When you travel around the city with your child, discuss the various places, workers, and activities you observe. This also would be the perfect time to take your child to some special city attraction.

Linking Up:

To help bring the "feel" of a crowded city into the classroom, create different degrees of population density for students to experience. Use a clothesline rope to make a circle 10 feet in diameter on the classroom floor. Tell the class that the area inside the circle represents a city. Select a student to "live in the city," and ask him to stand inside the circle. Repeat this process until enough students have been added to create a high population density situation. Ask students to express their feelings about the crowded conditions. Relate the overcrowdedness inside the circle to problems that exist in overcrowded cities, such as congestion, noise, and conflicts among individuals and groups.

Social Studies:

1. The Rise of Cities

Brief Background. Before towns and cities developed, bands of nomads roamed the earth. These hunters and gatherers could not live for very long in one place because they had to be on the move constantly in their unrelenting search for food. Around 9,000 years ago, farming and the domestication of animals first appeared. These two developments supported the rise of cities. Slowly but surely, humans started to change the way they lived. They began to live together in permanent settlements, produce a food surplus, and develop a variety of specialized jobs like weaving and pottery making. Ur, one of the world's first cities, was built by the Sumerians in Mesopotamia around 3500 B.C. All of the world's earliest civilizations developed in river valleys.

Begin by asking students to imagine a time long ago when there were no towns or cities anywhere on Earth. Have them speculate about what this world without cities might have looked like. What would people do? Where would they live and work? Ask students to list the needs of people in cities. Probe to see if students can identify any conditions that might have contributed to the development of cities. Probe to see if students recognize the significance of the connection between river valleys and the development of early cities (the river valleys provided an abundant water supply, fish and other natural food supplies, and rich soil

for agriculture). To give students additional insights into the development of cities, read aloud selections of *Timelines: Cities, Citizens, and Civilizations* by Fiona MacDonald (Franklin Watts, 1992), or another appropriate children's book.

2. Famous Ancient Cities

Let students use atlas and encyclopedia tools to learn about the world's great ancient cities. The locations of some of the greatest ones, which are shown in Figure 11-1, are listed below. The present-day countries in which the cities were located are in parentheses. Ancient cities: Babylon (Iraq), Thebes (Egypt), Mohenjo-Daro (Pakistan), Tenochtitlan (Mexico), Machu Picchu (Peru), Tikal (Guatemala), Timbuktu (Mali), Athens (Greece), and Rome (Italy).

3. Cities of Yesteryear

Many of the original graphics of nineteenth- and early twentieth-century American cities found in history books and other sources can give students a realistic picture of what cities then were like. Show them old photographs and illustrations that chronicle some of the miserable living conditions (air, traffic, housing, work, health, etc.) that existed in them. Discuss conditions in cities as they exist today. How are conditions similar, and different?

4. Many Kinds of Occupations

Have students generate a list of all the products and services found in their local community. Then help them sort the items generated into the following types of occupations: technicians; professional specialties; service; management; sales; transportation and material-moving; construction; mechanics, installers and repairers; clerical; helpers and laborers; agriculture, forestry, and fishing; and production.

5. Community Businesses: Past and Present

As an extension to Activity #4 above, students can use the Yellow Pages of the local telephone book to identify products and services found in the local community. Use old telephone books to compare the number and variety of products and services in the community at different points in time. The location of various past and present businesses and services can be plotted

FIGURE 11-1

on a large community map created by students. (Note: For comparison purposes, particularly if your local community is small, you might want to obtain the Yellow Pages for a large metropolitan area.)

6. Plan Your Own City

City planners advise people on ways to improve communities. They draw maps and make models of cities. In this activity, students will be making their own models of cities. Each student will need a variety of small, clean, empty paper and plastic containers to use to make miniature buildings and other structures for their model cities. (Note: Give students three or four weeks to gather materials from home for the activity.) To stimulate students' thinking about city planning, use an overhead projector to display a map of a "mixed-up" city, drawn by you, for the students to analyze. To make the "mixed-up" map transparency, draw a simple map of an imaginary, unplanned city that shows the land being used in "mixed up," or illogical, ways. For example, the map might show a railroad track cutting through an airport runway, a hospital next to a factory, or a waste dump across the street from a park. Label the buildings and other structures on the map to avoid confusion. After the students identify all of the problems in the "mixed up" city, challenge them to plan new, improved cities that would be sensible and pleasurable to live in. Tell them that city planners must decide how the city's land should be used. The students will need to decide how to divide up their cities into different areas, such as residential, business, and industrial. To make their models, each pair of students will need one 4 X 3 feet piece of light brown or white paper (for the "land"), the empty containers (for the "buildings" and other structures), and magic markers (to draw "streets," "rivers," "grass," etc.). Each pair will need space on the floor or at a table to spread out their piece of paper. Give the pairs plenty of time to discuss their plans and determine where facilities and services—such as schools, roads, factories, fire and police stations, homes, and shops—should be located. After the pairs have finished, the class can "visit" each model city and each pair can tell about their plan. Before the objects are removed from the pieces of paper, use a regular or Polaroid camera to take "aerial" photographs of each of the cities, and then direct students to trace around the miniature buildings and other structures with a felt-tipped pen to create maps of their model cities, which then can be displayed on the walls. To give students an idea of what cities might look like in the future, read aloud sections of and show illustrations from *Your World 2000: Cities* by Robert Royston (Facts on File Publications, 1985), or some other appropriate children's books.

7. Exploring the Ethnic Diversity of America's Cities

Each of America's cities reflects its own unique blend of ethnic diversity. For a look at New York, Los Angeles, Chicago, Detroit, San Francisco, New Orleans, Miami, and San Antonio from multicultural perspectives, read aloud sections of *A Multicultural Portrait of Life in the Cities* by David Wright (Marshall Cavendish, 1994). Have students gather stories, songs, poems, and recipes that reflect the ethnic diversity of cities and report them to the class.

8. Creating a Photographic Record

Help students create a photographic record of your city or one nearby. Take students on a field trip to the city. They or you can take photographs of various city happenings and structures. To make a display of the city scenes, attach the map of the city you have photographed to the wall, attach the photographs around the map, and use lengths of yarn to connect each photograph to its proper location on the map.

Math:

1. Population Graphs

Brief Background. Cities in the ancient world were much smaller than cities today. For example, Athens' population was around 155,000 in 430 B.C., during ancient Greece's Golden Age. In comparison, modern Athens has a population of over 3 million. Over 33 percent of the world's people live in urban areas containing one million or more people.

Help students locate the top five largest population centers (listed below) on a world map. Have students make bar graphs showing their populations. To help students grasp the magnitude of these large numbers, show them photographs of outdoor stadiums that hold 100,000 or more people, and then have them calculate how many 100,000-seat stadiums would be needed for 1 million people, 15 million, and so forth.

1. Tokyo-Yokohama, Japan	27 million
2. Mexico City, Mexico	21 million
3. Sao Paulo, Brazil	18 million
4. Seoul, Korea	16 million
5. New York City, USA	15 million

2. Land Area Measurements

Provide students with maps of the local community and/or various cities. Have students use the scale to measure the community's/cities' approximate land area.

Science:

1. Skyscraper Design

Brief Background. The four tallest buildings in the world are in American cities. The Sears Tower

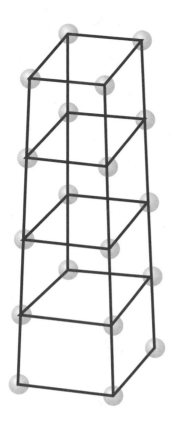

Pea and Toothpick Building
FIGURE 11-2

in Chicago is the tallest (1,454 feet), followed by the twin towers of the World Trade Center (1,368 and 1,362 feet) and the Empire State Building (1,250 feet) in New York City. Challenge students to identify the tallest building in their own community. How does it compare with the height of the Sears Tower? Let students grapple with some of the problems faced by building architects and engineers. Students can make their own skyscrapers from toothpicks and peas. To prepare for this hands-on project, students need to first learn about how real skyscrapers are constructed by consulting the library and other sources. Provide students with toothpicks and dried peas, which have been soaked overnight (Figure 11-2).

Language Arts:

1. The Joys and Miseries of City Life

Millions of tourists a year visit Washington, D.C., New York City, Chicago, San Francisco, Los Angeles, London, Paris, Rome, Hong Kong, Tokyo, and Rio de Janeiro, to name some of the most popular city destinations. They come to marvel at the architecture, exhibits, buildings, parks, monuments, and a host of other attractions. Amidst the splendor and luxury of cities, however, squalor and misery also exist. To look at the complexity of city life in depth, let the class choose a large American or foreign city as a case study. Help the class gather ample information from a variety of media sources about the city for use in the classroom. Then, assign pairs of students different aspects of the city to investigate; let some pairs examine problems, like traffic jams, crime, and the homeless, and other pairs deal with positive aspects of the city, such as access to a variety of attractions, contact with diverse cultures, and job opportunities. The pairs can prepare written and oral reports on their assigned topics, complete with drawings and other illustrations. Each oral report will make a unique contribution to the class's total understanding of their chosen city.

Music:

1. Songs About Cities

There are many popular, contemporary songs that refer to American cities, such as *Chicago, I Left My Heart in San Francisco, New York, New York, On the Way to San Jose,* and *The M.T.A.* (about Boston). You might want to share some of these songs with the class. Encourage students to write lyrics for a song about the city in which they live, or a city they have visited or studied.

Art:

1. Making City Landmarks

Students can use clay to create miniature replicas of famous city landmarks such as the Sears Tower (Chicago), Statue of Liberty (New York), Gateway Arch (St. Louis), Liberty Bell (Philadelphia), Washington Monument (Washington, D.C.), Space Needle (Seattle), U.S.S. Constitution (Boston), Alamo (San Antonio), Big Ben (London), Eiffel Tower (Paris), Colosseum (Rome), and St. Basil's Church (Moscow). After the clay bakes or dries, the replicas can be painted and displayed in the classroom.

Cooking:

1. City Cuisine

Many American cities are noted for special foods, like New Orleans for its Creole dishes or Kansas City for its steaks. New York City probably has a greater number and variety of restaurants than any other city, but it is still famous for one very simple and common food: the lowly, but delicious, hot dog, which can be purchased and eaten on the run from sidewalk vendors all over the city. To give your students a taste of New York, help them prepare a batch of hot dogs. Serve the dogs with an assortment of condiments: mustard, catsup, cole slaw, sauerkraut, relish, cucumber slices, and you name it. Or, if you prefer, pick your own favorite city and, together with your students, plan and cook a dish for which it is well known.

Books:

1. Royston, Robert. (1985). *Your World 2000: Cities*. New York: Facts on File Publications. Intermediate.

2. Wright, David K. (1994). *A Multicultural Portrait of Life in the Cities*. New York: Marshall Cavendish. Advanced.

3. MacDonald, Fiona. (1992). *Timelines: Cities, Citizens, and Civilizations*. New York: Franklin Watts.

4. Kalman, Bobby, and Hughes, Susan. (1986). *I Live In a City*. New York: Crabtree Publishing. Primary.

5. Knapp, Brian. (1994). *Cities of the World*. Danbury, CT: Grollier Educational Corporation. Intermediate.

6. Kalman, Bobbie. (1983). *Early City Life*. New York: Crabtree Publishing. Intermediate.

7. Beekman, Dan. (1982). *Forest, Village, Town, City*. New York: Thomas Y. Crowell. Primary.

8. Costa-Pau, Rosa. (1994). *The City*. New York: Chelsea House Publishers. Intermediate.

Software:

1. *Mathville* [Mac IBM]. Seattle, WA: Didatech. Primary, Intermediate, Advanced.

12

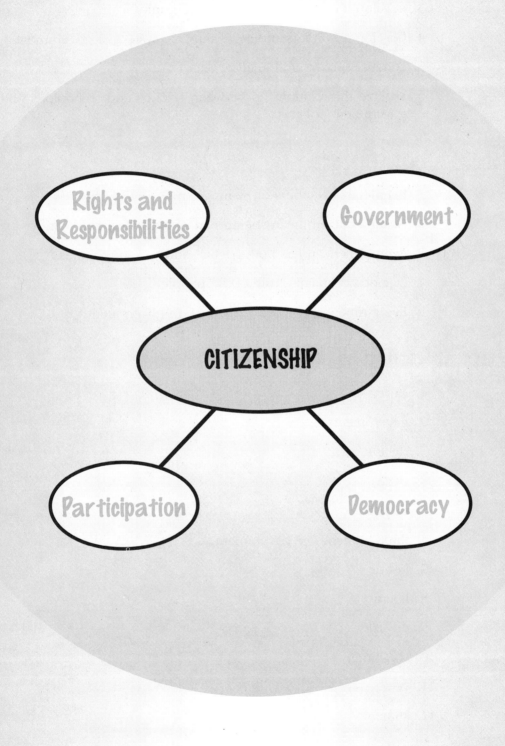

Rights and Responsibilities

Government

CITIZENSHIP

Participation

Democracy

Theme Goals:

Students will:

1. develop the concept of citizen.

2. distinguish between "rights" and "responsibilities."

3. develop a concept of political community.

4. develop an understanding of the U.S. system of government.

5. conduct surveys and analyze data.

6. analyze the relationship between science and technology and government policies.

Theme Concepts:

1. People are members of many groups.

2. Being a citizen means being part of a political community.

3. Every American has both "rights" and "responsibilities."

4. Democracy means "rule of the people."

5. Every American should participate in government.

Vocabulary:

1. citizen

2. government

3. rights

4. duties

5. democracy

6. three branches of government

7. justice

8. liberty

9. diversity

10. community

11. veto

12. anthem

Instructional Bulletin Board

The purpose of this bulletin board is to help students distinguish between "rights" and "responsibilities." Use a 2-inch-wide strip of colorful paper to divide the board into two equal left and right sides. Label the left side "responsibilities" and right side "rights." Make rights and responsibilities cards that are related to classroom and school experiences (some important national and state rights and responsibilities of United States citizens are listed below). Place the cards in an envelope attached to the lower corner of the bulletin board. The students' task is to categorize the cards by pinning the "responsibilities" cards on the right side of the board and the "rights" cards on the left side.

Citizen responsibilities cards: "Attend school until at least age 16"; "Obey the law"; "Serve on a jury"; "Defend the nation in war"; and "Pay taxes." Citizen rights cards: "Travel to a foreign country"; "Vote in an election"; "Gather together to discuss a public issue"; "Worship in a church, synagogue, or mosque"; "Live in the United States"; "Have a fair and speedy trial"; and "Express an opinion."

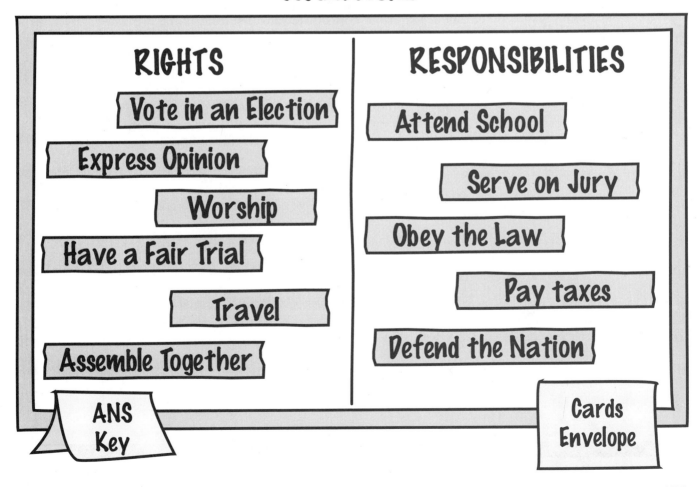

CITIZENSHIP

RIGHTS	RESPONSIBILITIES
Vote in an Election	Attend School
Express Opinion	Serve on Jury
Worship	Obey the Law
Have a Fair Trial	Pay taxes
Travel	Defend the Nation
Assemble Together	

ANS Key

Cards Envelope

Parent Letter

Dear Parent:

We will be beginning our study of citizenship soon. For children, "citizenship" is a very abstract concept. To make the concept more concrete, the children will be directly involved in a number of activities that will enable them to experience government firsthand. Included among the activities will be the following:

At School:

- Developing our own definition of the "good" citizen
- Making good citizen badges
- Exploring our "rights" and "duties"
- Meeting important citizens from the community
- Creating a democracy in our classroom
- Taking polls and surveys
- Learning important American values

At Home:

Some ways you can help teach the concept of citizenship at home are listed below:

- Give your child regular chores to do around the house.
- Talk about the work of community service organizations and agencies.
- Participate in a voluntary community service project with your child.
- Discuss community, state, national, and world issues at the dinner table.
- Next time you vote in an election, take your child to the polling place with you.

Linking Up:

For children, "citizenship" is a very abstract concept. To understand its meaning in their own lives, children need to feel that they can play a part in governing themselves. By modeling the role of decision maker and problem solver, you can help children see that citizenship refers not simply to things that happened a long time ago or far away—it is also about things all Americans, including the students, must *do*. Ask students to list things they must do to be a good citizen of the classroom and school.

Social Studies:

1. Collecting Evidence

Have students make observations in their classroom and at various locations in the school to determine whether or not school rules are being followed. For example, after a small group of students have reviewed the rules for conduct in the cafeteria, students can station themselves in the cafeteria and record any instances of rule breaking that occur there. The data collected, after they are tallied and interpreted, might suggest ideas for improving cafeteria conditions and conduct, and/or for modifying the rules.

2. Membership in Many Communities

Children are members of various groups—family, school, city, state, and nation. Discuss the various groups to which students belong. Draw the diagram in Figure 12-1 on the chalkboard to illustrate how someone can be simultaneously a member of many different, increasingly more inclusive groups. Have students name their nation, state, city, school, and family.

3. What is "Community"?

Bring in pictures of people (those with close-ups of faces are ideal) that represent the *diversity* of America—age, gender, race, religion, disability, and ethnicity. Ask students what all of these people share or have in common. Being part of a group gives people a sense of *community*, a Latin word that originally meant "in common" or "sharing." Have students give concrete examples of things they share and/or have in common with people in their families, school, city, state, and nation. Have students compile a list of the examples.

4. Qualities of Good Citizenship

Being a *citizen* means being part of a political community. A political community has to make wise and good decisions that affect what people in the community can and cannot do. To stimulate students' thinking about citizenship, tell them that a student from a foreign country is moving to the community and will be joining their class. Challenge students to develop a description of a "good" student. Have the class compile a list of characteristics of a good student. Do any of the characteristics on the list relate to making wise and good choices? Next, have the class compile a list of characteristics of a "good" American citizen to send to the student. Can the class agree on what makes a good citizen? How are the "good student" and "good citizen" lists alike? How are they different?

5. Students' Rights and Responsibilities

Have students compile a list of school "rights" and "responsibilities." "Rights" refer to things that students are usually allowed to do without interference. A list of "rights" might include "to hear and see the teacher's lesson," "to ask questions," "to learn," "to be treated fairly," and "to move throughout the school safely." "Responsibilities" refer to things students are required to do. A list of "responsibilities" might include "obey the teacher," "listen carefully," "do your own work," and "work quietly in the library." Have each student pick one right and one responsiblity from the list and explain how each one applies to her life.

6. Speakers from the Community

Expose your students to people who work to make the community better. Invite community leaders and helpers from all walks of life into the classroom to explain what they do and why they do it. Possible guests include the following: mayor, school board member, the principal, police officer, sanitation worker, fire fighter, health officer, and a volunteer from a service organization.

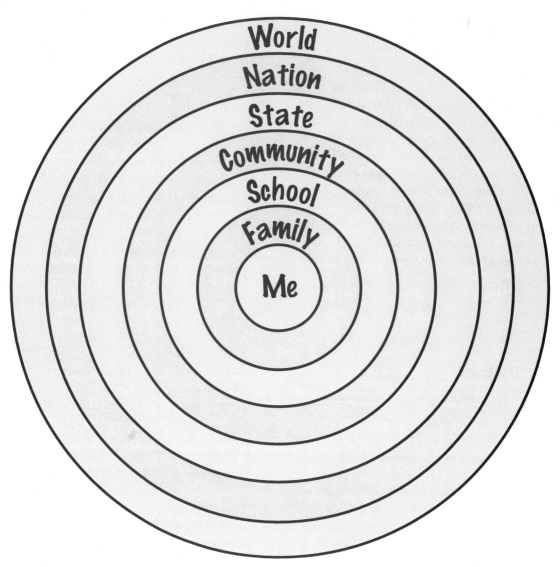

FIGURE 12-1

7. Community Service in Action

Involve the class in a school or community project. Some examples of projects include the following: tutoring younger or disabled students; cleaning the school grounds; planting flowers and shrubs or a tree on the school grounds; monitoring student behavior in the hallways, cafeteria, and on the playground; picking up litter; adopting a senior citizen; visiting the sick; collecting food for the poor; and earning money (car wash, bake sales, etc.) for needy causes in the community.

8. Mini-Government: A Student Simulation

You may not be able to travel to Washington, D.C., or to your state's capital, but you can create a mini-democracy in your classroom. Write

the word "democracy" on the chalkboard and ask students to tell you what they think it means. Tell students that democracy is a form of government that was invented by the ancient Greeks over 2,000 years ago. *Democracy* means "rule of the people." After you have given the class a brief overview of our three-branch system (legislative, executive, and judicial) of government, you can let students experience the dynamics of democracy firsthand through the following activities related to the legislative branch, which should be spread out over several days.

1. Help students conduct schoolwide surveys to identify issues of concern. The surveys might reveal issues related to things like hallway congestion, cafeteria food, playground equipment, classroom rules, consequences

128

for misbehavior, and field trip options. Based on the issues identified, let students assume the role of "legislators" and formulate "bills," which will be debated by the students later. For example, one bill prompted by the hallway congestion issue might create a "student hallway traffic monitor" position.

2. The legislative area can be decorated with a cardboard replica of the front of the Capitol Building. Arrange the chairs/desks in a semi-circle to facilitate discussion. Assign a "speaker" to preside over the legislature. The legislators must vote whether they are "for" or "against" each of the bills identified in step #1 above. Let legislators debate and vote on each bill one at a time. Allot a specific period of time for debate. You might want to let the legislators move around the legislative area and confer with one another for a few minutes before each vote is cast.

3. Before a bill becomes a law, the president (you) must sign it or veto it.

After the mini-democracy activity has concluded, debrief the participants by asking such questions as:

- What did you like best (least) about the role you played?
- What issues (bills) were the hardest (easiest) to deal with?
- What did we learn about the legislative branch of government from doing this activity?
- What parts of the activity were most difficult to do?
- How would you describe our legislature to someone who knew nothing about it?

(Note: A simulation is by its very nature an over-simplification of reality. Nevertheless, the activity should give students some insights into the legislative process. During the debriefing, make certain to clarify and correct any student misconceptions.)

9. Community Project

Identify a problem in the community on which students can act, such as a pollution problem, care of elderly, or a need for a stoplight. After students investigate the problem, they can write letters to local leaders stating their position, develop posters, make an action plan to help, and be a direct part of the solution by working for change.

Math:

1. Practical Applications

To help students become more confident and competent citizens, give them plenty of opportunities to act on decisions they have made. For example, with your help and guidance, your students might plan a party, collect money for a project, use the school bank or store, prepare a walking excursion or field trip, conduct a candy sale, or prepare a food recipe. All of these activities and many others involve the use of mathematics.

2. Survey Skills

The surveying activities described above provide many opportunities to apply math skills. The example below shows survey data that could be presented in either pictorial or numerical form, depending on the background of the learners.

Questions:	Pictorial	Number
How many students said our class rules were fair?		10
How many students said our class rules were unfair?		4
Total		14

Possible questions and tasks: Did more students say the class rules were fair? Did more than half the class say the class rules were fair? What percentage of students said the class rules were unfair? Make a bar graph that displays these data. Make a pie graph that displays these data.

Language Arts:

1. The Meaning Behind the Words

Have students discuss the meaning of terms found in familiar documents. One example is the "Pledge of Allegiance," which many students say every day. Write the Pledge on the chalkboard. Ask students to tell you what each of the following words means: pledge, allegiance, liberty, invisible, justice, republic, and nation. Relate these terms to the children's personal experiences. For example, children might not know the meaning of "justice," but they do have definite ideas about what "fair" and "unfair" mean. They can cite examples of fairness and unfairness on the playground, at the ballpark, and in the classroom, as well as many, many other places. Based on the students' responses, develop webs for the concepts, such as the one for "liberty" shown in Figure 12-2.

2. "Mayflower Compacts" for Modern Times

Tell students about the Pilgrim's voyage to New England, and read them sections of the "Mayflower Compact." Have them imagine that they are starting life over again in a new, unsettled land. What rules would they agree to follow? Have small groups of students develop a set of rules that they could live with. After they have finished their "compacts," the groups can share them with the class.

3. Position Papers

In conjunction with the mini-government activity described above in Social Studies Activity

#8, encourage students to draft or dictate position papers on school-related issues. Give students a specific writing format to follow. The paper should include a clear statement of the position on the issue, strong reasons that support the position, and a conclusion that summarizes the position.

Science:

1. Technology and the Community

Scientific discoveries and technology have made our lives easier and better, but they have also created many problems. As a result of unwise choices, humans have caused wildlife extinction, habitat destruction, natural resource depletion, and pollution. Help students create a chart, like the one at the bottom of page 131, that shows both positive and negative consequences of technological advances such as those listed. For example, the invention of the car made moving from place to place easier and faster, but the fumes from cars also pollute the air; a chain saw makes it easy to remove a dead tree limb that might otherwise fall on the

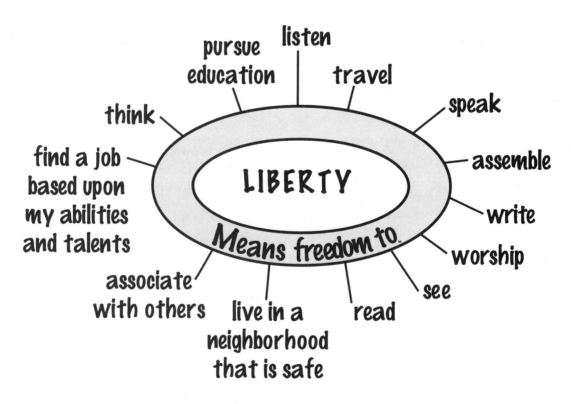

Mind Map of "Liberty"

FIGURE 12-2

roof, but it also makes it easy for loggers to cut down whole forests quickly.

2. Coping with the Challenges

Help students generate a list of examples of ways that we have tried to protect ourselves from the bad consequences of technology. Examples could include setting speed limits; monitoring the levels of air, water, and land pollution; requiring antipollution devices on vehicles and in factories; controlling access to television programs and the Internet; and monitoring and encouraging the recycling of materials like paper, plastics, and metal.

3. Local Decisions for a Global Community

Show students how local actions affect people everywhere. For example, increased world demand for construction materials like wood has led to the rapid destruction of the world's rain forests, acid rain created by factories in the United States has cause pollution problems in Canada; and over-fishing the world's oceans has led to serious reductions in the numbers of whales and certain species of fish worldwide. What policies (laws) does the world need to protect the environment?

Art:

1. Citizenship in Action

Let students work individually or in pairs to create scenes of citizenship in action. Some possibilities for illustrations include scenes depicting people helping other people, scenes from

FIGURE 12-3

American history, scenes showing people cleaning up the community, and scenes showing people voting in an election. Each picture can be glued to a large sheet of butcher paper to create a collage of the class's work.

2. Awards for Merit

Provide students with an assortment of ribbons, foil, glitter, glue, crayons, paints, and tagboard, and let them design and make "good citizen badges" like the one in Figure 12-3 that can be worn when merited by their good behavior.

	Good Consequence	Bad Consequence
Technology		
Car		
Bulldozer		
Chain saw		
Super tankers		
Nuclear plants		
Wood stoves		

Music:

1. The National Anthem

Before our national anthem became the nation's song it was a poem that Francis Scott Key wrote during the War of 1812. The words to the poem were inspired by the British naval attack on Fort McHenry in Baltimore, Maryland. Key, who was a prisoner on a British ship, watched the attack. Guns on the enemy ships bombarded the fort for two days, but the Americans refused to surrender, and the flag continued to fly above the fort. Filled with pride, Key decided to write a poem about the battle, which later became our national anthem. Write the words to "The Star-Spangled Banner" on the chalk board. Have children read the poem and discuss the meaning of the words. For example, students might check the dictionary for definitions for these italicized words: "and the rockets' red *glare*, the bombs *bursting* in air, gave *proof* through the night that our flag was still there." After the meaning of the poem has been discussed, play a tape of the national anthem, and let students sing along.

Books:

1. Scher, Linda. (1993). *The Vote: Making Your Voice Heard*. Austin, TX: Raintree Steck-Vaughn. Primary, Intermediate.

2. Ritchie, Donald. (1988). *Know Your Government: The Senate*. New York: Chelsea House. Advance.

3. Gourse, Leslie. (1994). *The Congress*. New York: Franklin Watts. Intermediate.

4. Swanson, June. (1990). *I Pledge Allegiance*. Minneapolis: Carolrhoda Books. Primary.

5. Fradin, Dennis. (1985). *Voting and Elections*. Chicago: Children's Press. Primary.

6. Schulz, Marjorie. (1990). *Community Services*. New York: Franklin Watts. Intermediate.

7. Hoose, Phillip. (1993). *It's Our World, Too! Stories of Young People Who Are Making a Difference*. Boston: Little, Brown and Company. Advanced.

Software:

1. *Origins of the Constitution* [Mac IBM Windows CD-ROM]. Fairfield, CT: Queue. Advanced.

2. *Capitol Hill* [Mac MPC CD-ROM]. Novato, CA: Mindscape Educational Software. Advanced.

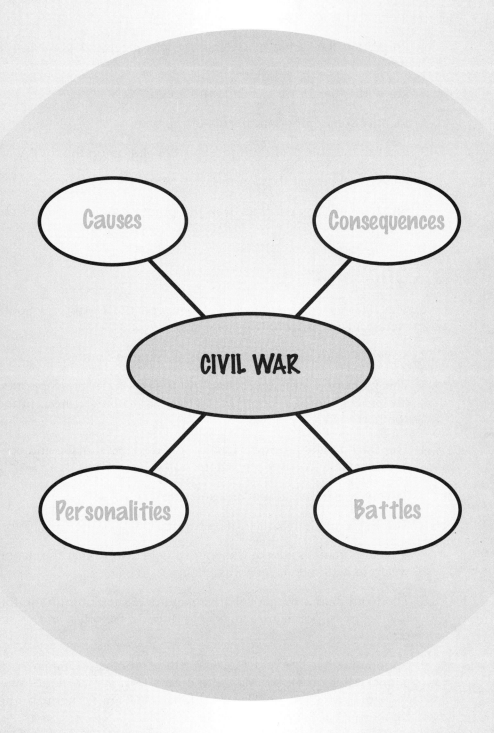

Theme Goals:

Students will:

1. describe major causes of the Civil War.

2. compare and contrast life in the North and South.

3. identify characteristics of slavery.

4. know that the Battle of Gettysburg was a turning point in the war.

5. know that the North defeated the South.

6. identify some important results of the war.

7. analyze the effects of the Industrial Revolution on the Civil War.

8. analyze numerical data on the Civil War.

9. write about the Civil War from the point of view of one of the contemporaries.

Theme Concepts:

1. The differences that developed between the North and South were a major cause of the Civil War.

2. Slavery was the key issue dividing North and South.

3. The plantation system and the institution of slavery supported the production of a single cash crop, particularly cotton, in the southern states.

4. The small family farm was ideally suited to the climatic and economic conditions of the northern states.

5. Slavery was cruel, inhumane, and unjust.

6. The Battle of Gettysburg was a turning point of the Civil War.

7. Two important results of the South's defeat were that the nation was reunited and slavery was ended.

8. The North had a numerical advantage over the South in the following areas: population, miles of railroads, factories, and workers.

9. Important Civil War era figures include Abraham Lincoln, U.S. Grant, Jefferson Davis, Matthew Brady, Harriet Beecher Stowe, William Lloyd Garrison, Harriet Tubman, William T. Sherman, and "Stonewall" Jackson.

Vocabulary:

1. slavery

2. Union

3. Confederacy

4. *E Pluribus Umum*

5. Battle of Gettysburg

Instructional Bulletin Board

The purpose of this bulletin board is to let students list important characteristics of the North and South during the time of the Civil War. Students can attach the characteristic cards inside the appropriate section of the diagram.

Cards

Large cotton plantations (South)

30,000 miles of railroad (North)

Seceded from the Union (South)

Supported slavery (South)

Wanted to end slavery (North)

Longer growing season (South)

Smaller population (South)

Better military leaders (South)

More manufacturing (North)

Fewer states (South)

Most of the Civil War battles fought here (South)

Colder climate (North)

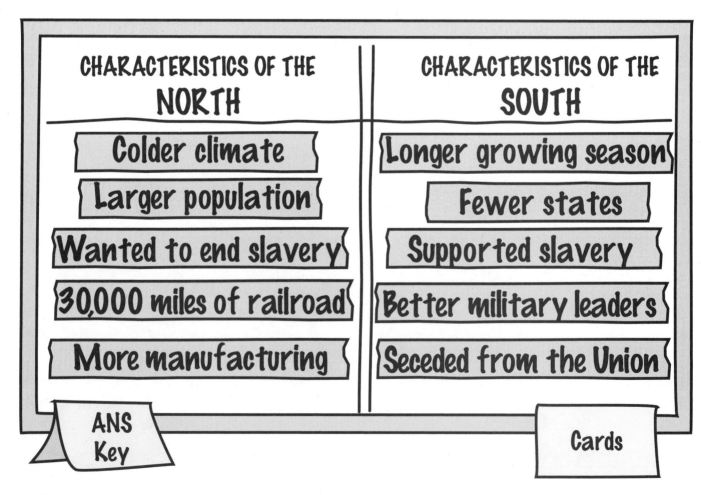

CHARACTERISTICS OF THE
NORTH

- Colder climate
- Larger population
- Wanted to end slavery
- 30,000 miles of railroad
- More manufacturing

CHARACTERISTICS OF THE
SOUTH

- Longer growing season
- Fewer states
- Supported slavery
- Better military leaders
- Seceded from the Union

ANS
Key

Cards

Parent Letter

Dear Parents:

We are beginning a theme on the the Civil War, our nation's bloodiest and most tragic conflict. The war divided the country—and sometimes families. Americans were not fighting a foreign enemy: They were fighting each other. The Northern victory preserved the Union, ended slavery, and strengthened the concept of American citizenship.

At School:

The students will be engaged in the following activities:

- Comparing life in the North and South
- Identifying the characteristics of slavery
- Enacting the Battle of Gettysburg
- Drawing and making models of Civil War soldiers and equipment
- Making charts on Civil War facts and figures
- Writing about the Civil War from the points of view of contemporaries

At Home:

If your community played a part in the Civil War, find information about it. Answer your child's questions about the conflict, and share your own feelings about the tragic struggle.

Linking Up:

The issue of slavery divided the nation and led to the Civil War. Talk about contemporary issues on which people disagree. How are political and social problems resolved today? The Civil War was the first conflict to be extensively photographed. See if your local library has *The American Heritage Picture History of The Civil War* edited by Richard M. Ketchum (American Heritage, 1960), or some other book displaying photographs of Civil War scenes. Together with the class, look at the photographs. What do they tell the students about this tragic war?

Social Studies:

1. Causes of the Conflict

Brief Background. Underlying causes of the Civil War were the economic, political, and social differences that developed between the northern and southern sections of the country. The northern region had become a center for commerce and industry, where large cities, industrial resources, railways, banks, factories, and shipping were concentrated. Industrial development created new jobs, and the North's population increased rapidly as European immigrants poured into the country to fill them. The northern states were called "free states" since they had declared slavery illegal. The southern region, in comparison, was more rural. An abundance of rich soil and a long growing season made the South ideally suited for agriculture, especially for raising the south's most important cash crop, cotton. Much of the cotton was grown on plantations, and its production depended on the labor of black slaves. Although not everyone in the South was a slave owner, most southerners accepted the institution of slavery and were opposed to northern attempts to abolish it. By the 1850s, slaves comprised about 40 percent of the South's population. Because slavery was legal within their borders, the southern states were called "slave states." The development of the western region of the United States was strongly influenced by the North. Most of the pioneers heading West had no interest in owning slaves or the spread of slavery. By 1859, there were many more free states in the Union than slave states. Some specific events that increased tensions between North and South included: (1) bloody fighting be-tween proslavery and antislavery forces occurred in Kansas; (2) the Supreme Court declared that perhaps slavery could not be outlawed anywhere; (3) the antislavery novel *Uncle Tom's Cabin* was published; and (4) John Brown tried to spark a slave revolt at Harpers Ferry. Finally, when a strong opponent of the spread of slavery, Abraham Lincoln, was elected president, the southern states seceded to form a new nation, the Confederacy.

Show students physical and climate maps of the United States. Compare and contrast the northern and southern sections. Using a political map, identify the following 23 states of the Union: Maine, Vermont, New Hampshire, Massachusetts, Connecticut, Rhode Island, New York, New Jersey, Delaware, Pennsylvania, Ohio, Michigan, Iowa, Illinois, Indiana, Kansas, Wisconsin, Minnesota, California, Oregon, Missouri, Kentucky, and Maryland. The 11 Confederate states of the South were as follows: Virginia, North Carolina, South Carolina, Georgia, Tennessee, Florida, Alabama, Mississippi, Louisiana, Arkansas, and Texas. Provide information about the states of the North and South. Have pairs of students select one state to study. They can investigate the following questions: What is the history of the state? What geographic and climatic factors help explain the state's development over time and its role in the war?

2. Life in the North and South Before the War

Allow students time to explore pictures of scenes that depict life in the pre–Civil War North and South. Using the following information, describe farm life in the North and life on a plantation in the South. Then, have students list differences and similarities noted between the two lifestyles. Help the class create a retrieval chart that compares and contrasts the two ways of life.

A SOUTHERN PLANTATION

Plantations are large farms with many workers that usually grow a single crop. Most southern plantation workers were black slaves who were forced to serve the landowner, or master. Like the land itself, the slaves were considered to be the property of the master. The biggest and grandest building on the plantation was the plantation owner's house, or mansion, which was often surrounded by gardens, orchards, and farm buildings. Back a distance from the mansion were the slave cabins. The plantation produced many things needed by the owner and slaves. There were usually stables, storehouses, a kitchen, carpenter shop, a weaver's house, a blacksmith shop, a tannery, a smokehouse, and barns. Although tobacco or rice was grown on some plantations, the most important money-making crop in the South was cotton. The back-breaking work of raising huge quantities of cotton was done by the slaves, who toiled in the fields from sunrise to sunset. Much of the cotton crop was sold to merchants and shipped to England.

A NORTHERN FARM

Northern farms were much smaller than southern plantations. The buildings and grounds on a farm usually included a small farmhouse, a barn, chicken coop, garden, and fields. Northern farms were called "family farms" because all of the work on the farms was done by family members. Each member of the family would usually have different chores to do. These chores included tasks like the following: building a stone wall, weeding the garden, feeding the chickens, milking the cow, and churning butter. At harvest times, everybody on the farm would help out in the wheat, corn, and barley fields. The family would eat and store some of the food produced, and then take the rest to town to sell.

3. Slavery

Before the Civil War resolved the issue, the institution of slavery divided the nation. Today, it is clear to every reasonable person that slavery was morally wrong. Back then, however, some people saw slavery as an economic and political necessity. Information presented in Social Studies Activity #1 above explores briefly some of the factors related to the issue of slavery. Provide students with period illustrations of slaves, including scenes of slaves being transported across the Atlantic, working on the plantations, and being sold at an action. To stimulate children's thinking about the experience of being a slave, invite them to talk about their feelings about the illustrations, and elicit their thoughts about the following situations experienced by slaves: being taken from your home, packed on a ship, and taken to another country; working every day for long hours and never getting paid; knowing that you could be separated forever from your loved ones; knowing that if you don't work hard or if you run away from your master, you will be sold and/or beaten; knowing that you will never enjoy the comforts and freedoms in life enjoyed by white people; and knowing that your children will have no chance for a better life.

4. Gettysburg: The Turning Point

Brief Background. The opening shots of the Civil War were fired in 1861 at Fort Sumter, a Union fort located on an island in Charleston Harbor, South Carolina. There were many subsequent bloody battles fought, and almost all of them took place in the South. The Union army was much larger and better equipped than the Confederates, but the better-led Rebel troops usually outfought the Yankees in the early campaigns of the war. The turning point of the war was a battle that took place in 1863 on northern soil near the town of Gettysburg, Pennsylvania shown in Figure 13-1. The Confederate and Union armies fought savagely there for three days. On the third day, in a head-on attack on Union forces called Pickett's Charge, the Confederates suffered terrible losses. The beaten Confederate army, led by their great general, Robert E. Lee, managed to retreat to Virginia. Although fighting would continue for almost two more years, the Battle of Gettysburg so weakened General Lee's troops that they were never again able to take the offensive against the Northern army.

Provide students with military maps and scenes, and let them draw pictures of the Battle of Gettysburg. Help students script a scene from the battle and make props and costumes a reenactment.

5. The Results of War

Brief Background. In 1865, General Lee's surrender to General Grant at Appomattox brought the Civil War to an end. Two very important results of the Northern victory were the reunification of the nation and the end of slavery.

Help students identify American symbols and scenes that tell us we are all part of one nation. For example, every state is represented by a star on the U.S. flag, and the nation's motto, *E Pluribus Unum*, which is on the Great Seal

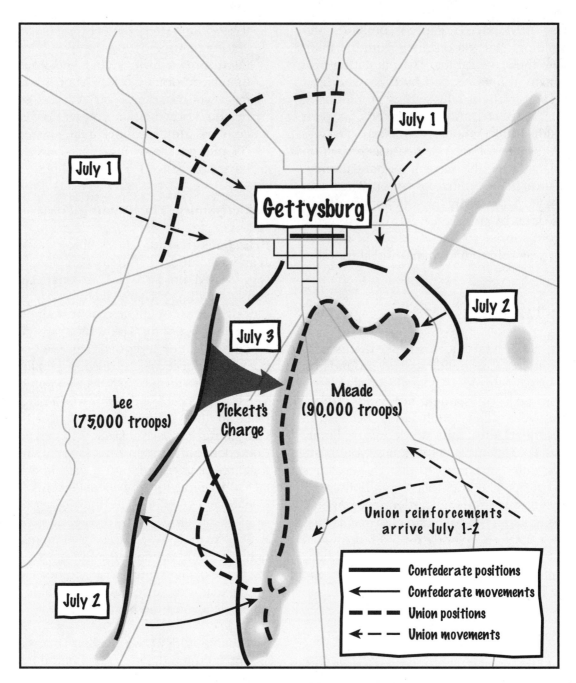

Gettysburg Battlefield

FIGURE 13-1

of the United States of America and all U.S. coins, means "from many, one." Encourage students to cite examples of values and habits shared by Americans.

6. Modern Connections

What places in the northern, southern, eastern, and western parts of the United States do all Americans today like to visit? Have students study a map of the United States showing high-ways and airline routes. Discuss how highways, telephones, television, computers, and faxes have linked people together. Ask students how modern transportation and communications systems have changed the United States, when compared to Civil War times.

7. Working for Change

Brief Background. After the Civil War, amendments were added to the U.S. Constitution to prohibit slavery (13th Amendment), to give all people equal citizenship and equal protect of the laws (14th Amendment), and to forbid all states from denying the vote to any person on the basis of "race, color, or previous condition of servitude" (15th Amendment).

Have students make a list of rights they think every citizen should have. Of course, the struggle for freedom and justice for all Americans continues to this day. Provide students with some examples of contemporary people and groups who have worked for change.

Science:

1. The Civil War and the Industrial Revolution

Brief Background. The Civil War was the first war to take full advantage of the technological advances created by the Industrial Revolution. One invention that played an important part in the war was the railroad. The North's extensive railroad system was used to move troops and supplies quickly over long distances. An invention that had a significant impact on wartime communications was the telegraph, which was used by President Lincoln and his generals, as well as by Southern leaders. New military weapons made the Civil War far deadlier than any previous conflict. At the start, foot soldiers on both sides were armed with one-shot rifles that were loaded much like Revolutionary War–era muskets. During the war, Union inventors developed repeating rifles that could fire 8 to 15 bullets without reloading. The ultimate rapid-fire weapon invented during the Civil War was the machine gun. The Gatling gun, which saw limited use late in the war, could fire 600 rounds a minute. The first naval battle between ironclad ships—the South's *Merrimack* and the North's *Monitor*—took place during the Civil War. Still another invention, photography, was used extensively for the first time in a conflict during the Civil War.

Show the class photographs of Civil War soldiers and scenes. Do the photographs "tell" the students anything about the Civil War? Do the faces in the photographs reveal feelings and emotions? To give students background on Civil War weapons and equipment, read aloud selections from *The Civil War Rifleman* by Martin Windrow (Franklin Watts, 1985), or another appropriate children's book. Provide interested students with art, modeling, and construction materials, and then let them make models and drawings of Civil War soldiers and their weapons and equipment.

Math:

1. Lopsided Numbers

Have students analyze the following numerical data on the North and the South. They can make pictorial, bar, and pie graphs for each of the factors. Help students calculate percentages to show comparisons between one side's figure and the total. Students can use subtraction to compare the two sides' figures on each factor. Do these numbers suggest that one side might have had an advantage over the other?

Factors	North	South
Population	22 million	9 million (incudes 3 million black slaves)
Miles of railroad	30,000	10,000
Factories	100,000	20,000
Workers	1.1 million	111,000

Language Arts:

1. Voices from the Past

Some of the interesting personalities of the Civil War era are listed below. Assign each student the task of learning about one of them. Students can make brief presentations to the class dressed in the costume of the personality.
U.S. Grant, Union general

Robert E. Lee, Confederate general
Jefferson Davis, President of the Confederacy
Abraham Lincoln, President of the United States
Matthew Brady, Civil War photographer
Harriet Beecher Stowe, author of *Uncle Tom's Cabin*
William Lloyd Garrison, Northern abolitionist
Harriet Tubman, agent of slaves' escape through "underground railroad"

William T. Sherman, Union general
"Stonewall" Jackson, Confederate general

2. Civil War Histories

After students have received sufficient background information about the Civil War, let each of them take the role of an ordinary person—teacher, shopkeeper, slave, soldier, or student—who lived during those times, and then write (or dictate) a brief personal history about their everyday experiences.

Books:

1. Reit, Seymour. (1988). *Behind Rebel Lines: The Incredible Story of Emma Edmonds, Civil War Spy*. San Diego: Harcourt, Brace, Jovanovich. Advanced.

2. Carter, Alden R. (1985). *The Civil War*. New York: Time-life Books. Intermediate, Advanced.

3. Weiner, Eric. (1992). *The Civil War*. New York: SMITHMARK Publishers, Inc. Advanced.

4. Windrow, Martin. (1985). *The Civil War Rifleman*. New York: Franklin Watts Limited. Intermediate, Advanced.

5. Reef, Catherine. (1993). *Civil War Soldiers*. New York: Twenty-First Century Books. Advanced.

6. Reef, Catherine. (1992). *Gettysburg*. New York: Dillon Press. Intermediate, Advanced.

7. Greene, Carole. (1989). *Robert E. Lee: Leader in War and Peace*. Chicago: Children's Press. Primary.

8. Davis, Burke. (1976). *Runaway Balloon: the Last Flight of Confederate Air Force One*. New York: Coward, McCann, & Geoghegan. Intermediate.

9. Kent, Zachary. (1992). *The Story of the Battle of Bull Run*. Chicago: Children's Press. Intermediate, Advanced.

10. Weinberg, Karen. (1991). Weinberg. *Window of Time*. Shippensburg, PA: White Mane Publishing Co. Intermediate, Advanced.

11. Ketchum, Richard M. (1960). *The American Heritage Picture History of the Civil War*. New York: American Heritage. Advanced.

Software:

1. *Turning Point Series: The Civil War* [Apple II Mac IBM Windows CD-ROM]. Victoria, British Columbia: Entrex. Advanced.

2. *U.S. History on CD-ROM* [Mac IBM CD-ROM]. Princeton: Bureau of Electronic Publications. Advanced.

3. *GTV: A Geographic Perpective on American History* [GS Mac IBM Laserdisc]. Washington, DC: National Geographic. Advanced.

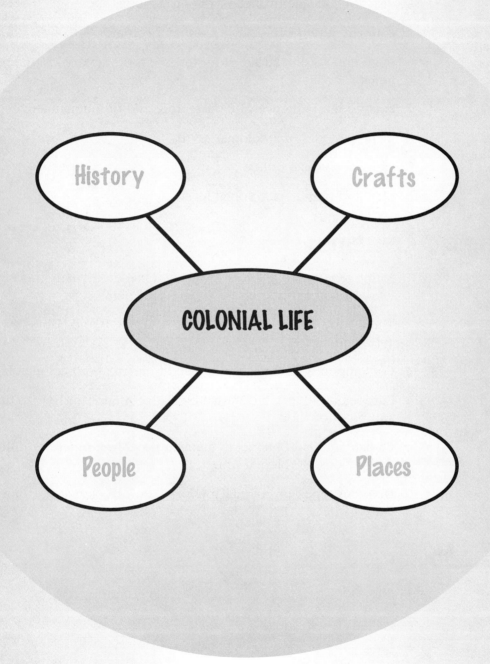

History

Crafts

COLONIAL LIFE

People

Places

Theme Goals:

Students will:

1. apply map skills.

2. compare and contrast early colonies.

3. make inferences about colonial life.

4. describe the significance of corn to colonial life.

5. compare and contrast the 13 original colonies.

6. write about colonial life from the point of view of contemporaries.

7. analyze the influence of climate and land on human activity.

8. make a model of a colonial town.

9. create a colonial quilt.

10. plan and prepare a colonial feast.

Theme Concepts:

1. Many geographic features must be considered when choosing the best place to locate a colonial settlement.

2. Three early English colonies were Roanoke Island, Jamestown, and Plymouth.

3. Contemporary sources can be used to learn about colonial life.

4. European settlers were shown by Native Americans how to find and produce food.

5. Climate and land factors influenced the development of different sections of colonial America.

6. Different types of colonial people viewed colonial life differently.

Vocabulary:

1. governor

2. planter

3. servant

4. slave

5. patriot

6. Pilgrim

Instructional Bulletin Board

The purpose of this bulletin board is to display students' stories written from the perspective of different types of colonists (see Language Arts Activity #1 on page 148). Large cutout illustrations of the different types of colonists (such as governor, planter, Native American, apprentice, goodwife or married woman, Pilgrim, servant, slave, constable, smuggler, patriot, newcomer, and fur trader) can accompany the stories.

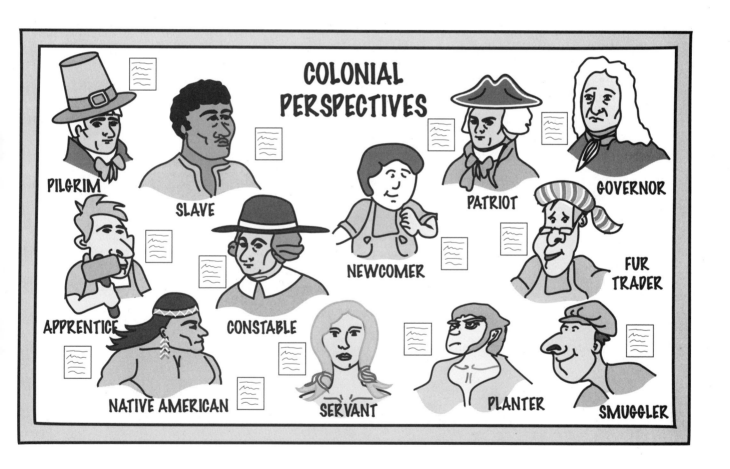

Parent Letter

Dear Parents:

The class is starting its study of the colonial period in America's history. The first colonists came to the Americas for different reasons. Some came to escape religious persecution; others for land and riches. However, they all had two things in common: a desire to start a new life and a lack of knowledge of the many dangers that lay ahead.

At School:

Our study of colonial life will involve the class in the following activities:

- Locating an ideal place for a colony
- Comparing the Roanoke Island, Jamestown, and Plymouth colonies
- Observing illustrations of colonial times
- Learning about amazing maize
- Investigating the 13 colonies
- Writing from a colonial perspective
- Analyzing how geography influenced the development of the different colonies
- Making a model of a colonial town
- Preparing a colonial feast

At Home:

This would be a a good time to read with your child about colonial times. Check the community library for an appropriate book. If there are any museums or historical societies nearby that feature colonial history, make a visit with your child. Tell your child about your favorite colonial personality. Does your child have a favorite, too?

Linking Up:

Write the word "colonist" on the chalkboard. Explain that a colonist is someone who settles in a new country. Ask students to imagine going to a new place to live. Would they want to leave their homes and friends and go to a new place? What would they hope to find at their new place? What would they want to take with them?

Social Studies:

1. Mystery Place

Brief Background. When the early colonists came to North America, they were not certain where to locate their settlements. They spent considerable time searching for the best spots, and with good reason. They knew that if they made a wrong decision, the results might be disastrous.

To give students a sense of the uncertainties and risks faced by settlers back then, provide small groups of students with maps of an island (the island can be imaginary or based on a real place). The map should show climate, mountains, rivers, lakes, vegetation, harbors, and other natural features, but no settlements. Tell students to imagine they are members of an English Land Company. Their goal is to establish a colony (settlement) on the island that will be profitable.

They want to use the resources of the new land to develop products that can be traded in England. Give the small groups time to analyze the map and decide on the best location for a settlement. After the groups have finished, let a spokesperson from each group show the class the group's choice for a settlement location. Group members should also explain the reasons for their choice (i.e. richness of land, nearness to fresh water, protection from sea storms, etc.)

2. Early Colonies

Brief Background. Three of the earliest English colonies formed were Roanoke Island, Jamestown, and Plymouth.

To provide students with information and visual images about these colonies, read aloud selections and show illustrations from appropriate children's books, such as *N.C. Wyeth's Pilgrims* by Robert San Souci (Chronicle Books, 1991), *Roanoke: The Story of the Lost Colony* by Peter Bosco (Millbrook Press, 1992), and *Jamestown: The Beginning* by Elizabeth Campbell (Little, Brown, 1974). As students discuss the colonies, help them create a retrieval chart as illustrated.

3. Inferring About Colonial Life

Provide students with pictures that show colonial American ways of life. These pictures should depict people (both Europeans and Native Americans), buildings, tools, dress, and

RETRIEVAL CHART

	When	Where	Why	Who	Trade	What Happened
Roanoke Island	1587	North Carolina	riches, trade	118 men	none	people vanished
Jamestown	1607	Virginia	riches, trade	105 men and boys	tobacco	became capital of expanding colony
Plymouth	1620	Massachusetts	escape religious persecution	102 Pilgrims	lumber, salt fish, and corn	successful

work and social activities. As students observe the pictures, have them write down what the pictures tell them about colonial America. Record their inferences on the chalkboard, and make certain they copy them down in their notebooks.

4. Maize—The Lifesaver

Brief Background. Without the help of Native Americans, it is doubtful the early colonies could have survived. Native Americans taught the settlers how to produce their own food. At Plymouth, a Native American named Squanto showed the Pilgrims where they could catch fish and find edible wild plants. Probably the most important lesson that the Pilgrims learned from Squanto was how to grow Indian corn (maize) using fish as fertilizer. Corn was easy and quick to grow, and it was also easy to dry and store. With plenty of dried corn, the Pilgrims could make it through the cold New England winter without starving.

Show students an ear of corn (if possible, use blue or multicolored Indian corn, and provide each student with an ear). Have students observe the ear of corn carefully. Ask them to orally describe the ear of corn. Next, have them draw the ear of corn and label the parts (husk, ear, kernel, and cob). Help the class make a list of all the ways in which they prepare and eat corn today. To conclude the discussion of corn, prepare roast corn on the cob or a cornbread snack for the class, or prepare a full-fledged colonial feast (see the menu in the Food Activity).

5. The Thirteen Colonies

Point to the red and white stripes on the American flag. Ask students to guess what the thirteen stripes symbolize. Each of America's original thirteen colonies has an interesting history. Assign small groups of two or three students the task of researching one of the thirteen colonies. They can draw a map of the colony and describe its people, resources, and products. To increase motivation, challenge students to identify the colony that matches each of these descriptions. The answers are in parentheses.

- Home of the first constitution (Connecticut)
- Swedes established the first permanent settlement (Delaware)

- Last of the original thirteen colonies to be founded (Georgia)
- Famous for its religious freedom (Maryland)
- "Live Free or Die" is its motto (New Hampshire)
- Dutch established its first permanent settlement at Bergen (New Jersey)
- Founded as New Amsterdam (New York)
- Its first settlement is now called "The Lost Colony" (North Carolina)
- A Quaker colony (Pennsylvania)
- The smallest colony (Rhode Island)
- A proprietary colony (South Carolina)
- Site of the first permanent English colony (Virginia)
- Established first college in the colonies (Massachusetts)

Language Arts:

1. Colonial Perspectives

What was colonial life like from the point of view of the different types of people who lived back then? Let each student answer that question by assuming the persona of one of the following colonial types: governor, newcomer, Pilgrim, servant, goodwife (married woman), Native American, apprentice, planter, slave, fur trader, constable, smuggler, and patriot. To give students insight into the lives of colonial people, read aloud selections from *Colonial People* by Sarah Howarth (The Millbrook Press, 1994), or some other appropriate children's book. After students have acquired sufficient background information, let them write a description of colonial life as it might be viewed through their subject's eyes. Encourage students to give an oral report in the voice and dressed in the costume of their colonial figure.

2. Writing Captions

Cover the text and/or captions and have students observe selected pictures from a large-size, profusely-illustrated book on colonial life. Help students develop a caption for each selected picture. Compare the students' caption and the book's caption (text). If necessary, help students rewrite their caption to make it more accurate historically. Each student can then draw the picture on a large piece of construction paper, and write the class's caption under their drawing.

Science:

1. Geographic Factors

Climate and land influenced the development of the thirteen American colonies. Provide students with atlases and other resources that show the geographic features of the Atlantic Seaboard region. Help students create a retrieval chart that contrasts the colonies' three distinct geographic regions. Then, discuss the relationship between these and other geographic factors and the regions' economic and social development. For example, New England's nearness to the ocean, short growing season, and poor soil influenced the development of small farms, cities, fishing and manufacturing industries, and trade, while the Southern colonies' rich soil and long growing season influenced the development of large-scale agriculture in the form of the plantation system, with special emphasis on tobacco and cotton.

Math:

1. Colonial Town

Students should enjoy applying their math skills as they make a model of a colonial town. Have pairs of students make different buildings and other places for the model town. Among the types of structures and areas that might be included are: meetinghouse, jail, church, gardens, tavern or inn, governor's house, harbor, fort, streets, post office, homes, shops, and surrounding corn and tobacco fields and hunting grounds. Miniature colonial figures can be fashioned from pipe cleaners and cloth. Twigs, clay, and dirt can be used to create a realistic town landscape. To create a permanent surface area for the town, use a piece of plywood, or for a temporary surface, tape a large sheet of brown paper to a tabletop. Provide students with information about colonial towns and buildings, and supply them with an assortment of construction materials (e.g., wood blocks, empty paper cartons, scissors and other cutting and sawing equipment, Styrofoam, cardboard, construction paper, pipe cleaners, glue, paint). To plan and construct the model, students will need to engage in the following math activities: measuring the area to be used, using chalk to show where various places will be located, deciding on the size and scale of structures and figures, and measuring the structures and figures.

Art:

1. Quilting Bee

Have students gather together to make a colonial-style quilt. These cloth bedcovers were

RETRIEVAL CHART

Region	Climate	Land
New England (New Hampshire, Massachusetts, Connecticut, Rhode Island)	four distinct seasons, very cold winters	mountains, hills, rocky and thin soil rugged shoreline
Middle Atlantic (New York, Pennsylvania, New Jersey, Delaware, Maryland)	warm, rainy summers and cool to cold winters with abundant snow in North	highland areas in Northwest and coastal pains in Southeast; excellent harbors
Southern (Virginia, North Carolina, South Carolina, Georgia)	warm winters; adequate rain-fall and long growing season	highlands in West, rolling pains in central area, and coastal plain in East

decorated with geometric designs and/or pictures of people, animals, plants, and places. Quilting bees were a popular social activity during colonial times. To recreate a quilting bee, give pairs of students a 1-foot square of white sheet material and some fabric pens. After the students have researched colonial quilt patterns found in library books and other sources, they can use the fabric pens to draw colorful designs or pictures on their squares of cloth. When the squares are finished, they can be attached to the bulletin board (or a larger wall area, if necessary) to form the quilt.

Food:

1. Colonial Feast

You can celebrate a bountiful colonial harvest with a classroom feast. Involve students and their parents in the planning and preparation of the meal.

First Thanksgiving Menu

squash	strawberries	grapes
corn	seafood	
turkey	cornbread	

Books:

1. Quackenbush, Robert. (1991). *Benjamin Franklin and His Friends*. New York: Pippin Press. Intermediate.

2. Waring, Gilchrist. (1976). *The City of Once Upon a Time*. Richmond: Dietz Press, Inc. Primary, Intermediate.

3. Kalman, Bobbie. (1992). *Colonial Crafts*. New York: Crabtree Publishing Company. Intermediate.

4. Howarth, Sarah. (1994). *Colonial People*. Brookfield, CT: Millbrook Press. Intermediate, Advanced.

5. Howarth, Sarah. (1994). *Colonial Places*. Brookfield, CT: Millbrook Press. Intermediate, Advanced.

6. San Souci, Robert. (1991). *N.C. Wyeth's Pilgrims*. San Francisco: Chronicle Books. Intermediate.

7. Fradin, Dennis Brindell. (1991). *The New Jersey Colony*. Chicago: Children's Press. Intermediate.

8. Bosco, Peter. (1992). *Roanoke: The story of the lost colony*. Brookfield, CT: Millbrook Press. Advanced.

9. Campbell, Elizabeth. (1974). *Jamestown: The Beginning*. Boston, MA: Little Brown. Intermediate.

10. Fradin, Dennis. (1988). *The Thirteen Colonies*. Chicago: Children's Press. Primary.

11. Johnston, Johanna. (1973). *Who Found America?* Chicago: Children's Press. Primary.

12. Beller, Susan Provost. (1992). *Women of Independence: The life of Abigail Adams*. White Hall, VA: Shoe Tree Press. Advanced.

Software:

1. *Life in Colonial America* [Mac MPC CD-ROM]. Fairfield, CT: Queue. Advanced.

2. *ColonyQuest* [Mac IBM CD-ROM]. San Ramon, CA: Decision Development Corp. Intermediate, Advanced.

3. *The First Thanksgiving* [Laserdisc]. Chicago: Clearvue/eav. Primary.

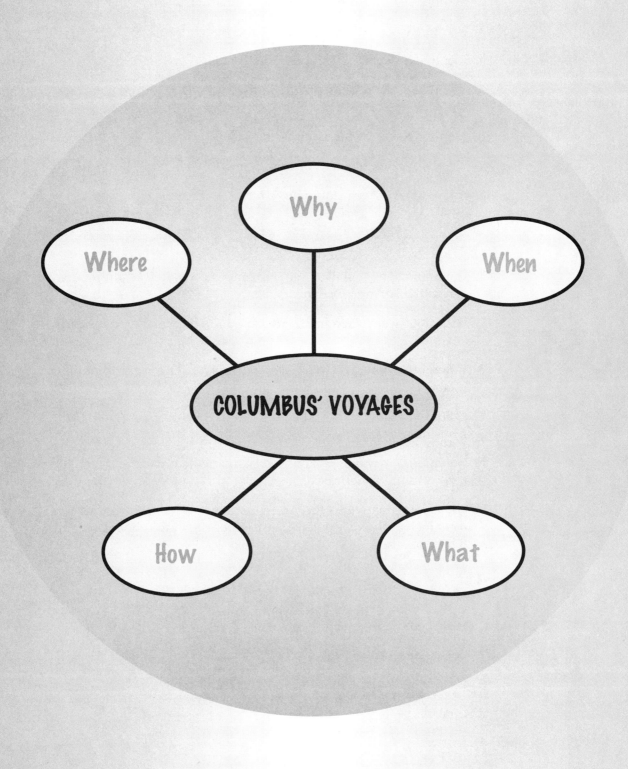

Theme Goals:

Students will:

1. trace the routes of Columbus' voyages.

2. identify significant events in Columbus's life.

3. know reasons why Columbus made his voyages.

4. identify effects of Columbus's discoveries.

5. describe the way of life in fifteenth-century Europe and the Americas.

6. identify plants of the New World.

7. use maps and calculate distances.

8. role-play events in Columbus's life.

Theme Concepts:

1. Columbus was a skilled sea captain who charted a true course across the Atlantic Ocean.

2. Columbus was a merchant, navigator, and map maker in his early years.

3. Columbus wanted to reach the Indies by sailing west across the Atlantic.

4. Columbus wanted to find a shortcut to Asia to secure gold, silk, gems, and spices.

5. Columbus's voyages established permanent contact between Europe and the Americas.

6. Some foods native to the Americas that were introduced to Europe included sweet potatoes, tomatoes, peanuts, chocolate, and white potatoes.

Vocabulary:

1. ethnocentricism

2. ocean currents

3. trade winds

4. caravel

5. scurvy

6. circumference

Instructional Bulletin Board

The purpose of this bulletin board is to help students recall the sequence of five important events in Columbus's life. Use sturdy paper to make a pocket chart 3 inches deep across the bulletin board as pictured below. After consulting illustrations of scenes from Columbus's life, make (or have students make) large, colorful drawings with labels of the following events, which are listed in chronological order: (1) Columbus asking King Ferdinand and Queen Isabella to finance his voyage; (2) Columbus's three ships—the *Pinta*, the *Nina*, and the *Santa Maria*—sailing on the open sea; (3) the sighting of land by a sailor on the Pinta; (4) Columbus meeting with Native Americans for the first time when he landed in the West Indies; and (5) Columbus reporting his findings to King Ferdinand and Queen Isabella upon his return to Spain. (Note: Leave a 3-inch margin blank at the bottom of each drawing.) Laminate the drawings. Put the drawings in a large envelope attached to the bottom right corner of the bulletin board. Attach an answer key to the bottom left corner.

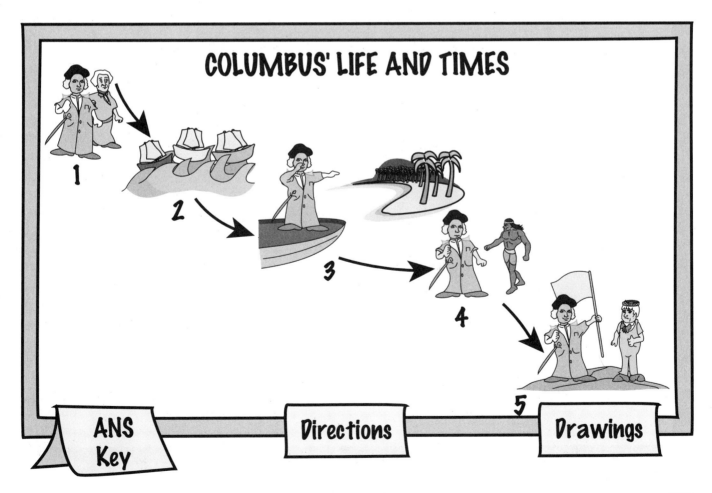

Parent Letter

Dear Parents:

Christopher Columbus's impact on history was monumental. His discoveries changed the size and shape of the known world. He was the bridge between the Old World and a New Land—the Americas. In our theme on Columbus, the children will travel into the past, focusing on the life and times of this famous historic figure.

At School:

The students' journey back in time will be enhanced by the following hands-on activities:

- Creating a personal history
- Sequencing important events in Columbus's life
- Examining the riches of the Indies
- Making "old" maps
- Sampling foods of the New World
- Charting voyages and calculating distances
- Keeping an explorer's journal

At Home:

To help your child discover his or her personal links to the past, take a journey through the family's history. Together with your child, look through the family album, talk about events in the lives of relatives from past generations, and visit older members of the family.

There are probably some children's books on Christopher Columbus at the community library. Help your child select one, then the two of you can read it together.

Linking Up:

Ask students about trips they have taken to new places. How did they feel? Were they excited? What did they expect to find there?

Social Studies:

1. Columbus's Accidental Discoveries

Brief Background. Columbus made four voyages westward between 1492 and 1504. He reached the following present-day places: the Bahamas, Cuba, Dominican Republic, Haiti, Marie-Galante, Puerto Rico, Jamaica, Trinidad, Venezuela, Martinique, Honduras, Nicaragua, Costa Rica, and Panama. Since Europeans before Columbus's voyages did not know the Americas existed, Columbus thought he had reached Asia instead of a new land.

Cover the areas of North and South American on a globe with blue construction paper (attach with EZTAK, or a similar product; it can be removed without harming the globe). Ask students to tell you where Columbus's voyage might take him if he sailed westward from Spain. Let students, using their fingers, trace a voyage westward on the globe until they reach land, that is, the Asian land mass. After everyone has had an opportunity to trace Columbus's *planned* trip, remove the construction paper and let them repeat the tracing exercise. This time of course, they will "bump" into North America before they can reach Asia, just as Columbus did (Figure 15-1).

2. Columbus' Life

Provide students with background information about Columbus's early life by reading aloud Joan Anderson's *Christopher Columbus: Voyager to the Unknown* (Dutton, 1990), or another appropriate children's book. Encourage students to illustrate scenes from Columbus's life. Have interested students research Christopher Columbus during his early years when he was a merchant, navigator, and map maker. Are there characteristics about young Columbus upon which to base a prediction that he would go on to make such great discoveries?

3. Personal Histories

To give students a personal sense of the past, let them create simple time ropes that lay out important events in their own lives. Provide students with an assortment of magazines, and let them cut out pictures to represent themselves, people they know, and things they have done. To make her time rope, each student can tape the pictures in chronological order on a length of string or yarn. Display the completed students' time ropes on the wall.

4. The Riches of the Indies

Brief Background. Back in Columbus's time, much of Asia—including India, China, Japan, and Indonesia—was called the Indies. Although Europeans knew almost nothing about this faraway place, they craved the Indies's luxurious silks, glittering gold and gems, and aromatic and tasty spices. European rulers and merchants wanted to find a shortcut to the Indies to secure more of these rare and valuable items.

Ask students why Columbus called the natives he met in the New World "Indians." To help them understand Columbus's confusion, let students trace the overland route from Europe to the Indies. Describe some of the hardships (mountains, deserts, bandits, etc.) faced by traders and merchants who used the overland route. Explain that before Columbus's voyages, this was the only route to the riches of the Indies. Provide students with examples of some of the riches of the Indies. Let students see and touch some gold costume jewelry and silk fabric, and smell clove, nutmeg, mace, and other Asian spices. Tell students that wealthy Europeans would pay a high price for these valuable items. Invite students to talk about valuable things they possess or would like to own. Are there special smells and tastes that students would not want to do without? Link students' wants to those of the people who lived in Columbus's time.

5. Life in the Old and New World

What was life like on both sides of the Atlantic Ocean at the time of Columbus's voyage? To help students answer that question, read aloud sections of *1492: The Year of the New World* by Piero Ventura (G.P. Putnam's Sons, 1991), or some other appropriate children's book. Ven-

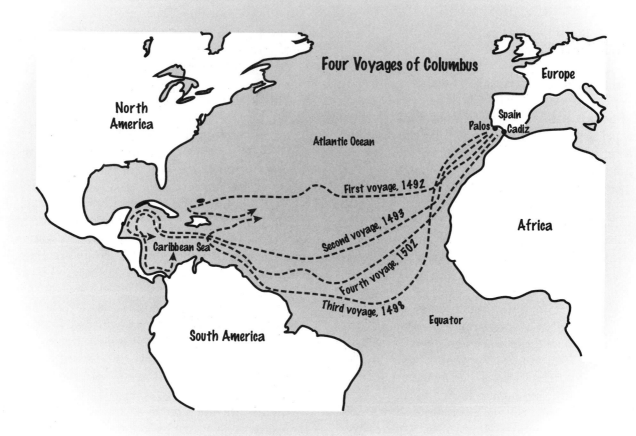

Four Voyages of Columbus

Europe

Spain

Palos
Cadiz

North
America

Atlantic Ocean

Africa

First voyage, 1492

Second voyage, 1493

Caribbean Sea

Fourth voyage, 1502

Third voyage, 1498

Equator

South America

Columbus' Route Across Atlantic

FIGURE 15-1

tura compares and contrasts conditions in fifteenth-century Europe with those of various Indian cultures in the New World. Make a list of similarities and differences between the Old World and the New World.

6. Cultural Conflict

Brief Background. Columbus and his crew thought the New World natives were "primitive" and "uncivilized." From the Spaniards' European-centered perspective, being "civilized" meant being literate, Christian, and fully attired. This unfavorable opinion helps account for Columbus's

often cruel treatment of the "Indians." Some New World groups, such as the Maya and Aztec, had civilizations that were just as complex—with elaborate writing, mathematical and religious systems—as any in Europe. The Spaniards' hostile attitude toward the Indians is an example of *ethnocentrism*, which is the tendency to regard one's own race or culture as superior to others.

Have students make a list of things they do, such as playing games, exchanging presents, doing chores, celebrating holidays, and wearing particular styles of clothing. How are the students' ways of doing things similar to those of the Indians? How are they different? Point out to students that all humans, past and present, have the same basic needs for food, clothing, shelter, and care. Emphasize that, although the ways basic needs are satisfied may differ across time and space, beneath the surface people are more alike than not. Ask students to create posters that celebrate diversity locally and globally.

7. The Americas: What's in a Name?

Brief Background. After four trips across the ocean in search of the spice islands of Asia, Columbus was extremely frustrated that he had failed to find them. Therefore, he made no claim that he was the first to land on a new continent. The upshot of Columbus's silence on this matter was that a later explorer of the New World, named Amerigo Vespucci, ended up getting the credit—and his name on the maps.

Have the students imagine they are passengers on a bus trip to visit Disney World. Those on the bus can't wait to get there, but unfortunately the bus never arrives at its destination. The driver keeps getting lost, and each night the children must stay overnight in a different motel somewhere along the way. How would the passengers on the bus feel? How would the bus driver feel? Explain that, like the bus driver, Columbus never reached his destination. Ask students to guess the source of the name "America." Help students find these Amerigo Vespucci namesakes: North America, South America, and the United States of America.

8. Geography Search

Many places in the United States are named Columbia or Columbus in honor of Christopher Columbus. In fact, many colonial Americans wanted to name our new nation Columbia. Seven well-known places named after Columbus are listed below. Have students track down their locations on maps. They can also find other places in atlases to add to the list.

District of Columbia
Columbia University
Columbia River
Columbia, Missouri
Columbia, South Carolina
Columbus, Georgia
Columbus, Ohio

9. "Before" and "After" Maps

Show students copies of late fifteenth-century and early sixteenth-century world maps. Let students draw their own "old" maps that show the shape of the known world before and after Columbus's journeys. The "before" maps should not show the Americas, since Europeans before Columbus's voyage did not know North and South America existed. The "after" maps should include the Americas. Have students compare their hand-drawn replicas of fifteenth- and sixteenth-century maps with today's modern maps of the world. Point out that map makers in the fifteenth century had very crude instruments and only limited and often faulty knowledge of the geography of the world, which accounts for their distorted map drawings.

10. Glory and Blame

Brief Background. Columbus Day is a legal, federal holiday celebrated on the second Monday in October. Columbus is honored for his historic voyages that established permanent contact between Europe and the Americas. Although Columbus failed to find the riches of Asia, later expeditions by other explorers carried huge amounts of gold and silver back to Europe, which helped make Spain a world power. Columbus is blamed by some for leading to the destruction of Native American cultures and the exploitation of natural resources.

As students learn about Columbus' voyages, help them construct a chart that lists the positive and negative impacts of these voyages on history.

Science:

1. The Voyages

Brief Background. Columbus was a very skillful sea captain who knew how to use the winds and currents to move his ships across a vast ocean. He took advantage of the westerly trade winds that blow at that latitude. The design of Columbus's ships also helped to ensure a successful voyage. The ships, called *caravels*, could sail against the wind.

Provide students with globes and atlases. Trace the route of Columbus's first voyage to the Americas. Encourage students to speculate about his route. Ask students why Columbus first headed south from Spain instead of heading west, which might appear on the map as the most direct route to his destination. Let students examine a map that shows Atlantic wind and current systems. Introduce the concept of ocean currents, or "rivers" of water that flow in circular paths. On the map, help students find the current system used by Columbus. Explain that currents are created by winds, and that the trade winds on Columbus's route to the Americas blow from the northeast. Have students trace the route of Columbus's return voyage. Point out that Columbus used a different ocean current on the return trip. Located at a more northern latitude, this current flowed from west to east. Show students pictures of Columbus's ships, the *Pinta*, *Nina*, and *Santa Maria*. Make certain students observe that the ships were made of wood and had sails. Point out that they had no motors or engines. Students can test the effects of wind on miniature sailing ships. To make their ships, each student will need a walnut shell half for the hull, one 2" to 3" wooden skewer for the mask, a small square of white paper for the sail, and a tiny piece of modeling clay to secure the mask in an upright position inside the walnut shell (Figure 15-2). Provide a large container of water and a plastic drop cloth, and let pairs of students take turns testing the seaworthiness of their vessels. They can create wind by fanning their ships with paper fans. Have students compare the simple design of their ships with the design of caravels and other fifteenth-century ships.

2. New World Plants

Brief Background. Because of Columbus's and other European expeditions, many foods native to the Americas were introduced into Europe. They include cassava, hot peppers, sweet potatoes, white potatoes, tomatoes, cayenne, paprika, peanuts, cashews, and chocolate.

Assign students the task of researching one of these foods. They can include illustrations, samples, and maps with their reports. To increase motivation, serve students bite-sized pieces of some New World foods.

3. Eating Right

Brief Background. Crew members on Columbus's voyages ate a diet that consisted mainly of salted meat or fish, hard biscuits, and watered-down wine. Sailors on long voyages often got scurvy, a disease resulting from lack of vitamin C that caused gums to bleed and teeth to fall out.

Have students research foods that are rich in Vitamin C. What foods do they eat that provide this valuable vitamin?

Math:

1. Global Miscalculation

Brief Background. Columbus knew the earth wasn't flat, but he did miscalculate the earth's circumference by about 25 percent. Columbus thought that by sailing 2,500 miles west from the Canary Islands (located off the coast of northeastern Africa), he could reach Japan (the actual distance is approximately 10,600 miles). Columbus also made one other big mistake: He thought more than 70 percent of the earth was covered by land (in fact, just the opposite is true; ocean covers 70 percent of the earth's surface). Based on these miscalculations, Columbus thought that Asia was both closer to Europe and easier to reach than it was.

Provide pieces of string and an assortment of different-sized balls, and let students measure the balls' circumference, or distance around at the center. Then, provide globes and review or

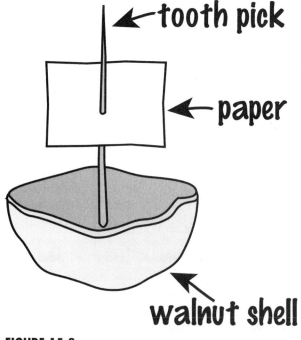

FIGURE 15-2

teach scale and measurement of distance on a globe. Using strings and globes, let students measure the circumference of the earth (approximately 24,000 miles), and the actual distances between the Canary Islands and Japan (approximately 10,600 miles). They can also measure the distance between the Canary Islands and the islands of the Bahamas (where Columbus landed on October 12, 1492). How far off was Columbus in his calculations?

2. Short Tons for a Long Trip

Brief Background. Ninety crew members made the voyage aboard Columbus's three ships, the *Pinta, Nina,* and *Santa Maria.* Each of the ships could carry around 60 short tons. A short ton is 2,000 pounds.

If each crew member weighed 150 pounds, how many short tons did the total of 90 crew members weigh? (6.75 short tons) How many pounds of cargo could the ships carry?

3. How Old Was Columbus When . . . ?

Brief Background. Christopher Columbus was born sometime between August 25 and October 31, 1451, in Genoa, Italy.

Have students calculate Columbus's age when he sailed from Spain on his first voyage (August 3, 1492), second voyage (September 25, 1493), third voyage (May 30, 1495), and fourth voyage (May 9, 1502), and when he died (May 20, 1506).

4. The High Costs of Travel

Unlike in Columbus's time, when a voyage across the Atlantic took over a month, people today can move around the world easily and quickly in high-speed cars, trains, and planes. Gather information on travel costs and times to various destinations, including Spain. Help students plan an itinerary and calculate the expenses of a trip from their home city to a place they would like to visit and explore. Invite a travel agent to class to help students plan their imaginary trip.

5. Columbus Board Game

Provide drawing and construction materials, and challenge more independent students to create a board game that focuses on Columbus's voyages to the New World.

Language Arts:

1. The Power of Persuasion

Columbus was an eloquent and forceful speaker who first convinced Spain's King Ferdinand and Queen Isabella to finance the risky expedition, and later, on the high seas, persuaded his unhappy crew not to mutiny. Have interested students role-play Columbus's presentation of his plan to the Spanish monarchs. Questions students should consider are: Why was Columbus so confident he could reach Asia? Why were the Spanish monarchs at first reluctant to help him? Why did they finally agree to help? After a month at sea and with no land in sight, many crew members wanted to mutiny and turn back. Let students role-play Columbus in this difficult situation. What might Columbus say to his crew to persuade them to continue the voyage?

2. Accurate Attributes

After students have studied Columbus in depth, let them generate a list of attributes that describe him. Make certain they can think of examples for each attribute. Some possible attributes that students might mention include brave, persistent, cruel, dependable, persuasive, ambitious, and skillful. For each attribute, have students complete the following sentence: "Columbus was _____ when he _____ ."

3. Explorer's Journal

Brief Background. Columbus kept a personal account of his voyages. His private notes sometimes differed from his daily entries in the ship's log, which was open to the crew. Columbus sometimes intentionally underestimated the distances he recorded in the ship's log to fool the crew into thinking it had not journeyed as far as it had. He feared that if crew members knew the real distances traveled, they might loose confidence in him and mutiny. Conditions on the ships for crew members were terrible. The ships had no tables, chairs, beds, or bathing facilities for the crew. Crew members slept on the open deck. Their diet was extremely limited and monotonous, and consisted mainly of biscuits, pickled fish, watered-down wine, and a few other items. Columbus sailed from

Spain on August 3, 1492, and arrived at the Canary Islands on August 12. He departed the Canary Islands on September 6, and the crew did not sight land again until October 12, 1492, when they reached the island they named San Salvador (Holy Savior) in the present-day Bahamas.

Ask students to imagine that they were with Columbus on that long and arduous journey into the unknown. Have each "crew member" make three entries in his diary, one for August 3 (the day of departure), a second for October 6 (after one month on the open sea), and a third for October 12 (after land had been sighted). Let partners or small groups of students share their diary entries.

4. Inventing Signs

Brief Background. Columbus and his crew spoke Spanish, the Indians spoke their own languages, and neither group understood the language of the other. Challenge students to invent a sign language for these words: animals, food, hungry, ship, Europe, friend, gold, spices, water, and "hello."

Art:

1. Ship Diagrams

Display pictures of caravels and other fifteenth-century ships. Provide students with pencils, rulers, and large sheets of paper, and let them draw large diagrams of these ships, showing the deck plans and major ship parts.

2. Murals

Have small groups of students make murals of Columbus's voyage. Let them sketch their scenes first, and then use colored chalk or tempera paint to create bold and eye-catching murals.

Books:

1. Brenner, Barbara. (1991). *If You Were There In 1492*. New York: Bradbury Press. Intermediate, Advanced.

2. Dyson, John. (1991). *Westward with Columbus: Set Sail on the Voyage That Changed the World*. New York: Scholastic Press Books. Advanced.

3. Fradin, Dennis. (1991). *The Nina, the Pinta, and the Santa Maria*. New York: Franklin Watts. Advanced.

4. Krensky, Stephen. (1991). *Christopher Columbus*. New York: Random House. Primary.

5. Poole, Frederick King. (1989). *Early Exploration of North America*. New York: Franklin Watts. Intermediate, Advanced.

6. Levinson, Nancy. (1990). *Christopher Columbus: Voyager to the Unknown*. New York: Lodestar Books. Advanced.

7. Ventura, Piero. (1991). *1492: The Year of the New World*. New York: G. P. Putnam's Sons.

Software:

1. *Multimedia U.S. History: The Story of a Nation* [MPC CD-ROM]. Princeton: Bureau of Electronic Publishing. Advanced.

2. *Explorers of the New World* [Mac MPC CD-ROM]. Cambridge, MA: Softkey/Future Vision. Intermediate, Advanced.

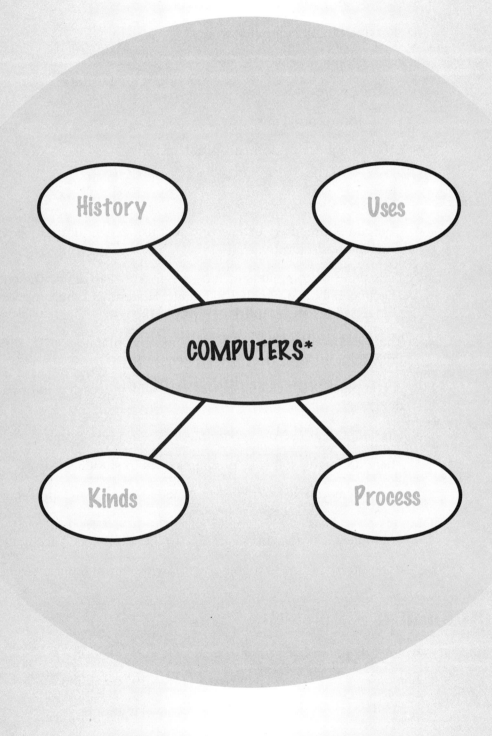

Theme Goals:

Students will:

1. identify how computers are used in school and at home.

2. trace the development of computers over time.

3. identify and label the parts of a computer.

4. describe how a computer works.

5. define common computer terms.

6. practice word processing.

7. use software programs.

8. use a computer to do math problems.

Theme Concepts:

1. Computers are used extensively in business, education, government, and industry.

2. Early types of computers include the abacus, Pascal's Arithmetic Machine, Babbage's Analytical Engine, Hollerith's Tabulating Machine, and Wozinak and Jobs's Apple II.

3. The basic components of a computer are monitor, CPU, disk drive, mouse, keyboard, and printer.

4. A computer is a machine for storing and processing information.

5. One important use of the computer is word processing.

6. There are many software programs to help students learn.

7. Computers can help create multimedia reports and presentations.

8. Computers can do many tasks with tremendous speed accuracy.

9. Computers are linked together worldwide through the Internet.

Vocabulary:

1. computer	5. CPU	9. memory
2. mouse	6. keyboard	10. operation
3. monitor	7. disk drive	11. output
4. printer	8. input	

---

*Barbara V. Wheeler contributed many of the activities for this theme.

Instructional Bulletin Board

The purpose of this bulletin board is to give students an opportunity to label the parts of a computer. Make a drawing of a computer and attach it to the bulletin board. Make labels for the components and place them in the pocket. Let students take turns identifying the components by pinning the correct label next to the component. Attach an answer key to the bulletin board so students can check their answers.

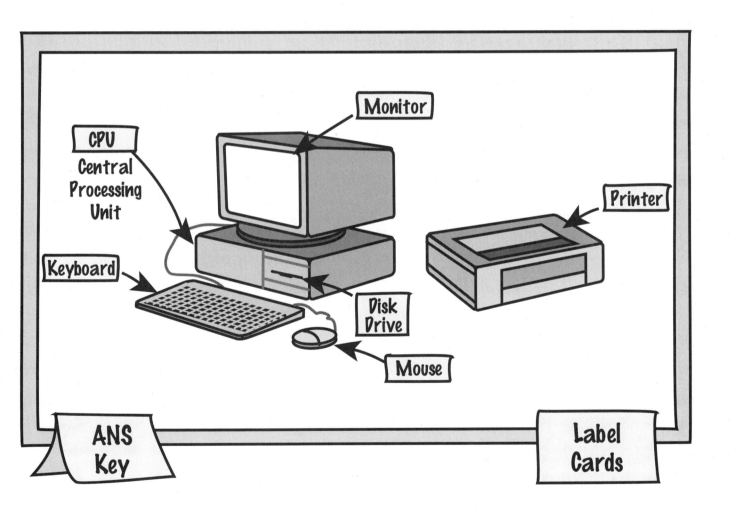

Parent Letter

Dear Parents:

We are beginning our study of one of society's most indispensable tools—the computer. Computers are everywhere and they do just about everything. They give us cash, call us on the phone, calculate our grocery bill, and monitor our health, to name just a few of the jobs they do. Some of the activities designed for this unit are described below.

At School:

This theme will include the following activities:

- Tracking down the many computer uses
- Investigating early computers
- Labeling the parts of a computer
- Finding out how a computer works
- Developing a computer vocabulary
- Practicing word processing
- Creating a class newspaper

At Home:

If your child is already using a computer at home, he or she can assist us with some of the planned activities. If your child's experiences with computers are limited, this theme will introduce the basics and beyond.

Thank you for your support and cooperation.

Linking Up:

Chances are probably good that the computer experiences of your students vary greatly. A portion of your students may already be travelers on the information super highway. Some may use Internet regularly and chat live via electronic mail with cyber friends on their own personal computers at home. Other students' access to and familiarity with computers may be quite limited, or confined solely to school use.

To help students understand the pervasive role that computers play in their lives, take them for a walking tour of places in the school where computers are used to get work done. Have students answer these questions: Do some or all classroom teachers use computers to keep class lists and schedules and compute grades? Do students use computers in their classrooms, the media center, special computer labs, or elsewhere in the school? Do the school nurse, librarian, secretaries, counselor, and other support faculty and staff use computers? How extensively are computers used in the principal's office? Try to track down each and every computer use in your school. Make certain students have a record of their observations of computer use.

Social Studies:

1. The Community–Computer Connection

Computers have become one of society's most indispensable tools. Have students find examples of computer use in the community. To give students firsthand knowledge of the community–computer connection, arrange a field trip to places where computers are extensively used. Some possiblities include the following:

- business, industry, and government offices
- factories
- banks
- hospitals
- newspaper companies
- supermarkets
- retail stores
- fire departments

2. Computer Time Line

With *TimeLiner 4.00* software (Tom Synder Productions), students can use the computer to make time lines of the history of computers. Examples of early computers are listed below.

(1) Abacus—The first computing device was probably the abacus, which was used in ancient China and elsewhere. Over two thousand years old, the abacus is still used today by shopkeepers in some parts of Asia.

(2) Arithmetic Machine—In 1642, Blaise Pascal invented the Arithmetic Machine, a device that could do simple addition and subtraction calculations.

(3) Analytical Engine—In 1835, Charles Babbage, in collaboration with Lady Ada Augusta Lovelace, designed the Analytical Engine, but failed to build a working model of the device.

(4) Tabulating Machine—In 1887, Herman Hollerith developed the Tabulating Machine to do the 1890 U.S. population census. Using Hollerith's machine, the 1890 census was tabulated in six weeks instead of almost five months, which was the length of time it took to do the 1880 census.

(5) Apple II—In 1977, Stephen Wozinak and Steven Jobs introduced the Apple II, the first widely accepted personal computer.

Science:

1. Computer Anatomy

Have students identify and label the basic parts of a computer: monitor (screen), CPU (central processing unit; the "brain" of the computer), disk drive (where the disk is inserted), mouse, keyboard, and printer. (Note: You may want to include other components, such as modem and scanner, depending on the background of your students.)

2. How the Computer Works

A computer is a machine for storing and processing information, or data. Terms used to describe how a computer works are as follows:

The Computer:		Example:
accepts data	(*input*)	random list of names
stores data	(*memory*)	names
processes data	(*operation*)	alphabetizes names
gives out data	(*output*)	alphabetized list of names

Have students compare how a computer works with how they process information. Give them three simple words (input), tell them to remember the words for a minute (memory), ask them to alphabetize the words (operation), and say or write the words in alphabetical order (output). Repeat the same process with numerical data, and have students compute a simple arithmetic problem.

Language Arts:

1. Computer Vocabulary

Students can search for definitions and make vocabulary cards for these and other common computer terms:

bits = In binary system, a bit is either the digit 0 or 1. The bit is the basic unit for storing data.

byte = a group of eight bits that represent an alphabetic or numeric character

CPU = acronym for *C*omputer *P*rocessing *U*nit, integrated circuits that form the memory and processing of computer

character = letter, digit, or symbol used in programming

COBOL = acronym for *C*ommon *B*usiness *O*riented *L*anguage

cursor = blinking line marking spot on monitor

data = information

Fortran = *For*mula *tran*slation language for science and math

flowchart = graphic outline of the steps needed to do a certain job

hardware = monitor, external hard drive, keyboard, printer, and other computer equipment

software = computer programs

variable = stored bit of information identified with a name

Internet = a worldwide network of interconnected computers

BASIC = acronym for *B*eginning *A*ll-Purpose *S*ymbolic *I*nstruction *C*ode

RAM = acronym for *R*andom *A*ccess *M*emory

PASCAL = programming language named after famous mathematician

E-mail = electronic-mail, typed messages that can be transmitted from one computer to another

modem = acronym for *mo*dulator-*dem*odulator; piece of equipment that links your computer through the telephone to on-line, interactive services

CD-ROM = acronym for *C*ompact *D*isk, *R*ead *O*nly *M*emory; compact disks that can contain text, audio and video clips, animation, photos, illustrations, and other information that run on a CD-ROM drive

2. Getting Started

Muppet Learning Keys (Pleasantville, NY: Sunburst) is an excellent keyboard to introduce young children to computers. Tailored for little hands, it features upper- and lowercase letters in alphabetical order, keys to activate the letters, number keys, a paintbox of colors, action buttons, and a print button. Students can learn beginning word processing, math, and reading skills with these software programs: *Muppets on Stage, Muppetville, Muppet Word,* and *Muppet Slate* (all from Sunburst).

3. Word Processing

One important use of the computer is word processing. With *ClarisWorks* (Claris Corporation), or other integrated applications packages, students can do word processing, drawing, and painting. *ClarisWorks'* step-by-step instructions and on-screen organization make word processing easy. Students can do prewriting activities, such as outlining, that require them to categorize and organize information in outline format. To familiarize students with the word processing capabilities of the computer, let them type their names using different fonts and type sizes. Make certain each student saves his work on a personal disk.

4. Software Programs That Stimulate Thinking

A sampler of outstanding early-learning software programs follows: *Kid Pix* (Broderbund),

Hands-On Math (Ventura Software), *Storybook Weaver* (MECC), *Millie's Math House* (Edmark), and *TimeLiner 4.0* (Tom Snyder Productions). Two excellent electronic encyclopedias for children are *My First Encyclopedia* (Knowledge Adventure) and *Encarta* (Microsoft). For more advanced students, use interactive CD-ROM programs, such as *Wagon Trail 1848, Oregon Trail II, Africa Trail, Maya Quest* and *The Amazon Trail* (all from MECC), and the Carmen Sandiego "detective" series *Where in the USA Is Carmen Sandiego?* and *Where in the World Is Carmen Sandiego?* (both from Broderbund).

5. Class Newspaper

Your class can publish its own newspaper with easy-to-use software like *Writing Center* (The Learning Company). With this program, students' articles are formatted into columns with headlines, just like a regular newspaper. Different fonts and graphics can be used to give the newspaper a professional look.

6. Beyond the Classroom

Is your school wired for the Internet—called by many the "Information Superhighway"? With a modem and electronic mail software, your students can use the Internet to exchange information with distant audiences. Internet tools like Gopher, World Wide Web, and Mosiac can help students locate information from almost anywhere. For advice on finding curriculum materials and getting students on line, consult Marc Gascoigne's *You Can Surf the Net!* (Puffin Books, 1996), or, if you're already on line, use the Internet to get up-to-the-minute information from these sites:

http://www.classroom.net
gopher://ericir.syr.edu

7. Researching the Net

Show students how to use the Internet search engines, such as Lycos, Yayoo, Alta Vista, and Infoseek, to track down information on topics of interest to them. Have them identify Internet sites that have information on their favorite topics. Show them how to use "Bookmark" to save these sites on their personal disks. Let them practice using Bookmark to access sites they have listed on their topics.

Math:

1. Computing: Who's Smarter and Faster?

Brief Background. Computers can solve huge math problems with incredible quickness. A computer is so fast that its computing time is measured in nanoseconds (a nanosecond is one billionth of a second). It takes 4 nanoseconds for a computer to solve $27,548 \times 579,110,989$!

Despite the computer's tremendous speed, students (depending on math background and capability, of course) can do some types of math problems faster in their heads than by using their computers. For example, many students have memorized the answers to simple addition, subtraction, and multiplication problems such as $2 + 2$, $10 - 5$, and 3×3. Let half the class use the computers' built-in calculators to do simple math problems (a,b, and c below), and let the other half of the class use their heads to do the same problems. Which group, computer or noncomputer, does the problems correctly faster? (Of course, the reason the computer group would be slower in this case is not really the computer's fault; the students simply cannot use the keyboard as fast as they can recall the answers.) Next, let the two groups do more difficult math problems (d, e, and f below), and compare speed and accuracy. (Why might the computer group be a lot faster with these last three problems?)

	Conditions	
	Computer Group	Non-computer Group

Math Problems

a. $2 + 2 =$

b. $10 - 2 =$

c. $3 \times 3 =$

d. $234 + 763 =$

e. $789,436 - 499,589 =$

f. $79,953,020 \times 4,810 =$

Other types of problems where a person has an advantage over the computer are novel problems that require unique solutions. For example, your students have probably never been asked to solve the following problem (select an easier or more difficult word problem, depending on your students' math ability), but many of them probably can solve it quickly, either in their heads or with pencil and paper:

Divide the number of players in a basketball game by the number of wheels on a bicycle and then add the total stars on the American flag.

The above word problem would have to be translated into a numerical problem ($10 \div 2 + 50$) before it would make any sense to a computer. When it comes to solving novel and unique problems, the artificial intelligence of the computer cannot match the human brain's ability to combine, associate, relate, transform, and synthesize information.

Books:

1. Atelsek, Jean. (1993). *All About Computers*. Ameryville, CA: Ziff-Davis Press. Advanced.

2. Richardson, Peter, and Richardson, Bob. (1993). *Great Careers for People Interested in Math and Computers*. Detroit: UXL. Advanced.

3. Koehler, Lora. (1995). *Internet*. Danbury, CT: Children's Press. Intermediate.

4. Pederson, Ted, and Moss, Francis. (1995). *Internet for Kids! A Beginner's Guide to Surfing the Net*. New York: Price Stern and Sloan. Advanced.

5. Armstrong, Sara. (1996). *Kidstuff on the Internet*. San Francisco: Sybex Inc. Advanced.

6. Gascoigne, Marc. (1996). *You Can Surf the Net!* New York: Puffin Books. Advanced.

Software:

1. *Oregon Trail II* [Mac MPC CD-ROM]. Minneapolis: MECC. Advanced.

2. *Wagon Trail 1848* [Mac]. Minneapolis: MECC. Advanced.

3. *Maya Quest* [Mac Windows MPC CD-ROM]. Minneapolis: MECC, Advanced.

4. *The Amazon Trail* [Mac IBM Windows MPC CD-ROM]. Minneapolis: MECC. Intermediate, Advanced.

5. *Africa Trail* [Mac Windows CD-ROM]. Minneapolis: MECC. Intermediate, Advanced.

6. *Where in the World Is Carmen Sandiego?* [Apple II Mac IBM CD-ROM]. Novato, CA: Broderbund. Intermediate, Advanced.

7. *Where in the USA Is Carmen Sandiego?* [Apple II GS Mac IBM CD-ROM]. Novato, CA: Broderbund. Intermediate, Advanced.

8. *Kid Pix 2* [Mac IBM Windows]. Novato, CA: Broderbund. Primary, Intermediate, Advanced.

9. *Hands-On Math* [Apple II Mac IBM]. Grover Beach, CA: Ventura Educational Systems. Primary, Intermediate, Advanced.

10. *Storybook Weaver* [GS Mac IBM]. Minneapolis: MECC. Primary, Intermediate.

11. *Millie's Math House* [Mac IBM Windows CD-ROM]. Redmond, WA: Edmark. Primary.

12. *TimeLiner 4.0* [Apple II IBM Mac Windows]. Watertown, MA: Tom Snyder Productions. Primary, Intermediate, Advanced.

13. *Encarta* [Mac MPC CD-ROM]. Redmond, WA: Microsoft. Primary, Intermediate, Advanced.

14. *My First Encyclopedia* [Mac MPC CD-ROM]. Glendale, CA: Knowledge Adventure. Primary.

15. *Writing Center* [Mac CD-ROM]. Fremont, CA: The Learning Company. Primary, Intermediate, Advanced.

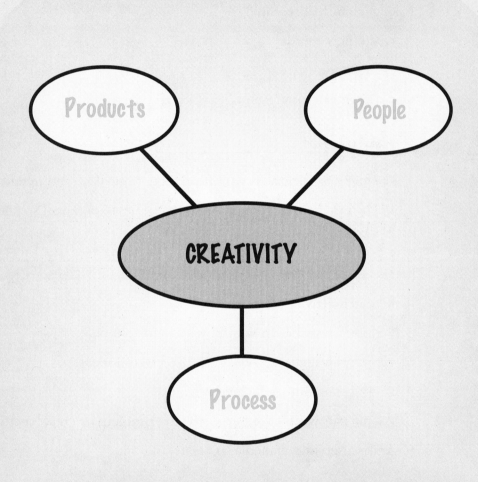

Theme Goals:

Students will:

1. investigate meaningful problems.

2. use brainstorming as a technique to generate potential solutions to problems.

3. investigate the lives of creative people.

4. create a future city.

5. think of different uses for common objects.

6. engage in real research.

7. create new words.

8. create stories.

9. create artistic products.

Theme Concepts:

1. Creativity is associated with flexibility, originality, and fluency.

2. Brainstorming is a technique used to generate potential solutions to problems.

3. Some creative people in history include Thomas Edison, Michelangelo, Leonardo da Vinci, and William Shakespeare.

4. Research activity creates knowledge.

5. People can come up with new uses for old objects.

6. People can come up with new objects and ideas.

7. Every generation creates new words.

8. People can work together to solve a problem or create a story.

9. Artists use various media to create artwork.

Vocabulary:

1. brainstorming

2. research

Instructional Bulletin Board

The purpose of this bulletin board is to provide an opportunity for all students to display their creative products, such as poems, inventions, papier-mache or clay sculptures and models, collages, murals, drawings, paintings, cartoons, stories, research projects, and the like. Make certain each child's very best creative work is included. Make small cardboard shelves and attach them to the bulletin board to display small three-dimensional creative products. Large creative products can displayed on a table located near the board. Attach a card with the student's name and photo next to the creative product. After a few days, rotate the bulletin board display so that all of the students have an opportunity to showcase their work.

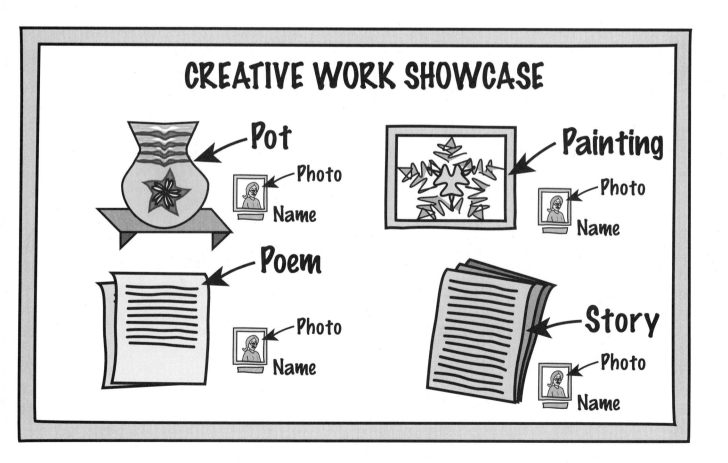

Parent Letter

Dear Parents:

The focus of our next theme of study is creativity. This theme will explore the creative abilities of students in both intellectual and artistic activity.

At School:

To encourage creativity, we have planned the following activities for students.

- Investigating concrete problems identified by students
- Using brainstorming to come up with many different solutions to a problem
- Reading about creative people and their accomplishments
- Creating a future city
- Figuring out different uses for common objects
- Creating stories
- Creating artwork

At Home:

There are numerous opportunities for students to engage in creative activities at home. Take stock of your child's interests and talents, and then provide him or her with ways to explore and expand in those areas. Ideas for exploration can be found in how-to children's books on arts, crafts, nature study, story writing, music, theater, and a host of other topics at the local library.

Thanks for your support!

Linking Up:

Creativity means the ability to create. To create means to bring into existence. An important step in getting students to think creatively is helping them to recognize it when it occurs. Three characteristics often associated with creative thinking are: *flexibility*, or the ability to come up with unusual uses for familiar objects or ideas; *originality*, or the ability to come up with new objects or ideas; and *fluency*, which refers to the quantity of output.

To initiate critical thinking, provide ample opportunities for students to identify and solve meaningful problems. To be meaningful, the problems should deal with children's concrete and immediate concerns. These concerns might relate to keeping track of time, money, or personal items, choosing items to purchase, caring for pets, making models, or doing homework effectively. To encourage critical thinking, as students generate ideas and solutions, make certain you show them that you value their thinking.

Social Studies:

1. Brainstorming

Brief Background. Brainstorming is a technique used to generate many different potential solutions to a problem. In brainstorming, the objective in quantity. During brainstorming, no criticism of potential solutions is allowed, no matter how silly or impractical they might appear, and students' analysis and evaluation of ideas is deferred until after the process is completed. Brainstorming solutions to problems will also expose students to one another's point of view. The more brainstorming students do, the better they should become at doing it.

To get students started, use hand puppets, a skit, or illustrations to present a situation that demonstrates the problem. Start with simple problems, such as "How can we decorate our classroom better?" or "How can we earn money for a class pizza party?" Based on the backgrounds and interests of your students, you may want to move to serious environmental problems, such as how to deal with water waste and pollution. For this problem, students could use brainstorming to generate practical ways to conserve water and reduce pollution. Finally, after a list of solutions is generated, students could evaluate their practicality. Are some solutions better than others? Why?

2. Creative People Past and Present

Brief Background. Throughout history, the world's greatest creative people have demonstrated rare intellectual and artistic insights, sensitivities, and appreciations. Because of their unique literary, scientific, and/or artistic perspective(s), they saw the world differently—and as a result, they created what ordinary people of the time could not imagine. Thomas Edison has been called America's greatest creative genius. As a child, Edison was mischievous and his formal schooling was brief. He loved science, however, and he would spend many hours at home experimenting with chemicals and building model steam engines. While working as a telegrapher, young Edison became intrigued by electricity and its potential uses.

Henry Ford	Thomas Jefferson	Leonardo da Vinci
Michelangelo	Copernicus	Aristotle
Isaac Newton	George Washington Carver	Beethoven
Rembrandt	Grandma Moses	Albert Einstein
Picasso	Mark Twain	William Shakespeare
Benjamin Franklin	Orville and Wilbur Wright	Walt Disney
Marie Curie	F. W. Woolworth	Squanto

Highlight some of Edison's more important inventions like the telephone transmitter, phonograph, electric light, and motion pictures, as well as his development of electric utilities and electrical manufacturing, which made electrical lighting a commercial success. Have students imagine what life would be like without Edison's inventions. On the preceding page is a short list of some other creative geniuses for students to investigate. Encourage students to add other names to the list.

3. City Scape

Discuss city problems with which students are familiar, such as pollution, noise, and traffic congestion. Challenge small groups of students to design a new problem-free city of the future.

Have students decide what materials to use to construct their model cities. (Note: Be prepared to help them find an assortment of construction items, such as blocks, tapes, empty paper containers, and construction paper.)

Science:

1. _____ **Ways to Use** _____

Challenge students to come up with as many different uses as they can for common objects, such as an *empty milk carton*, *brick*, *coat hanger*, *dime*, *paper clip*, and *ruler*. For example, a plastic milk carton, with simple modifications, might be used for the purposes shown in Figure 17-1.

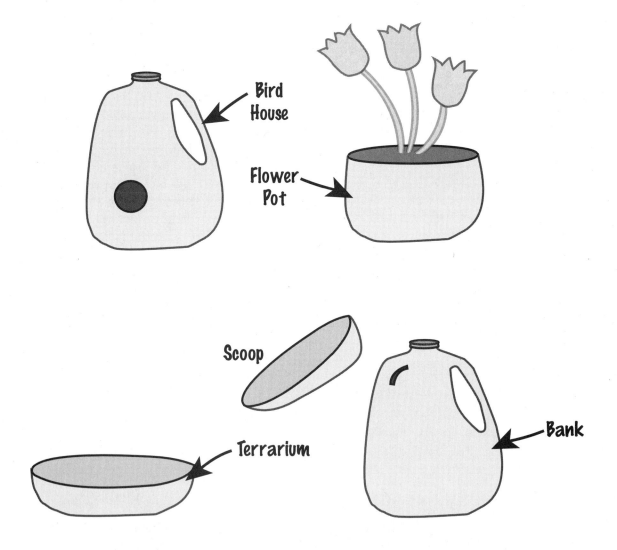

Bird House

Flower Pot

Scoop

Terrarium

Bank

Uses for 1 Gal Milk Carton

FIGURE 17-1

176

- birdhouse
- scoop
- beverage container
- flower pot
- terrarium
- coin bank
- pet food bowl

2. Creative Research

When students do real research they are engaged in a knowledge-creating process. Children's research can take many forms, some of them quite simple. For example, students can formulate hypotheses about the world, such as "gerbils love lettuce," and then test the hypothesis through observation and analysis of gerbils' eating preferences. The results of such activities create new data, or information. Of course, to make certain that research data are not only interesting but accurate, students would have to follow procedures carefully for collecting and analyzing data, which is what science is all about. Some possibilities for creative researching, stated in hypothesis form, include the following:

- Plants grow better in sunshine than darkness.
- Students in our class prefer ice cream over yogurt.
- Vegetables are a popular food in the school cafeteria.
- Rain and cloudless sky can occur together at the same moment in time.
- People who study their spelling words will score higher on a test than those that don't.
- In our class, boys weigh more on average than girls.
- Sneakers are more popular than shoes.
- Language Arts (reading) is our class's favorite subject.

Math:

1. A New Dessert Topping

Let students invent a new topping for an ice cream or yogurt sundae. They can draw pictures of their desserts and label the ingredients. Have students determine the amounts of the ingredients that would be needed in making the dessert. If possible, hold a sundae snack party, and let students make, distribute, and share

equal portions of the dessert. At the party, hold a contest to name the new sundae topping.

2. Counting Solutions

During brainstorming, creative research, and other activities described in this unit, there will be opportunities for students to tabulate student-generated data and solutions to problems.

3. Finding Shapes

Challenge small groups of two or three students to discover examples of simple shapes (circle, oval, square, triangle, and rectangle) that are part of the classroom environment (i.e. circular clock on the wall, rectangular desktops, square notepads). Challenge students to find shapes at home.

Language Arts:

1. Creating New Words

Back in the 1960s, "groovy" was a popular expression, especially for young people. Every generation invents and uses slang words to describe people, places, and actions. Have students create new words to express the following conditions:

beautiful	great
terrible	loud
hard	delicious
easy	exciting
funny	mysterious
stupid	large

2. Chain Fairy Tales

Challenge students to create a fairy tale from beginning to end. Guide students through a consideration of the elements below. Let students take turns adding to the developing story. Dramatize and/or illustrate segments of the fairy tale as they are created. When they are creating their fairy tale story, make certain that students consider the following elements: setting (Where does the story take place?); characters (Who are the good characters? Who are the bad characters?); and plot (What problem are the good characters trying to solve? In what actions do the bad characters try to interfere with the good characters?). To get students focused, begin with "Once upon a time, . . ." then ask "What happens first?" then "What happens next?" and so on. The ending should describe how the good characters triumph over the bad characters, so that the story has a happy ending.

3. Picture Stories

Collect and laminate an assortment of pictures with scenes that show rural, urban, and natural landscapes, animal and plant life, technology in action, and various activities of people around the world. Provide each child with a random selection of the pictures. Direct students to gather around a large open area of the floor. Place a picture on the floor and let it serve as the vehicle to begin the story. For example, let's say the picture shows an airplane flying in the sky. You could begin the story by saying that the Ryan family is taking a vacation, and the family is traveling to _____. Then have students check their pictures to identify one that could be connected to the first picture to extend the story. Let's suppose a child has a picture of an Arizona desert scene. That child could place his picture next to yours and explain that the Ryan family was traveling to the desert. Another child could then add a picture, and on and on until everyone had an opportunity to contribute to the story.

Art:

1. Something from Nothing

Provide students with large sheets of butcher paper, tape, glue, a stapler, and throw-away items. Have students use items that normally would be thrown away to create a three-dimensional collage. Throw-away items might include such things as empty cans, bags, paper containers and food wrappers, used pencils, waste paper, string, yarn, and bottle caps.

2. Seed Pictures

Give each student an assortment of different kinds of dried seeds (black-eyed peas, green peas, lima beans, kidney beans, corn, rice, etc.), glue, and heavy card paper. Have students create a design with the seeds, and then glue the seeds to the card paper. (Note: Apply a coat of varnish to the completed seed picture.)

3. Printing with What?

Have students think of all the possible objects they might use for printing. Possibilities include leaves, sponges, different-textured cloth and paper, pieces of carpet, rope, string, potatoes, and hands. Provide paper, paint, and various objects, and let students make prints on sheets of white paper. For step-by-step instructions on printing, consult *Printing* by Ruth Thompson (Children's Press, 1994), or some other appropriate craft book for children. After the students complete their prints, display them on the wall.

4. Cereal Box Design

To attract customers, creative advertisers want to make their products appealing. For example, they try to create colorful, eye-catching pictures and designs to put on the fronts of breakfast

Art from Shape
FIGURE 17-2

cereal boxes. Popular sports heroes and cartoon characters often adorn the box fronts. Messages suggesting that the cereals are fun, tasty, and/or nutritious to eat are usually prominently displayed. Provide poster board and art materials, and challenge students to design their own cereal box fronts. Display the completed designs on the wall.

5. Creating Art from Shapes

Provide each student with a piece of drawing paper displaying one of the following shapes: square, circle, rectangle, triangle, or oval. Challenge students to create a picture (people, animals, plants, places, etc.) using the shape as a starting point, such as shown in Figure 17-2.

Music:

1. Making Music Instruments Creatively

To engage students creatively in music, consult Rebecca Anders' excellent book, *Making Musical Instruments* (Lerner Publications Company, 1975), which describes sound and rhythm and gives instructions on how to make different kinds of instruments from flower pots, cartons, plastic bottles, and other materials.

Books:

1. MacLeod-Brudenell, Iain. (1993). *Animal Crafts*. Milwaukee: Gareth Stevens Publishing. Intermediate, Advanced.

2. Guerrier, Charlie. (1994). *A Collage of Crafts*. New York: Ticknor & Fields. Advanced.

3. Winter, Jeanette. (1991). *Diego*. New York: Alfred A. Knopf. Primary, Intermediate.

4. Kallen, Stuart A. (1993). *Eco-Arts and Crafts*. Minneapolis: Abdo Consulting Corporation, Inc. Intermediate, Advanced.

5. Tuttell, Jervis, and Cawley, Frank. (1991). *Ideas from Nature*. North Bellmore, NY: Marshall Cavendish Corporation. Primary, Intermediate.

6. Anders, Rebecca. (1975). *Making Musical Instruments*. Minneapolis: Lerner Publications Company. Intermediate, Advanced.

7. Thomson, Ruth. (1994). *Printing*. Chicago: Children's Press. Primary.

8. Milford, Susan. (1995). *Tales Alive*. Charlotte, VT: Williamson Publishing. Intermediate, Advanced.

9. Fleisher, Paul. (1993). *The Violin Master*. Boston: Houghton Mifflin Company. Intermediate.

Software:

1. *Thinkin' Things Collection 1* [Mac IBM Windows MPC Cd-ROM]. Redmond, WA: Edmark. Primary, Intermediate.

2. *Thinkin' Things Collection 2* [Mac IBM Windows MPC CD-ROM]. Redmond, WA: Edmark. Primary, Intermediate, Advanced.

3. *Thinkin' Things Collection 3* [Mac MPC CD-ROM]. Redmond, WA: Edmark. Intermediate, Advanced.

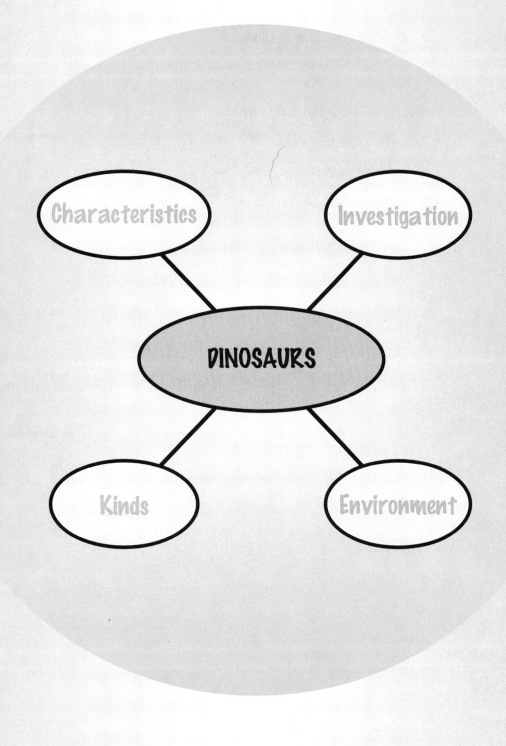

Theme Goals:

Students will:

1. identify different kinds of dinosaurs.

2. create a dinosaur time line.

3. measure the lengths of dinosaurs.

4. graph the lengths of dinosaurs.

5. analyze the possible reasons for the disappearance of the dinosaurs.

6. identify endangered animals.

7. write a creative story.

8. make fossil replicas.

9. make cutouts of dinosaurs.

Theme Concepts:

1. There were many different kinds of dinosaurs.

2. Dinosaurs lived millions of years ago, long before humans arrived on Earth.

3. Dinosaurs came in many different shapes and sizes.

4. Scientists have developed hypotheses about why dinosaurs disappeared from the Earth.

5. Because of human activity, many animals today are in danger of extinction.

6. Fossils give us our only record of what dinosaurs looked like and when they lived.

Vocabulary:

1. era

2. hypothesis

3. reptile

4. fossil

5. extinction

6. paleontologist

7. geologist

Instructional Bulletin Board

The purpose of this bulletin board is to let students use data on dinosaur length listed under Math Activity #1 to make a bar graph. To construct the bar graph, cover the bulletin board with a large sheet of white paper. Draw a horizontal axis for the graph that will show dinosaur length and a vertical axis that will display kinds of dinosaurs. Assign each student the task of making a bar on the graph to represent the length of one of the kinds of dinosaurs. Let a 1-inch length of construction paper represent one foot on the bar graph. Have students measure and cut strips of construction paper that represent their dinosaurs' lengths, using a different color of construction paper for each kind of dinosaur. For example, the strip for Plateosaurus would be 20 inches long to represent the creature's length of 20 feet. (Note: The strips of a few giant dinosaurs, such as the 70-foot-long Brachiosaurus, might extend beyond the area of the bulletin board.) Have students arrange the strips for each dinosaur on the graph. When each strip is positioned correctly, glue it to the paper to form one bar on the graph.

BAR GRAPHS OF
DINO LENGTHS

Name of
Dino

"

"

"

"

Parent Letter

Dear Parents:

Children have an inexhaustible curiosity about dinosaurs. Although no human has ever seen these creatures, they have still managed to capture our imagination. What makes them so interesting? At one time there were hundreds of different kinds of dinosaurs. They were the largest and fiercest animals ever to roam the Earth. Yet all of them disappeared mysteriously millions of years ago, leaving only fossilized bones and eggs as proof that they were once here. During our study of dinosaurs, your child will be engaged in a variety of activities, including those listed below.

At School:

In this theme, students will be:

- Identifying different kinds of dinosaurs
- Creating a giant dinosaur time line
- Measuring and graphing dinosaurs
- Analyzing reasons why dinosaurs disappeared
- Writing a creative story about dinosaurs
- Making fossil replicas

At Home:

Now would be a great time to talk with your child about dinosaurs. In addition, you might want to consider doing one or more of the following: Together with your child, read aloud a book on dinosaurs; make a dinosaur model from clay; and/or visit a museum that displays dinosaurs. The more interest you show in dinosaurs, the more excited your child will be with learning about these fascinating creatures.

Linking Up:

Ask students to bring some of their dinosaur "things" to school to share with the class. Let students show and tell about their dinosaur toys, dolls, cards, pictures, books, and assorted other items. Encourage students to disclose their knowledge about dinosaurs and note any misinformation they might have about these creatures.

Math:

1. Dinosaur Time Line

Brief Background. Dinosaurs lived millions of years ago, and they disappeared from the face of the Earth long before humans arrived on the scene. Dinosaurs first appeared about 220 million years ago. They roamed the Earth during the *Mesozoic Era*, which is divided into the following three time periods: the *Triassic* (240 million to 205 million years ago), the *Jurassic* (205 million to 138 million years ago) and the *Cretaceous* (138 million to 63 million years ago).

To give students a sense of the magnitude of these huge expanses of time, help them construct a giant time line in the school's hallway, gym, or outside play area. The time line will demonstrate for students approximately when various dinosaurs lived and give them a sense of how long ago this time period was from the present. First, assign small groups of students the task of researching one or more of the following dinosaurs listed below under the time periods in which they lived. (Note: the approximate length of each dinosaur is in parenthesis.)

TRIASSIC

1. Plateosaurus (20 feet)
2. Procompsognathus (3 feet)

JURASSIC

3. Heterodontosaurus (3 1/2 feet)
4. Stegosaurus (20 feet)
5. Scelidosaurus (12 feet)
6. Brachiosaurus (70 feet)
7. Apatosaurus (70 feet)
8. Ornitholestes (6 feet)
9. Camptosaurus (15 feet)
10. Compsognathus (2 1/2 feet)
11. Allosaurus (30 feet)

CRETACEOUS

12. Iguanodon (30 feet)
13. Deinonychus (9 feet)
14. Ornithomimus (14 feet)
15. Ankylosaurus (25 feet)
16. Tyrannosaurus (40 feet)
17. Corythosaurus (30 feet)
18. Pentaceratops (25 feet)

Each small group will need to make a large poster that includes the following: name of the dinosaur, a colorful drawing of the dinosaur, and the time period in which the dinosaur lived on Earth. Then, provide groups with measuring instruments and 220 feet of string or twine, and let them create the time line based on the following scale: 1 foot = 1 million years. (To reach back to the appearance of the first dinosaurs, the time line will need to be 220 feet long.) Once the approximate points on the time line that correspond to the three time periods have been determined, place the posters along the time line within the correct time period segment. Compared to the dinosaurs' long time line, it seems that people arrived on the scene only yesterday. Tell students that the fossil remains of our ancient ancestors date back approximately 4 million years (represented by the last 4-foot segment on the time lime), and that the earliest civilizations on Earth were established about 10,000 years ago (represented by 1/100 of a foot segment at the end of the time line (the end of the time line represents the present time).

2. Sizing Up Dino's Shadow

Dinosaurs came in a great variety of shapes and sizes (Figure 18-1). To show students how long some of the dinosaurs were, involve students in the following outdoor activity. For this activity, you will need a large, flat, hard surface (i.e. concrete or asphalt) outside. Besides measuring instruments, students will need the posters created in Math Activity #1, as well as extra-large pieces of chalk. Pair up the students and have them spread out to give them plenty of room to work. Assign each pair one of the dinosaurs listed above to draw. Let pairs measure the lengths of the dinosaurs (which are shown in parenthesis above) on the asphalt or

2. Procompsognathus

3. Heterodontosaurus

1. Plateosaurus

4. Stegosaurus

5. Scelidosaurus

6. Brachiosaurus

7. Apatosaurus

FIGURE 18-1a

concrete surface. They can use the large chalk to outline a "shadow" of each dinosaurs body.

Science:

1. Dinosaur Mysteries

Brief Background. Although numerous fos-silized dinosaur bones and eggs have been found, scientists still do not know a whole lot about these fascinating creatures. The ideas scientists have about dinosaurs are called hypotheses, which are generalizations about what is believed to be true. For a long time scientists believed that dinosaurs were most closely related to reptiles, that they were very slow and clumsy, and that, as a group,

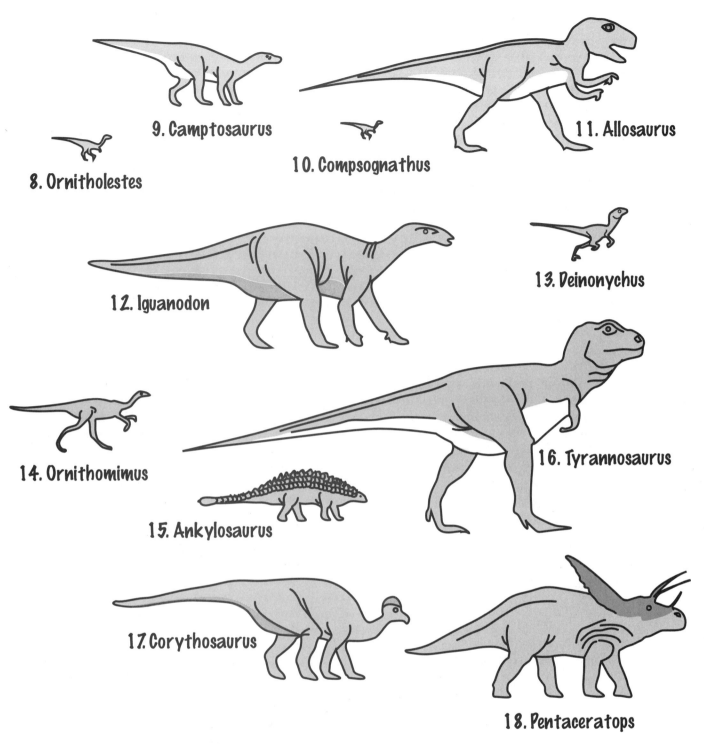

9. Camptosaurus

8. Ornitholestes

10. Compsognathus

11. Allosaurus

12. Iguanodon

13. Deinonychus

14. Ornithomimus

15. Ankylosaurus

16. Tyrannosaurus

17. Corythosaurus

18. Pentaceratops

FIGURE 18-1b

they were not very bright. But, new evidence has caused scientists to revise their ideas. Now, they tend to believe that many kinds of dinosaurs were more like birds than reptiles, that many were probably quite agile, and that they were probably not as dumb as first imagined. One of the biggest mysteries to scientists is why dinosaurs died out.

Show students pictures and models of dinosaurs. Ask students to hypothesize about what happened to them. List their ideas on the chalkboard, and discuss each one. Then, read aloud selections from *What Happened to the Dinosaurs?* by Franklyn Branley (Thomas Y. Crowell, 1989), or another appropriate children's book, that discusses some of the possible causes of the creatures demise. Let students consider the following hypotheses suggested by experts. Which hypothesis seems to be the most sensible?

HYPOTHESES

1. Dinosaurs died out because their food source (plants) disappeared as a result of the development of new kinds of plants.
2. Dinosaurs died because their food source died out when Earth's climate changed, resulting in colder temperatures.
3. Dinosaurs died because an asteroid hit the Earth, causing great fires and dust storms and resulting in darkness that killed their food source.

2. Dinosaur Museum

Have students create museum exhibits of various kinds of dinosaurs. Each student can make a diorama that displays a particular kind of dinosaur in its natural environment. Students can use modeling clay or papier-mache to form the dinosaurs. Provide each student with a small box (for the diorama), paint supplies, and an assortment of natural objects, such as dirt, rocks, and plant foliage, and let them create dinosaur dioramas to exhibit in their museum.

3. Ask the Expert

If a natural history museum or college is nearby, ask a scientist who collects and studies fossils, such as a paleontologist or geologist, to visit the class. Ask the expert to talk about dinosaurs, or other extinct and mysterious creatures, and ask him or her to bring along a few fossils for students to examine up close.

Social Studies:

1. Our Endangered Earth

Brief Background. For most of Earth's history, extinction was the result of natural causes, as in the case of the dinosaurs. Today, the main cause of animal and plant extinction is people. Hundreds of animals, including the dodo and passenger pigeon, have become extinct. Hunting, fishing, logging, farming, mining, and manufacturing activities continue to cause habitat destruction and endanger increasing numbers of living things.

Read aloud selections from *Will We Miss Them? Endangered Species* by Alexandra Wright (Charlesbridge Publishing, 1992), or another appropriate children's book on endangered species. Have each student select an endangered animal to investigate. They can draw pictures of the animals, describe their natural habitats, and explain why the animals are endangered. Have students brainstorm actions they can take to protect the natural environment, both locally and globally.

Language Arts:

1. Dinosaur Stories

Make a transparency of the following blueprint for a dinosaur story, project it on the screen, and then let students fill in the colorful and exciting details.

Sam had the greatest collection of toy dinosaurs in the world! He kept some of his favorites lined up on his desk next to his bed. They included the giant _____, the terrifying _____, and the three-horned _____. But the two he loved to play with the most were _____ and _____.

One night he dreamed he was somehow transported back in time to the Mesozoic Era, where he had to outsmart a bunch of real dinosaurs that were definitely not plant eaters. What follows is his account of what happened.

_____

_____

_____

_____

_____

_____

"Sam! Sam! Get up! It's time for school."

"O.K. mom. I hear you," mumbled Sam as he crawled out of bed. Wow, was he glad to

Fossil #1 Imprint

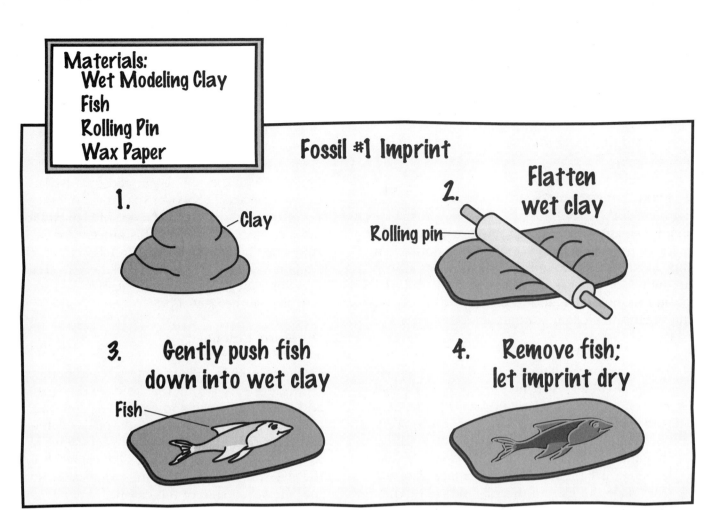

1. Clay

2. Flatten wet clay
Rolling pin

3. Gently push fish down into wet clay
Fish

4. Remove fish; let imprint dry

Fossil #2
3-D Duplicate

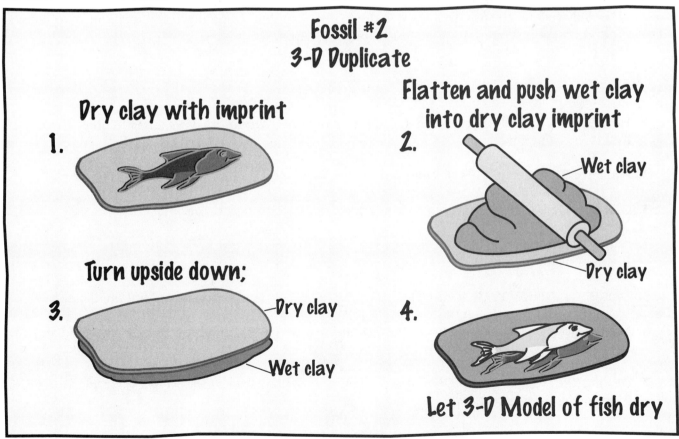

1. Dry clay with imprint

2. Flatten and push wet clay into dry clay imprint
Wet clay
Dry clay

3. Turn upside down;
Dry clay
Wet clay

4. Let 3-D Model of fish dry

Diagram for Making Fossils

FIGURE 18-2

189

be back home with his toy dinosaurs. They were a lot smaller than the ones he had just left behind. Then suddenly, he exclaimed to himself, "I think I'll just put you guys in the closet for safekeeping."

Art:

1. Make Your Own Fossil Replicas

Brief Background. Fossils give us our only record of what dinosaurs looked like and when they lived. Fossils are formed when the imprint of an animal or plant is preserved in a mineral deposit, or when mineral deposits replace a decaying organism, creating a three-dimensional image of it.

To make replicas of fossils, follow the directions in Figure 18-2. You'll need to bring an intact small (5"–7") fish to class. Provide each student with clay and a piece of wax paper to place it on. Help each student flatten the clay with a rolling pin until it is about 1" thick and its surface area is large enough to accommodate the fish. Place the fish on the clay and roll gently until the fish's body is pressed down into the clay. Carefully remove the fish, trying not to disturb the impression. Repeat this process with each student. When the clay is dry, each student will have a fossil imprint of the fish. The clay fossil imprints can be used to make another type of fossil, a three-dimensional replacement of one side of the fish's body. To make the three-dimensional fossil, place a flattened piece of wet clay on the dry clay imprint of the fish. Gently push the wet clay down into the impression with the rolling pin and fingers. Turn the two pieces of clay over so that the dry piece is on top. Remove the dry piece of clay and let the wet piece dry. Repeat this process for each student. When the wet pieces of clay dry, each student will have another fossil of the fish—only this time, the clay has duplicated or replaced one side of the fish's body.

2. Dinosaur Cutouts

Provide students with art materials and outlines on poster board of different kinds of dinosaurs, and let them cut out and color their dinosaurs. Have them color only one side of the cutout. Since no one knows for sure what dinosaurs looked like, invite students to be creative about their choice of colors for their dinosaurs. On the uncolored side of the cutout, students can write the name of the dinosaur and briefly describe it. Hang the completed dinosaur cutouts from the ceiling.

Books:

1. Horner, John R., and Lessem, Don. (1992). *Digging Up Tyrannosaurus Rex*. New York: Crown Publishers, Inc. Intermediate.

2. Penner, Lucille Recht. (1991). *Dinosaur Babies*. New York: Random House Inc. Primary.

3. Gibbons, Gail. (1987). *Dinosaurs*. New York: Holiday House. Primary.

4. Sattler, Helen Roney. (1981). *Dinosaurs of North America*. New York: Lothrop, Lee and Shepard Books. Advanced.

5. DuBosque, Doug. (1993). *Draw Dinosaurs*. Molalla, OR: Peel Productions. Intermediate.

6. Nardo, Don. (1994). *The Extinction of Dinosaurs*. San Diego: Lucent Books. Intermediate, Advanced.

7. Dewan, Ted. (1993). *Inside Dinosaurs and other Prehistoric Creatures*. New York: Delacorte Press. Intermediate, Advanced.

8. Simon, Seymour. (1990). *New Questions and Answers About Dinosaurs*. New York: William Morrow and Co., Inc. Primary, Intermediate.

9. Sattler, Helen Roney. (1992). *Stegosaurs: The Solar Powered Dinosaurs.* New York: Lothrop, Lee and Shepard Books. Intermediate.

10. Branley, Franklyn M. (1989). *What Happened to the Dinosaurs?* New York: Thomas Y. Crowell Junior Books. Primary.

11. Wright, Alexandra. (1992). *Will We Miss Them? Endangered Species.* Watertown, MA: Charlesbridge Publishing. Primary, Intermediate.

Software:

1. *Dinosaur Discovery* [Mac MPC CD-ROM]. West Chester, PA: Romtech. Primary, Intermediate, Advanced.

2. *3-D Dinosaur Adventure* [Mac IBM CD-ROM]. Glendale, CA: Knowledge Adventure. Primary, Intermediate, Advanced.

3. *Dinosaurs* [Laserdisc]. Washington, DC: National Geographic. Intermediate, Advanced.

4. *Encyclopedia of Dinosaurs* [Mac MPC CD-ROM]. San Diego, CA: Gazelle Technologies. Intermediate, Advanced.

5. *Fossils! Fossils!* [Laserdisc]. Chicago: Clearvue/eav. Advanced.

6. *Dinosaur Museum* [Mac Windows CD-ROM]. Cambridge, MA: Softkey International. Intermediate, Advanced.

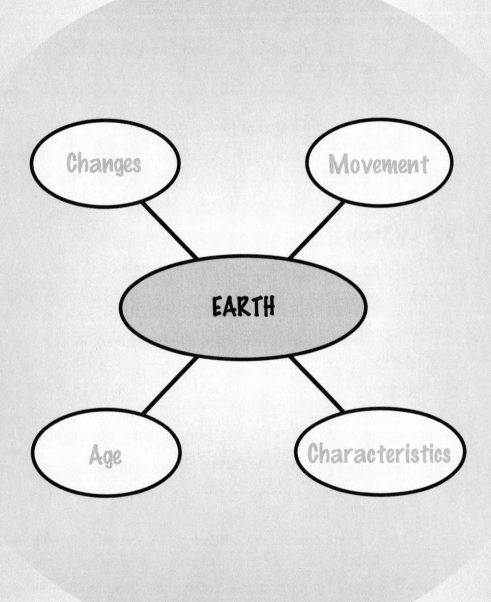

Theme Goals:

Students will:

1. gather current events articles on Earth changes.

2. complete a jigsaw puzzle activity on Pangaea.

3. demonstrate the Earth's seasonal changes.

4. observe and sort substances in soil.

5. take a geologic field trip.

6. conduct an experiment to demonstrate the effects of the Sun's energy on plants.

7. construct a time line.

8. make a scale drawing of the Sun and planets.

9. make creative products that describe various aspects of the Earth.

10. construct a model of the Earth's layers.

Theme Concepts:

1. Physical changes on Earth occur constantly.

2. According to plate tectonics theory, the Earth's surface is divided into moving plates.

3. The seasons change because the Earth is tilted on its axis as it moves around the sun.

4. A variety of substances can be found in soil.

5. Evidence of geological changes can be observed on the surface of the Earth.

6. The chief source of the Earth's energy is the Sun.

7. The three major types of rocks are igneous, sedimentary, and metamorphic.

8. The development of life on Earth has occurred over billions of years.

9. The Earth, from surface to center, is divided into the following four layers: crust, mantle, outer core, and inner core.

10. The Earth is the third planet from the sun.

Vocabulary:

1. Pangaea

2. plate tectonics theory

3. crust

4. mantle

5. inner core

6. outer core

7. continental drift

Instructional Bulletin Board

The purpose of this bulletin board is to help students learn the relationship between the tilted Earth's revolution around the Sun and the change of seasons as they occur in the northern hemisphere. Place a picture of the Sun in the center of the bulletin board. Draw a diagram of the Earth's position (draw a circle with an imaginary axis at 23 degrees) at the start of each of the four seasons. Make four cutouts of the earth showing Western Hemisphere, equator, and some meridians (north/south lines) to indicate poles. Darken each of the Earth cutouts (as shown in Figure 19-2) to represent the sun's rays at one of the four seasons. Make labels for "winter," "summer," "spring," and "autumn." Place Earths and labels in the pocket. Have students attach Earth's labels correctly (as shown) with pins.

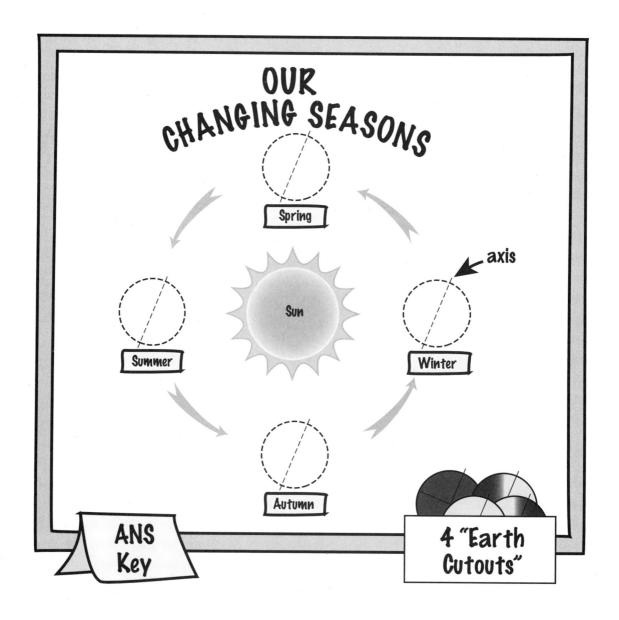

Parent Letter

Dear Parents:

In our current theme of study the class will be learning about their home, the Earth. The Earth is a special place: Of all of the planets in the solar system, only the Earth is known to support life.

At School:

Here are some activities planned for the theme:

- Collecting clips from newspapers and magazines about changes occurring on Earth
- Putting together the jigsaw puzzle pieces of a moving Earth
- Using models to learn about the Earth's changing seasons
- Observing the Earth (soil) up close
- Taking a geologic field trip
- Experimenting with the Earth's energy
- Constructing an Earth time line
- Making a scale drawing of the planets
- Making a model of the earth's layers

At Home:

Ask your child where he or she lives. Does the answer mention the Earth? We are asking students to gather articles from magazines that are about changes that occur on the Earth's surface, including earthquakes, storms, volcanic activity, flooding. Please help your child hunt for articles, and encourage him or her to take them to school so they can be shared with the rest of the class.

Linking Up:

Ask students to tell you about their favorite places on Earth. Make a list of them on the chalkboard. Help students find a basis for grouping and labeling the places. For example, some favorite places might be grouped together under the label "mountains," other places under the label "on or near water," others under "amusement parks," and so on.

Social Studies:

1. Earth Watch

Have students save clippings from newspapers and magazines that are about physical changes occurring on Earth. Specifically, direct students to look for articles dealing with earthquakes, volcanic activity, mud slides, flooding, storms, and other weather conditions. The articles can be attached around a map of the world. Yarn can be used to identify the place described in the article.

Science:

1. The Moving Earth

Brief Background. The theories of plate tectonics and continental drift provide scientists with an explanation of why the Earth looks the way it does. According to the theory of plate tectonics, the earth's crust and outermost mantle are divided into moving plates. The thickness of the plates ranges from 5 to 120 miles (60 miles is average), and they move about four inches a year. Provide students with a world map showing the Earth's plate boundaries. Point out that most of these boundaries are on the ocean floor. Because of the Earth's moving plates, the continents are in constant motion, drifting slowly across the Earth's surface. Scientists believe that about 200 million years ago there was one single land mass on Earth. This supercontinent, called Pangaea, broke into smaller land masses that slowly drifted to their present locations around the world (Figure 19-1). A vast amount of geological evidence has been collected to support the theory. The most striking evidence is the shapes of the land masses themselves. The theory explains, for example, why the east coast of South America seems to fit together with the west coast of Africa.

Bring in a simple jigsaw puzzle and let students take turns putting the pieces together. Then, have pairs of students carefully study globes and world maps. Challenge the pairs to find land areas on the globes and maps that might fit together like a puzzle. Tell students that scientists believe that long ago (200 million years) there was a single giant continent called Pangaea, which was centered at the equator. Arrange large poster board cutouts of the seven continents (make a separate cutout of India) on the floor so that they resemble a world map. Introduce or review the seven continents, and ask students to name them. Then, mix up the pieces. Ask students to imagine that the continents are pieces of a jigsaw puzzle. Have volunteers take turns putting pieces together to form one giant continent. If they need additional direction, display the map below, which shows the pieces arranged to resemble the supercontinent of Pangaea. Provide art materials and large sheets of drawing paper, and let students draw maps of Pangaea for display on the wall.

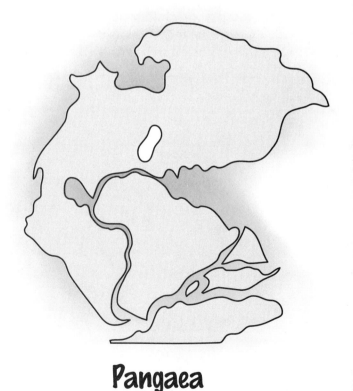

Pangaea

FIGURE 19-1

2. Continental Drift

Brief Background. According to scientists, about 65 million years ago Pangaea divided into two land masses: Laurasia, consisting of North America, Europe, and Asia; and Gondwanaland, consisting of South America, Africa, India, Australia, and Antarctica. These two land masses then broke into smaller pieces and drifted to their present locations.

After the pieces are arranged on the floor to form a map of Pangaea in Science Activity #1, ask students to predict the direction each of the continents will drift over the next 200 million years. Tell students that the wall map of the world provides clues about the movement of the drifting continents. Invite volunteers to take turns slowly moving the pieces to their present-day positions. (If possible, take photographs or a videotape of the activity to document the "movement" of the continents to their present-day locations.)

3. Earth's Seasonal Changes

The seasons change as the Earth goes around the Sun because the earth is tilted about 23 degrees. The Earth is always tilted the same way as it revolves around the Sun. Summer occurs in the Northern Hemisphere when the North Pole is tilted toward the Sun; winter in the Northern Hemisphere occurs when the North Pole is tilted away from the Sun (Figure 19-2). Use a globe and a spotlight to show how the higher latitudes get more sunlight in summer than in winter. Provide students with oranges or styrofoam balls and let them make their own models of the Earth. They can stick a pencil or bamboo skewer all the way through the center of their "earths" to represent the imaginary tilted axis. Make certain students hold their globes tilted constantly at about 23 degrees as they take turns moving around the "sun." Rotate the spotlight so that its beam stays constantly on the globe as the student walks around it.

4. Observing the Earth

Tell the class that today they are going to investigate a tiny portion of the Earth's surface. Take students outside to collect soil samples in small plastic bags, or provide each student with a small bag of soil, a hand lens, and a small

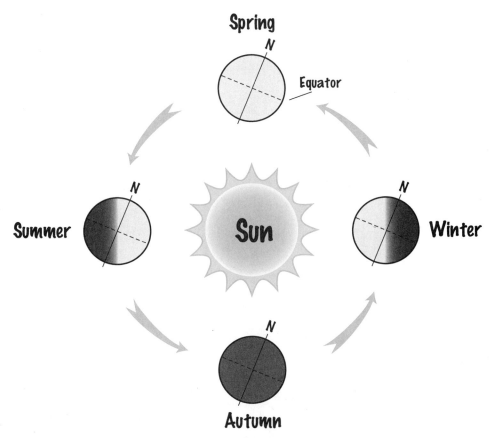

FIGURE 19-2

stick. Have students use their sticks to spread the soil out on large sheets of white paper. Encourage them to examine the soil carefully with their hand lenses and probing sticks. What substances can they find in the soil? Ask them to sort different substances found in the soil into piles—small rocks, sand, gravel, humus, trash, dead animals, live animals (worms, bugs, etc.). What do the students' analyses of the soil tell them about its composition?

5. Geologic Field Trip

If possible, take students on a field trip to areas that demonstrate how the Earth changes. Ask a geologist at a nearby college to suggest the most interesting places to visit. He or she may also be willing to accompany your class on the trip. Land areas containing marine fossils provide evidence that many parts of the United States were once ocean beds. Shorelines have changed because of the composition of the area, its elevation, river and ocean currents, and increased and decreased amounts of water in the oceans. In some sections of the northern United States, glacial action has shaped the Earth. On the Pacific Coast, earthquakes have uplifted the land. Mines, quarries, river gorges, and road cuts can all reveal interesting information about an area's geologic history. After the field trip, let students make dioramas of the place.

6. The Earth's Energy

The chief source of the Earth's energy is the Sun. To demonstrate the use of the Sun's energy, secure two potted plants that are alike in every way—kind, size, condition, potting soil, and so forth. Place one plant near sunlight and the other in darkness. Give both plants the same amount of water. Have students examine the two plants periodically and note any differences. They can make a chart like the one in Figure 19-3 to show the growth rates. What do the students' observations tell them about the Sun's energy?

7. Sorting Rocks

Brief Background. The three major types of rocks are igneous (formed by volcanic action), sedimentary (formed by compression of sediments, or particles of soil), and metamorphic (formed by great pressure on igneous and sedimentary rocks). Some rocks of each type are listed below.

Igneous	Sedimentary	Metamorphic
basalt	chalk	marble
pumice	sandstone	slate
granite	coal	gneiss
obsidian	shale	schist

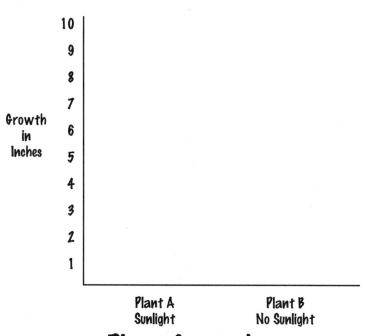

FIGURE 19-3

Plant Growth

Secure a mineral map of the state and local area from a geologist or government agency. Have students collect rocks of the local area, or provide students with an assortment of rocks. Let students classify the rocks using the following characteristics: size, shape, weight, hardness, roughness, roundness, color, luster, and magnetism.

Math:

1. Earth Time Line

Some important events in the development of life on Earth are listed below. Have students create a time line that places the events in chronological order. Challenge students to create a scale so that events can be placed in proper relationship to one another on the time line.

What Happened?	When Did It Happen?
(a brief description of event)	(years ago)
The birth of the Earth	4.5 billion
Bacteria in sea	3.5 billion
Jellyfish and worms in sea	1.1 billion
Trilobites and mollusks in sea	570 million
Land plants appear	435 million
Fish, amphibians, and insects appear	410 million
Reptiles appear	330 million
Seed plants appear	290 million
Turtles, crocodiles, dinosaurs, and mammals appear	240 million
Flowering plants appear	138 million
Dinosaurs had died out	63 million
Bats, camels, cats, horses, monkeys, and whales appear	55 million
Apes appear	38 million
Humanlike creatures appear	5 million
Human beings appear	2 million
Civilizations develop	10 thousand

2. Scale Model Solar System

Provide graph paper and measuring instruments, and have students make a scale model of the solar system using the following scale: 3 mm = 8,000 miles (Figure 19-4).

3. Time and Motion

Brief Background. Units of time are based on the Earth's motion in relation to the sun. A fifteen-degree rotation of the Earth relative to the sun requires one hour of time.

Ask students to imagine a world without clocks or watches. How would units of time on Earth be measured without these inventions? Introduce or review the imaginary lines—latitude, longitude, the equator, the tropic of Cancer, the tropic of Capricorn, the Arctic Circle, the Antarctic Circle, and the poles—used to establish time and location. Demonstrate with a projector and globe that a fifteen-degree rotation of the earth relative to the sun represents one hour of time. Provide students with Styrofoam balls and have them draw lines of longitude and lines of latitude on them. Let students take turns rotating their globe in front of a projector to demonstrate the relationship between time and the Earth's motion.

Language Arts:

1. Where on Earth

Have students write about faraway places they would love to visit. Encourage them to include plenty of details in their descriptions. Call on volunteers to read their descriptions, and challenge the rest of the class to guess their locations. Follow up with *Earth Treks* (Sanctuary Woods), a software program that lets students explore the Earth, its people, and the environment.

2. Our Place

Provide students with an assortment of well-illustrated magazines. Have students cut out

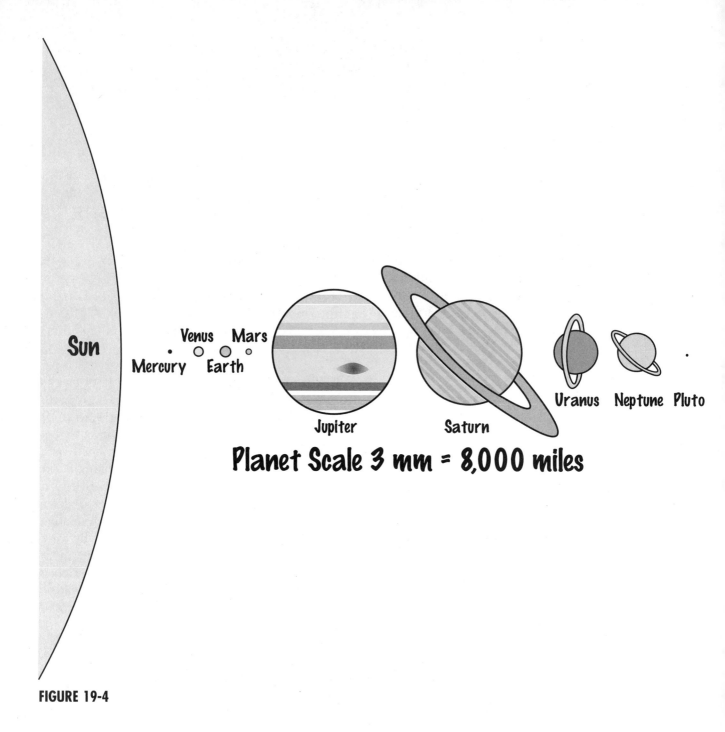

Sun

Mercury

Venus
Earth

Mars

Jupiter

Saturn

Uranus

Neptune

Pluto

Planet Scale 3 mm = 8,000 miles

FIGURE 19-4

photographs, draw pictures, and write stories and poems that describe the climate, weather, landscape, and plants and animals that make up the area in which they live. Collect the students' work and use it to compile a scrapbook entitled "Our Place."

Art:

1. Model of the Earth

From surface to center, the earth is divided into the following four layers (the approximate thickness of each layer is in parentheses): crust (5 to 25 miles), mantle (1,800 miles), outer core (1,400 miles), and inner core (800 miles). Provide modeling compound, paint, and brushes, and have students make colorful three-dimensional, cross-sectional models of the Earth (Figure 19-5).

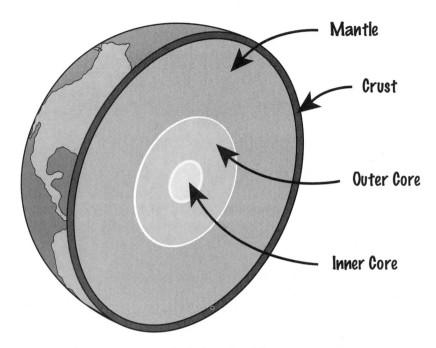

FIGURE 19-5   **Cross-Section of Earth Showing Layers**

Books:

1. Simon, Seymour. (1988). *Volcanoes.* New York: Mulberry Paperback Books. Intermediate, Advanced.

2. Simon, Seymour. (1987). *Icebergs and Glaciers.* New York: Morrow. Intermediate.

3. Branley, Franklyn. (1986). *What Makes Day and Night?* New York: Crowell. Primary.

4. Lye, Keith. (1980). *The Earth.* Morristown, NJ: Silver Burdett Co. Advanced.

5. Bramwell, Martyn. (1987). *Planet Earth.* New York: Franklin Watts. Advanced.

6. Berger, Melvin. (1980). *The New Earth Book: Our Changing Planet.* New York: Crowell. Advanced.

7. Branley, Franklyn. (1972). *The Beginning of the Earth.* New York: Crowell. Intermediate.

8. VanRose, Susanna. (1994). *The Earth Atlas.* New York: Dorling Kindersley. Advanced.

9. Ride, Sally, and O'Shaughnessy, Tarn. (1994). *The Third Planet: Exploring the Earth from Space.* New York: Crown. Advanced.

Software:

1. *Earth Treks* [Mac IBM]. San Mateo, CA: Sanctuary Woods. Intermediate, Advanced.

2. *Alfred Wegener: Continental Drift* [Laserdisc VHS]. Chicago: Clearvue/eav. Intermediate, Advanced.

3. *Our Biosphere* [Laserdisc]. Denver: Lumivision. Intermediate, Advanced.

4. *Violent Earth* [Mac MPC CD-ROM]. Austin, TX: Steck Vaughn. Intermediate, Advanced.

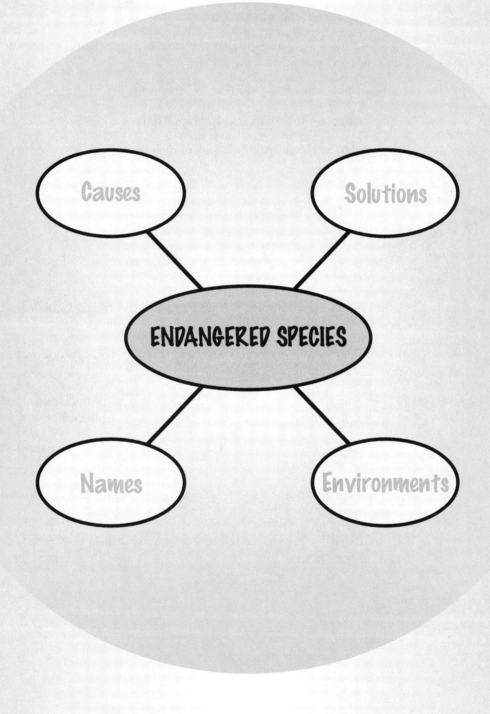

Causes

Solutions

ENDANGERED SPECIES

Names

Environments

Theme Goals:

The students will:

1. investigate an endangered species in depth.

2. describe natural habitats.

3. participate in conservation/preservation activity.

4. examine cause and effect relationships.

5. describe the past, present, and future usefulness and value of an endangered species.

6. engage in a simulated search for an endangered species.

7. infer patterns and relationships from data.

8. empathize with the plight of an endangered species.

9. create a species.

Theme Concepts:

1. Many people are unaware of the many animals and plants that are endangered or threatened.

2. The Endangered Species Act (1973) gave the federal government power to protect endangered animals and plants.

3. People can get involved locally and globally to help endangered species and their habitats.

4. Major causes of environmental problems are habitat loss, predation, exploitation, competition, disease, and pollution.

5. Many little-known endangered animals and plants are useful and valuable to humans.

6. The current condition of endangered species must be carefully monitored.

7. Humans will not help endangered species unless they know and care about them.

Vocabulary:

1. habitats

2. endangered

3. conservation

4. preservation

Instructional Bulletin Board

The purpose of this bulletin board is to provide students with an opportunity to practice categorizing endangered and threatened mammals, fish, birds, and reptiles. Divide the bulletin board into four columns. Head the columns *mammals* (hair/fur), *fish* (gills, fins, swims), *birds* (feathers), and *reptiles* (body usually covered with scales or bony plates). Place pictures of a variety of endangered and threatened mammals, fish, birds, and reptiles in a pocket (encourage students to find pictures of other animals to add to the pocket). Place a table directly under the bulletin board. Have students spread out the pictures on the table, and then attach them with pins under the correct headings.

ENDANGERED ANIMALS

WHICH AM I?

MAMMALS	FISH	BIRDS	REPTILES
hair/fur	gills, fins	feathers	scales, bony plates

ANS Key

Picture Endangered Animals

Parent Letter

Dear Parent:

This theme highlights the importance of protecting endangered plants and animals. Every day natural environments are being destroyed to make way for farms, factories, roads, mines, towns, and other types of development. Since an animal or plant is gone forever once it becomes extinct, helping children become aware of our role as guardians of the planet is surely worthy of our respect and our time.

At School:

Some of the activities in which students will be engaging are:

- Making "Wanted Alive!" posters
- Finding information about an endangered species
- Conserving and preserving resources locally
- Connecting with global conservation groups
- Tracing cause and effect relationships
- Tracking down endangered animals
- Giving animals a voice
- Creating an unknown species

At Home:

Now would be a great time to take a nature walk with your child. As you walk, identify plants and animals observed. Help your child learn about any local endangered and threatened species. If local species are threatened, have efforts been taken by local authorities to protect them?

Linking Up:

Ask students what kinds of things might harm plants and animals. Record their responses on the chalkboard. Encourage students to ask questions and share some of their thoughts and concerns about plants and animals. Explain that they will be discussing ways to protect plants and animals from danger.

Social Studies:

1. "Wanted Alive" Posters

Brief Background. Tigers, cheetahs, leopards, giant pandas, gorillas, black rhinoceroses—some of the world's most magnificent and well-known animals—are on the endangered species list. But most of the animals on the list are not household names. For example, few people have ever heard of the Coffin Cave moth beetle, Oahu tree snail, or blunt-nosed leopard lizard.

Have students make "Wanted Alive" posters for animals on the endangered species list. Challenge them to track down unknown endangered animals to highlight on their posters. Each poster can include the following information: the caption "Wanted Alive" in large, bold letters; a colorful picture of the animal; and the name of the animal in large, bold letters (Figure 20-1). After students complete their posters, display them in high-traffic areas, such as the school cafeteria, hallway, or media center. You can also ask permission to place posters in local banks, supermarkets, and other businesses.

2. Protecting Animal Habitats

Brief Background. The Endangered Species Act (ESA) was passed in 1973. This act gave the United States Government the power to protect endangered animals and plants, most of which are at risk because of habitat loss. Environmentalists support the ESA because they believe that, without it, there would be uncontrolled development of America's natural areas. They point to the multitude of agricultural, industrial, and residential projects that have caused environmental problems in the past. Developers, on the other hand, believe that people should have the right to exploit the economic potential of their own land; if that means cutting down trees, building roads and homes, or raising crops and livestock, then so be it. Since many people gain their livelihood from the land, the problem of achieving a proper balance between environmental protection and economic activity is not easy.

WANTED ALIVE POSTERS

FIGURE 20-1

Some of the animals endangered by habitat loss are listed below. Assign pairs of students the task of learning about one of the animals and its habitat needs. To illustrate the reports, students can draw a picture of the animal in its natural environment.

American crocodile
Bald eagle
California condor
Columbian white-tailed deer
Ivory-billed woodpecker
American alligator
Brown pelican
American peregrine falcon
Masked bobwhite
Whooping crane
Woodland caribou
West Indian manatee
Gorilla
Leopard
Arabian gazelle
Puerto Rican parrot

3. Taking Action

Read aloud the following scenario, and then let students discuss the best course of action to take.

Scenario: To help save an endangered species of owl from extinction, the government is considering making millions of acres of forest in the Pacific Northwest off-limits to chain saws. Hundreds of loggers do not want this to happen because they would lose their jobs. What do you think the government should do?

4. Getting Involved

You and your students can get involved locally and globally to help endangered species and their habitats. Locally, you can help the class become conservers of natural resources. They can recycle glass, aluminum, and paper. Introduce students to the "multiplier effect," which works this way: If each student can encourage two or three other family members to practice recycling, then she has become an instrument for multiplying or intensifying the effect, which is to increase the amount of recyclable materials collected. Globally, you can connect with organizations that work worldwide to preserve

natural habitats for endangered plants and animals, such as those listed below.

The Nature
Conservancy
P.O. Box 17056
Baltimore, MD 21298

Rainforest Action
Network
300 Broadway Suite 28
San Francisco, CA 94133

Science:

1. Investigating Causes and Effects

The causes of environmental problems are complex and varied. Some of the main general causes and examples of effects are presented in the chart on page 211. Challenge students to add examples to the chart.

2. Revealing Important Connections

Since most of the over 3,000 endangered species worldwide are relatively obscure organisms that most people have never heard of, some students may wonder why they should be saved from extinction. To help answer the "What good is it anyway?" question, bring some freshwater mussels to class for the students to examine. Ask students if they have every heard of the fine-rayed pigtoe mussel. This particular mussel is one of 56 that are listed as threatened or endangered. Trace the connections between freshwater mussels and the rest of the world, which are displayed on the diagram in Figure 20-2. Challenge each student to create a similar diagram that shows connections for a species of his choice and the rest of the world.

3. Keeping Track of Endangered Animals

Brief Background. Scientists throughout the world are always trying to identify new endangered animals. Scientists also want to learn more about the changing conditions of identified endangered animals. One effective way to study animals in the wild is to capture the animals, fit them with harmless identification tags and/or monitoring devices, and then set them free. Large, dangerous animals, like grizzly bears, are subdued with tranquilizing darts. Scientists work quickly to weigh, measure, and attach electronic monitoring collars to the animals before they wake up. At Florida's Everglades National Park, scientists place tiny metal tags on hundreds of baby alligators no larger than the palm of the

Causes of Environmental Problems	Examples
Habitat destruction caused by humans	Clear-cutting of Amazon rain forest has reduced the total population of golden lion marmosets in Brazil to around 300
Predation which occurs when a consumer kills a living organism and then eats it	Pigs and goats have consumed many different kinds of Hawaiian plants (e.g., Hawaiian vetch, kio'ele, oha wai, haha)
Exploitation of animals and plants by humans	Tigers are killed for their prized skins; wolves are shot because they are hated by ranchers
Competition for food and space	Cattle introduced on the tropical African savanna have devoured the grasses on which native herbivores (i.e., zebras, gazelles, and antelopes) also feed
Disease carried by introduced species that spread to vulnerable native species	Hawaiian native birds are threatened by diseases carried by birds introduced from the mainland
Pollution caused by chemicals, oil spills, and other contaminants	Chemical runoffs into the Everglades National Park have polluted the wetland habitat of the American crocodile

hand. By tagging the animals, scientists can keep track of how large they get and how far they travel.

Of course, scientists have to find the animals in the wild before they can be tagged. Invite your students on an endangered animals expedition. Without the students' knowledge, place ten colored plastic paper clips (of different sizes) and two dozen regular metal paper clips in various places around the room. (Note: Don't hide the clips from view, but don't make them too easy to find either. Students should be able to find the clips with moderate difficulty.) Place the students in pairs. Tell the pairs that they are teams of scientists. Each team's task is to track down endangered animals that are lurking around the room. Explain that the 24 regular paper clips represent animals that are not on the endangered list and the ten colored paper clips represent endangered animals. When the pairs find an endangered animal (colored paper clip), they should do the following: make an accurate, life-size drawing of the animal; draw a map of the environment (classroom) showing the exact spot where the animal was found; measure and record the precise length of the animal; and state the animal's color. After the pairs complete this

project, they can report their findings to the class. The next day, place the paper clips in different locations and repeat the activity. Have the class compare their day one and day two findings, and then calculate how far each of the endangered animals traveled. Follow up this hands-on activity with library research on the scientific monitoring of real endangered animals.

Math:

1. Endangered and Threatened Species

Brief Background. Over 1,000 species of animals and plants worldwide have been identified as endangered or threatened. The animal species at risk have been enumerated by groups as follows: mammals (336 species); birds (243); reptiles (112); amphibians (19); fishes (106); snails (20); clams (57); Crustaceans (12); insects (28); and arachnids (3).

Have students make a bar graph to display these data. To focus students' attention on the graph, ask these questions: How many total animal species are endangered or threatened? Why are there more animal species than plant species?

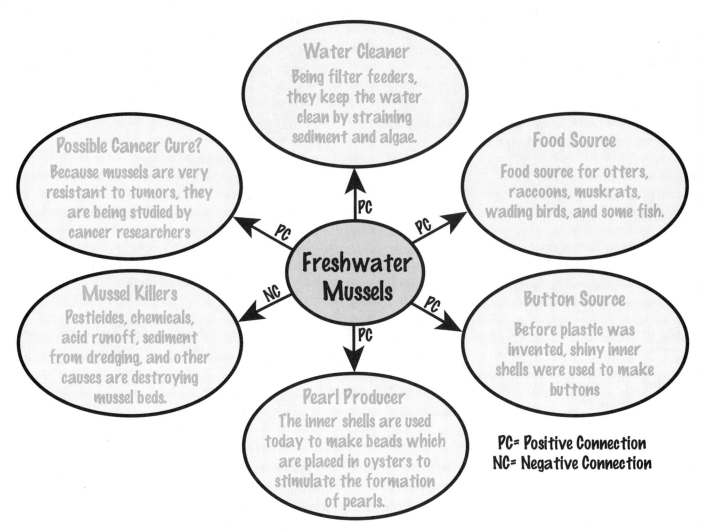

FIGURE 20-2 Connections between mussels and the rest of the world

Among the animal groups, why are mammals the largest group?

Language Arts:

1. Giving Endangered Species a Voice

Plants and animals cannot, of course, speak for themselves. They can't appear on talk shows or write letters to government officials. They are silent about their current condition and about their prospects for the future. Only humans can talk (and write) about the problems faced by endangered species. But humans won't speak for animals and plants unless they first care about them. After each student has had an opportunity to study one endangered organism in depth, let him become that plant or animal and describe the world from its perspective. Once students have decided on the content of their messages, let them design different vehicles to communi-cate them. They can choose from a variety of possibilities, such as writing poems, songs, and jingles, creating newspaper, radio, and TV ads, and developing skits and puppet shows.

Art:

1. Creating Unknown Species

Because of human activity, many animals, like the dodo and passenger pigeon, have become extinct. The dodo died out about 1680. Show students a picture of the dodo (found in an encyclopedia or other source). Explain to students that an indeterminate number of unknown species have vanished form the earth without a trace. Since they are now extinct, we will never know what these plants and animals looked like. Provide students with a variety of art and construction materials (art paper and tissue, card paper, glue, wire, pipe cleaners, Styrofoam, balsa wood, paint, magic markers, etc.). Ask each student to imagine what one of these unknown species of plants and animals might have looked like. Then, let students use their imaginations and the materials to create plants and animals that have died out. After they make their plants and animals, they can write epitaphs for them. Explain to students that an epitaph is a brief statement commemorating a deceased person. The epitaphs for their creations can commemorate the imagined lives of the vanished plants and animals.

Books:

1. Maynard, Thane. (1993). *Endangered Animal Babies.* New York: Franklin Watts. Advanced.

2. Taylor, Dave. (1992). *Endangered Wetland Animals.* New York: Crabtree Publishing Company. Advanced.

3. Steele, Philip. (1991). *Extinct Land Mammals and Those in Danger of Extinction.* New York: Franklin Watts. Intermediate, Advanced.

4. Goodall, Jane. (1990). *Gorillas.* New York: Macmillan Publishing Company. Intermediate, Advanced.

5. Bailey, Jill. (1990). *Mission Rhino.* Austin, TX: Steck-Vaughn Company. Advanced.

6. Arnold, Caroline. (1993). *On the Brink of Extinction: The California Condor.* New York: Harcourt, Brace, Jovanovich. Advanced.

7. Barrett, Norman. (1988). *Pandas.* New York: Franklin Watts. Advanced.

8. Hirschi, Ron. (1992). *Where Are My Prairie Dogs and Black Footed Ferrets?* New York: Bantam Books. Primary, Intermediate.

9. Wright, Alexandra. (1992). *Will We Miss Them? Endangered Species.* Watertown, MA: Charlesbridge Publishing. Primary, Intermediate.

Software:

1. *What Is a Habitat? What Is a Niche?* [Laserdisc]. Coronet/MTI. Primary, Intermediate, Advanced.

2. *Valuing Predators/Saving Endangered Spe-cies* [Laserdisc]. Coronet/MTI. Intermediate, Advanced.

3. *Total Amazon* [MPC CD-ROM]. Torrance, CA: Davidson/Simon & Schuster. Intermediate, Advanced.

4. *Total BioPark* [MPC CD-ROM]. Torrance, CA: Davidson/Simon & Schuster. Intermediate, Advanced.

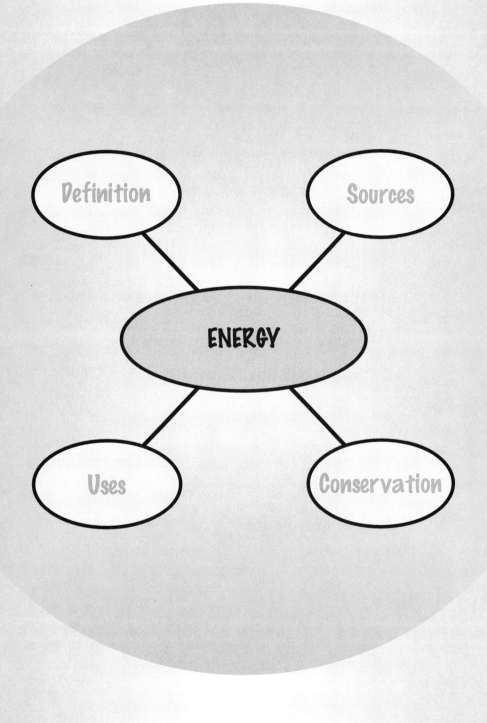

Theme Goals:

Students will:

1. define energy and list sources of energy found in the environment.

2. describe the uses of energy.

3. distinguish between different types of energy and their uses.

4. study the impact of energy on the environment.

5. research energy sources of the past.

6. discuss the safe uses of electricity.

7. write stories and poems about energy.

8. count calories and discuss how humans burn energy.

Theme Concepts:

1. Energy is the ability to get work done.

2. Living things depend on the flow of energy from the Sun.

3. Primary energy sources are: coal, oil, natural gas, nuclear, solar, wind, water, and geothermal.

4. Electricity is a secondary energy source.

5. Energy is used to generate heat and to power vehicles and machines.

6. The production and use of energy have changed the Earth's environment.

7. The supply of many energy sources is limited.

8. People should practice energy conservation.

9. New energy technologies are being developed.

10. People should learn to use electricity safely.

Vocabulary:

1. pollution

2. electricity

3. energy

4. conservation

5. work

6. energy conversion

7. geothermal energy

8. fossil fuels

9. calories

Instructional Bulletin Board

The purpose of this bulletin board is to allow students an opportunity to express and display their creative talents through the construction of an energy "quilt." Each student can choose one energy type, scene, or symbol to depict on a piece of 8 × 11" white sheet material. Let students use fabric pens to draw and color. They can decorate their work with small pieces of fabric, yarn, string, ribbon, foil, and other things that can be glued to the sheet. When completed, the pieces can be attached to the bulletin board to form a quilt design. This activity is a good way to culminate the theme on energy.

ENERGY QUILT

Lightening	Wind Mill	Waterfall Gravity	Dam	Sun
Nuclear	Ocean	Solar	Oil	Geothermal
Electricity	Muscle	Oil	Charcoal	
Wind	Wood	Wind		

Types of Energy

Parent Letter

Dear Parents:

Energy is a great theme for study in the classroom. First, children are literally full of energy. They can learn about the concept from their own bodies. Second, because we are surrounded by energy from a variety of sources and in a variety of forms, children can use their powers of observation to understand it. Third, energy is an extremely important topic: Our future depends on abundant, clean energy that does not pollute the air, land, and water.

At School:

During our study of energy your child will be involved in the following activities:

- Searching for evidence of energy at home and school
- Studying how energy changes from one form to another
- Unlocking the mysteries of electricity and learning how to use it safely
- Identifying our many uses of energy
- Investigating how energy use can pollute
- Counting, eating, and burning calories

At Home:

There are plenty of examples of energy use at home. Take your child on a guided tour of the kitchen and other rooms in the home (including garage, if applicable), pointing out examples of energy use, and cautioning against potential misuse. Energy is a fascinating subject. If your child would like to learn more about the topic at home, contact me for a list of books on energy for young readers that might be available at the school or community library.

Linking Up:

Energy can be defined as the capacity to do work. *Work*, in turn, is done when a force causes an object to change movement or shape. Write the words "energy" and "work" on the chalkboard. Ask students to think of other words that describe energy and work. List their words on the chalkboard (possible responses include: activity, power, force, drive, and strength, which are all good answers). Introduce the definition of energy given above. To demonstrate the concept of energy, show the class a small ball of clay, then squeeze the ball until it changes shape. Explain that food gave you the energy, or capacity, to work, which happened when you squeezed the ball and changed its shape. Have pairs of students create brief skits in which they pantomime a work activity. After each pair performs the pantomime, let the class try to guess the type of work, including the force and effect.

Science:

1. Sources of Energy

Have students make a list of things that supply energy. To increase motivation, tell students that most of these things are either in or near the school and/or at home. Help students identify the following energy sources: solar, gravity, wood, food, geothermal, nuclear, wind, oil (fuel oil, kerosene, and gasoline), natural gas, and coal (charcoal). Write the following examples of energy in action on the chalkboard and let students identify the correct energy sources, which are shown in parentheses. Encourage students to add items to the list.

walking (food)
boat sailing (wind)
plant growing (solar)
steaks cooking (wood, charcoal, natural gas, or
    electricity)
car moving (gasoline)
talking (food)
kite flying (wind)
light bulb shining (electricity)
geyser erupting (geothermal)
clothes drying outside (solar)
dirt flowing down a sink drain (gravity)
radio playing (electricity)

listening (food)
dog barking (food)
fire burning in fireplace (wood)
snow melting (solar)
apple dropping (gravity)

2. Uses of Energy

As an extension of Science Activity #1, assign students the task of taking one of the energy sources and examining how that source is connected to various kinds of work or changes. For example, what kinds of work does the energy source, gasoline, allow us to do? (Possible answers: power cars, trucks, boats, lawnmowers, chainsaws, etc.) Provide an assortment of old magazines and let students find and cut out illustrations that show the multiple kinds of work done by different energy sources. After they sort and label the cutouts, students can paste them on large sheets of paper to create an energy collage.

3. The Energy Conversion Process

Brief Background. Energy can change into different forms. Through the food chain, living things continuously interchange energy with their environment. By the process of *photosynthesis*, the Sun's energy is absorbed by plants and converted to carbohydrates, a primary energy source for animals. Three very important fossil fuels—coal, oil, and natural gas—were formed from plants buried in the earth for hundreds of millions of years. When they are burned, the chemical energy in them is converted to thermal or heat energy. Heat energy, in turn, can convert water into steam. Steam is used to power engines directly, and also to run turbines that generate another important energy source, electricity.

To demonstrate the energy conversion process, use a hot plate to boil water in a pan. As the steam rises, place a pinwheel above the pan. The force of the steam will cause the pinwheel to move. Ask students to diagram the conversion process, which is shown in Figure 21-1.

4. Energy Story Chains

Have students create energy story chains, like the one in Figure 21-2, that show specific examples of energy, work, and/or the conversion of energy from one form to another.

Electricity

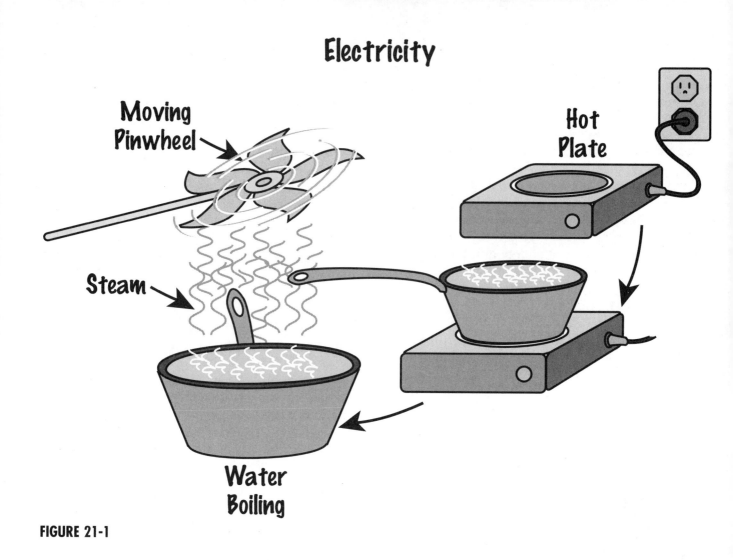

FIGURE 21-1

5. Electricity: Don't Take It for Granted

Brief Background. It is easy for children to take electricity for granted. It is always there at the flick of a switch. Electricity is called a secondary energy source because its generation requires a primary energy source—solar, falling water, oil, coal, natural gas, or nuclear.

Invite a spokesperson from the local electric utilities company to the classroom to discuss the generation, transmission, and distribution of electricity in your community. Let small groups of students make large, colorfully illustrated diagrams showing the following flow of energy as shown in Figure 21-3 on page 222.

6. Understanding the Atom

Brief Background. To understand how electricity works requires some knowledge about electro-

magnetic interactions of the atom. All matter is made up of atoms. Each atom consists of a positively charged nucleus surrounded by negatively charged electrons. All atoms contain some free electrons that are capable of moving from atom to atom. Some substances, like copper, contain many free electrons that are capable of carrying an electric circuit.

Without going into any complex details, you can demonstrate the flow of electrons through a circuit by hooking up an insulated copper wire to a battery and bulb as diagrammed in Figure 21-4 on page 223. For the bulb to light, electrons must be allowed to flow completely through the circuit. Provide students with sets of materials and let them try to light the bulb.

7. Fossil Fuel Pollution

Brief Background. Burning fossil fuels causes pollution. For example, when coal is burned, the

FIGURE 21-2   An energy story chain

sulfur in it combines with oxygen to form sulfur dioxide, which is a major source of air pollution.

Ask students to predict what will happen to the classroom environment if a match is lighted. List their predictions on the chalkboard. Let students discuss the basis for their predictions. Then, light a wood match and stand it in a lump of clay so students can watch it burn. Ask students to raise their hands if and when they think the burning

221

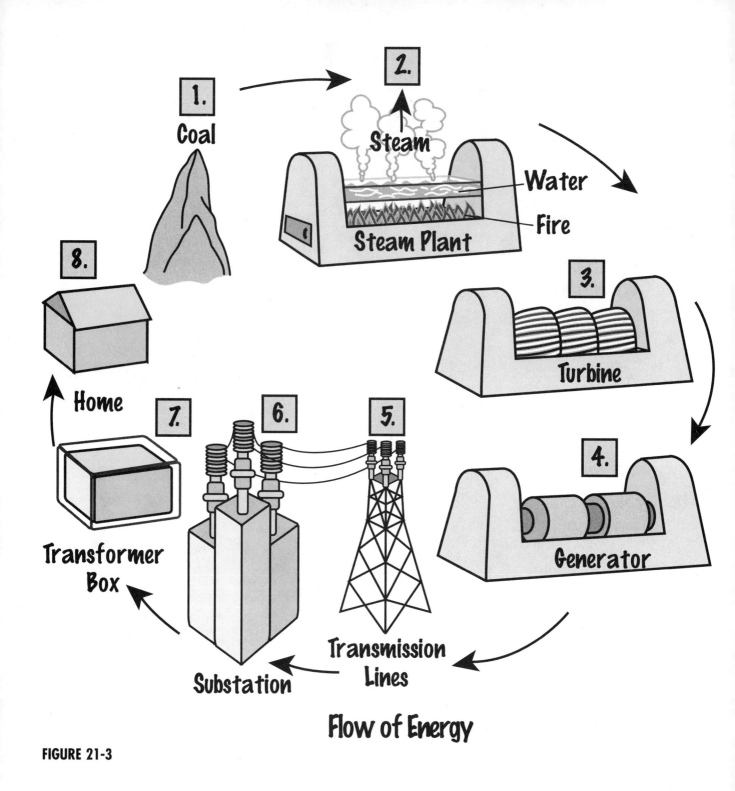

1. Coal

2. Steam

Water

Fire

Steam Plant

8.

3. Turbine

4. Generator

7. Transformer Box

6.

5.

Home

Substation

Transmission Lines

Flow of Energy

FIGURE 21-3

match has changed its surroundings. (Note: As the match burns, it adds a variety of pollutants to the air, including sulfur oxide, which has a distinct odor.) One major pollution problem in the United States is acid rain, which is caused by pollutants discharged from the smokestacks of various industrial plants. Have students investigate acid rain and other environmental problems caused by energy production and use.

Social Studies:

1. Energy in the Workplace

Ask students to explain how the following jobs depend on energy: farmer, police officer, teacher, fast-food worker, supermarket clerk, dentist, TV newscaster, chef, scientist, office

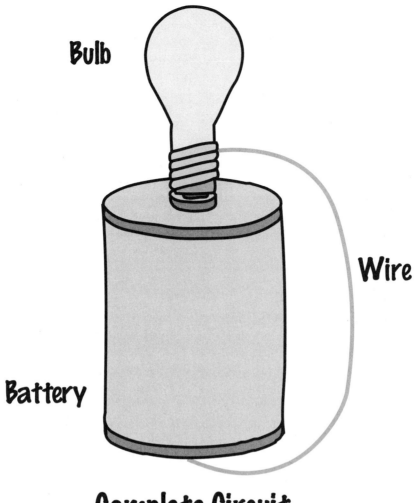

Bulb

Wire

Battery

Complete Circuit

FIGURE 21-4

worker, carpenter, truck driver, and jet pilot. Have students draw pictures of workers using energy.

2. Safety Tips

When used properly, electricity is a safe and convenient form of energy. Discuss the electrical safety rules listed below. Then assign students the task of creating a poster showing a scene in which electricity is being used safely. Students should also include a safety rule on their poster. Students can use pencils to sketch possible designs for their posters. Then, after they have chosen a design, provide sheets of heavy, white paper, felt-tip pens, and tempera paint in an assortment of colors to use in creating the posters.

- Don't play near power company equipment.
- Stay away from power lines.

- Never climb a tree or ladder that is near a power line.
- Never fly a kite near a power line.
- Never touch an electrical cord or appliance if your hands or feet are wet.
- Keep electrical appliances away from water.
- Never touch a broken wire, plug, or electrical appliance.

3. Energy Conversion

Brief Background. People have unlimited energy needs, but there are limited energy resources. The world's supply of fossil fuels— oil, coal, and natural gas—is limited and will run out eventually.

Discuss things the children can do at home to save energy. For example, under the supervision of their parents, they can keep a record of how frequently the family follows these energy conservation tips: Turn off electrical devices and appliances, such as TVs and lamps, that are not being used; shut the door tight to keep heat in and cold air out; avoid frequent trips to the refrigerator and don't leave the door open while you "look around"; take quick showers; walk, ride a bicycle, or carpool, if possible; make sure water faucets don't drip; keep the chimney damper closed when fireplace is not in use; set the thermostat at 65° F in winter; and keep the temperature at no lower than 78° F when running the air conditioner in summer. To increase motivation, award students who demonstrate sustained conservation habits "Energy Saver" certificates.

4. Energy in the Early 1800s

When compared to 200 years ago, our current energy needs and uses are very different. Challenge students to research energy needs and uses around the year 1800. What was life like back then? What kinds of work did people do? What tools and technology were available? Was life easier, or harder? Have students make a chart showing energy conditions and concerns then and now.

Language Arts:

1. Tales of Work

Bring an assortment of office, garage, and garden tools and gadgets to the classroom. Display the items and encourage students to examine them. Ask each student to imagine someone engaged in using one of them. Have each student compose a brief story that includes a character using the item in some way. The story should demonstrate the use of energy.

2. Powerful Poems

Invite students to write energy poems that include *power*ful sounds, such as *boom, gurgle, gush, bubble, pound, hammer, clang,* and *zoom.*

Math:

1. Calorie Counter

Brief Background. The energy provided by the foods we eat is measured in calories. When it comes to calories, all foods are not equal. Each gram of carbohydrate or protein equals four calories, but each and every gram of fat equals nine calories. Food packages and labels on cans and jars usually list information about calories in addition to other nutritional facts.

Bring a bunch of food labels and empty packages to the classroom and distribute two or more to each student. Let students add up the number of calories they would consume if they ate the "whole thing," or all of the food that had been in their packages and containers. Collect the containers and redistribute them so that students can get plenty of practice counting calories for a variety of different food items.

Art:

1. Fuel Savers

Challenge students to invent brand-new, energy-saving machines to replace fuel-guzzling machines currently in use. Provide a variety of art and construction materials and let them make diagrams and three-dimensional models of their inventions.

2. Energy Landscapes

Let students use pencils to draw simple landscapes showing one or more of the following energy sources: the Sun, a geyser, fire, wind, waterfall, volcano, and plants. They can fill in color by applying tempera paint with cotton swabs.

Cooking:

1. Pizza Party

Involve students in preparing pizza using the recipe on the facing page. Then have students identify how energy was used and/or converted in each step of the pizza-making process.

Movement:

1. Energy and Exercise

This activity can be related to two activities above, calorie counting and pizza eating. We measure our energy intake by counting food

RECITE

Pizza Dough:

4 cups sifted all-purpose flour
1 cup milk
4 tablespoons olive oil
1 ounce yeast

Pizza Sauce:

1 onion
1 large can of tomatoes
2 tablespoons tomato puree
1 tablespoon sugar
1 teaspoon oregano
1 tablespoon olive oil

Toppings:

Mozzarella cheese
Let children choose other toppings.
Directions: In a large bowl, mix flour, yeast, and part of the milk until mixture has the consistency of breadcrumbs. Leave to ferment 15 minutes. Add olive oil and rest of milk and knead. Wait 30 minutes. Divide dough into four equal balls and roll out each into circles. Spread pizza sauce on dough and cover with toppings. To make sauce, heat chopped onion in olive oil in saucepan until onions are translucent. Add remaining ingredients and heat. (Note: For purposes of comparison, use a manual can opener to open one can, and an electric can opener for the other.) Let sauce cool before spreading on dough. Put pizzas on cookie sheet and bake at 400° F until edges are golden brown. Cut each pizza into small slices and serve.

calories. If we consume too many calories, especially fat calories, and exercise too little, we gain weight. Maintaining a proper balance between diet and exercise is not easy. Lead your students in a series of gentle exercises, such as stretching and bending. Explain to students that as they exercise (do work), they are also burning up food calories.

Books:

1. Ardley, Neil. (1992). *The Science Book of Energy*. London: Gulliver Books. Primary.

2. Podendorf, Illa. (1982). *A New True Book Energy*. Chicago: Children's Press. Primary.

3. Taylor, Barbara. (1990). *Energy and Power*. New York: Franklin Watts. Primary, Intermediate.

4. Lafferty, Peter. (1992). *Force and Motion*. New York: Darling Kindersley, Inc. Advanced.

5. Jennings, Terry. (1982). *The Young Scientist Investigates Energy*. Chicago: Children's Press. Intermediate.

6. Gardner, Robert. (1987). *Energy Projects for Young Scientists*. New York: Franklin Watts. Advanced.

7. Asimov, Isaac. (1975). *How Did We Find Out About Energy?* New York: Walker and Company. Advanced.

8. Hawkes, Nigel. (1994). *New Technology Energy*. New York: Twenty-First Century Books. Intermediate, Advanced.

Software:

1. *Learning About Electricity* [Laserdisc VHS]. Chatsworth, CA: AIMS. Primary, Intermediate, Advanced.

2. *New A+ Science* [Mac IBM Windows]. Oklahoma City: American Education Corporation. Primary, Intermediate, Advanced.

3. *All About Science I* [Mac IBM CD-ROM]. Fairfield, CT: Queue. Advanced.

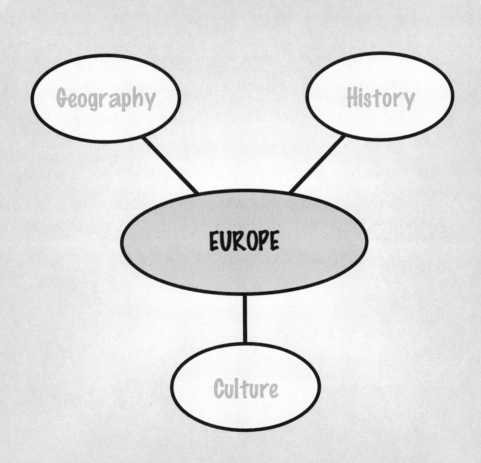

Theme Goals:

Students will:

1. examine European influences on American history.

2. identify important geographic features of Europe.

3. identify cultural characteristics of Europe.

4. study a European country in depth.

5. identify important European scientists and inventors.

6. use math skills to identify countries by shape and size.

Theme Concepts:

1. Many Americans can trace their cultural heritage back to Europe.

2. Europe is a continent with many peninsulas.

3. Europe and the United States are about the same size.

4. Europe is made up of many countries and cultures.

5. Wars and conflicts have played a big part in Europe's history.

6. European scientists and inventors have made many outstanding contributions to scientific knowledge.

Vocabulary:

1. peninsula

2. nationalism

3. European union

4. Bundestag

5. Bundesrat

Instructional Bulletin Board

The purpose of this bulletin board is to give students opportunities to identify important European landmarks. Attach pictures of a variety of European landmarks on the bulletin board, such as the Eiffel Tower (Paris, France), Big Ben (London, England), the Colosseum (Rome, Italy), the Parthenon (Athens, Greece), the Matterhorn mountain (Alps, Switzerland), windmills (Holland), and fjords (Norway). Make label cards for the pictures. Place labels in a pocket, and have students attach labels to the correct pictures.

EUROPEAN LANDMARKS

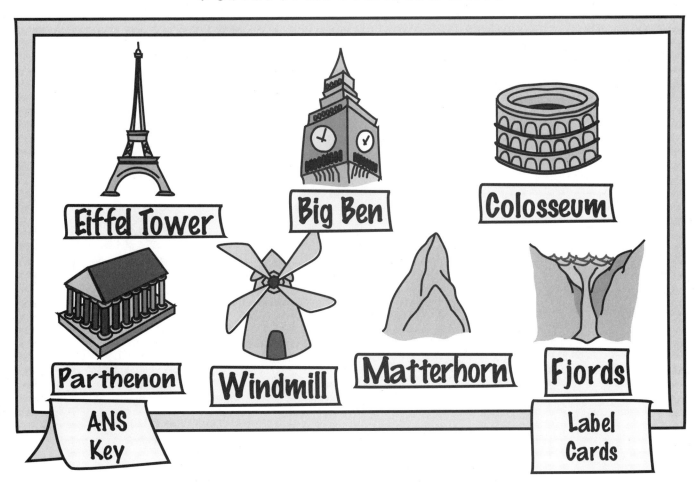

Eiffel Tower Big Ben Colosseum

Parthenon Windmill Matterhorn Fjords

ANS Key Label Cards

Parent Letter

Dear Parent:

No part of the world has had a stronger influence on American history than Europe. During our study of Europe, students will be looking at some of the United States–Europe connections. Some of the activities planned for the theme are listed below.

At School:

Your child will be:

- Tracing our European heritage on a time line
- Mapping the continent of Europe
- Sampling some European languages
- Exploring Europe's diversity
- Taking a European tour (in the classroom)

At Home:

Here are some things you can do to stimulate your child's interest in Europe.

- Make your child aware of any family connections to Europe
- Read aloud an illustrated travel book on Europe
- Ask your child what he or she would want to do on a trip to Europe

Thanks for your support.

Linking Up:

Many Americans can trace their cultural heritage back to Europe. No region of the world has influenced the course of American history more. America's major language, English, as well as American music, religious institutions, industries, educational system, government, and foods have all been heavily affected by European exploration, colonization, and immigration. Encourage students to brainstorm United States–European connections. Write their reponses on the chalkboard. Ask students to tell you what they would like to learn about Europe.

Social Studies:

1. Mapping Europe

Provide students with maps of Europe found in atlases and other sources. Make a transparency of an outline map of Europe that shows polit-ical borders. Invite volunteers to identify various countries and other geographic features on the transparency. Encourage students to share any information they have about the various countries and cultures. Ask students to describe the shape of Europe (Figure 22-1). Point out to the students that Europe is a land of peninsulas. See how many peninsulas the students can find on the map. Point out that much of Europe is near the sea. Many major European cities are located either alongside the sea or on rivers that have access to the sea. Historically, some of world's most important centers of commerce and trade were European cities that had direct access to the sea, such as Genoa, Venice, Amsterdam, and London. Ask students to locate some of Europe's major population centers on their maps. How many of these centers are on or near the sea? Europe's climate is also influenced by the sea. The winds blowing toward Europe from the Atlantic Ocean have a warming effect on the continent. Most of Western Europe has a maritime climate. Southern Europe also has a mild climate that is influenced by the Mediterranean Sea. Have students locate the At-

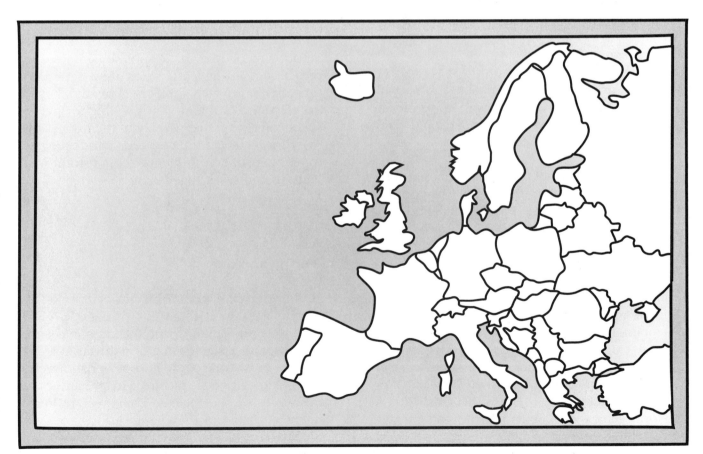

Map of Europe

FIGURE 22-1

lantic Ocean, Mediterranean Sea, and other bodies of water that border Europe.

2. European Heritage

Teach or review important events that show early European influences on our nation. Provide students with maps and index cards. Then help them create a time line of the following events:

- Columbus lands in Bahamas and claims the Americas for Spain (1492)
- Sir Francis Drake claims San Francisco region for England (1579)
- Sir Walter Raleigh establishes England's first American colony at Roanoke Island, North Carolina (1585)
- First permanent English settlement established at Jamestown, Virginia (1607)
- First African slaves brought to Virginia (1619)
- Dutch colony of New Amsterdam founded on Manhattan Island (1626)
- Swedish colony established in Delaware (1638)
- Jews arrive in New Amsterdam (1654)
- Germans arrive in Philadelphia (1683)
- Massive Irish immigration begins (1845)

3. European Languages

Brief Background. The United States is basically an English-speaking country with a significant Spanish-speaking minority. In comparison, over 35 major languages are spoken in Europe.

Compare the sizes of the United States and Europe on a wall map of the world. Point out that the United States and Europe are almost the same size. Have students look at the names of countries on the map of Europe. Tell students that many of the names are clues about the languages. As an example, point to Germany, and explain that the language spoken in Germany is German. Encourage students to guess the names of other European languages based upon these clues. Among the major languages of Europe are English, French, Spanish, Greek, German, Italian, Polish, Russian, English, Portuguese, Dutch, Czech, Danish, Swedish, Finish, Norwegian, and Ukrainian. Invite students who speak European languages to teach a few words or phrases to the whole class. Play cassette tapes of some European languages and encourage students to repeat words and phrases. Have students create brief skits in which they greet each other in a European language (other than English).

4. Cultural Tensions

Brief Background. Deep-rooted ethnic and religious tensions and conflicts have plagued Europe for centuries. Much of Europe's history is about the nations of Europe fighting among themselves. In the twentieth century, two bloody European wars—World Wars I and II—spread to almost every corner of the planet. One major cause of these wars was nationalism, or the belief that the interests of one's own nation are more important than regional or international concerns. Current European trouble spots include Northern Ireland, Bosnia, and the Basque area of Spain. Fortunately, the nations of Europe are finding ways to work together—ways that will hopefully lead to greater European cooperation and prosperity. The most significant example of European collaboration is the European Union, which is an organization designed to promote free trade among its member nations.

Have students explore pervasive issues and problems, such as hunger, pollution, and resource depletion, that require cooperation among nations to solve. Have students talk about why people and groups sometimes don't get along. In the past, when they have been upset or angry with someone, how did they try to solve the problem? Is it possible for people to become so concerned about themselves that they forget about the concerns and feelings of others? Encourage students to brainstorm ways nations can work together.

Language Arts:

1. European Tour

Take your class on an imaginary tour of Europe. First, select three to five nations in Europe to visit. Then, divide the class into small groups, and assign each group the task of "getting to know" one of the European nations chosen. Gather books, pictures, maps, and other resources on the selected countries and make them available in the classroom for your students. The background information and language arts activities that follow are for Germany, France, and Italy. Other activities can be added, of course, to extend and enhance the "tour." After the groups become "experts" on their assigned countries, they can share their knowledge with the whole class. Students can make a chart to compare and contrast the three countries, as shown in Figure 22-2.

Brief Background on Germany. Germany is a democracy like the United States. Germany's two legislative chambers are called the *Bundestag* and the *Bundesrat*. The English and German languages come from a common source. That's why many English and German words are similar (e.g., father = vater, water = wasser, apple = apfel). Some Americans drive German cars, like BMW, Mercedes-Benz, and Volkswagen. Most American children go to "kindergarten," which was a German invention. While there is no one "typical" German town, some frequent and distinctive German city-scenes include narrow cobblestone streets, sidewalk cafes, parks, fountains, statues, and stone buildings. There are also castles throughout Germany that were built in the Middle Ages. Some of the world's outstanding classical music was composed by Germans. The most popular sport in Germany is soccer. After World War II, a defeated Germany ended up divided into two parts. In 1990, however, East Germany and West Germany became one country again.

To involve students in a "trip" to Germany:

1. Get travel brochures on Germany from travel agencies. Have students cut out pictures from the brochures and write (or dictate) captions for them.
2. Read aloud some German fairy tales, such as "Rumpelstiltskin," "Hansel and Gretel," and "Snow White." Have students identify characters, setting, plot, and ending.
3. Have students study a physical map of Germany, and then write sentences that describe Germany's shape and terrain.
4. Play selections from the works of Ludwig van Beethoven, Johann Sebastian Bach, or other world-renowned German composers. Have students draw pictures that show how the music made them feel. Then, ask them to describe those feelings orally.

Brief Background on France. A love for liberty and freedom is intertwined with the history of the French people. During the Hundred Years War (fifteenth century), a young peasant girl, Joan of Arc, was inspired to lead the French against the English and save her country from defeat. France's national day is the 14th of July, which is the date of the fall of the Bastille in 1789. That is the day that the French

monarchy was overthrown and the citizens of France took control of their government. Today, France is a democratic republic with a president and two houses of parliament. Paris, the capital of France, is one of the world's most beautiful cities. Millions of tourists visit Paris annually. They come to see the Eiffel Tower, Notre Dame Cathedral, the Arch de Triumph, and many other scenic attractions.

To engage students in their "tour" of France, implement the following activities:

1. Play the national anthem of France, "La Marseillaise." This rousing song was inspired by the French Revolution. How does the music make the students feel? Have students draw pictures and write captions about their feelings.
2. The two most popular participation sports in France are soccer and tennis. Play a game of soccer on the school playground. Have a soccer player or coach show students how to play soccer. (If some students already know how to play, they can help teach the others.) Have students explain the rules of soccer and write them down in their notebooks.
3. The French tricolor flag represents much of French history. The blue is nearest the staff, the white in the middle, and the red on the outside. These three colors first became associated together when the great Frank king, Charlemagne, tied a red, white, and blue ribbon to his banner. A white flag had long been associated with the kings of France. At the time of the French Revolution, the red and blue colors that symbolized the rebellion were combined with white. The three vertical bands of colors came to stand for the people of France as a whole, rather than for the authority of the king. Provide students with rectangles of white sheet material and red and blue fabric markers, and then let them make French flags. The flags can be displayed along with a short paragraph on the significance of the flag.

Brief Background on Italy. Italy's shape is unique. The country forms a bootlike peninsula that juts southward into the Mediterranean Sea. The towering Alps divide Italy from the rest of Europe to the north. The capital of modern Italy, Rome, was the center of the western world for centuries. The remains of ancient Roman spas, temples, roads, and aqueducts, which can be found throughout Italy, are evidence of some of the splendid architectural accomplishments of the Roman Empire. Dazzling works of art from the Middle Ages and the Renaissance periods can be seen today in Rome, Florence, Venice, and Milan, as well as in smaller cities. Opera was first performed in Italy in the sixteenth century. Today, Italy is a center for fashion and handicrafts such as ceramics, glasswork, embroidery, jewelry, and violins. Italian food is popular throughout the world. Italian cooking specialties include scampi (prawns), pasta, and minestrone (soup).

To give students a flavor of Italy, give them opportunities to participate in the following activities.

1. Let students plan and cook a simple Italian meal. Help them write the menu and directions for cooking the food.
2. Provide students with illustrations of Italian paintings and sculpture, and then encourage them to describe the works of art in their own words.
3. Have students draw a large map of Italy. Students can write a paragraph description of Italy's geography to accompany their maps.

Math:

1. Sizing Up Europe's Countries

Over 30 major countries make up Europe. Have students count the countries of Europe (they can number each one on a blank political outline map.) Ask students to identify countries based on their shape, size, and location. They can identify the following: the largest countries, the smallest countries, countries that border water, landlocked countries, countries that are peninsulas, and countries that are islands.

Science:

1. Europe's Great Scientists

European scientists and inventors made outstanding contributions to scientific knowledge. Have interested students investigate one or more of the scientists listed below. The report

Comparing and Contrasting

	France	Germany	Italy
Government			
People			
Location			
Work			
Landmark			

FIGURE 22-2

should include a drawing of the invention or discovery, along with a written explanation of its significance.

Galileo (Italy; invented the telescope)
Galvani (Italy; discovered that electricity can be produced by chemical action)
Volta (Italy; discovered electric magnetism to turn dynamo)
Marconi (Italy; invented radio)
Fermi (Italy; caused first atomic chain reaction)
Newton (Britain; discovered law of gravity)
Watt (Britain; invented an "improved" steam engine)
Stephenson (Britain; invented the first successful steam locomotive)
Zeppelin (Germany; invented rigid airship)
Diesel (Germany; invented diesel engine)
Gutenberg (Germany; invented movable type)
Daguerre (France; invented photography)
Turong and others (France; invented microcomputer)
Blanchard (France; invented parachute)
de Mestral (Switzerland; invented Velcro)
Nobel (Sweden; invented dynamite)

Books:

1. Coote, Roger. (1993). *The Anglo-Saxons*. New York: Thomson Learning. Intermediate.

2. Leitner, Isabella. (1992). *The Big Lie*. New York: Scholastic Press. Intermediate, Advanced.

3. Miquel, Pierre. (1977). *18th Century Europe*. Morristown, NJ: Librairei Hachette. Advanced.

4. Roberts, Elizabeth. (1990). *Europe 1992*. New York: Gloucester Press. Advanced.

5. Miquel, Pierre. (1976). *Europe's Age of Steam*. Morristown, NJ: Librairei Hachette. Advanced.

6. Moran, Tom. (1986). *A Family in Ireland*. Minneapolis: Lerner Publications Company. Primary, Intermediate.

7. Reynolds, Jan. (1992). *Far North*. New York: Harcourt Brace Jovanovich. Primary, Intermediate.

8. Clark, Colin. (1994). *Journey Through Italy*. Mahwah, NJ: Troll Associates. Intermediate, Advanced.

9. Montanfier, Poupa. (1983). *One Summer at Grandmother's House*. Minneapolis: Carolrhoda Books, Inc. Intermediate.

10. Pellicer, Maria Eugenia D. (1988). *Spanish Food and Drink*. New York: The Bookwright Press. Intermediate, Advanced.

11. Hills, Ken. (1988). *World War I*. New York: Marshall Cavendish. Advanced.

Software:

1. *Code: Europe!* [Mac IBM]. Redmond, WA: Compu-Teach. Advanced.

2. *Swamp Gas Visits Europe* [Mac Windows]. Lake View, CN: Inline Software/Davidson. Intermediate, Advanced.

3. *World History: 20th Century* [Mac MPC CD-ROM]. New Rochelle, NY: MultiEducator, Incorporated. Advanced.

23

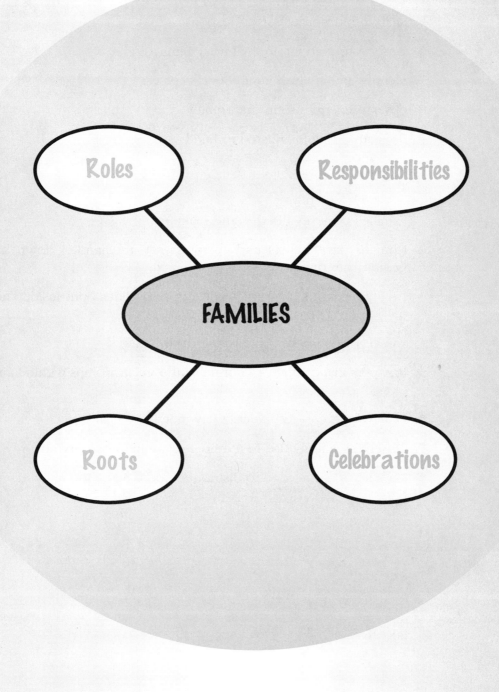

Roles

Responsibilities

FAMILIES

Roots

Celebrations

Theme Goals:

Students will:

1. make a family tree.

2. identify family traditions.

3. describe the work families do.

4. research family's ethnic/cultural heritage.

5. analyze birth-order survey responses.

6. write a story about an imaginary family.

7. identify and analyze family food choices.

8. observe energy use in the home.

9. do math problems related to family size.

Theme Concepts:

1. Families come in all sizes and makeups.

2. Families have beliefs and customs that are handed down by mouth from one generation to the next.

3. Family members have roles and responsibilities both inside and outside the home.

4. Families have ethnic/cultural ties to the past.

5. Interpersonal conflict is a normal part of relationships within families.

6. Family food choices affect family members' health.

7. Observing energy use in the home may help conserve energy.

8. Math skills are needed to distribute food equally to family members.

Vocabulary:

1. extended

2. tradition

3. adoptive

Instructional Bulletin Board

The purpose of this bulletin board is to let students display their families' photographs, using yarn to show their families' ancestral ties to countries and cultures around the world.

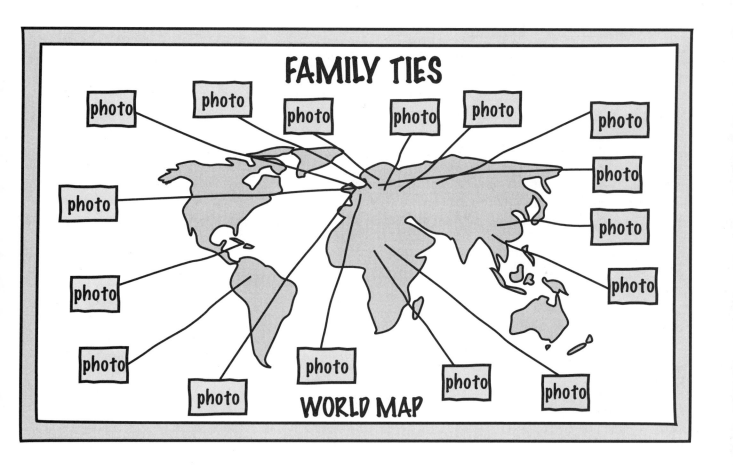

Parent Letter

Dear Parents:

It is hard to overstate the significance of the family. The family is the most important transmitter of values from one generation to the next. It is within a family structure that children acquire a sense of belonging. For our theme on families to be meaningful, much of the content must be drawn from the children. Since no topic is more personal or complex than families, we want you to look over the planned activities listed below, and to let us know if any of them appear inappropriate, given your child's feelings and sensitivities. If you have any questions or concerns, please contact us. At your request, we would be happy to provide other activities that your child would enjoy.

At School:

During our study of families, the following activities are planned:

- Constructing family trees
- Sharing family traditions
- Identifying family roles and responsibilities inside and outside the home
- Researching family ties to the past
- Conducting a birth-order survey
- Writing stories about imaginary families
- Surveying family energy use, food choices, pet choices, and family TV show, vacation, supermarket, and dessert preferences

At Home:

Since our topic is families, please spend some time talking to your child about family values and traditions. You are invited to come to our class to talk about your family's cultural heritage, and also to participate in Family Ethnic Heritage Day. Please contact us as soon as possible if you would like to join us on that day.

Hope to see you in class.

Linking Up:

No topic is more personal and complex than "families." Each family is different and each child is unique. For a unit on families to be meaningful, much of the content must be drawn from the children. Before you begin the unit, inform parents and caregivers about the assignments and activities. Ask them to convey any concerns they might have about their child's feelings and sensitivities regarding the topic (see "Parent Letter" on the preceding page). Based on feedback you receive, you may want to modify or omit one or more of the activities below. If some children do not wish to participate in a certain activity, find some other activity they would enjoy doing. Write the word "family" on the chalkboard. Ask students to tell you what they think of when they hear the word "family." As students make word associations with family, write their associations on the chalkboard.

Social Studies:

1. Family Composition

Brief Background. Families come in all sizes and makeups. Some are composed of only one child and one adult, while other families have many children and adult members. Words to describe the diversity of families include two-parent, single-parent, nuclear, extended, blended, adoptive, and foster. Words to describe family members include: mother, father, husband, wife, son(s), daughter(s), brother(s), sister(s), foster child, foster children, foster parent(s), adopted child, adoptive parent(s), natural parent(s), stepbrother(s), stepsister(s), stepparent(s), half brother(s), half sister(s), divorced parent(s), and widowed parent(s). Some families extend to grandparents, great-grandparents, great-uncles, great-aunts, uncles, aunts, nieces, nephews, and/or cousins.

To introduce students to relationships within families, read aloud *Who's Who in My Family?* by Loreen Leedy (Holiday House, 1995), or some other appropriate children's book. In Leedy's engagingly illustrated book, animal characters are cleverly used to show different types of family relationships. Provide students with an assortment of illustrated magazines and scissors, and let them cut out pictures of peo-

ple to represent family members. Each student can then paste her pictures on a large sheet of paper labeled "My Family."

2. Family Traditions

Brief Background. Most families have beliefs and customs that are handed down by word of mouth or by example from one generation to the next. Traditions vary from family to family. There are major traditions that occur annually, like sitting down to turkey dinner on Thanksgiving Day, and lesser traditions, like the family sharing a big bowl of popcorn while watching a movie or TV video on Friday night.

To encourage students to talk about how their families do various things, describe some of your own family traditions. Invite students to talk about family birthday and holiday celebrations, interests and hobbies, trips and vacations, and recreation and leisure-time activities. Do some families get together for annual picnics or reunions? Do children do things with their parents that the parents also did with their own parents? Are there certain family activities that students look forward to doing year after year? Make a list on the chalkboard of the different family traditions. Ask students to describe how the traditions make them feel. Have students compile a family traditions scrapbook for the whole class. Allot one page in the scrapbook per child. Students can include photographs, symbols, drawings, and documents that represent the traditions.

3. Working Families

Family members have roles and responsibilities both inside and outside the home. Discuss the work that parents do, and the responsibilities that children have assumed. Do children have pets they care for? Do they do chores around the house? Do they do their homework? To give students insights into how different working families cope with the demands placed on them, read selections from *Both My Parents Work* by Katherine Leiner (Franklin Watts, 1986), or some other appropriate children's book. Have students make lists of the chores they do at home. They can graph the data as shown in Figure 23-1.

4. Family Ties

Describe your own ethnic/cultural heritage. On a world map, show students where your an-

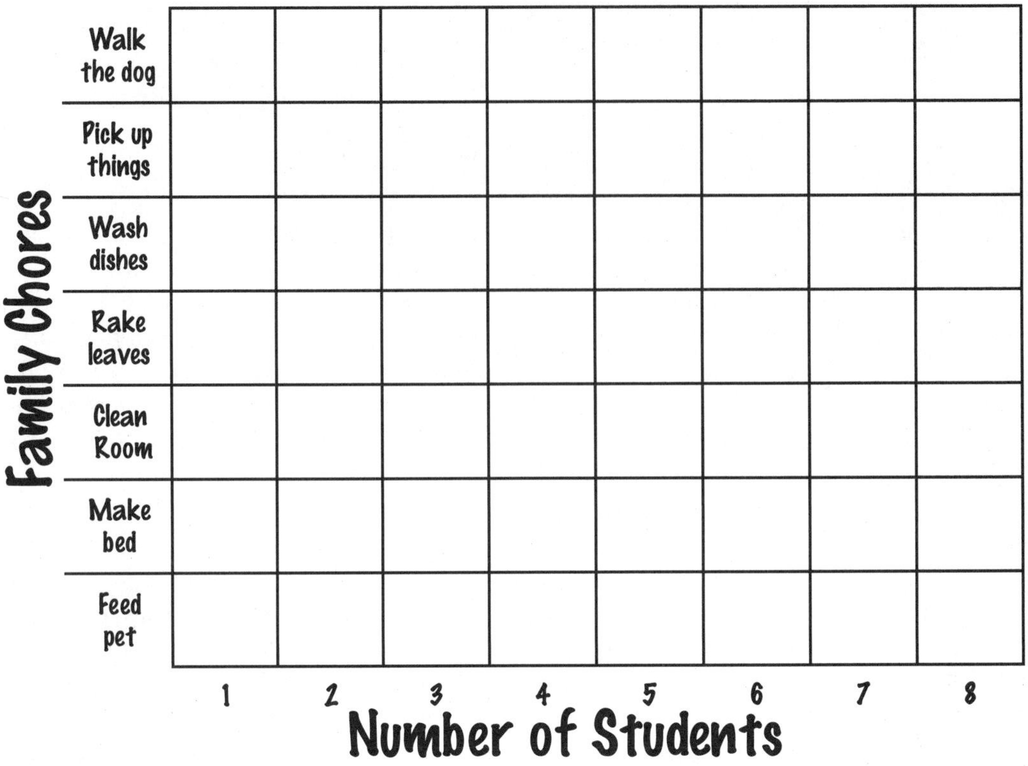

FIGURE 23-1

cestors once lived. Provide students with examples of family traditions and activities that reflect your ethnic/cultural background. For additional multicultural insights, read aloud selections from *How My Family Lives in America* by Susan Kuklin (Bradbury Press, 1992), or another appropriate children's book. Kuklin explores the customs of three families—an African American, a Chinese American, and an Hispanic American. Have students research their own families' ethnic and cultural backgrounds. Plan and hold a family heritage-day celebration. Let students decorate the room with flags, maps, symbols, and drawings that represent their families' ethnic/cultural background. Some students might volunteer to make and wear costumes that reflect their ethnic/cultural heritage. Invite members of the students' families to class to talk about or demonstrate some aspects of their cultural roots. Encourage them to bring ethnic dishes to share with the class.

Language Arts:

1. Birth-Order Survey

To encourage students to talk and write about their own experiences, help students conduct

a birth-order survey. Inspiration and procedures for the survey can be found in *The Birth-Order Blues* by Joan Drescher (Viking Penguin, 1993). In the book, children disclose their feelings about being the oldest, youngest, somewhere-in-the-middle, or only child. After your students answer the questions on birth order, help them tabulate and analyze the responses. Then, after discussion of the results, let students write about where they fit into the family, how they feel about their place, and/or how it would feel to trade places with someone in the family.

2. Imaginary Families

Growing up in families can be difficult, even under the best of circumstances. Conflict is a natural part of life, including family life. When not handled constructively or left unresolved, however, conflicts can lead to major fears and problems for children. Students can learn about themselves from stories that deal with relationships within families. "Hansel and Gretel," "Cinderella," and other familiar fairy tales, as well as other classics of children's literature, often deal with generational conflicts, sibling rivalries, and other interpersonal conflicts. Have students talk about characters, settings, plots, and endings of fairy tales they have read, or other familiar stories. Moving beyond the magic that occurs in most fairy tales, see if students can cite examples of realistic accomplishments performed by fairy tale heroes. By asking probing questions, you can determine whether or not students sense virtues, such as love, justice, and courage, in the actions of the "good" fairy tale characters. Have pairs of students make up their own fairy tales about a family. Each pair can make an illustrated book out of large pieces of construction paper, and/or the pair can write a script, make hand puppets of their fairy tale characters, and then perform a fairy tale puppet show for the class.

Science:

1. Food Choices

Draw a large food guide pyramid on the chalkboard like the one in Figure 23-2. Have students list the foods their families ate the previous day. Then, have students determine in which food groups they would be found. Have students survey family members to determine each member's favorite foods. Then, have them sort the choices into the food pyramid categories, which are as follows: (1) bread, cereal, rice, and pasta; (2) fruit; (3) vegetables; (4) milk, yogurt, and cheese; (5) meat, poultry, fish, dry beans, and nuts; and (6) oils, fats, and sweets. Which food groups are the more frequent choices of family members? Less frequent?

2. Energy Use

How much energy do family members use in the home? Have students make a list of all the household appliances and devices that use electricity. Students can ask family members to keep logs of their use of appliances and devices for one day. After the logs are completed, student can compare the results.

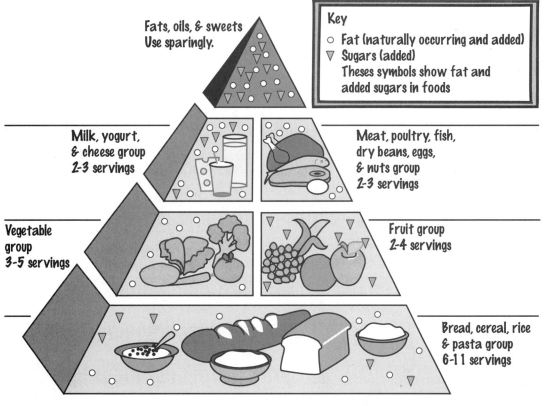

FIGURE 23-2

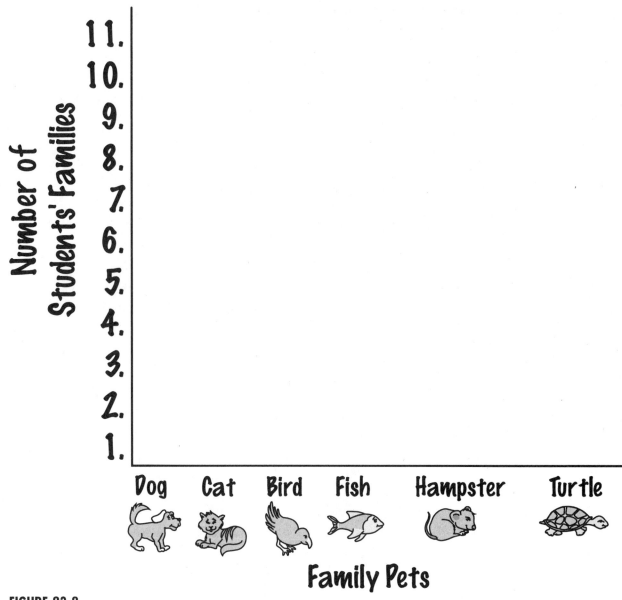

Number of Students' Families

11.
10.
9.
8.
7.
6.
5.
4.
3.
2.
1.

Dog   Cat   Bird   Fish   Hampster   Turtle

Family Pets

FIGURE 23-2

3. Family Pets

Survey the class to determine the numbers and kinds of family pets. Make a graph of the results as shown in Figure 23-2. Have students report on the care of their family pets.

4. Family Habits

Discuss ways families can control and conserve the amount of waste they produce. Have them identify natural resources that are overused and at risk. Do they recycle metal, glass, and paper? Can they eliminate or extend the use of some products? Let students brainstorm ways to decrease their use of various resources.

Math:

1. Family Size

Have each student count the total family members for his or her family. What is the total number of family members for the whole class? What is the class average?

2. Counting Members of Families

Provide students with paper and pencils. Have students take turns telling the class the number of total people in their respective families. Have students record the numbers. How many people are in all of the families? What is the average number of people in a family?

3. Sharing Food

To introduce or reinforce division, ask students how a student's family with three members could equally share six pieces of pizza or 12 cookies. Have students compute similar division problems for families with different numbers of members sharing fixed numbers of various items equally.

4. Graphing Family Data

Under your direction, students can gather, enumerate, and process data in response to the following questions about their families:

- What is your family's favorite TV show?
- Where does your family like to go on a trip or vacation?
- What is your family's favorite supermarket?
- What is your family's favorite dessert?

Books:

1. Drescher, Joan. (1993). *The Birth-Order Blues.* New York: Viking Penguin Group. Primary.

2. Leiner, Katherine. (1986). *Both My Parents Work.* New York: Franklin Watts. Intermediate.

3. Patrick, Diane. (1993). *Family Celebrations.* New York: Silver Moon Press. Intermediate, Advanced.

4. Super, Gretchen. (1992). *Family Traditions.* Frederick, MD: Twenty-First Century Books. Primary.

5. Loredo, Betsy. (1995). *Faraway Families.* New York: Silver Moon Press. Advanced.

6. Drescher, Joan. (1980). *Your Family, My Family.* New York: Walker and Company. Primary.

7. Berger, Melvin, and Berger, Gilder. (1993). *Where Did Your Family Come From?* Nashville: Ideals Children's Books. Intermediate.

8. Leedy, Loreen. (1995). *Who's Who in My Family?* New York: Holiday House. Primary.

9. Kuklin, Susan. (1992). *How My Family Lives in America.* NY: Bradbury Press. Intermediate.

Software:

1. *Family Tree Maker* [IBM Windows MPC CD-ROM]. Novato, CA: Broderbund/Banner Blue. Advanced.

24

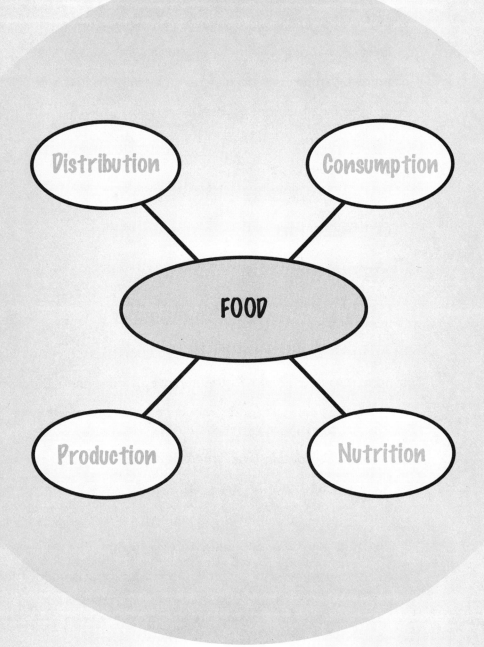

Theme Goals:

Students will:

1. categorize foods into the following nutrient groups: protein, fats, and carbohydrates.

2. compare diets from different cultures.

3. know that food resources are not distributed evenly throughout the world.

4. test food products to determine the best buy.

5. keep a food diary.

6. predict changes that occur when foods are heated and frozen.

7. analyze fat content of foods.

8. distinguish fruits and vegetables.

9. create a class cookbook.

10. make predictions.

11. conduct a survey.

Theme Concepts

1. Foods contain protein, carbohydrates, fats, water, vitamins, and minerals.

2. Cultures around the world have developed very diverse diets.

3. Food resources are not distributed evenly throughout the world.

4. Consumers can test food products to evaluate whether or not they are the best buys for the money.

5. Some foods contain large amounts of fat.

6. Seed-bearing structures are fruits.

7. Students can work together to create a class cookbook.

8. Vegetables are an important part of a healthy diet.

9. A survey is a way to gather information about students' food preferences.

Vocabulary:

1. nutrient

2. protein

3. fat

4. carbohydrates

Instructional Bulletin Board

The purpose of this bulletin board is to give students practice conducting a survey and constructing a pictograph of the resultant data. Have each student cut out the front side of an empty box of his or her favorite cereal and bring it to class. Have each child attach the cereal box so that the same brand/kind are in the same column on the board to form a pictograph. After the pictograph is finished, let students answer the following questions: How many cereal boxes are in each column? What does each box represent? What does the pictograph tell us about our class's cereal preferences?

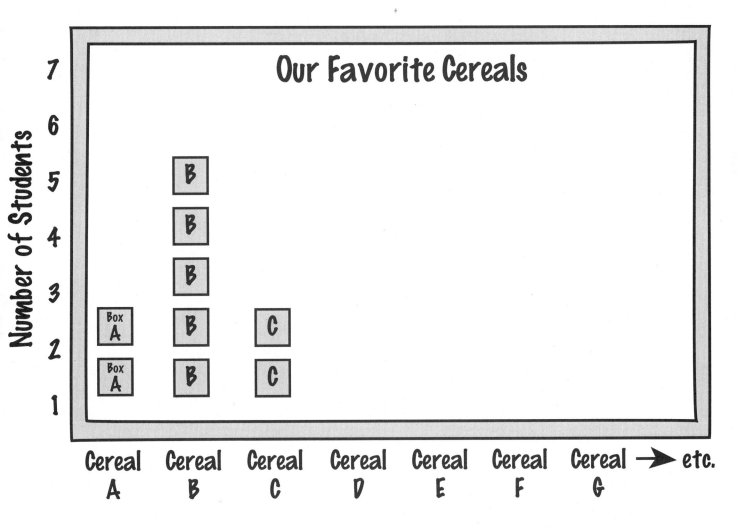

Parent Letter

Dear Parents:

Nothing can get children's attention any faster than food. During our study of this theme, your child will have a chance to examine food from many different perspectives. Specifically, the class will be engaged in the activities listed below.

At School:

- Investigating the nutrients in foods
- Comparing diets from different cultures
- Working to find food for all
- Testing brands of foods
- Keeping a food diary
- Analyzing fat in foods
- Creating a class cookbook
- Conducting a food-preferences survey

At Home:

As mentioned above, we are going to develop a class cookbook. Our goal is to include recipes from all of the families represented in the class. We know it will mean a lot to your child to have his or her family's recipe in the cookbook. Please talk to your child about the cookbook project. We look forward to receiving a family recipe from you as soon as possible.

Linking Up:

The quickest way to link this topic to your students' lives is to ask them about their favorite and least favorite foods. After students have discussed their preferences, have them make predictions regarding the food preferences of students in other classrooms. Then, let them conduct a schoolwide favorite food survey. If other teachers agree, let students visit other classes to conduct the survey. Respondents can write down (or dictate) their answers to the following two questions: What is the food you like best? and What is the food you hate most? Help students process, analyze, and graph the results. Are there differences in students' food preferences across grade levels? Were the students' predictions accurate?

Social Studies:

1. Eating Healthy

Brief Background. Foods contain protein, carbohydrates, fats, water, vitamins, and minerals. The human body needs certain amounts of these nutrients daily to maintain good health.

Some important sources of these nutrients are listed below. Introduce or review the sources, and then make certain students have a basic understanding of them. Ask students to list some of the common foods they eat. After they have compiled the list, ask the following: "What foods on your list supply you with one or more of these nutrient sources?"

Sources of protein: meat, fish, eggs, milk, poultry, soybeans, and nuts.
Sources of fats: butter, margarine, salad oils, nuts, cream, ice cream, egg yolks, cheese, and meat.
Sources of carbohydrates: sugars, vegetables, grains, beans, nuts, potatoes, and fruit.

2. Diet Diversity

Although everyone, everywhere must eat, people around the world have developed very diverse diets. Have students compare the typical foods they eat with the traditional diets from other cultures below. What food items are also on the students' list? What might account for differences in diet around the world?

Pacific Islands	Central America	Japan
Taro*	Tortillas	Rice
Breadfruit**	Black beans	Oranges
Bananas	Pineapple	Fish
Fish	Papaya	Soybean soup
Coconuts	Cheese	Seaweed
Taro leaves	Chard	Strawberries
Limes	Squash	Green onions

*Potato-like vegetable
**Grows wild on trees; when baked, tastes like bread

To give students additional insights into cross-cultural cookery, read aloud selections from Yvonne McKenley's *A Taste of the Caribbean* (Thomson Learning, 1995), *Cooking the Spanish Way* by Rebecca Christian (Lerner, 1982), and Lucille Penner's *A Native American Feast* (Macmillan, 1994), or other appropriate children's books.

3. Sharing Food and Good Fortune

Brief Background. Natural resources are not distributed evenly throughout the world. America has more than its fair share of optimum climate and soil conditions necessary for the production of agricultural goods. As a result, the United States produces much more food than it can consume. Some parts of the world, especially in the developing nations of Asia, Africa, and Latin America, do not have enough food to feed their large populations. One of the big problems the world must solve is how to feed so many people. It has been estimated that about 16 percent of the world's population (800 million) are unable to grow, or buy, the food they need.

To introduce the concept of *scarcity*, start with classroom supplies and show that there are not always enough pencils, computers, reference books, and other desired items for all children. To demonstrate the problem of food scarcity and global hunger, involve students in the following activity. If we imagined that a class of 20 students represented the earth's total population, then three students (slightly less than 16 percent) in the class would go hungry. To give students a sense of the magnitude of the world food problem, open a small package of M&Ms (any highly desired food can be used) and distribute them equally to 84 percent of your class (put the M&Ms on small paper plates and tell students to look but don't touch). Tell the students that the M&Ms on their plates represent all of the world's food. Do students think it's fair that some of them get candy while others don't? Let students discuss this issue. Are they sensitive to others' needs? Conclude the activity by redistributing the M&Ms equally to all members of the class. Are the students happy that everyone in the class received an equal share of M&Ms?

Science:

1. Consumer Research

Discuss the effects of cereal, candy, and cookie ads and commercials on students' brand pref-

erences. Introduce the idea that consumers can test products to evaluate whether or not they are the best buys for the money. Have students compare different brands of chocolate chip cookies to determine which is best in terms of cost per ounce, taste, crumbling, and average number of chips per cookie. Select three (or more) brands of chocolate chip cookies to test. Show students how to test the brands as follows:

1. To determine the cost per ounce, divide the cost of the package by the total number of ounces in the package to find the unit cost.
2. To test for taste, have a group of students taste each brand of cookie and award from 1 to 5 points, with 1 = bad taste and 5 = great taste. To ensure objectivity, cover up the brand labels during the taste test so students do not know the names of the brands they are tasting.
3. Crumbling can be determined by measuring the amount of crumbling caused by shaking the cookie inside a paper bag.

	Brand A	Brand B	Brand C
Cost per ounce			
Crumbling			
Taste			
Number of chips per cookie			

Comparing Brands

FIGURE 24-1

4. The average number of chocolate chips contained in a cookie can be measured by counting the number of chocolate chips in each of three cookies, and then adding the three numbers and dividing the total by three.

To ensure valid results, make certain that students make careful measurements and keep accurate records. Have students make a chart like the one in Figure 24-1 to organize and display their research.

2. What Happens?

Have students predict changes that occur when different foods are heated and frozen. Let students record their observations on a retrieval chart as shown in Figure 24-2.

3. Heavy and Empty Calories

Brief Background. The energy provided by the food we eat is measured in calories. People gain weight when they consume more calories than they burn up. One gram of fat has more than twice as many calories as one gram of carbohydrates or protein (9 calories, compared to 4). That is why consumption of fat is so hard to limit to only 30 percent or less of total daily calories, yet this is the amount that dietary guidelines allow. Consumption of some simple carbohydrates, like cake, soft drinks, and other "junk" foods, also should be

What Happens?		
	Heat	Freeze
Milk		
Chocolate bar		
Green bean		
Marshmallow		
Sugar		
Jello		
Syrup		

FIGURE 24-2

limited. Rather, than being heavy on sweets, a healthy diet should include plenty of complex carbohydrates, like grains, fruits and vegetables.

Distribute empty food packages to students. Have them imagine they have just finished eating the foods that were in the empty packages. Help them calculate the protein, carbohydrate, and fat calories they would have consumed if they had eaten the foods. Have students keep a daily diet diary in which they record all of the foods (and calories) they eat.

4. Testing for Fat

Many foods Americans love to eat, such as pies, ice cream, and candy bars, contain a high percentage of both fat and sugar. Provide students with small pieces of different kinds of fatty and non-fatty foods (e.g., hot dogs, salad oils, avocadoes, bananas, cheese, broccoli, carrots), and then have them place a small amount of the foods on absorbent brown paper hand towels. Print the name of the food on a card and place the card next to the food. After one hour, have students remove the foods and observe any fat residue that remains on the paper. Which foods left the biggest fat spots? The smallest? Which foods left no fat spots at all? Have students make charts and graphs to display their findings.

5. Resolving the "Is It a Fruit or Vegetable" Question

Brief Background. Since some fruits are called vegetables and vice versa, it's sometimes easy to get confused about the two. To help students distinguish between them, have them apply the following rule: If the plant part contains seeds, it is a fruit; and if it doesn't, it is a vegetable. Given this rule, the tomatoes, cucumbers, and green pep-

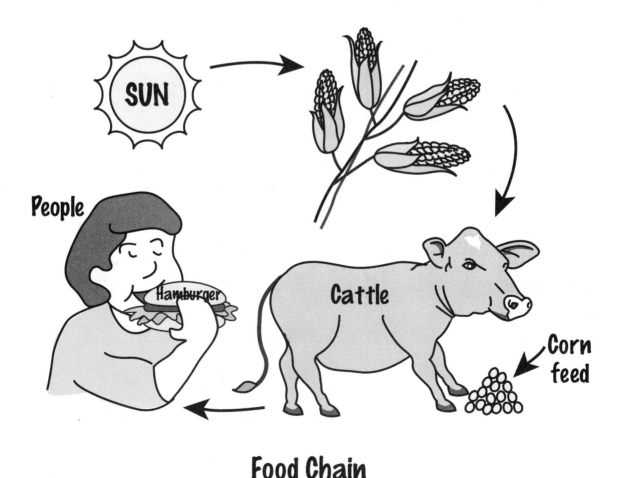

Food Chain

FIGURE 24-3

254

pers found in the supermarket would be classified as fruits since all three are seed-bearing plants.

Provide students with the edible parts of a variety of plants, and let them search for seeds in them. They can classify the plant structures into the following groups: fruits (seed-bearing) and vegetables (non–seed bearing).

6. The Food Chain

Brief Background. Through the food chain, matter and energy are constantly interchanged. The food chain shows the relationship between energy sources. Plants store energy from the Sun and are basic to the food supply of all living things. Some animals eat only plants, and they, in turn, are eaten by animals that, in turn, are eaten by other animals. For example, grain from corn is used for cattle feed, and cattle, in turn, are slaughtered and reach the consumer as food in restaurants or fresh meat in supermarkets.

Provide students with pictures of plants and animals (including people), and have them arrange two, three, or more pictures to show the relationship of energy sources in a food chain as shown in Figure 24-3.

Language Arts:

1. Class Cookbook

From hearty stews, fruity pies, creamy casseroles, flavorful soups, and homemade breads, to scrumptious deserts—almost every family has a cherished recipe or two that they enjoy preparing and eating again and again. Have students gather family recipes from home. You may want to call parents and relatives to elicit their support. After the recipes are collected, have each student use a standard format to neatly copy down his or her recipe on a regular sheet of 8 1/2" × 11" paper. The heading for each recipe should read "The _____ Family Recipe for _____." If possible, have each student attach a photograph of her family to the recipe page. The recipes can then be duplicated and collated to create the cookbooks. Personalized covers for the cookbooks can be laminated and bound (use a 19-hole binding machine if available).

2. Love a Vegetable

It seems that many kids love to hate vegetables. To counter this nutritionally disastrous attitude, challenge each student to "become" a particular vegetable while trying to convince the class that the vegetable should be loved—read "eaten"—by the class. Let each student create a poem or brief skit about the nutritional benefits of his vegetable. Encourage students to create vegetable costumes for their presentations.

Math:

1. Predicting Amounts

First, have students predict the number of pieces contained in small packages of the foods listed below. Then, let students open the packages and count the pieces inside. How close were their predictions to the actual numbers?

Food Package	Number Predicted	Number Counted
M&Ms		
Reese's Pieces		
pretzels		
peeled baby carrots		

Art:

1. Papier-Mache Fruits and Vegetables

Provide students with an assortment of firm, hard-surfaced fruits and vegetables. Let students cover the plant structures with wet paper and paste. After the paper dries, you can use a sharp modeling knife to cut the papier-mache in half and separate it from the plant. Let students use more wet strips of paper and paste to reattach the two halves. Students can paint the papier-mache so that it looks like the real plant. Display the colorful papier-mache plants in trays and baskets placed around the classroom.

Cooking:

1. Cooperative Soup

Make a pot of vegetable soup for the students to enjoy, and let everyone in the class contribute an ingredient. Start with six to eight cans of beef broth. Then, let children add the following vegetables (cut in small pieces) to the pot:

1/4 cup fresh parsley
4 large potatoes
2 onions
1 turnip
1 cup mushrooms
3 carrots
2 small zucchinis

Books:

1. Steele, Philip. (1994). *Food and Feasts In Ancient Rome*. New York: New Discovery Books. Intermediate.

2. Steele, Philip. (1994). *Food and Feasts Between the Two World Wars*. New York: New Discovery Books. Intermediate.

3. Dawson, Imogen. (1994). *Food and Feasts in the Middle Ages*. New York: New Discovery Books. Intermediate.

4. Badt, Karin. (1994). *Good Morning, Let's Eat*. Chicago: Children's Press. Primary, Intermediate.

5. Baldwin, Margaret. (1983). *Thanksgiving*. New York: Franklin Watts. Intermediate.

6. McKenley, Yvonne. (1995). *A Taste of the Caribbean*. New York: Thomson Learning. Primary, Intermediate.

7. Christian, Rebecca. (1982). *Cooking the Spanish Way*. Minneapolis: Lerner Publications Company. Intermediate.

8. Zubrowski, Bernie. (1981). *Messing Around With Baking Chemistry*. Boston: Little, Brown and Company. Primary, Intermediate.

9. Kaur, Sharon. (1989). *Food in India*. Vero Beach, FL: Rourke Publications, Inc. Intermediate, Advanced.

10. Penner, Lucille. (1994). *A Native American Feast*. New York: Macmillan Publishing Company. Intermediate.

Software:

1. *What Is an Ecosystem?/What Is a Food Chain?* [Laserdisc]. Coronet/MTI. Primary, Intermediate, Advanced.

25

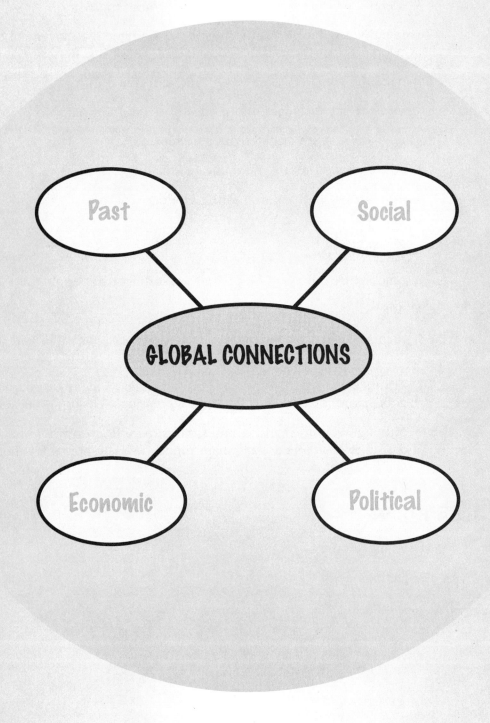

Theme Goals:

Students will:

1. identify family connections to countries and cultures.

2. describe groups that immigrated to the United States.

3. identify products made in countries around the world.

4. identify geographic features that have inhibited the movement of people across the Earth.

5. trace the spread of ideas over time and space.

6. measure the distances and modes of travel from place to place.

7. read stories with an international theme.

8. create a mural representing the world's people.

9. listen to music from around the world.

Theme Concepts:

1. America is comprised of a diverse assortment of people.

2. America is a land of immigrants.

3. Immigrants have come to America to seek a better life, and to escape starvation, persecution, and poverty.

4. Advances in technology have made the movement of people, goods, and ideas across the Earth increasingly easier and faster.

5. Although countries and cultures differ, people everywhere have the same basic needs and share the same basic hopes for their children's future.

Vocabulary:

1. immigration

2. technology

3. culture

Instructional Bulletin Board

The purpose of this bulletin board is to highlight the world's people, products, and ideas, and connect them to the students' lives. Attach a consumable, blank wall map of the world to the bulletin board. (Note: The map should show the political boundaries of nations, but no other geographic features.) Assign each student the task of finding examples of our international connections. Encourage them to bring in pictures of people and products, as well as news articles, about other countries and cultures. When a student brings in an international item, he can attach it to the bulletin board, color in the appropriate country on the world map, and then connect them with pins and yarn.

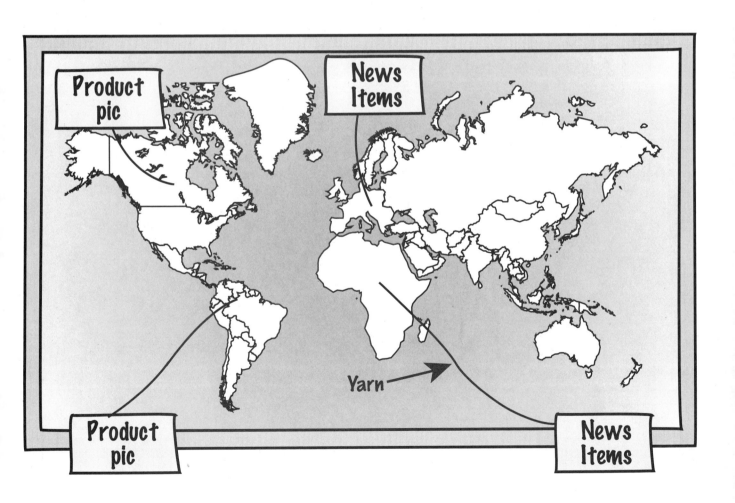

Parent Letter

Dear Parents:

The United States is a diverse nation. We can trace our roots back to people and places around the globe. In our shrinking world, it is very important that students both appreciate different countries and cultures and understand the many ways in which they are connected to them. During our study of global connections, we will focus on what has brought the world's people closer together. Listed below are some of the activities we have planned for your child.

At School:

During our theme of study, students will be:

- Creating an ethnic heritage album
- Collecting oral histories
- Studying an immigrant group's country and culture
- Identifying products in the global marketplace
- Tracing how ideas spread from place to place
- Reading international stories
- Making a mural of the world's peoples
- Enjoying music from around the world

At Home:

Evidence of global connections can be found all over the home. Furniture, appliances, tools, foods—the list of products made in other countries seems to get longer and longer. Together with your child, identify products in the home that come from other countries. After you compile a list, your child can bring it to school to share with the class. Finally, if you and your family have any special international connections that you would like to share with the class, please let us know.

Linking Up:

In today's global marketplace, people buy products made in countries around the world. Have students check labels on clothing, shoes, and other personal and classroom items to determine where they were made. Make a list of the nations that made the products and help students find their locations on a globe and on a wall map of the world. Which parts of the world supplied the most products? What other products that come from other countries can students list?

Social Studies:

1. America's Roots

Brief Background. America is comprised of a diverse assortment of individuals. Native Americans were the first people who lived on the land we know as America. On the other hand, some people living in the United States today were born in other countries and arrived here only recently. The ancestors of most African Americans were forced to come to the United States. Most Americans, however, are the descendants of immigrants who came here willingly in search of a better life.

Have students check with parents to find out about their roots. How many countries and continents are represented? Make a list of them. Compare the class's ethnic composition with other classes across the nation (students can write or E-mail other schools).

2. Ethnic Photo Album and Scrapbook

You will need a large-size photo album book. Devote one page of the book to each of your students. Encourage each student to gather or develop materials, suitable for placement in the album, that reflect his or her ethnic heritage, such as the following: family photographs, a map and a flag or other symbol that represents the student's ethnic background, and drawings and pictures that reflect some aspects of the student's ethnic background.

3. Collect Oral Histories

Let students interview older family members to find out about their elders' recollections of any family connections in the past to other countries and cultures. Among the questions students can ask are the following: What makes you proud of the country/culture? What are some of the country's/cultures's important geographic features, historical characters, beliefs, customs, holidays, and special events?

4. Compile an Ethnic Cookbook

Students can bring favorite family recipes, which can be compiled in an ethnic cookbook. What ingredients are in the recipes? What is the origin of the ingredients?

5. Ethnic Pride

On a rotating basis, highlight each student in the classroom with a bulletin board display that includes photographs and information that reflect the person's ethnic heritage.

6. Immigration in the Past

Explain to students that an immigrant is someone who comes to a country to live. Millions of immigrants have come to America. Show students historical photographs of immigrants who have just landed at Ellis Island in New York or at other port cities in the United States. Ask students why people would leave their homeland and go to a strange land. Probe to see if students are aware that people have many reasons for coming here, including to escape war, poverty, starvation, and religious persecution, as well as to find a better job and living conditions. Divide the students into small groups. Assign each group the task of assuming the roles of family members coming to the United States in the nineteenth century from one of the immigrant groups listed below. Read aloud selections that describe these different immigrant groups and tell about their experiences. Provide each student group with pictures, books, and other resources about its immigrant group. Family members in each group can study their immigrant group's country and culture, discuss reasons for leaving, list items to take with them to America, and discuss where they would like to live and what they would like to do once they arrive. Have each "family" present a short skit on its experiences as it prepares to leave home, journeys across the ocean, and arrives in America.

Who	When	Why
Irish	1840s and 1850s	To escape starvation caused by potato famine
Germans	1840s to 1880s	To escape unemployment and political turmoil
Scandinavians	1870s to 1890s	To escape bad harvests and starvation
Jews	1880s to 1920s	To escape religious persecution
Eastern Europeans	1880s to 1920s	To escape poverty, overpopulation, and/or political repression
Italians	1880s to 1920s	To escape poverty and overpopulation

7. Immigration Today

Since the 1950s, Asians and Latin Americans have become major immigrant groups. Help students identify the major immigrant groups in the local community. Invite a recent immigrant to your class to talk about why he or she came to America to live.

Science:

1. The World Is Getting Smaller

Provide students with globes and world maps that show topographical features. Help students locate features on the Earth's surface that are natural dividing barriers, such as lakes, canyons, oceans, rivers, mountain ranges, and deserts.

Have students discuss any obstacles to the movement of people during different periods of history. Write "The world is getting smaller" on the chalkboard and read it aloud to the class. Invite students to explain what the statement means. Tell students that, of course, the world isn't really getting smaller. It just seems that way, because the invention of new machines makes it easier and easier to move people, goods, and ideas around faster and faster. Provide students with an assortment of magazine and scissors, and let them cut out pictures of machines that have helped make the world smaller. As students come up with examples, help them sort the examples into broad categories, such as transportation and communication. Students can glue their pictures to a large sheet of paper to create a collage suitable for displaying on the wall.

INVENTIONS AND DISCOVERIES

What	Who	Where	When
			B.C.
Potter's wheel	?	Mesopotamia	3500
Paper	?	China	140
			A.D.
Rubber	?	Latin America	?
Microscope	Jannsen	Holland	1590
Barometer	Torricelli	Italy	1643
Steam engine	Watt	Scotland	1765
Photography	Daguerre	French	1839
Diesel engine	Diesel	Germany	1893
Early Tape Recorder	Poulsen	Denmark	1898
Jet engine	Whitte	England	1930

2. The Spread of Ideas

People in the United States, including the students, have benefitted from the contributions of inventors and discoverers from around the world. Show students the list on the preceding page, and have them do one or more of the following activities.

- Find each inventor's or discoverer's homeland on a map.
- Explain how the invention/discovery affected people's lives.
- Make a time line of the inventions and discoveries.

3. Faraway Foods

Many of the foods we eat are grown and produced in other countries. Bring in an assortment of imported foods (both produce and packaged or canned foods) for students to examine. Make a list of where they come from. Have students observe the produce and package labels close up. Help students classify the foods into the following categories: vegetables, fruits, meats, dairy products, and grains. What do the foods tell the students about the countries that produced them? Over time, foods spread from their places of origin to places throughout the world. Help students locate on a map the place of origin of the following popular foods:

Hot dogs or frankfurters (Germany)
Pizza (Italy)
Ice cream (United States)
Popcorn (South America)
Coffee (Ethiopia)
Potato (South America)
Chocolate (Mexico and Central America)

Math:

1. How Far Is Far

Provide students with road maps and world atlases, as well as schedules of airplane, bus, train, and ship departures to, and arrivals from, different places around the world. To compare distances and travel times between places, help students fill in the chart below.

2. Counting Our Global Connections

Have students identify and count objects in the classroom that come from other countries. Make certain they check items carefully; the identification data are sometimes hard to spot. What is the total number? Are there many or few? If all of these foreign-made objects were removed from the classroom, would it affect students' ability to learn? Encourage other teachers in the school to do the same activity, and then compare their totals with your classroom's. How many more (less) items are there in one classroom compared to another? Which classroom has more, less, the most, the least? What is the average number for all of the classrooms?

Language Arts:

1. International Stories

Children's literature can take students anywhere, anytime. Through books, they can travel to tropical jungles, frozen wildernesses, ancient ruins, and glittering cities. They can discover how other people live and work, find out how they feel about their world, and ex-

DISTANCES AND TRAVEL TIMES						
		Days, Hours, and Minutes				
	Miles	Airplane	Ship	Train	Bus	Car
To:						
From:						
To:						
From:						
To:						
From:						

perience cultural commonalities and connections. To encourage reading and heighten interest in other cultures, create a "Worldly Readings Passport" for each child. To make each passport, following these steps: Cut two sheets of letter-size plain white paper in half, put the resultant four strips of paper on top of each other, fold the stack of paper strips in half, spread the sheets open, staple them together at the crease, and then refold in half to form a 16-page booklet. Let each student personalize his or her book by decorating the cover. Inside the cover (page 1), have each student list the following "passport" information: name, address (including state and country), height, weight, hair color, and eye color. Each student can attach a small photograph of himself on page 1. Each time a student reads (or is read aloud to, if appropriate) a book with an international theme, have her print the book's title and the name of the country/culture it is about on a passport page. After you have verified that the task was accomplished, you can officially "stamp" the passport by attaching a postage stamp or miniature flag sticker of that country to the page. (Note: Inexpensive packages of canceled stamps from around the world can be purchased at stamp and coin shops, and world

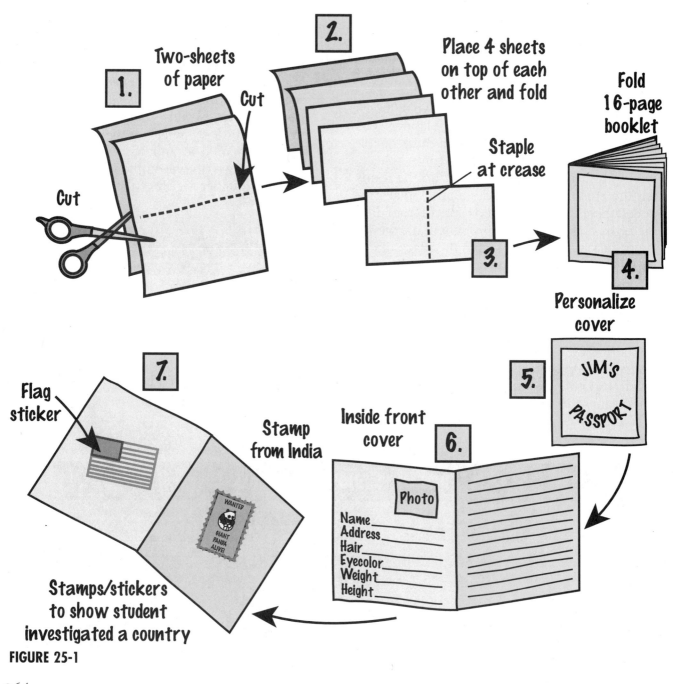

1. Two-sheets of paper Cut Cut

2. Place 4 sheets on top of each other and fold Staple at crease

3.

4. Fold 16-page booklet Personalize cover

5. JIM'S PASSPORT

6. Inside front cover Photo Name___ Address___ Hair___ Eyecolor___ Weight___ Height___

7. Flag sticker Stamp from India WANTED GIANT PANDA ALIVE! Stamps/stickers to show student investigated a country

FIGURE 25-1

flag stickers can usually be found at teacher supply stores.)

Art:

1. Peoples of the World Mural

Pair up students. Assign each pair the task of researching the traditional clothing worn by an important cultural group within a particular country. Have the students make a large class mural of the world. Provide art materials, and have the pairs of students take turns drawing or painting people dressed in appropriate clothing for the country. A flag of the country should also be painted next to each drawing.

Music:

1. World Music

Because of the global entertainment industry, people everywhere are enjoying each other's music. Encourage students to share their favorite music with the class. Play selections of music from different countries and cultures, such as the following (audiotapes, laserdiscs, and CD-ROMs may be available from the music teacher or media center): reggae (Jamaica), mariachi band (Mexico), opera (Italy), polka (Poland), samba (Brazil), sitar music (India), and blues (the United States). Have students compare and contrast the sounds of the different music.

Books:

1. Riquier, Aline. (1984). *Cotton in Our T-shirt*. Ossining, NY: Editions Gallimard. Primary, Intermediate.

2. Ganeri, Anita. (1992). *France and the French*. New York: Gloucester Press. Advanced.

3. Ganeri, Anita. (1992). *Germany and the Germans*. New York: Gloucester Press. Advanced.

4. Badt, Karin Luisa. (1994). *Greetings*. Chicago: Children's Press. Intermediate, Advanced.

5. Knapp, Brian. (1994). *People of the World, Population and Migration*. Danbury, CT: Grolier Education Corp. Advanced.

6. Stepanchuk, Carol. (1994). *Red Eggs and Dragon Boats: Celebrating Chinese Festivals*. Berkeley: Pacific View Press. Intermediate, Advanced.

7. Brice, Raphaelle. (1984). *Rice: The Little Grain That Feeds the World*. Ossining NY: Editions Gallimard. Primary, Intermediate.

8. Kendall, Russ. (1994). *Russian Girl: Life in an Old Russian Town*. New York: Scholastic Inc. Intermediate.

9. Beirne, Barbara. (1993). *Siobhan's Journey: A Belfast Girl Visits the U.S.* Minneapolis: Carolrhoda Books. Intermediate.

10. Morris, Scott E., ed. (1993). *Using and Understanding Maps*. New York: Chelsea House Publishers. Intermediate, Advanced.

Software:

1. *Children's Songs Around the World* [Laserdisc VHS]. Baldwin, NY: Educational Activities. Primary, Intermediate.

2. *Global Language Series* [MPC CD-ROM]. Novato, CA: Mindscape Educational Software. Intermediate, Advanced.

3. *Regard for the Planet* [Mac Laserdisc]. New York: Voyager. Primary, Intermediate, Advanced.

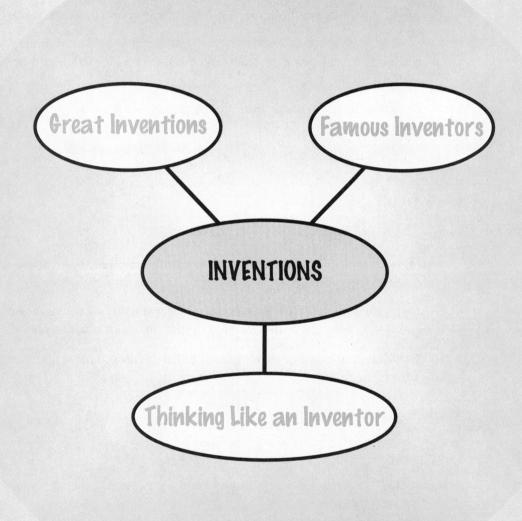

Great Inventions

Famous Inventors

INVENTIONS

Thinking Like an Inventor

Theme Goals:

Students will:

1. disassemble and reassemble simple machines and categorize various machine pieces.

2. design new inventions.

3. design and test paper airplanes.

4. create invention chains showing how past inventions have affected the development of newer inventions.

5. identify inventors who have made significant contributions to our way of life.

6. distinguish between copyrights, patents, and trademarks; and design their own trademarks.

7. use calculators to view the effects that computers have had on solving problems.

8. invent a musical instrument.

Theme Concepts:

1. Inventions changed the world.

2. Most inventions were planned; they were developed as responses to particular situations.

3. Great inventors based their ideas on careful study of the past and present, combined with a keen imagination about what might be.

4. Early inventions help make possible the development of later inventions

Vocabulary:

1. lever

2. pulley

3. axle

4. inclined plane

5. wedge

6. patent

7. copyright

8. trademark

Instructional Bulletin Board

The purpose of this bulletin board is to have children match some of the world's great inventors with their inventions. Draw, cut, and laminate the inventions. The children can place each invention inside the proper circle by using "fun tack" or magnetic strips on the inventions.

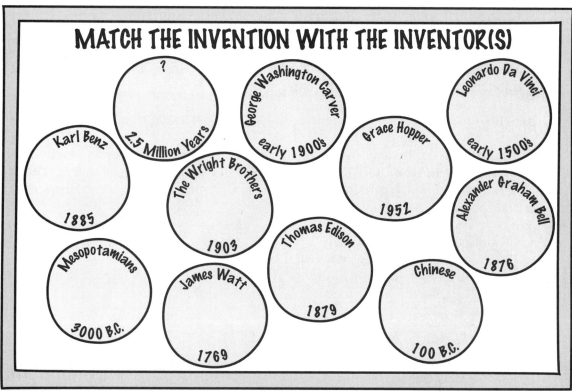

MATCH THE INVENTION WITH THE INVENTOR(S)

- ? — 2.5 Million Years
- George Washington Carver — early 1900's
- Leonardo Da Vinci — early 1500's
- Karl Benz — 1885
- Grace Hopper — 1952
- The Wright Brothers — 1903
- Alexander Graham Bell — 1876
- Mesopotamians — 3000 B.C.
- Thomas Edison — 1879
- James Watt — 1769
- Chinese — 100 B.C.

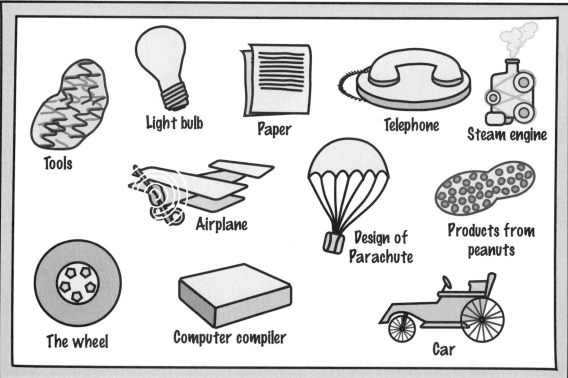

Tools · Light bulb · Paper · Telephone · Steam engine · Airplane · Design of Parachute · Products from peanuts · The wheel · Computer compiler · Car

Parent Letter

Dear Parents:

Change is coming faster and faster. Only a century ago, there were no airplanes, radios, televisions, or computers. Today, these inventions, which have changed the world, are taken for granted. The future will bring even more profound changes to our children's lives. We will be studying some of the great inventions and inventors that have changed the world.

At School

This theme on inventions covers a variety of amazing people—such as Leonardo da Vinci and the Wright Brothers—and their accomplishments. The children should enjoy participating in a variety of "hands-on" learning experiences, including the following:

- Creating their own inventions
- Designing a "better-flying" paper airplane
- Inventing a new musical instrument
- Making a healthful snack food

At Home

To make your child aware of all the inventions found in the home, take him or her on a tour of your home, noting all of the inventions, such as the toaster or microwave oven, that help the family get work done. To help your child think creatively, check out a library book on inventions that features projects you and your child can do together.

Linking Up:

Children and inventors share some identical characteristics. Both display an insatiable curiosity about the world around them and both have a knack for coming up with new uses for old materials. Let children examine inventions from the past that are no longer in use or are in the process of becoming obsolete. They can compare "old" inventions with "new" inventions that have replaced them. For example, 45 rpm records could be compared to CDs, or a manual typewriter could be compared to a personal computer and printer. Discuss the consequences of the changes. Ask children if the new inventions are better than the old ones, and if so, why. Are they more productive, comfortable, or convenient? Do they make our lives simpler, or more complicated?

Science:

1. What's Inside Machines?

Brief Background. Curiosity is a characteristic common to most inventors. When he was a young man, Thomas Edison loved to take machines apart to see how they worked. After he mastered the mechanism, he usually was able to think of ways to improve it. He went on, of course, to greater things. Among Edison's many inventions were the electric light, mimeograph machine, movie projector, and phonograph.

Make an assortment of discarded machines and common tools available for children to investigate. Let the children disassemble and reassemble the machines. Have them categorize the parts of each tool based on the six simple machine types: lever, screw, pulley, wheel and axle, inclined plane, and wedge which are shown in Figure 26-1. If possible, let them demonstrate the use of each tool.

2. A Class of Inventors

The scope of Leonardo da Vinci's (1452–1519) artistic talents, scientific curiosity, and inventive genius knew no bounds. Although probably best known for his world-famous painting, the *Mona Lisa*, many of his sketches of machines were remarkably similar to modern-day inventions. Long before the technology existed to make them, Leonardo drew designs for such things as parachutes, helicopters, tanks, and rapid-firing guns.

Show students copies of da Vinci's futuristic designs, which can be found in history and art reference books. Encourage children to imagine the world to come and to invent machines for that distant future. To guide their thinking, have them follow these three steps: (1) look closely at how some particular task is currently done; (2) think of new ways to accomplish the same task; and (3) design a device to complete the task faster and/or better.

3. First in Flight

Brief Background. The Wright Brothers made the world's first flight by powered aircraft at Kitty Hawk, North Carolina, on December 17, 1903. Before that time no one had been able to devise a practical way to keep a flying machine stably balanced in the air. Using insights gained by watching pigeons fly, the Wrights developed a method that enabled the pilot to adjust the shape of the wings in flight, thereby controlling the stability of the aircraft.

Challenge students to design "The World's Best Flying Paper Airplane." Encourage them to experiment with a variety of wing designs for their aircraft. A "traditional" design is shown in Figure 26-2 on page 272. After students have made their planes, help them identify fair and accurate procedures to determine their airworthiness. Pose these questions: When thrown, can the paper airplanes reach a specified destination (target)? To determine the planes' accuracy, what type of target should be constructed? To determine the planes' reliability, how many times should each plane be thrown, and by whom? How should accuracy be measured? Who should do the measuring?

Social Studies:

1. From the Wheel to Locomotive

Brief Background. One invention or discovery invariably leads to others. For example, the locomotive, which was invented by Richard Trevithick in 1804, called for literally thousands of other inventions, such as passenger rail cars, sleeping cars, dining cars, freight cars, air brakes, couplers, tracks, block signals, and switching systems. The

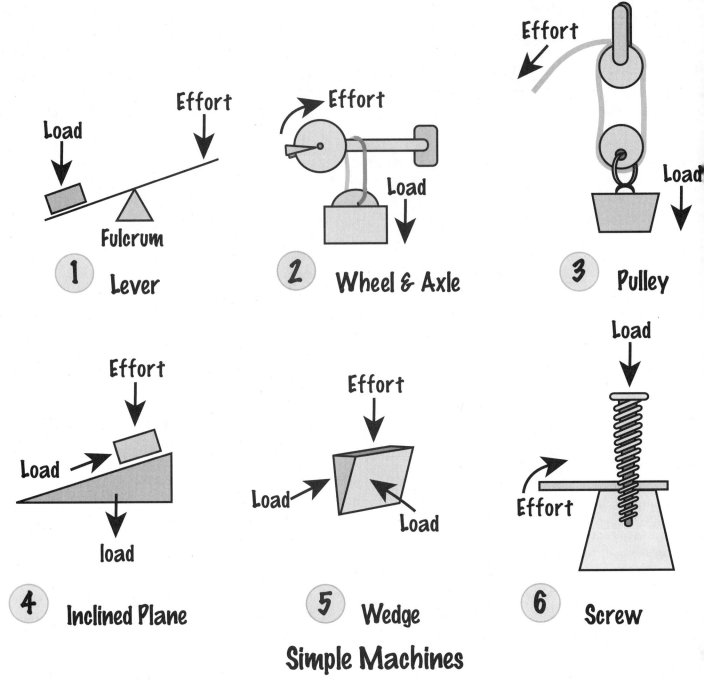

① Lever

② Wheel & Axle

③ Pulley

④ Inclined Plane

⑤ Wedge

⑥ Screw

Simple Machines

FIGURE 26-1

locomotive could never have been developed without other inventions. The machine that powered the first locomotive was the steam engine, which was invented by James Watt in 1769. Steam locomotives pulled most trains in the United States until the switch to diesels in the 1940s and 1950s. Named after Rudolf Diesel, who invented it in 1892, the diesel engine was more practical and efficient than the steam engine. Of course, the invention that made the development of the loco-

motive possible in the first place was the wheel, which was invented over 3,000 years ago.

Show children pictures and models of various inventions (cutaway pictures showing the parts of the invention are especially good). Ask them to consider how each invention made dozens of others necessary. Have the children create "Invention Chains" using words and pictures for inventions, like the one for locomotives illus-

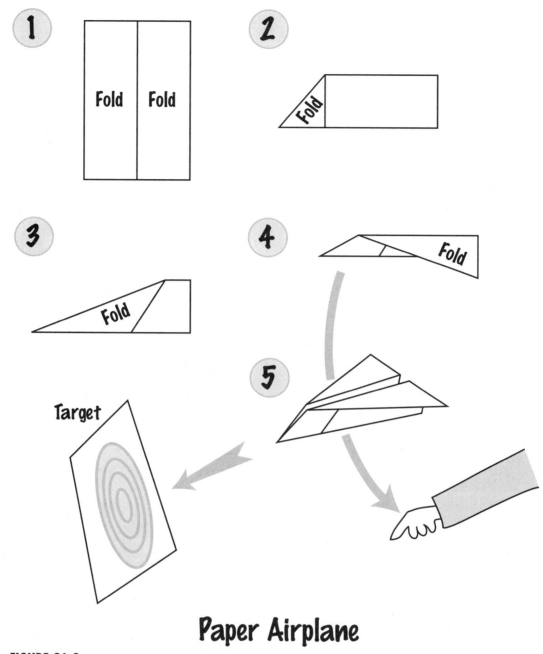

Paper Airplane

FIGURE 26-2

trated in Figure 26-3 on page 274. Display the chains on the classroom wall.

2. Ignored Inventors

Brief Background. The accomplishments of women and minority inventors are frequently ignored in history books, yet they are considerable. For example, over 350 inventions by African Americans were recorded from 1834 to 1900.

Introduce children to the following inventors (their inventions are in parentheses): Elizabeth Pinckney (developed an important commercial crop, indigo, a dye used in printing and dying cotton); Martha Coston (developed signal lights); Fannie Farmer (wrote first modern-day cookbook); Barbara McClintock (made Nobel Prize–winning discoveries in the field of plant genetics); Stephanie Kwolek (developed bullet-resistant fiber called Kevlar); Benjamin Banneker (built first clock made in the United States); Charles Browne (developed new system to refine sugar); Jan Matzeliger (developed a shoe-lasting machine); Lewis Latimer (develped first electric light with a carbon filament); George Washington Carver (developed hundreds of products from peanuts); and Garrett Morgan (develped first traffic light).

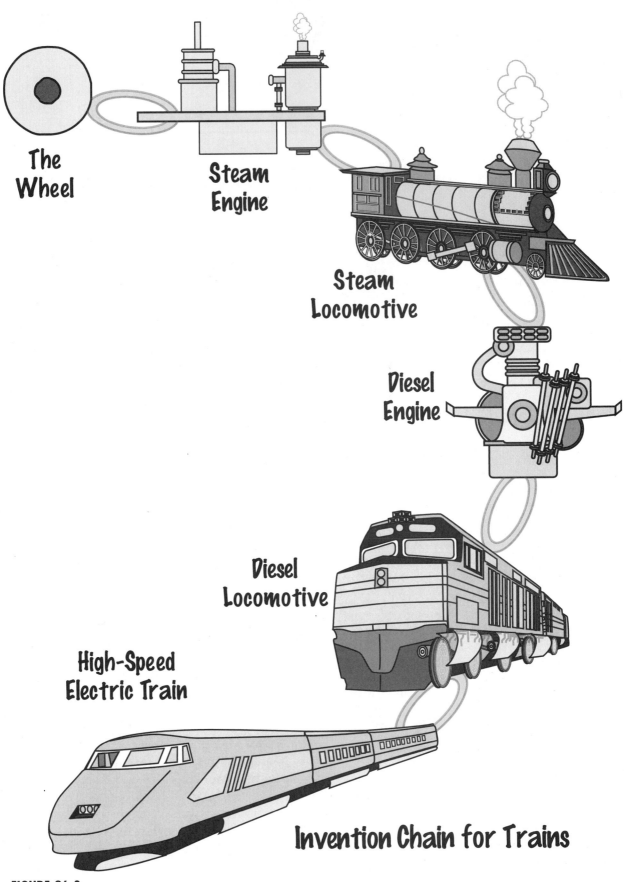

The Wheel

Steam Engine

Steam Locomotive

Diesel Engine

Diesel Locomotive

High-Speed Electric Train

Invention Chain for Trains

FIGURE 26-3

Language Arts:

1. Class Investigation

Brief Background. Patents, copyrights, and trademarks are issued to inventors, authors, and entrepreneurs to protect their creative works. A *patent* is a legal document issued by the U.S. government that gives an inventor the exclusive right to make, use, or sell an invention. A *copyright* gives the author or owner the exclusive right to reproduce, publish, and sell a literary, musical, or artistic work. A *trademark* is a device, such as a word, symbol or both, that is legally reserved for the exclusive use of the owner.

Lead the children on a search for products in the classroom and school that are protected by patents (indicated by a patent number), copyrights (indicated by the symbol © or the word "Copyright"), or trademarks (indicated by a small ™ or the symbol ®).

2. Applications for Patents

To involve the children in protecting their own intellectual property, they can create funny inventions and then apply for patents for them. They might invent a new mail box, basketball shoe, fuel-efficient car, or perhaps a device to assist in watering a plant, walking the dog, brushing their teeth, or cleaning their room. When applying for a patent, an inventor must submit a drawing and a brief narrative description of the invention. Have the children draw a picture of the invention, and then describe it briefly (one paragraph) in clear and concise language.

3. Copyrights for Students' Stories

Have the children copyright their own original short stories and poems. To copyright their works, students must attach the follow elements to them: the symbol ©, or the word "Copyright;" the year the work was created; and the name of the owner of copyright to the work (e.g., the child's name).

Art:

1. Trademarks and Logos

Show the children pictures of well-known trademarks, for example, McDonald's golden arches, Nike's swoosh, Campbell's red and white soup can. Challenge students to identify the companies' names. Let students create and draw original trademarks for different types of products, such as sports equipment, medical supplies, fast food, shoes and sneakers, television and electronics, automobiles, and super-markets.

Math:

1. A Time-Saving Device

Brief Background. The invention of the computer has lead to the on-going information revolution. One of America's greatest computer geniuses was a gifted mathematician and rear admiral in the U.S. Navy named Grace Hopper. In 1952, she developed a device, called a compiler, that enabled a computer to understand English-like commands. Hopper also led projects to make the computer solve problems faster. When Hopper started her career, the most powerful computers were over 50 feet long and could do just three additions every second. In comparison, today's small computers can perform millions of calculations a second.

Have children compare how long it takes them to do a specified set of math problems with and without the aid of pocket calculators (or use the personal computer's built-in calculator). First, one group can solve the problems with the aid of calculators while the other group can work the same problems without them. Then, they can switch roles to solve another set of similar math problems. Make certain that the children record the time needed to complete the problems under the two conditions, and then compare the results.

Art:

1. Classroom Banner

Have students make a class banner. To encourage inventiveness, challenge small groups of students to design several banners for consideration. Each group can make their preliminary designs on large sheets of paper and present them to the class. After students have discussed the different designs, they can make any agreed-upon modifications and select the design to be used. To make the banner, cut a piece of white cotton cloth into a banner shape. Draw the design lightly in pencil on the cloth.

To make the design, cut out pieces of colored cloth and sew them on. Sew a hem across the top of the banner. Put a dowel through the hem and tie a piece of yarn to both ends. Hang the banner on a wall inside the classroom or outside next to the classroom door. An example of a class banner is shown in Figure 26-4.

Music:

1. Making a Little Music

Brief Background. People have been making music for a long time. The drum is probably the world's oldest instrument. The ancient Egyptians played trumpets. Lutes and harps were in use over 4,000 years ago. The piano was invented in 1709 by an Italian named Bartolommeo Cristofori. The saxophone was invented in 1846 by Adolphe Sax. The electronic synthesizer was developed by Robert Moog in 1954. The sound of music is made when something vibrates. Percussion instruments—drums, maracas, and xylophones—are made to vibrate by striking.

Let children construct their own drums and other percussion instruments. They can use an assortment of objects, such as cans, pebbles, cartons, boxes, bottles, and sticks, in a variety of combinations to make sounds. After the children make their instruments, play a tape of one of their favorite songs and let them provide the background rhythm.

Health:

1. Invent a Snack

Let children invent healthful snacks. Place different snack food items on trays for the children to sample. Include nuts, raisins and other dried fruits, pretzels, raw vegetable, and so forth. Challenge small groups of three or four children to create a tasty snack food by combining some or all of the items into a healthful mix. Each group can share its new snack invention with the rest of the class.

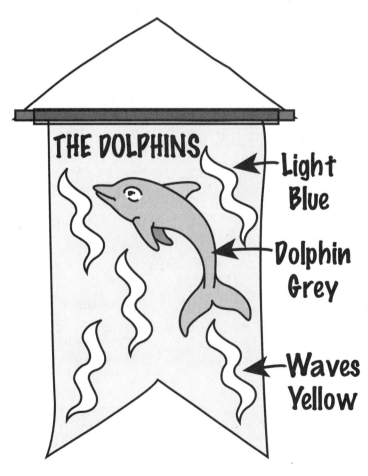

Class Banner

FIGURE 26-4

Books:

1. Binder, Lionel. (1991). *Invention*. New York: Alfred A. Knopf. Primary, Intermediate, Advanced.

2. Endacott, Geoff. (1991). *Discoveries and Inventions*. New York: Viking. Intermediate, Advanced.

3. Flatow, Ira. (1992). *They All Laughed . . .* New York: HarperCollins. Advanced.

4. Gardner, Robert. (1990). *Experimenting with Inventions*. New York: Franklin Watts. Advanced.

5. Haskins, Jim. (1991). *Outward Dreams: Black Inventors and Their Inventions*. New York: Walker and Company. Advanced.

6. Hooper, Meredith. (1976). *Everyday Inventions*. New York: Taplinger. Advanced.

7. McCormack, Alan. (1981). *Inventors Workshop*. Carthage, IL: Fearon Teacher Aids. Intermediate, Advanced.

8. Murphy, Jim. (1978). *Weird and Wacky Inventions*. New York: Crown. Intermediate, Advanced.

9. Jones, Charlotte Folitz. (1991). *Mistakes That Worked*. New York: Doubleday. Intermediate, Advanced.

10. Turvey, Peter. (1992). *Inventions, Inventors and Ingenious Ideas*. New York: Franklin Watts. Primary, Intermediate, Advanced.

11. Vare, Ethlie Anne, and Ptacek, Greg. (1993). *Women Inventors and Their Discoveries*. Minneapolis, MN: The Oliver Press. Advanced.

12. Cooke, David. (1968). *Inventions That Made History*. New York: G. P. Putnam's Sons. Advanced.

13. Manchester, Harland. (1976). *New Trail Blazers of Technology*. New York: Charles Scribner's Sons. Advanced.

Software:

1. *Simple and Compound Machines: How They Work* [Laserdisc VHS]. Chatsworth, CA: AIMS. Advanced.

2. *Inventors and the American Industrial Revolution* [Laserdisc]. Van Nuys, CA: Churchill Media. Intermediate, Advanced.

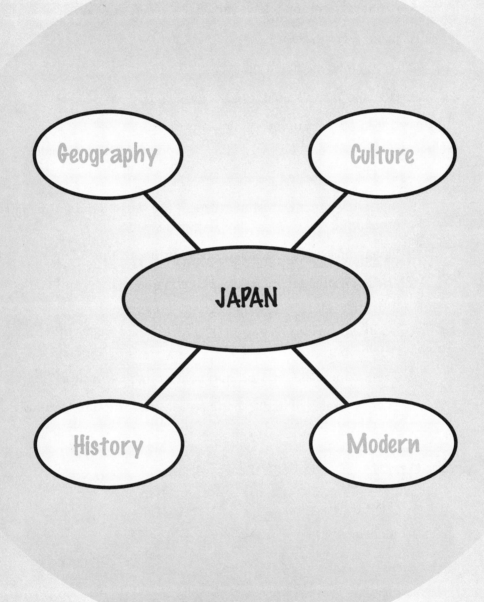

Geography

Culture

JAPAN

History

Modern

Theme Goals:

Students will:

1. practice Japanese etiquette.

2. identify the locations of Japan's major islands and cities.

3. investigate Japanese-made products in students' homes.

4. plan and eat a Japanese meal.

5. contrast "old" and "new" Japan.

6. make a Japanese toy.

7. write Japanese haiku poetry.

8. examine Japan's unique geology.

9. conduct a car survey using math skills.

Theme Concepts:

1. Rules of etiquette to show respect are very important in Japanese culture.

2. Japan consists of four major, heavily populated, islands.

3. The traditional Japanese diet is high in vegetables and grains and low in fat.

4. Japan is a modern nation that has retained many of its ancient traditions.

5. The Japanese depend on trade with other countries.

6. Two examples of traditional Japanese art forms are Daruma dolls and haiku poetry.

Vocabulary:

1. haiku poetry

2. etiquette

3. samuri

4. export

5. import

6. kimono

7. daruma dolls

8. calligraphy

Instructional Bulletin Board

The purpose of this bulletin board is to allow students an opportunity to classify and display information they have gathered on Japan. To make the bulletin board, find and attach an attractive large map of Japan to the center of the bulletin board; then divide the board into sections and make labels for them as shown. Direct students to do the following: Gather pictures about Japan; decide the category in which the picture ought to be placed; and attach each picture inside the appropriate category with a pin. Remember to check the accuracy of each student's work.

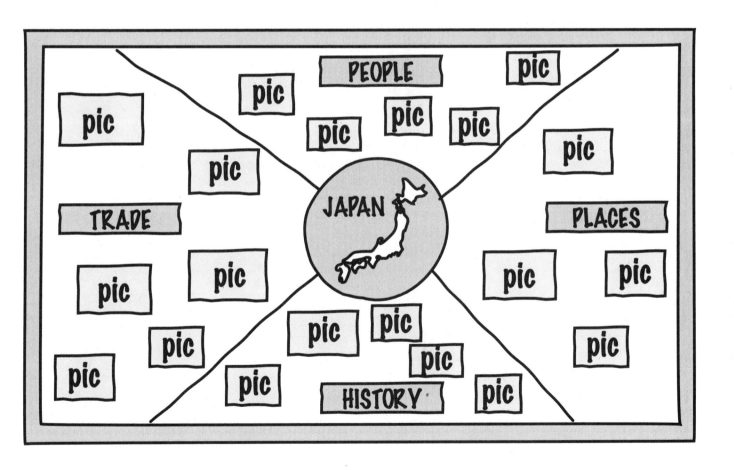

Parent Letter

Dear Parents:

Japan is a country that is a blend of the old and the new. There are ancient temples, shrines, and thousand-year-old festivals, as well as giant global companies—like Honda and Sony—which are headquartered in Japan's modern, crowded cities. In this theme on Japan, students will explore some of this small, but important, island nation.

At School:

Some activities planned for this week include:

• Practicing Japanese customs
• Mapping the locations of Japan's cities and volcanoes
• Searching for Japanese-made products in the home and school
• Tasting Japanese-style food
• Making a traditional Japanese toy
• Writing haiku poetry

At Home:

Japan is one of the world's most important economic powers. Chances are good that one or more Japanese products are in your home. Please help your child find and list Japanese name-brand products located in your home. Back at school, the completed lists will be combined to form a master list. If you have any special knowledge about Japan, now would be an ideal time to share it with your child.

Linking Up:

Bring several photographs of Japan to class. Try to include illustrations that show both traditional and modern scenes. Ask students to imagine they are going to visit Japan. Have students look for similarities and differences between scenes in the pictures of Japan and places with which they are familiar. Challenge students to identify as many similarities and differences as they can. Write the similarities and differences on a chart. Tell students that, during their study of Japan, they will check the accuracy of their list of similarities and differences.

Social Studies:

1. Japanese Etiquette

Brief Background. The Japanese are a very polite people. Instead of shaking hands when they meet, the Japanese bow by bending the head and upper body toward the person being addressed. When bowing, arms are held rigidly to the sides of the body, fingers pointed to the ground. The deeper the bow, the greater the sign of respect. When two Japanese meet, the person who usually commands more respect is the one who is older and/or holds a superior rank in business, government, or some other field of endeavor. To determine status, strangers will exchange business cards when they meet. In traditional Japanese society, males usually assumed roles of superior rank or status, compared to women. Teachers are highly respected in Japanese society.

Have students create personal business cards for themselves, and then exchange cards and greet one another in the Japanese fashion. Invite a Japanese person to class to discuss and demonstrate Japanese customs and traditions.

2. Japan's Geography

Brief Background. Japan is around the same size as California, but its population is about three times greater.

Have students locate Japan and California on a globe and world map (Figure 27-1). Ask students to contrast the two places. (Possible observations include the following: Japan is located in Asia, while California is part of North America; Japan is an island nation, while California is part of the United States mainland; Japan and California are located at about the same latitude; and Japan and California are separated by a huge body of water, the Pacific Ocean.) Provide blank, outline maps of Japan, and help students identify Japan's four major islands, which are Honshu, Hokkaido, Shikoku, and Kyushu. Have students predict locations of Japanese cities by marking them with an "x" on the map. Compare their predictions with a map of Japan that shows the actual locations of major Japanese cities, including Sapporo, Tokyo, Yokohama, Nagoya, Kyoto, Osaka, Kobe, Hiroshima, and Fukuoka. Ask students to make a list of reasons why they live where they do in the United States. Then, ask students to speculate about why the Japanese might live where they do. How are the two lists similar and different?

3. Japan's Trade

Brief Background. Japan is a small country with many people, yet it is one of the world's richest nations. Japan and the United States are major trading partners. Japan's most important source of imports is the United States, and Japan's most important export destination is the United States.

Chances are good that students, together with their families, possess many goods made in Japan. Have students search for Japanese-made items in their homes. What items show up most frequently on their lists? Japan is a major exporter to the United States of the following goods: watches, cameras, cars, televisions, calculators, computers, and computer parts. Japan's major imports are oil, natural gas, coal, iron ore, timber, meat, and wheat. Have students predict how Japan's imports might be used.

4. Eating "Healthy"

Brief Background. The traditional Japanese diet is high in vegetables and grains and low in fat. The Japanese eat lots of fresh and dried fish and seafood, fresh and pickled vegetables, tofu (bean curd), soups, noodles, and rice. Green tea is a favorite beverage.

Have students compare their diets with a traditional Japanese diet. Encourage students to find recipes of favorite Japanese dishes. List the

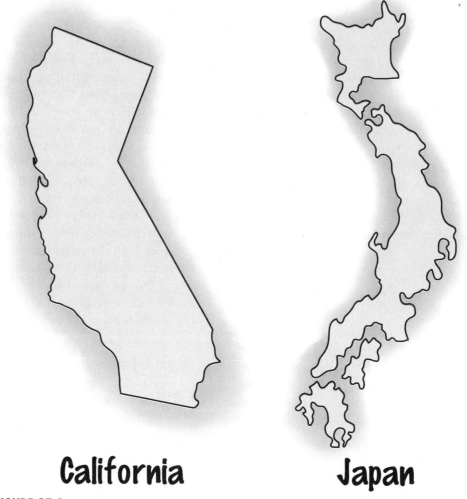

California   Japan

FIGURE 27-1

ingredients of these foods, and compare them with the ingredients of favorite American dishes. Help students plan and prepare a Japanese meal. Choose tasty, easy-to-prepare foods, such as skewered meat (yakitori) or a noodle soup (soba), or pick precooked selections, which can often be found in the frozen food section of the supermarket. Some parents also might volunteer to prepare some Japanese dishes for the occasion. Provide students with—and teach them how to use—Japanese-style chopsticks (they are shorter than Chinese chopsticks, and also have a more pointed tip), which can be purchased in bulk at Oriental food shops.

5. Japanese History

Brief Background. Japan's history goes back thousands of years. Some important events include the arrival of Mongol invaders from Asia (300 B.C.); the introduction of Buddhism and the Chinese writ-

ing system (around 500 A.D.), the development of military rule under the leadership of *shoguns* and their warriors, or *samuri* (twelfth century); the arrival of Europeans (mid-1500s); the arrival of Americans led by Commodore Matthew Perry (1854); the defeat of Japan, ending World War II (1945); and the development of Japan into a major economic power (present). Included among Japan's rich cultural traditions are calligraphy, painting on silkscreen, woodblock prints, *ikebana* (flower arranging), and *chanoyu* (tea ceremony).

Have students discuss traditional customs or practices that are part of their culture, such as celebrating birthdays and certain holidays. To make certain the traditions are truly "old," they can check to see if their parents and grandparents also engaged in them when they were the students' age. Then, contrast those traditional customs with relatively recent or modern practices, such as going to multiplex theaters in giant shopping malls, or listening to CDs on Walkmans. Finally, provide students with an assortment of pictures from books and magazines that depict events and scenes representing the lifestyles of both modern Japan (fast trains, ships, cars, tall city buildings, etc.) and traditional Japanese culture (ancient religious shrines and temples, *samurai* warriors, people dressed in *kimonos*, rice paddy fields, rituals like the tea ceremony, etc.). Have children sort the pictures into two groups, one labeled "Traditional Japan" and the other "Modern Japan." Compare and contrast the traditional and modern American and Japanese events and scenes. Point out similarities and differences.

Art:

1. Daruma Dolls

Brief Background. Named after the founder of Zen Buddhism, one of Japan's most influential religions, the Daruma doll, represents the importance of balance and orderliness in life. No matter how the Daruma doll is pushed around, it always lands upright.

To make the dolls, follow the directions in Figure 27-2.

2. Japanese Prints

Show students examples of Japanese woodblock prints found in art magazines and books and encourage them to make their own designs using potatoes and plastic knives to carve images. After the images are pressed into tempera paint, they can be stamped on their papers.

Language Arts:

1. Stories of Japan

Brief Background. Japan's literary tradition started around a thousand years ago when *The Tale of the Genji*, the world's oldest novel, was written. It is the story of the adventures of Prince Genji, a son of the emperor.

Help the class create their own story based upon their study of Japan. Begin the story "On a trip to Japan we saw some of the most in-teresting things," and let them fill in the supporting details.

2. Haiku Poetry

Brief Background. Haiku is a traditional Japanese form of poetry. A haiku poem has only three lines. The first line has five syllables, the second seven, and the third five. Many haiku poems celebrate the beauty of nature.

Read and discuss the haiku poem below. Then encourage students to write their own haiku poetry.

Glistening, quiet.
A thousand raindrops falling
in the warm moonlight.

Science:

1. Japan's Geology

Brief Background. One of Japan's most sacred and well-known symbols is Mt. Fuji, just one of Japan's many volcanic mountains. Japan is located on the "Ring of Fire," which is the name given to a circle of volcanoes that extend around the Pacific Ocean.

Show students pictures of Japan's mountainous landscape, and let them examine physical and relief maps of Japan. Have students compare Japan's geological features with conditions locally. Encourage them to make papier-mache or clay relief maps of Japan.

2. Japan and the Ocean

Brief Background. Japan is an island nation and its people depend on the ocean as a source for much of their food. Both raw and cooked fish and seafood are standard items in the Japanese diet. A main vegetable is mineral- and vitamin-rich seaweed, which is found in Japan's coastal waters.

Let students investigate and then write or transcribe an illustrated report on the following mainstays in the Japanese diet: tuna, salmon, eels, flatfish, mackerel, pollock, sardines, octopus, squid, clams, oysters, crabs, scallops, shrimp, and seaweed. Have students keep a

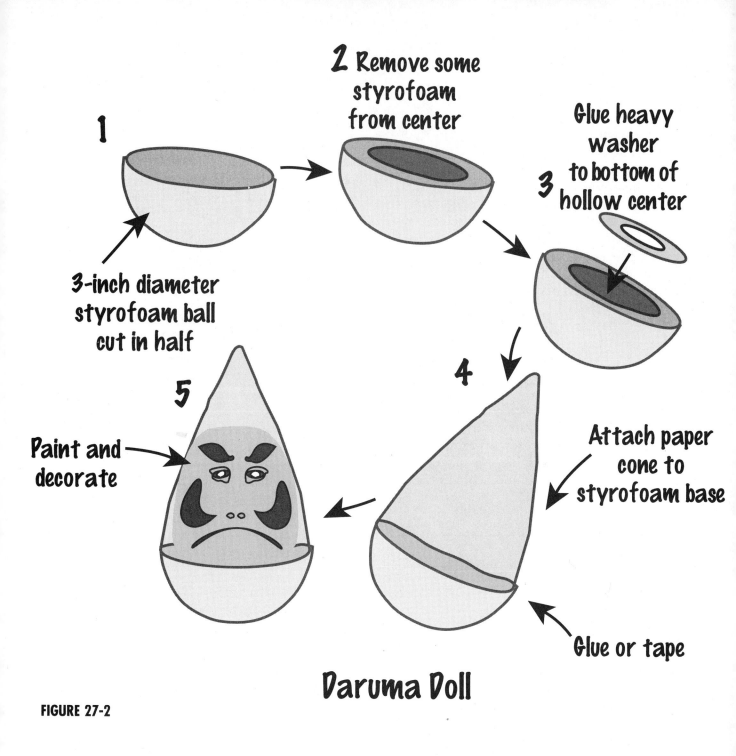

1 3-inch diameter styrofoam ball cut in half

2 Remove some styrofoam from center

3 Glue heavy washer to bottom of hollow center

4 Attach paper cone to styrofoam base

Glue or tape

5 Paint and decorate

Daruma Doll

FIGURE 27-2

record of their diets for one week. Did students eat any of the same ocean foods?

Math:

1. Counting Cars

Brief Background. Japan exports cars to countries around the world. Some Japanese-brand cars are also built in the United States. Many Americans drive Hondas, Toyotas, and other Japanese-brand cars. Have students conduct a car search in the school's parking lot to determine the number of Japanese-brand and non-Japanese-brand cars driven by administrators, teachers, and staff. To extend the investigation, have students conduct a survey to identify the brands of cars driven by parents. Help students tally, graph, and interpret the results.

Books:

1. Jacobsen, Karen. (1982). *Japan*. Chicago: Children's Press. Primary.

2. Tames, Richard, and Tames, Sheila. (1994). *Japan*. New York: Franklin Watts. Intermediate.

3. Morimoto, Junko. (1987). *My Hiroshima*. New York: Viking Press. Primary.

4. Paterson, Katherine. (1974). *Of Nightingales That Weep*. New York: Thomas Y. Crowell Company. Advanced.

5. Roberts, Jenny. (1990). *Samurai Warriors*. New York: Gloucester Press. Intermediate.

6. Lavallee, Barbara. (1992). *This Place Is Crowded: Japan*. New York: Walker and Company. Intermediate.

7. Kawamata, Kazuhide. (1984). *We Live in Japan*. New York: Bookwright Press. Intermediate, Advanced.

8. Stein, Conrad. (1982). *World at War: Hiroshima*. Chicago: Children's Press. Intermediate, Advanced.

Software:

1. *Meiko: A Story of Japanese Culture* [MPC CD-ROM]. Novato, CA: Broderbund/Digital Productions. Advanced.

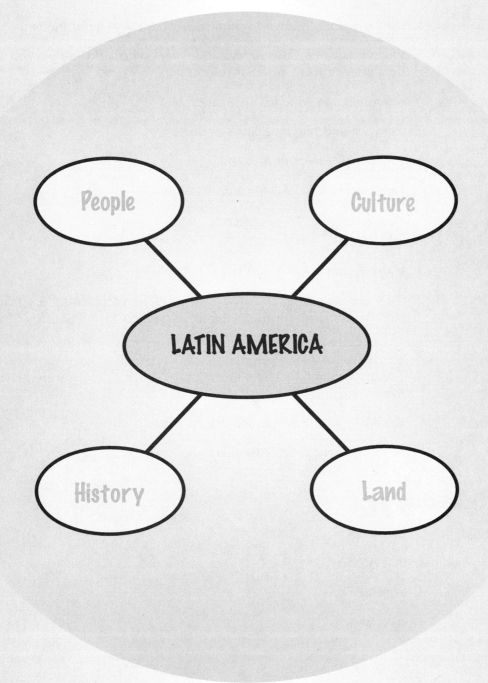

People

Culture

LATIN AMERICA

History

Land

Theme Goals:

Students will:

1. identify Spanish words used in English.

2. map Latin America.

3. describe the Latin American people.

4. compare and contrast Latin America's ancient civilizations.

5. identify famous Latin American leaders who led the fight for independence from colonial rule.

6. describe Latin America's climate.

7. use Inca and Mayan math systems.

8. create a picture writing system.

9. create replicas of Aztec calendar stones.

Theme Concepts:

1. Many Spanish words are used in English.

2. Latin America consists of over 30 independent countries from Mexico in the North to Chile and Argentina in the South.

3. Latin American is a diverse mix of races and cultures.

4. The three major ancient civilizations of Latin America were Maya, Aztec, and Inca.

5. The Maya and Aztec used picture writing.

6. The Maya and Aztec calendars were very accurate.

Vocabulary:

1. mestizo

2. independence

3. tropical

4. climate

5. quipu

6. tun

7. katun

8. baktun

Instructional Bulletin Board

The purpose of this bulletin board is to give students practice making inferences. Put some data clues that are related to a particular Latin American country on the bulletin board, and then challenge students to use these data to figure out which country it is. The example spotlights Mexico (as indicated by the following data: silver jewelry, Aztec ruins, Mexican flag, and bullfighting). Have students write down the name of the country and the reasons why they believe they are right on an index card. At the end of the day, reveal the name of the mystery country and discuss the students' answers and reasoning. Challenge students to create different mystery country puzzles for display on the bulletin board.

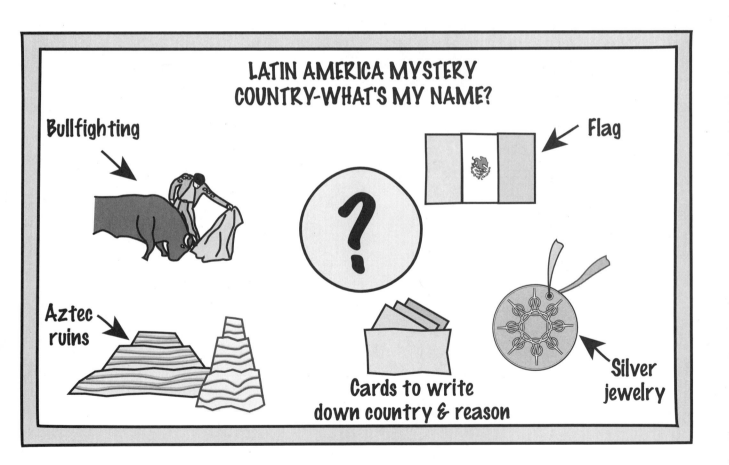

LATIN AMERICA MYSTERY COUNTRY—WHAT'S MY NAME?

Bullfighting

Flag

Aztec ruins

Cards to write down country & reason

Silver jewelry

Parent Letter

Dear Parents:

We are beginning our study of Latin America, which covers a vast landscape. It includes over 30 nations, including Mexico, the Caribbean island countries, Central America, and South America. Some of the activities in which students will be engaged are listed below.

At School:

In their study of Latin America, students will be:

- Identifying Spanish words used in English
- Mapping Latin America
- Exploring the ancient Maya, Aztec, and Inca civilizations, including sampling their foods
- Analyzing Latin America's climate
- Making Inca counting devices
- Using the Mayan number system

At Home:

This would be a fine time to explore the United States' Latin or Hispanic heritage with your child. What examples of Latin or Hispanic influence can you find in your community?

Linking Up:

Provide students with globes and atlases. Help the class plan a pretend trip to Latin American. Which nation would students want to visit? How would they get there? What would they want to see and do? Make a list of the students' associations with and understandings of Latin America. Let students look at some travel brochures on Latin America. Do any of the pictures in the brochures make Latin America seem like an interesting, exciting, or exotic place to visit?

Social Studies:

1. Languages of Latin America

Brief Background. Latin America gets its name from the fact that the three major languages spoken there—Spanish, Portuguese and French—are all Romance languages, which are derived from Latin. The vast majority of Latin Americans speak Spanish. Portuguese is the language spoken in Brazil, and French is spoken in Haiti and French Guiana. English is spoken in Belize, Guyana, and some Caribbean islands, as well as by many people throughout Latin America. Dutch is spoken in Suriname and Aruba. Native Indian languages are also spoken throughout Latin America.

Survey the class to determine if any students are native speakers of Spanish, Portuguese, or French. Many Spanish words are used in English. Write the following words on the chalkboard and see how many students know their meaning.

adobe	flamenco	patio	tapioca
amigo	guerrilla	plaza	hacienda
armadillo	llama	rodeo	tango
bonanza	machete	siesta	ole
cafeteria	mosquito	sombrero	fiesta
corral	nacho	taco	coyote

2. Mapping Latin America

Brief Background. Provide students with globes and world maps. Show them the location of Latin America on the globe and a wall map of the world. Latin America covers a vast landscape. It includes the southern part of the continent of North America, which covers Mexico, the countries of the Caribbean Islands and Central America, and the whole continent of South America.

Have students trace the shape of Latin America on their maps with their fingers. Help students find the equator. Point out to students that Mexico, the Caribbean region, Central America, and northern South America are north of the equator and in the Northern Hemisphere, while most of South America is south of the equator and in the Southern Hemisphere. To help students remember the locations, from north to south, of Mexico and the seven countries of Central America, try this mnemonic device: "My great big elephant hid Nick's costly pan." Each word in the mnemonic represents a country as follows: *M*y (Mexico), *g*reat (Guatemala), *b*ig (Belize), *e*lephant (El Salvador), *h*id (Honduras), *N*ick's (Nicaragua), *c*ostly (Costa Rica), *p*an (Panama).

To provide practice locating and identifying the countries of Latin America, give students individual sets of small outline maps of individual Latin American nations, and then let them find the countries represented in their sets on the globe and world map. For additional practice, provide blank maps of Latin America, and let students locate and label all of the Latin American countries in North, Central, and South America (Figure 28-1).

3. Geographic Questions

Have students use their map-reading skills to help them answer these questions: What country borders Latin America on the north? (the United States) What direction is Latin America from the United States? (south and east) Is Latin American as big as Canada and the United States combined? (Latin America is larger) What is the world's largest rain forest? (the Amazon rain forest in South America) What is the longest mountain range in the world? (the Andes Mountains in South America). Encourage students to create their own geographic questions to ask the class.

4. Latin American Peoples

Brief Background. Latin America is a region of great cultural and ethnic diversity. Some countries

Map of Latin America

FIGURE 28-1

in Latin America have large Indian populations. Many Indian groups live as they have for centuries. They wear traditional clothing made from cloth woven on hand looms, and they grow traditional food crops, such as potatoes or corn. Some Latin Americans are descendants of black slaves, or of blacks and Europeans who intermarried. Others are *mestizos*, or mixed Indian and European ancestry. Two countries, Argentina and Uruguay, are populated mainly by people of European ancestry. Some of the world's largest cities are in Latin America. There, business and professional people in urban centers dress and act much like city people do anywhere. However, life for large numbers of poor people who have come to Latin America's cities is not easy. Poverty, unemployment, and homelessness are real problems faced by many people throughout Latin America.

Gather photographs and pictures of people from different Latin American countries and share them with your students. Discuss the clothing worn by the people in the photographs and pictures, as well as the work or other activities in which they are engaged. Relate the clothing and activities to climate and cultural factors. Let students sort the pictures into two groups, one labeled "Urban" and the other "Small Village/Rural."

5. Ancient Civilizations

Brief Background. Before the arrival of any European explorers, there were three great native Indian civilizations—Maya, Aztec, and Inca—located in Latin America. A main crop of all three Indian groups was corn. The Aztec and Inca made popcorn. They all grew beans, pumpkins, squash, and chili peppers. Both the Maya and Aztec loved choco-late, which is made from cocoa beans. They drank hot cocoa flavored with honey and vanilla. The Aztec believed that chocolate was a gift from the gods, and that eating it would give a person wisdom. The Maya and Aztec also had chewing gum, which was made from chicle, the sticky sap of the itz tree. Another food staple of the Incas was potatoes, which they would freeze-dry in the high Andes mountains.

As a tasty way to introduce students to these ancient civilizations, share some of their favorite foods with your students. Treat students to a snack of popcorn, chocolate squares, tortilla chips, or potato chips made from dried pota-toes. You may also want to include a piece of chewing gum for each child. Tell students that these foods are gifts to the world from these three ancient civilizations.

6. Comparing Cultures

Provide students with appropriate books about the three cultures and have them complete a retrieval chart like the one presented below.

7. Struggles for Independence

Brief Background. Shortly after their arrival, the Spaniards had destroyed the Aztec and Inca civiliza-tions. Colonial rule of Latin America was often harsh and unjust. Like the United States, many Latin Amer-ican countries had to fight for their independence.

Have students research the following Latin Amer-ican patriots who led the revolt against colonial rule: Miguel Hidalgo y Costilla in Mexico; Jose de San Martin and Simon Bolivar in Peru; Bernardo O'Higgins and Jose de San Martin in Chile; Jose de San Martin in Argentina; Simon Bolivar and Antonio Jose de Sucre in Bolivia; and Simon Bo-livar in Colombia, Ecuador, and Venezuela.

Science:

1. Latin America's Climate

Brief Background. Because of Latin America's topography and location, some of its climate fea-tures are the reverse of the United States. Since most of Latin American is in the Southern Hemisphere, the seasons are opposite those of the United States. Since much of Latin America is located near the equator, there are no severe winters anywhere except in the sparsely populated tip of southern South America. In the United States, winds blow from west to east, but they blow from east to west in South America. In the mountainous regions of Latin America (including Mexico, Colombia, Ar-gentina, Ecuador, Peru, Chile, and Bolivia), there are three vertical climate regions: hot, temperate, and cold. The tropical conditions found in the Ama-

	MAYA	AZTEC	INCA
People	Indians	Indians	Indians
Location	Guatamala, Mexico, Belize, Honduras, El Salvador	Mexico	Peru, Ecuador, Chile, Bolivia, Colombia, Argentina
Time Period	800 B.C.–900 A.D.	1200 A.D.–1520 A.D.	1200 A.D.–1530 A.D.
Language	Mayan	Nahuatl	Quechua
Writing	Picture Symbols	Picture Symbols	None
Counting	Dot and bar symbols	Symbols	Knots on string
Food	Corn, squash, chocolate, honey, turkey, duck, deer, beans, sweet potato, chili peppers	Corn, chili pepper, chocolate, turkey, duck, beans, dog	Corn, white potatoes, ducks, geese, *oca* (edible root), quinoa (grain)

zon basin, located along the equator, have resulted in the creation of the world's largest rain forest.

Show a video of Latin America that highlights the region's mountain ranges, rivers, rain forests, and deserts, and then let students locate these features on a physical or topographical map of Latin America. Have students gather weather information found in daily newspapers and reported on TV for selected cities in the United States and Latin America. They can make a weather map showing temperatures and weather conditions for the cities. Discuss the temperatures, and relate any differences and similarities among places to the topography and location features described above.

Math:

1. Inca Counting

Brief Background. The Incas had no written symbols for numbers. Instead, they used a *quipu*, which consists of knots on colored string, to keep records.

Have students make quipus by tying one end of 3 or 4 strands of colored string to another string as shown in Figure 28-2. Each colored string is used to enumerate a different type of phenomenon. For example, a red string could be used to record the frequency of rainy days, while a blue string could be used to record quantities of food, and so on. Let students observe and record (by knotting the string) the

occurrence of everyday happenings of their choice for a specified period of time.

2. The Mayan Number System

Brief Backgound. The Maya devised a series of dot and bar symbols to indicate numbers as shown. The Mayan mathematical system was based on 20. Place values for numbers were arranged in rows. The bottom row indicated ones, or *tun*, the next row up 20's, or *katun*, the next 400s, or *baktun*.

Have each student use the ancient Mayan number system shown in Figure 28-3 to answer the following questions:

1. How old are you?
2 To the nearest hour, what time is it now?
3. How many legs does a spider have?
4. How many wheels does a car have?
5. How many players are on a baseball team?

3. Population Figures

Have students predict where people might live in Latin America, and why they might live there. They can record their predictions by putting marks to indicate the locations of population centers on a blank map of Latin America. Students can compare their predictions with actual locations. Let students use atlases and almanacs to gather geographic facts and population figures on each Latin American country, and then make bar graphs to compare the populations of these countries.

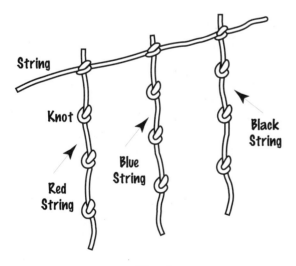

Quipu

FIGURE 28-2

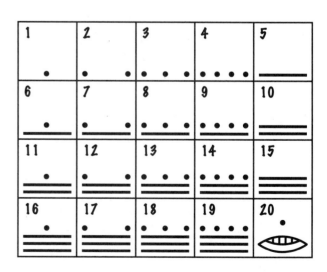

Mayan Number System

FIGURE 28-3

Language Arts:

1. Picture Writing

Brief Background. Both the Aztec and Maya used picture writing. For example, the Aztec symbol for "tree" was:

Show students other examples of Aztec and/or Mayan picture writing. Ask students to talk about why reading and writing are important. Discuss the importance of a writing system to a civiliza- tion (e.g., it provides a record of the past, information can be handed down from one generation to the next, it helps people learn about the past). Challenge students to invent their own picture writing systems and to use them to write a brief statement. Then, have pairs of students exchange statements and try to read them. If students experience difficulty reading one another's statements, explain that many years of study were necessary before experts were able to decipher the meaning of Aztec and Mayan picture writing.

Art:

1. Aztec Calendar Stones

Brief Background. Both the Mayans and Aztecs made careful celestial observations, and both developed 365-day calendars. The Aztec calendar consisted of 18 months of 20 days each, plus five

Rendition of Aztec Calendar Stone
FIGURE 28-4

extra days. At the center of the circular stone is the face of the Aztec's sun god. In circular patterns around the god are carvings that represent Aztec months and days.

Probe to determine if students understand the basis for the 365-day calendar, which is the earth's annual journey around the sun. Provide white paper plates and art materials, and encourage interested students to make renditions of the Aztec's stone calendar, such as the one shown in Figure 28-4.

2. Indian Weaving

Brief Background. Indians in Latin America still weave cloth with the same types of looms they have used for centuries. Sticks and pegs are used to fashion the looms.

Show students pictures of Indian looms and woven cloth with Indian designs, which can be found in books on Latin America. Let students make looms from pieces of cardboard as shown in Figure 28-5 . Provide students with different colors of yarn and large, dull needles, and let them weave. Display their weaving on the classroom wall.

1. Latin American Rhythms

Let students listen to examples of Latin American music. Check with the music teacher or media center for audiotapes and CDs of appro-

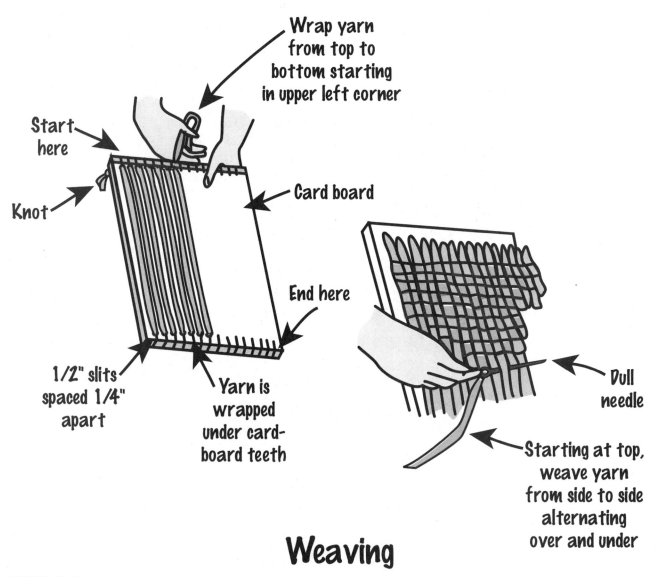

Weaving

FIGURE 28-5

priate music. Some popular songs that children in Latin America sing are listed below:

"La Viudita" (The Widow)—Mexico

"Palomita Blanca" (Little White Dove)—Argentina, Chile, Ecuador, Nicaragua, Uruguay, Venezuela

"Las Tres Cautivas" (The Three Captives)—Brazil

"Dame la Mano" (Pumpkin)—Dominican Republic

"Naranja Dulce" (Sweet Orange)—Costa Rica

"Cancion de Cuna" (Lullaby)—Puerto Rico

Books:

1. Lourie, Peter. (1991). *Amazon*. Amesdale, PA: Caroline House. Intermediate.

2. Morrison, Marion. (1994). *Brazil*. Austin, TX: Raintree Steck-Vaughn. Advanced.

3. Daniel, Jamie. (1992). *Nicaragua Is My Home*. Milwaukee: Gareth Stevens Publishing. Primary.

4. George, Jean Craighead. (1990). *One Day in a Tropical Rain Forest*. New York: Thomas Y. Crowell. Intermediate, Advanced.

5. Mathews, Sally Schofer. (1994). *The Sad Night: The Story of an Aztec Victory and a Spanish Loss*. New York: Clarion Books. Primary, Intermediate.

6. de Varona, Frank. (1993). *Simon Bolivar: Latin American Liberator*. Brookfield, CT: Gallin House Press, Inc. Advanced.

7. Georges, D. V. (1986). *South America*. Chicago: Children's Press. Primary.

8. Chrisp, Peter. (1993). *The Spanish Conquests in the New World*. New York: Wayland Publishers Ltd. Primary, Intermediate.

9. Lye, Keith. (1983). *Take a Trip to Brazil*. London: Franklin Watts Ltd. Primary.

10. Morrison, Marion. (1992). *Uruguay*. Chicago: Children's Press. Advanced.

Software:

1. *The Amazon Trail* [Mac IBM Windows MPC CD-ROM]. Minneapolis: MECC. Intermediate, Advanced.

2. *Children's Songs Around the World* [Laserdisc VHS]. Baldwin, NY: Educational Activities. Primary.

3. *Maya Quest* [Mac Windows MPC CD-ROM]. Minneapolis: MECC. Advanced.

4. *Let's Visit Mexico* [Mac IBM CD-ROM]. Fairfield, CT: Queue. Advanced.

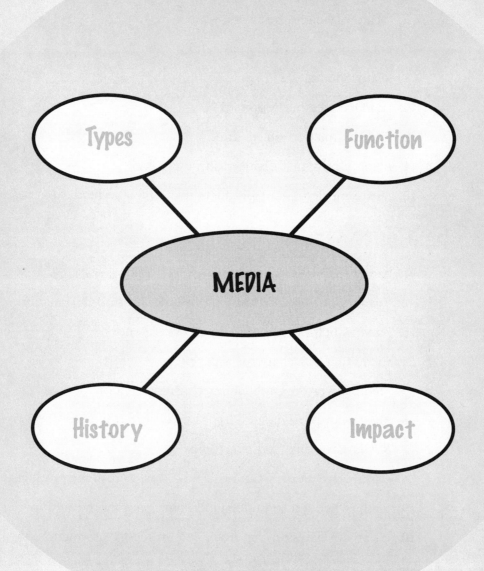

Theme Goals:

Students will:

1. identify the sections of the newspaper.

2. use the newspaper index to find information.

3. produce a class or school newspaper.

4. conduct surveys.

5. analyze media advertisements.

6. locate places in the news.

7. compare media of the past and present.

8. test products.

9. produce weather reports.

10. find information on Internet.

11. identify how math is used in newspapers.

12. create music and art products related to the media.

Theme Concepts:

1. A newspaper is divided into many sections.

2. Readers can use the newspaper index to find information.

3. Surveys help identify habits and preferences.

4. Creating a newspaper is a cooperative effort.

5. Media advertising influences consumers' choices.

6. Media can present stereotypes or distorted images of groups.

7. Media have changed over time.

8. Careful procedures can be used to test consumer products.

9. Math is needed to understand some parts of the newspaper.

10. Creativity plays an important role in media production.

Vocabulary:

1. media

2. index

3. stereotype

4. advertisements

5. survey

Instructional Bulletin Board

The purpose of this bulletin board is to help students process and interpret data on the class's media preferences. Separately label four large envelopes with one of the following statements: (1) My favorite TV program is _____; (2) My favorite song is _____; (3) My favorite movie is _____; and (4) My favorite computer game is _____. Attach the envelopes to the bulletin board. Let students indicate their favorites in these categories on index cards and deposit them in the appropriate envelopes. Let pairs of students take turns processing and interpreting the cards in one of the envelopes. For example, if a pair of students chose TV programs, the pair would first sort the cards into categories (TV Program A, TV Program B, Program C, and so on), and then create a bar graph of the resultant data as shown below. (Because of space limitations, there may be room on the graph for only the top five favorites in each category.) Students can use a felt-tipped pen (that washes off) to record their tallies on a laminated, large graph template that is attached to the bulletin board. Finally, pairs of students must answer the following question: What does the graph tell you?

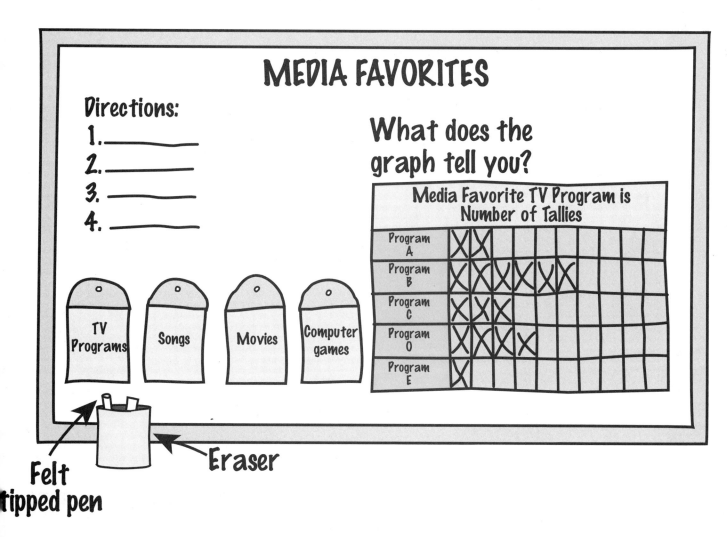

303

Parent Letter

Dear Parents:

Children are often unaware of how the media affect them. Yet every day, messages from TV, radio, film, records, and newspapers and other print media bombard their senses and flood their environments. This theme on media is designed to help children critically examine media messages.

At School:

During our study of media, your child will be engaged in the following activities:

- Using newspapers to find information
- Producing a class newspaper
- Conducting surveys on students' media preferences
- Analyzing media advertisements
- Finding places in the news
- Testing consumer products
- Searching for numbers in the news
- Creating multimedia presentations

At Home:

Here are some media experiences you can share with your child:

- Watch your child's favorite TV show with him or her.
- Talk to your child about his or her favorite movies, cartoons, magazines, books, music, and/or computer games.
- Ask your child to tell you about a favorite toy, cereal, game, etc. (Have any of the items been advertised on TV?)

Linking Up:

Each and every day, children are influenced by what they see, hear, and read in the media. Draw the outline of a TV on the chalkboard. Ask students to imagine that a picture has appeared on the screen. Have them describe the picture. What sorts of images do students associate with a TV screen? Put their associations and comments on the chalkboard.

Social Studies:

1. Development of Media

Bring in an assortment of old (e.g., a rotary telephone, a 45 rpm record) and new (e.g., mobile cellular telephone, CD) media technologies.

Have students write reports, draw illustrations, and make time lines that describe and show the following important events in the development of media: cave paintings (20,000 B.C.); first written documents made of clay tablets (3200–2850 B.C.); Chinese invented paper (1 A.D.); Chinese invented movable type for printing (about 1045); Europeans reinvented movable type for printing (mid-1400s); an improved photograph developed (1830s); electric telegraph invented (1840); typewriter invented (1868); telephone invented (1876); phonograph invented (1877); movies (late 1890s and early 1900s); television broadcasts made (1936); photocopying machine perfected (1960); cassette videotape recorder developed (1970s); personal computers introduced (late 1970s); compact disc players and mobile cellular telephones introduced (early 1980s); and the Internet, a global network of millions of computers, reached a mass market (1990s).

Name _____

Directions: Circle the answer that most accurately describes you.

1. On average, how much time do you spend daily watching TV?
   less than   1–2 hours   3–4 hours   more than
   1/2 hour   4 hours

2. How often do you read a newspaper or magazine?
   almost   once a   2–4 times   almost every
   never   week   a week   day

3. How often do you go to a movie theater?
   almost   once or twice   once   more than
   never   a month   a week   once a week

4. How often do you watch a movie on video at home?
   almost   2–3 times   once   more than
   never   a month   a week   once a week

5. How often do you listen to the radio?
   never   2–3 times   3–4 times   almost
                     a month   a week   every day

6. How often do you listen to CDs or audiotapes?
   never   2–3 times   3–4 times   almost
                     a month   a week   every day

7. How often do you use a computer to access information?
   never   2–3 times   3–4 times   almost
                     a month   a week   every day

8. Which of the following do you like to do the most? Place a 1 on the space before the thing you like to do most often, a 2 on the space before your next favorite thing, and so on.
   _____ Read a newspaper, magazine, or book
   _____ Watch TV
   _____ Listen to the radio
   _____ Listen to CDs or tapes
   _____ Go to a movie theater
   _____ Access information on a computer

FIGURE 29-1

2. Media Survey

Help students conduct a preference survey. Students can complete a simple questionnaire, such as the one shown in Figure 29-1. Younger learners can take the questionnaire orally and tape-record their answers. Before they take the survey, have students make predictions of possible results.

3. TV Preferences

Help students conduct a class survey to find out their TV program preferences. Ask: What is your favorite TV program? and Why do you like it best? Have students write down (or tape) their responses. After the results of the survey are compiled, ask students to tell you what they have learned about their preferences. Did a particular TV program emerge as a clear class favorite? What do they like best about their favorite programs?

4. Hidden Persuaders

Discuss the ads aired during students' favorite TV programs. Do students remember the advertisements (the sponsors, products, and commercials) associated with their favorite programs? Do students want and use particular product brands that are advertised during their favorite programs? If so, why are these brands better than other brands? Does advertising influence their brand choices? (See Science Activity #1 for a related activity.)

5. Media Stereotypes

A *stereotype* is an oversimplified, distorted mental image of a group of people that is based on inadequate and erroneous information. Bring in some ads from magazines and newspapers. Show students examples of ads that reflect stereotypes. Let students search for examples of stereotypes in various print media. Provide videotaped segments of TV programs for student viewing. Assign students the task of observing and recording how various groups of people are portrayed on the TV programs and commercials. What images are TV viewers receiving? Among the groups on which the students might focus are women, men, children, the elderly, African Americans, Hispanics, and Native Americans.

6. Classified Ads

Students can investigate job announcements found in the classified section of the newspaper. Do certain types of careers seem to be emphasized? Have students search the classified ads to find specific products and services, such as the following: washing machine, piano, music lessons, pets, furniture, home repair work, yard cleaning and landscaping, and sports equipment. What do the ads tell students about people's wants and needs? Provide local maps, and have students locate homes and apartments listed "For Sale" and "For Rent."

7. Mapping

Provide atlases, and let students locate places mentioned in local, state, national, and international news stories.

8. Change

Give students an assortment of well-illustrated magazines, both old and new. Using the illustrations as their data base, let students locate and describe changes in a variety of areas, such as the following: tools, clothing, transportation, appliances, foods, fashions, entertainment, and businesses.

9. Oral History

Let students ask parents, grandparents, and other older adults the following questions about their media habits when they were the students' age: What were some of the radio (TV) programs you liked to listen to (watch) when you were my age? What were some of your favorite movies? What are some differences between radio (TV) when you were my age and radio (TV) today?

Language Arts:

1. Newspaper Index

Provide pairs of students with copies of old newspapers. Point out the index. Explain that the index tells the reader where to find the different sections of the newspaper. Have students use the index to find different sections, such as the following: advice, arts and leisure, astrology, books, editorials and opinions, comics, local news, national news, world news, obituaries, travel, classified, weather, and sports. Younger students can focus on the illustrations to help them discover a basis for the paper's organization.

2. Identify Examples

Have students find specific examples of items found in different sections of the newspaper.

3. Topic Search

Challenge students to find information in newspapers related to an assortment of topics that they have identified. If the class has difficulty coming up with topics, offer a few suggestions from the following list:

Dogs	Famous athletes
Cars	Oceans
Clothes	Temperatures
Food	Europe
Movies	Judges
Sales	The President
TV shows	Animals
Film stars	Big numbers
Large cities	Homes

4. Comic Sequencing

Cut up comic strips into separate frames. Store frames for each comic strip in separate manila envelopes. Let individual students put the mixed-up comic frames in correct order.

5. Comic Captions

Delete dialogues and captions from comic strips. Have students create their own dialogues and captions.

6. Make a Newspaper

Have students make their own school newspaper. Divide students into cooperative learning groups, and assign each group one of the following sections of the newspaper: advice, sports, editorial, advertisements, classroom news, news from the principal, media center/book news, food, and health news. Help students interview important sources for school news, such as the physical education teacher, school nurse, custodian, principal, media center specialist or librarian, cafeteria manager, and other students. The newspaper can be formatted using *Writing Center*, or some other software program. Have each group enter its information on its section at the computer. After all groups have finished, print out a copy, and let them proofread and correct their work. The final step: Distribute newspapers to students, teachers, and staff.

7. Multimedia Approaches

Challenge students to develop a multimedia presentation of a favorite topic. If possible, introduce students to *Kid's Pix Studio*, or any other computerized-multimedia presentation tool. Even without computers, students under your guidance can combine text, graphics, and sound to create multimedia presentations. Let them use one or more of the following approaches in their presentations: opaque projector, overhead projector, posters, chalkboard, audiotape recorder, videotape recorder, slides or photographs, diagrams, charts and other graphics, and models.

Science:

1. Product Testing

Have students sample different brands of products advertised on TV. For example, they might sample several brands of cereals or cookies to determine which brands were tastier—crunchier, sweeter, fruitier, nuttier, and the like. Help students design procedures for testing the products and recording the results.

2. Weather Report

Students can create their own TV-style weather reports based on weather information found in the daily newspaper. Laminate a large, white blank map of the United States, including Alaska and Hawaii. Create ten or more maps symbols for each of the following different weather conditions: sunny, partly cloudy, cloudy, rain, snow, and thunderstorms. Laminate the map symbols and cut them out. Let small groups of students take turns researching and presenting the daily weather report. The map symbols can be attached to the wall map with EZTAK, or a similar product, that can be removed easily.

3. Field Trip

Arrange a field trip to the local newspaper company. Students can see the people and machines that produce the morning or evening news. What skills and resources are needed? What career fields are represented? Let students draw pictures to illustrate what they learned on the field trip.

4. Computer Info

Show students how to track down information on various topics through the Internet. With Netscape, or other Web browser software, students can point-and-click to track down information on practically any subject. (Note: Check your school system's policy on students' use of the Internet.)

Math:

1. Shopping List

Provide students with an assortment of ads that show prices for specific items. Let students make shopping lists, and then calculate the total costs for all of the items on their lists.

2. Looking for Bargains

Have students calculate the sale prices of various ad items if they are "50% off," "30% off," "40% off," and so on.

3. Sport Page Numbers

Let students identify the different ways numbers are used on the sports page. For example, they are used for identification (numbers on uniforms, race cars, in photographs), rankings (golf money winners, top teams), averages (field goals, hits), totals (yardage, at bats, time of possession, errors, fouls), and statistics (individual and team).

4. Measuring Winners

Challenge students to identify the unit of measurement in determining winners in various sports, such as golf (strokes), baseball (base

runners reaching home plate), running (hours, minutes), tennis (opponent not returning ball over net and inside court), and jumping and vaulting (feet and inches).

5. Page Finders

Have students use the tables of contents and indexes found in newspapers and magazines to look up articles and information.

6. Comparing Pages

Students can compare the average number of pages, illustrations, advertisements, columns, and the like in different newspapers and magazines.

7. Measuring Ads

Provide rulers, and let students measure the surface areas of full-page, half-page, quarter-page, and smaller ads. Help students check the newspaper company to find out how much different-size ads costs. Then, have students figure out the advertising costs for various-size ads.

Music:

1. Ad Jingles

Encourage students to create catchy ad jingles that are designed to sell products on TV or radio.

2. Top Twenty Countdown

Help students take a survey of their music preferences. Identify the types of music played on popular radio stations. What do the results indicate about students' and the general population's popular music preferences?

Art:

1. Create a Comic

Have students create original comic strips.

2. Poster Art

Let students create colorful, eye-catching posters that are designed to promote a service or sell a product.

Books:

1. Gibbons, Gail. (1987). *Deadline! From News to Newspaper*. New York: Thomas Y. Crowell. Primary.

2. Koral, April. (1989). *In the Newsroom*. New York: Franklin Watts. Intermediate.

3. Fisher, Leonard. (1981). *Nineteenth Century America: The Newspapers*. New York: Holiday House. Intermediate.

4. English, Betty Lou. (1985). *Behind the Headlines at a Big City Paper*. New York: Lothrop, Lee, and Shepard Books. Advanced.

5. Miller, Margaret. (1985). *Hot Off the Press: A Day at the Daily News*. New York: Crown Publishers, Inc. Primary.

6. Trainer, David. (1980). *A Day in the Life of a TV News Reporter*. Mahwah, NJ: Troll Associates. Primary.

7. Granfield, Linda. (1993). *Extra! Extra! The Who, What, Where, When, and Why of Newspapers*. New York: Orchard Books. Intermediate.

8. Craig, Janet. (1990). *What's It Like to Be a Newspaper Reporter?* Mahwah, NJ: Troll Associates. Early Elementary.

9. Waters, Sarah. (1989). *How Newspapers Are Made*. New York: Facts on File. Middle Elementary.

Software:

1. *Writing Center* [Mac CD-ROM]. Cambridge, MA: The Learning Company. Primary, Intermediate, Advanced.

2. *Hollywood* [Mac MPC CD-ROM]. Emeryville, CA: Theatrix. Intermediate, Advanced.

3. *Kid Pix Studio* [Mac MPC CD-ROM]. Novato, CA: Broderbund. Primary, Intermediate, Advanced.

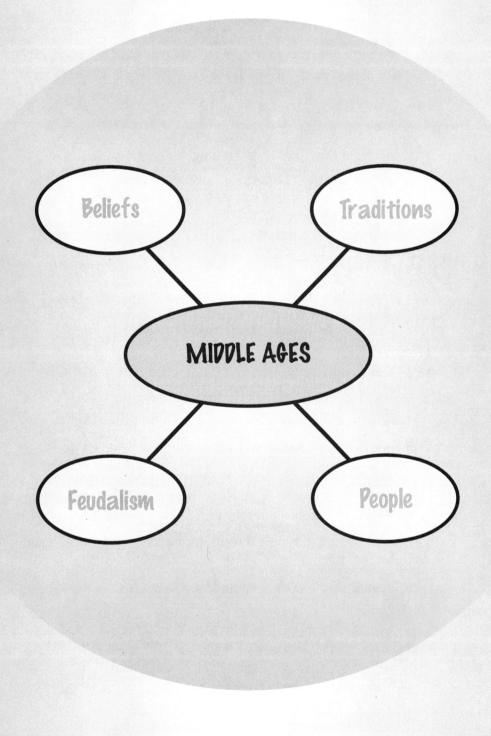

Beliefs

Traditions

MIDDLE AGES

Feudalism

People

Theme Goals:

Students will:

1. identify the period of history known as the Middle Ages.

2. use pictures of primary sources to describe the way of life during the Middle Ages.

3. describe the main characteristics of feudalism.

4. describe the role of knights.

5. experience how scribes copied manuscripts by hand.

6. contrast medieval people's beliefs about the Earth with current understandings.

7. describe how medieval buildings were constructed.

8. examine medieval games.

9. make replicas of stained glass windows.

Theme Concepts:

1. The Middle Ages covered the period from 500 A.D. to 1500 A.D.

2. Primary sources reveal aspects of everyday life in the Middle Ages.

3. The political system that developed during the Middle Ages is called feudalism.

4. Knights played an important role during the Middle Ages.

5. Books were copied by hand during the Middle Ages.

6. People during the Middle Ages believed erroneously that the Earth did not move, and that it was at the center of the universe.

7. Some popular games during the middle ages emphasized military strategy.

8. Beautiful stained glass windows were created during the Middle Ages.

Vocabulary:

1. manuscript
2. tapestry
3. feudalism
4. knight
5. manor

6. serf
7. lord
8. scribe
9. calligraphy
10. parchment

Instructional Bulletin Board

The purpose of this bulletin board is to spotlight students who engage in exemplary classroom behavior by recognizing them as members of the Knights of _____ (name to be decided by the teacher). Explain to students that, like the code of honor that guided a knight's conduct, the code of conduct for the classroom is a standard to which everyone should aspire. Decorate the border of the bulletin board with pictures of knights. List the code of conduct (classroom list of rules stated in positive terms, e.g., "Raise your hand if you want to talk.") on the left side of the bulletin board. On the right side of the bulletin board attach the photos and names of those students whose behavior exemplifies the code of conduct.

Parent Letter

Dear Parents:

The Middle Ages was a time of sharp contrasts. For the rich lords and ladies and their courts, there were festive banquets and knights in shining armor. For the poor peasants, however, there were backbreaking work, miserable food, and huts with dirt floors. During our study of the Middle Ages, we will be focusing on this interesting period in world history. Some of the activities and events planned for the theme are listed below.

In School:

In our theme on the Middle Ages, students will be:

- Identifying the Germanic tribes that replaced the Romans in western Europe
- Using pictures to learn about the past
- Building a feudal system in the classroom
- Copying old manuscripts by hand
- Learning about a knight's code of conduct
- Making paper replicas of stained glass windows

At Home:

Together with your child, take some time to do any or all of the following:

- Read aloud a story about the legend of King Arthur and his Knights of the Round Table.
- Watch a video of one of the film versions of "Robin Hood."
- Listen to music from *Camelot*, a Broadway musical based upon the legend of King Arthur.

Linking Up:

Show students a picture of a medieval castle. Ask them if they think it would be fun to live in a castle. (Most likely, some students will say that it would be fun.) Help students make a list of all the things that make their homes and school comfortable places in which to live and learn. The students' list will probably include such things as heating and air conditioning, electric lights, plumbing (including bathroom and rest room facilities), microwave ovens, water fountains, televisions, computers, frozen foods, carpeting, chairs, sofas, and beds, to name a few items. After the list is compiled, dramatically cross off each item on the list that would not be available to people of the Middle Ages. Ask students to guess why you are crossing items off the list. Can students discover the reason for your action? If not, explain that a medieval castle had none of the luxuries you crossed off; point out that people today take such luxuries for granted. Would the students want to live in a castle without such comforts? Encourage students to discuss their feelings and thoughts.

Social Studies:

1. Medieval History

Brief Background. The Middle Ages is the name given to a period of western European history from about 500 A.D. (it began with the fall of the Roman Empire) to 1500 (it ended with the "rebirth" of interest in classical learning). As Rome declined in power, warring Germanic tribes took over Western Europe. The tribes created many kingdoms and replaced Roman civilization with their own rough customs and traditions. The Romans called these invaders barbarians because of their fierce appearance and ignorance (most could not read or write). Charlemagne, a powerful king of the Franks, who ruled from 768 to 814 A.D., conquered many of the tribes and much of Europe. He helped establish a new political system to unify and maintain control over his kingdom. That system, called *feudalism*, formed the social structure for people of the Middle Ages. Because of the support of Charlemagne and subsequent European rulers, the Christian Church became very powerful and influenced all aspects of medieval life.

Show students maps of the Roman Empire before and after its decline. Let students trace the invasion routes of the following Germanic tribes: Visigoths, who invaded Spain; Angles, Jutes, and Saxons, who invaded Britain; the Franks, who invaded Gaul (present-day France); and the Vikings, who raided the coasts of Northern and Western Europe (Figure 30-1).

2. Everyday Life in the Middle Ages

Provide students with an assortment of colorfully illustrated books on the Middle Ages. They should include lots of photographs of paintings, armor, weapons, stained glass windows, manuscripts, sculpture, tapestry, and other things created by people of the time. Then, help students use the visual information to describe different aspects of medieval life including the following: warfare and weapons, the way people dressed, the way they traveled, the work they did, the tools they used, the foods they ate, the structures they built, the beliefs they had, and the kinds of things they valued. Write students' statements down on a retrieval chart. As they learn more about the Middle Ages, they can recheck their statements for accuracy and modify them if necessary.

3. Living in Medieval Times

Brief Background. Life in the Middle Ages was based on the social system called feudalism. At the top of the feudal social system was the king. The king granted land, called fiefs, to men of noble rank or birth, called *lords*. In return, each lord pledged his loyalty to the king and vowed to protect him. Serving the lords and their king in battle were mounted men-at-arms, called *knights*. The lord's land was called a *manor* and included an estate house or castle, church, fields, pastures, and a village. Craftsmen in the village produced almost everything that was needed on the manor. Most of the people on the manor were *serfs*, who were bound to the land and could not leave the service of the lord. The serfs lived outside of the walls of the castle in small villages. The serfs did the hard work. They labored in the fields, made the food, tended the animals, and served the lord in the manor house.

To give students a vivid picture of the Middle Ages, read aloud selections from *The Middle Ages* by Sarah Howarth (Viking Press, 1993), or another appropriate children's book. Gather

315

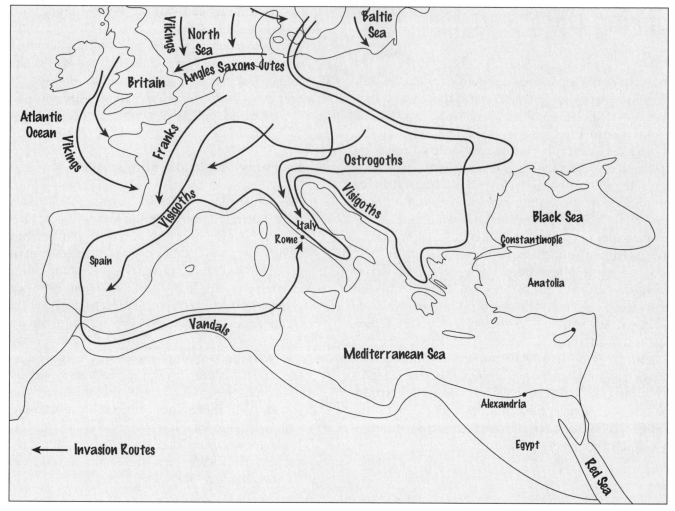

Invasion Routes

FIGURE 30-1

other books on the Middle Ages and make them available for students to read at a "Middle Ages Learning Center." Then, transform your classroom into a medieval manor. Students can use cardboard boxes (try to get lots of large boxes from appliance and furniture stores) and other construction materials, tape, and art supplies to create a scaled-down version of a castle, other manor buildings, church, stone walls, a moat, a plow for the fields, and additional tools. Let some students create costumes and assume the roles of lords, knights, and serfs. These students can explain their medieval ways of living to other students, who can assume the roles of "time travelers" from the present. The time travlers can explain their own modern lifestyles to the medieval role-players. Help students create simple skits to demonstrate and reinforce their understanding of the Middle Ages.

4. Knights

Brief Background. Knights were retained by lords to serve and protect them. Training for knighthood consisted of a long and difficult apprenticeship under the guidance of a knight. A boy preparing to be a knight began his training as a page at around the age of seven. A page learned the customs and courtesies of proper behavior, practiced using small weapons, and played chess and other games of military strategy. At age 15, a page advanced to the position of squire. A squire learned to fight skillfully on horseback, and he often accompanied his knight in battle. After about five years of service as a squire, the young man was eligible for knighthood. In the knighthood ceremony, the squire would kneel before the knight, who would say "I dub you knight," as he tapped his sword on the squire's back.

Read aloud selections of *Knights in Shinning Armor* by Gail Gibbons (Little, Brown, and Company, 1995), or some other appropriate children's book that describes knights. Discuss the knights' training, code of chivalry, clothing, armor, and weapons. Ask students why soldiers today don't wear armor. When knights were dressed head to toe in armor, the only way to tell one knight from another was by their coats of arms like the one shown in Figure 30-2. A knight's coat of arms was painted on his shield. Provide students with art materials and triangular pieces of poster paper, and let them design coats of arms that symbolize personal qualities and characteristics.

Language Arts:

1. Preserving the Past

Brief Background. During the Middle Ages, manuscripts were written by hand on parchment made from the skin of a sheep or goat. Monks and other religious people had the responsibility of copying

Coat of Arms

FIGURE 30-2

documents. The best manuscript writers, or *scribes*, as they were called, were also artists who frequently embellished their beautiful handwriting with colorful designs or paintings. Because handwritten manuscripts were produced in extremely limited quantities, only a relatively small group of people of wealth and/or prestige and scholarship had access to them during the Middle Ages.

Show students examples of manuscripts from the Middle Ages found in library sources, and let them try their hands at being medieval scribes. Choose a writing script for them to copy, such as Old English, that looks similar to the writing style of the Middle Ages. Today, the art of fine handwriting is called *calligraphy*. If available, use calligraphy pens and ink (provide brown paper to simulate parchment) and ask a skilled calligrapher to help supervise the activity. After students finish copying letters and words, remind them that, during the Middle Ages, the only way to preserve a text for future generations was to write it down word for word. Have students contrast the time and effort required to copy a page of text by hand and that required to capture a page by typewriter or word processor. Discuss modern machines (i.e., typewriters, photocopiers, computers, printers, computerized printing presses and publishing houses) that have replaced the scribes. Has technology made the job of knowledge-spreading easier and faster? If possible, take students to a newspaper company to observe the machines used to produce newspapers.

Science:

1. Where in the World Is the World?

Brief Background. People during the Middle Ages erroneously believed that the Earth was the center of the universe and that it did not move. They accepted the view of early Greek astronomer Ptolemy, and thought that the planets, the Sun, and all of the stars revolved around the Earth. (It was not until the sixteenth century that Copernicus published his theory of the solar system.)

Show students a diagram (Figure 30-3) of the Ptolemaic view of the Sun and planets, which shows the Earth at the center. Have students list any everyday observations that might lead someone to believe that this erroneous notion was true (such as the apparent daily movement of the Sun

317

across the sky from east to west). Demonstrate the revolution of the Earth and planets around the Sun. Help students see how the Earth's rotation on its tilted axis (once every 23 hours and 56 minutes) and its journey around the Sun (once every 365 1/2 days, traveling at 18 1/2 miles a second) cause the change in seasons in the temperate zones. Show students NASA photographs of the view of the Sun, Earth, and other planets of the solar system taken by deep space probes. Have students tell you what they see in the photographs. Use Styrofoam balls to make a model of the solar system.

2. Medieval Machines

Brief Background. Among the most magnificent buildings ever constructed in the history of the world are the cathedrals and castles of the Middle Ages. Today, these massive architectural marvels still dot the landscape of Europe, and millions of tourists flock to see them annually. The huge interiors of medieval churches were made possible by the development of *flying buttresses*. These stone arms, which extend from the ground to the exterior walls, provided additional structual support and made it possible to build the churches taller.

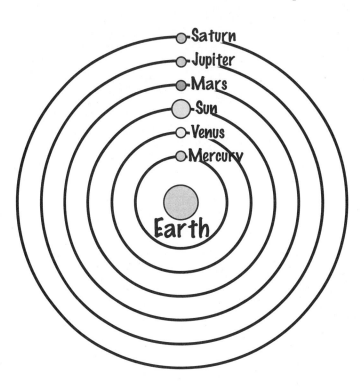

Ptolemy's Earth-Centered System

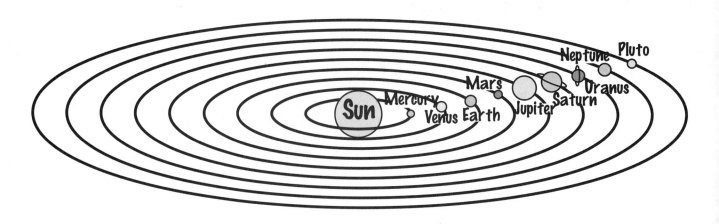

Solar System

FIGURE 30-3

Show students pictures of medieval churches and castles during different stages of their construction. Two excellent sources of illustrations and information on castles are *Medieval Castles* by Brian Adams (Gloucester Press, 1989) and *Castle* by David Macaulay (Houghton Mifflin, 1977). Provide students with drawing paper and construction materials, and let them make drawings and models of medieval castles and churches to display in the classroom. Challenge students to apply the principle of the flying buttress to the construction of their models of churches.

3. Medieval Maladies

Brief Background. The Middle Ages was not a healthy or safe time in history. Knowledge of proper hygiene and disease prevention was nonexistent. Garbage and sewage were thrown in the streets and left to rot. Drinking water was polluted. Meats and other foods were badly preserved and often contaminated. Neither the castles of the rich nor the huts of the peasants were very liveable. Both were damp, cold, drafty, and dirty. Periods of famines and plagues, as well as everyday unhealthy conditions, caused great pain, suffering, and death. For most people of the Middle Ages, life was harsh and short.

Help students gather information about recent or on-going famines. What places around the world experience food shortages? What recent bad weather conditions in the United States have resulted in crop failures? Devise a plan to gather food for soup kitchens, homeless shelters, and needy people in the local community. Invite the school nurse to the classroom to present a brief program on communicable diseases that spread quickly from person to person. During the Middle Ages, European trade with the Orient was drastically curtailed. This meant that Asian spices were in extremely short supply. Since these rare spices were needed to keep food from spoiling, they were more highly prized and sought after than gold and precious gems. Bring in samples of the following Asian spices for students to view and smell: ginger, pepper, cinnamon, clove, cardamom, and nutmeg. Serve some cookies and cakes flavored with ginger and cinnamon along with glasses of milk flavored with nutmeg.

Math:

1. Making Props

To give students a vivid impression of the Middle Ages, help them construct a classroom-sized manor complete with castle, church, moat, walls, fields, and costumed characters, as described in Social Studies Activity #3. Students will apply many math skills as they engage in the following construction activities: measuring area for structures; estimating amounts of construction materials (cardboard boxes, poster board, foil, cloth, etc.) needed; measuring materials; and cutting materials to correct size.

2. Medieval Games

Brief Background. Two popular games of the Middle Ages that required reasoning and mathematical skills were checkers and chess. In both games pieces, called men, are moved around by two players on a board divided by squares. These pieces represent two armies, and the goal of both games is to win the battle. In chess, each army includes foot soldiers, called pawns, and a king, a queen, two rooks (castles), two bishops, and two knights. In checkers, one player wins by capturing (or blocking) all of the other player's pieces, while in the game of chess, one player wins by capturing or blocking the other player's king.

If they are interested and able, let students play the two board games at appropriate times during their study of the Middle Ages. If students are unfamiliar with the more complex game of chess, you many want to simply show them the chess pieces and relate the game to the medieval way of life, in which warfare played a large role.

Art:

1. Stained Glass Windows

Some of the most beautiful examples of medieval art were the stained glass windows that adorned churches. The pieces of colored glass that formed the design were held together by strips of lead. Show students pictures of medieval stained glass windows (Figure 30-4). Help students make their own stained glass windows. Provide pieces of heavy, shiny paper of different colors (from old magazines), and let each student first use a pencil to lightly outline a window frame and scene or design for the window on a sheet of white poster board, then cut the paper into shapes and glue the shapes onto the paper to fill in the design; and lastly, cut narrow strips of black construction paper and glue on the design to represent the lead strips.

FIGURE 30-4 Stained Glass Window

Cooking:

1. Medieval Banquet

Brief Background. During the Middle Ages, the manor provided everything that was needed by the lord and peasants. Foods produced and consumed on the manor included grapes, bread, beans, cabbages, turnips, poultry, and beef. The lord and his court would have fancy banquets where huge portions of food were served. Wild game was especially popular at these banquets. Wild boar stuffed with garlic and roasted on a spit was a favorite delicacy. Wine and beer were the preferred beverages. In contrast, the poor peasants' diet was bland and sparse. The standard fare was a watery porridge, called gruel, and moldy bread.

Have students make a list of their favorite foods, treats and snacks. Explain to students that many foods that they take for granted were either unavailable or unknown to medieval people. As described in Science Activity #3, because there was very little trade with the Orient during the Middle Ages, spices were very rare and expensive. And since the Americas had not yet been "discovered," Europeans had no knowledge of New World foods, such as chocolate, potatoes, and corn. An excellent way to culminate the unit is to plan and stage a feast. To give students a realistic picture of medieval banquets, read aloud selections from *A Medieval Feast* by Aliki Brandenberg (Thomas Y. Crowell, 1993) or *Food and Feasts in the Middle Ages* by Imogen Dawson (Macmillan, 1994), or another appropriate children's book. You can serve fresh grapes, pears, and apples, a stew of beans, cabbage, and turnips, roast pork or chicken, and fresh-baked bread. Students can dress in the costumes of lords, ladies, knights, and peasant servants. If the talent is available, student troubadours can sing medieval songs, and jugglers can entertain the court.

Books:

1. Day, James. (1989). *The Black Death*. New York: The Bookwright Press. Intermediate, Advanced.

2. Dawson, Imogen. (1994). *Food and Feasts in the Middle Ages*. New York: Macmillan Publishing Co. Intermediate, Advanced.

3. Gibbons, Gail. (1995). *Knights in Shining Armor*. New York: Little, Brown, and Company. Primary.

4. Adams, Brian. (1989). *Medieval Castles*. New York: Gloucester Press. Intermediate.

5. Brandenberg, Aliki. (1993). *A Medieval Feast*. New York: Thomas Y. Crowell. Primary.

6. Caselli, Giovanni. (1986). *A Medieval Monk*. New York: Macdonald & Co. Publishers, Ltd. Intermediate.

7. Corbishley, Mike. (1993). *The Medieval World*. New York: Peter Bedrick Books. Advanced.

8. Howarth, Sarah. (1993). *The Middle Ages*. New York: Viking Press. Advanced.

9. Maria, Rius, Verges, Gloria, and Verges, Oriol. (1988). *The Middle Ages*. New York: Barron's Educational Series, Inc. Primary.

10. Macaulay, David. (1977). *Castle*. Boston: HoughtonMifflin.

Software:

1. *Battle Chess* [Mac IBM CD-ROM]. Irvine: CA Interplay. Intermediate, Advanced.

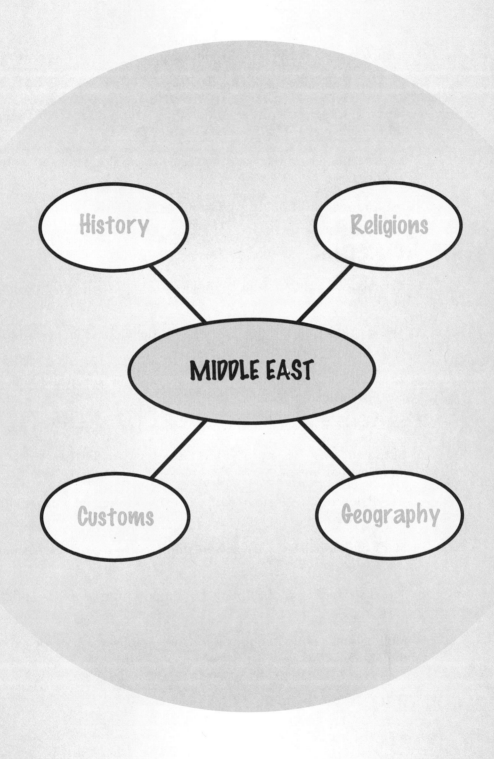

History

Religions

MIDDLE EAST

Customs

Geography

Theme Goals:

Students will:

1. identify significant characteristics of the Middle East.

2. locate nations of the Middle East on a map.

3. describe Jerusalem's history.

4. compare the Jewish and Moslem religions.

5. contrast Arab and United States customs.

6. describe the effects on the Middle East of the discovery of huge oil reserves.

7. analyze numerical data and solve math problems related to the Middle East.

8. explore ways to bring peace to the Middle East.

Theme Concepts:

1. The Middle East was the birthplace of important early civilizations.

2. The world's first writing system was developed in the Middle East.

3. The following three major world religions began in the Middle East: Judaism, Christianity, and Islam.

4. The Middle East is located where Africa, Europe, and Asia meet.

5. Jerusalem was the site of important events in Jewish, Moslem, and Christian history.

6. Israeli Jews and Moslem Arabs speak different languages and practice different religions.

7. Many traditional Arab customs are different from customs in America.

8. The discovery of oil has played an important role in the Middle East.

9. Multinational efforts continue for the establishment of peace in the Middle East.

Vocabulary:

1. religion   5. emotion

2. Judaism   6. latitude

3. Christianity   7. longitude

4. Islam

Instructional Bulletin Board

The purpose of the bulletin board is to give students practice locating the nations of the Middle East on a map. Cover the bulletin board with a large sheet of white paper. Using a transparency of a blank political map of the Middle East projected on the paper, trace the map on the bulletin board. Make individual name cards for the following nations of the Middle East: Israel, Saudi Arabia, Iraq, Syria, Jordan, Kuwait, Yemen, Oman, United Arab Emirates, Bahrain, Qatar, Iran, and Turkey. Students can attach name cards to the map, then check answer the key and correct mistakes. Store name cards in a large envelope.

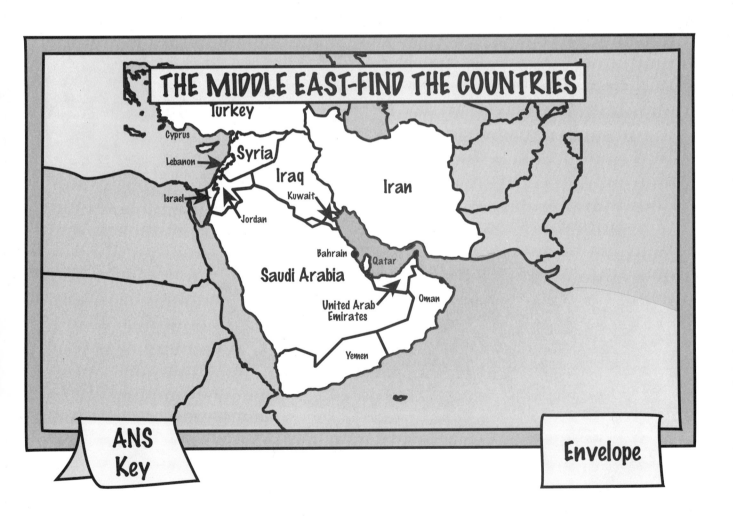

Parent Letter

Dear Parents:

We are beginning our study of the Middle East. The story of the Middle East spans thousands of years. It is a fascinating and often turbulent history that includes the rise and fall of ancient civilizations, the birth and spread of three world religions, the discovery of tremendous oil reserves, and the ongoing conflict between Arabs and Jews. To introduce the Middle East to students, we are planning many interesting activities, of which some are listed below.

At School:

Our theme on the Middle East will involve students in the following:

- Identifying symbols of the Middle East
- Exploring the sacred city of Jerusalem
- Comparing the Jewish and Moslem religions
- Dramatizing Arab customs
- Brainstorming ways to resolve conflicts
- Looking at the important role oil plays in the Middle East

At Home:

To help reinforce the concepts learned in this theme, we encourage you to take your child to the library and check out a book on the Middle East. Read the book aloud with your child, and talk about the national customs and histories of Middle Eastern peoples.

Linking Up:

Read selections from "Aladdin" from *The Arabian Nights* (many versions of this story adapted for children are available in most libraries). Many children know the story of Aladdin by heart; they have heard it many times, and they have seen the Disney movie. What appeals to children most about this famous story is the magic. Aladdin rubs his wonderful lamp and a genie appears. The genie possesses the bewildering power to grant his master's wishes. Most of Aladdin's wishes are associated with his efforts to marry the Princess Badroulboudour (named "Jasmine" in the Disney story and movie version). Provide students with copies of the lamp (Figure 31-1). Ask students what they would do if they had Aladdin's lamp. Their list might include money, toys, games and trips for themselves, vacations and cars for their families, or food and shelters for the needy. Have each student draw a picture of a "wish" inside the outline of Aladdin's lamp. Discuss their wishes and then display their drawings on the wall. Explain that today, in the Middle East, some nations possess a real substance that is almost as powerful as Aladdin's magical lamp—oil. Oil-rich nations in the Middle East have the wealth to make many of their wishes come true.

Social Studies:

1. Introduction to the Middle East

Brief Background. The story of the Middle East spans thousands of years. It is a fascinating and often turbulent history that includes the rise and fall of ancient civilizations, the birth and spread of three great religions, the discovery of tremendous oil reserves, and the ongoing conflict between Arabs and Jews.

To introduce the Middle East, show students the following items and ask them to speculate about how they are related to the Middle East.

Items	Significance
Pencil	World's first writing system was invented in Middle East
Drawings of the star of David, a crescent and star, and a lamb and cross	Three major religions began in Middle East; the three religions and their symbols are Judaism (star of David), Islam (crescent and star), and Christianity (lamb and cross)
A can of oil	The world's largest oil reserve is in the Middle East
drawing or picture of a white dove	Represents the peace process that will hopefully bring peace to the countries of the Middle East

2. Middle East Geography

Provide students with globes and world maps (Figure 31-2). Help them find the Middle East. Ask students to describe what the map tells them about the Middle East (e.g., nearness to major bodies of water, place where other large land areas—Europe, Asia, and Africa—meet). Give students cardpaper cutouts of Middle Eastern nations, and have them match the shape of the cutouts with the shapes of the nations on maps and globes. Introduce or review the following nations of the Middle East: Israel, Saudi Arabia, Iraq, Syria, Lebanon, Kuwait, Yemen, Oman, United Arab Emirates, Bahrain, Qatar, Jordan, Iran, and Turkey. Have students use atlases to compare and contrast the location, shape, area, population, topography, vegetation, climate, natural resources, and access to waterways of the different countries. Provide blank maps showing political boundaries, and have students label the countries.

Aladdin's Lamp

FIGURE 31-1

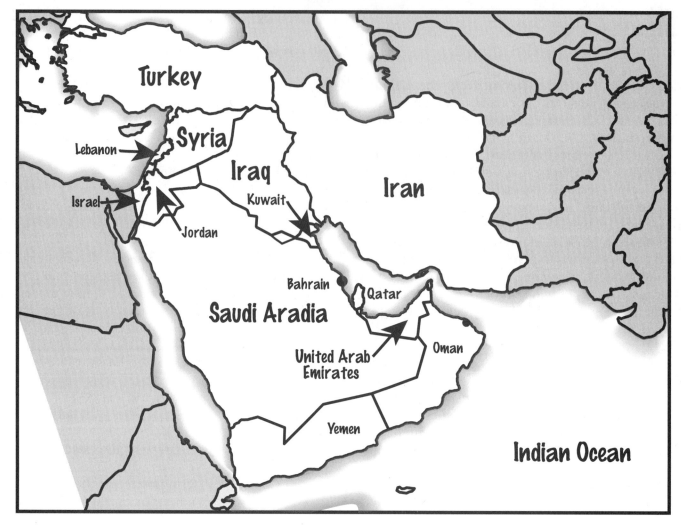

The Middle East

FIGURE 31-2

3. Gifts From the Ancient Middle East

Brief Background. Archaeologists and historians have recorded many ingredients of civilization that probably originated in the Middle East. The world's first civilization probably arose in Mesopotamia, in present-day Iraq, over 5,000 years ago. The Sumerian civilization in Mesopotamia developed the world's first system of writing, called *cuneiform.* The Sumerians made wedge-shaped symbols using a reed stylus that was pressed into wet clay tablets.

Some of the inventions and developments attributed to the ancient Mesopotamians are listed below. Ask students to provide examples of how these ancient "gifts" to us are related to or present in today's world. As a follow-up activity, provide each student with flattened wet clay and a popsicle-stick stylus, and let them experiment with the writing tools of the Sumerians. Show students pictures of Sumerian cuneiform tablets to copy, and also let them practice writing messages in their own language (see Figure 31-3).

Ancient Gifts	*Connections to Modern World*
Writing system	
Farming	
Potter's wheel	
Sailboats	
Wheeled carts	
Animal-drawn plows	
System of laws	
Algebra and geometry	

328

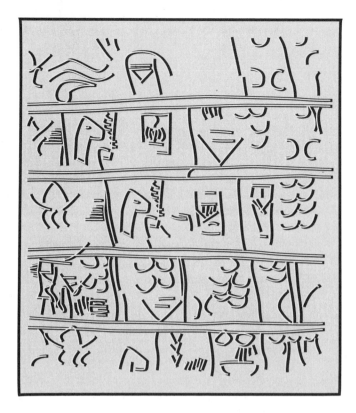

Child's Clay Tablet

FIGURE 31-3

4. The Sacred City of Jerusalem

Brief Background. During Jerusalem's 4,000-year-old history, the city was conquered, destroyed, and rebuilt many times. Babylonians, Greeks, Romans, Persians, Moslems, Crusaders, Ottoman Turks, and the British all came and went. Today, the ancient city is the capital of the Jewish nation of Israel. For the members of three major world religions—Judaism, Christianity, and Islam—Jerusalem is a holy place. The Wailing Wall, which is sacred to the Jews, is there, as is the site of the Prophet Muhammad's ascent to heaven. Jerusalem was visited many times by Jesus, and it was there that he was killed. Among the places in the city associated with Jesus' life are the Garden of Gethsemane and the Church of the Holy Sepulchre.

Read aloud selections from *Jerusalem, Shining Still* by Karla Kuskin (Harper & Row, 1987), or another appropriate children's book, that describes Jerusalem's colorful and often violent history. Have students locate the geographical origins of Jerusalem's conquerors. Encourage students to be aware of recent news reports about the city.

5. Religions in the Middle East

Brief Background. For many years, Jews and Moslem Arabs have fought over Jerusalem and the land of Israel. Israel was created in 1948 as a homeland for the Jewish people. At that time, most of the people who lived there were Moslem Arabs, called Palestinians. Since 1948, Jews from all over the world have settled in Israel, displacing the Palestinians and causing many of them to leave the country. A series of wars between Israel and its Arab neighbors have left the Middle East in turmoil. Although both sides have taken important steps toward peace (a peace accord was signed in 1993), much still remains to be done before trust and harmony can develop between Arabs and Jews.

To help students understand each side's religion, read selections from *Oasis of Peace* by Laurie Dolphin (Scholastic, 1993), or some other appropriate children's book. Using a chart format, help students list similarities and differences between the two groups. Invite a Jewish person and a Moslem person from the community to

	JEWS	MOSLEM ARABS
Language	Hebrew	Arabic
Religion	Judaism	Islam
Religious obligations	Do not eat pork; cannot eat milk and meat together; pray at the synagogue; read the holy book, Torah; celebrate Hanukkah and other holy days; obey the laws of Judaism, including the Ten Commandments	Do not eat pork; eat milk with meat; pray five times a day; read the holy book, Koran; celebrate the holy month of Ramadan; pray at the mosque; make a pilgrimage (hajji) to Mecca, site of holy shrine; give alms to the poor

class to talk about their respective ways of life.

6. Saudi Arabian Customs

Brief Background. Saudi Arabia, largest nation on the Arabian Peninsula, is a mixture of traditional and modern. Islam's holy prophet, Muhammad, lived and died in Saudi Arabia, and Mecca, site of one of Islam's holiest shrines, is located there. Traditional costumes and customs are a part of everyday Saudi Arabian life. However, despite Saudi Arabia's adherence to tradition, the nation has not spurned modern technology and conveniences. Wealth from oil has allowed Saudis to build modern schools and colleges, communications and transportation systems, and apartment and public buildings. Saudis in the cities drive cars, watch television, live in air-conditioned houses and apartments, and some wear western clothing in addition to tradition dress, which is shown in Figure 31-4.

Students can make Arabian costumes and dramatize some Arabian customs, which are described below. How do these customs compare with the students' customs? Have students complete the personal side of the chart below.

Language Arts:

1. Write It Down

Have students imagine they are either a Jew or Moslem Arab in Israel, and let them write or dictate accounts of how they felt when they heard that an Israeli-Arab peace accord was to be signed.

2. Solving Problems

Have students brainstorm ways to keep Jews and Arabs in the Middle East from fighting. Then, let students decide if some ways are better than others, and why. Finally, students can write or dictate a brief paragraph describing the best way.

3. Reading Expressions

Provide students with pictures of Middle Eastern people gathered from books and magazines. Write words that convey feelings—such as happy, sad, angry, frustrated, tense, troubled, calm, content, glad, and excited—on the chalkboard. Have students pick a feeling and match it with a facial expression that shows that emotion.

Science:

1. All About Oil

Brief Background. One of the world's richest oil reserves is located in the Middle East. Because of the great world demand for oil, some countries in the Middle East, like Saudi Arabia and Kuwait, have become very wealthy.

Have interested students investigate oil. Specifically, they can draw a map showing where it is found, and then write or dictate a report de-

ARABIAN CUSTOM	OUR CUSTOMS
Arabian women wear long dresses called darr'as. In public, Arabian women wear a black cloak. Arabian menwear long robes called dishdashas. On their head they wear a large white or red checked cloth, called a gheetra, that is held in place by a black rope.	
Arabians go to the marketplace to buy food, clothing, and other items.	
Arabian marriages are often arranged by the parents.	
During the holy month of Ramadan, children go from house to house singing songs of praise to those who fast. The children receive nuts and candy in return.	

330

Arabians in Traditional Attire
FIGURE 31-4

scribing its characteristics, how it is processed, what its uses are, and who its biggest users are. What have oil-producing nations done with the money they have earned from the sale of oil?

2. "Ships of the Desert"

Brief Background. In ancient and modern times, camels have transported Middle Eastern people and their possessions across the desert. Camels are ideally adapted to their desert environment. They have eyelashes that screen their eyes from sand, they can drink over 50 gallons of water in one day, and they sweat very little. Camels can carry over 300 pounds, travel up to 40 miles a day, and live for more than a week without water.

Read aloud selections from *Bedouin: The Nomads of the Desert* by Muhammad Alotaibi (Rouke Publications, 1989), or another appropriate children's book that describes the important role that camels play in the survival of nomadic people. Encourage interested students to research camels and the people who depend on them.

Math:

1. Bar Graphs

Provide students with population figures from atlases and almanacs, and have them construct bar graphs showing the population of each country in the Middle East.

2. Empty or Crowded?

Students can find the average population per square mile for each country in the Middle East, and then compare the figures with those for the United States.

3. Traveling to the Middle East

Have students measure distances between their community and cities in the Middle East. Then, let them compute travel times to destinations in the Middle East traveling 600 mph by nonstop jet.

4. Latitude and Longitude

Let students find the latitude and longitude coordinates for various nations of the Middle East.

Books:

1. Alotaibi, Muhammad. (1989). *Bedouin: The Nomads of the Desert.* Vero Beach, FL: Rourke Publications, Inc. Intermediate, Advanced.

2. Fakhro, Bahia, and Walko, Ann. (1978). *Customs of the Arabian Gulf.* Hamden, CT: Arab Customs. Intermediate.

3. Fox, Mary Virginia. (1991). *Iran.* Chicago: Children's Press. Advanced.

4. Kuskin, Karla. (1987). *Jerusalem, Shining Still.* New York: Harper & Row, Publishers. Intermediate.

5. Foster, Leila Merrell. (1991). *Jordan.* Chicago: Children's Press. Advanced.

6. Taylor, Allegra. (1987). *A Kibbutz in Israel.* Minneapolis, Lerner Publications Company. Primary, Intermediate.

7. Dolphin, Laurie. (1993). *Oasis of Peace.* New York: Scholastic Inc. Primary, Intermediate.

8. Marston, Elsa. (1994). *Lebanon: A New Light in an Ancient Land.* New York: Dillon Press. Advanced.

9. Pimlott, John. (1991). *Middle East: A Background to the Conflicts.* New York: Gloucester Press Book. Advanced.

10. *Arabian Nights.* (1995). Retold by Brian Alderson. NY: Morrow Junior Books. Intermediate.

Software:

1. *The Middle East: A Closer Look* [Laserdisc]. Chicago: Clearvue/eav. Intermediate, Advanced.

2. *Jerusalem* [Mac MPC CD-ROM]. Torrance, CA: Davidson/Simon & Schuster. Advanced.

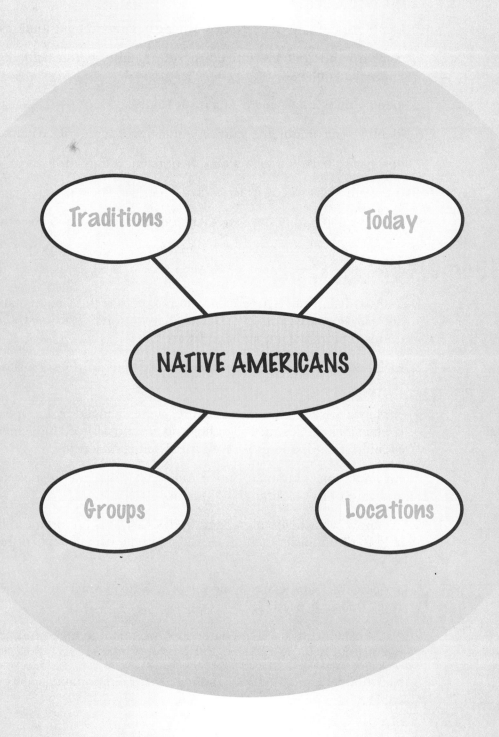

Traditions

Today

NATIVE AMERICANS

Groups

Locations

Theme Goals:

Students will:

1. identify the names of important Native American groups.

2. know the names, locations, and important characteristics of Native American cultural areas.

3. identify some important Native American cultural contributions.

4. compare and contrast Native American culture before and after European contact.

5. identify traditional Native American values.

6. identify some important Native American words and place names.

7. distinguish between factual and fictional accounts of history.

8. use math skills to construct Native American shelters.

9. participate in traditional Native American art, music, and customs.

Theme Concepts:

1. The six main Native American cultural areas in the United States are: Far North, Eastern Woodland, Plains, Northwest Coast, California-Intermountain, and Southwest.

2. Included among Native American contributions are the snowshoe, toboggan, canoe, corn, squash, and lacrosse.

3. Some ways Native American cultures were changed by European contact include destruction of hunting grounds, forced movement to inferior land, and erosion of tribal self-sufficiency.

4. An important traditional Native American value was respect for and care of the natural environment.

5. To know what really happened in the past, it is important to be able to distinguish between factual and fictional accounts of history.

6. To construct an accurate model of a Native American shelter, math skills are needed.

7. Native Americans used the natural environment in ingenious and resourceful ways.

8. Native American art, music, and legends are important aspects of culture.

Vocabulary:

1. myth   3. powwow

2. adobe   4. heritage

Instructional Bulletin Board

The purpose of this bulletin board is to help students identify representative Native American groups by geographical/cultural areas. Make a map of Native American cultural areas as shown below. Make individual labels for each of the six cultural areas and some of the groups listed in Social Studies Activity #2. Place Velcro patches on the labels and on appropriate spots on the map. Let students match cultural areas and groups to their geographic locations. Store labels in a large envelope attached to the lower right corner of bulletin board. Attach a covered answer key to the lower left corner of the board.

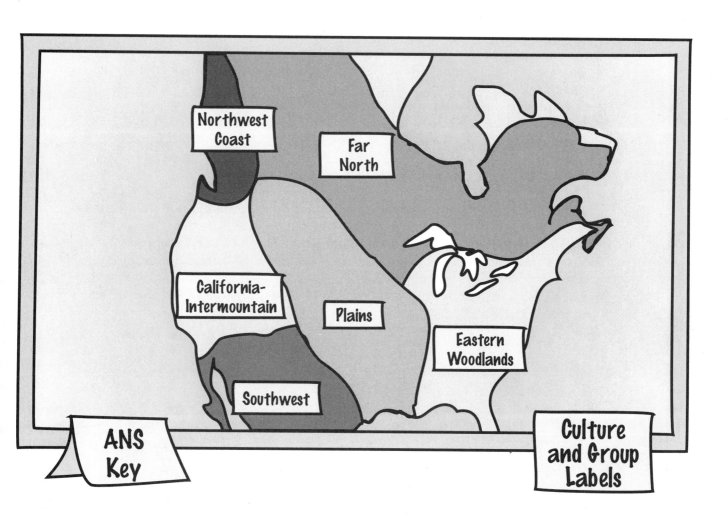

Parent Letter

Dear Parents:

We are beginning our study of Native Americans. The ancestors of contemporary Native Americans were the "first" Americans. There are over 500 different native American groups in America. During our theme on Native Americans, students will be engaged in a variety of activities, including those listed below.

At School:

Your child will learn about the history and culture of Native Americans by:

- Researching representative Native American tribes in six geographical/cultural areas
- Exploring Native American beliefs about nature
- Comparing Native American cultures before and after European contact
- Sampling Native American legends and myths
- Distinguishing between factual and fictional historical accounts about Native Americans
- Constructing a Native American shelter
- Making sand paintings
- Participating in a powwow

At Home:

To reinforce our theme study of Native Americans, you and your child can:

- Gather and discuss current stories in the media about Native Americans.
- Visit a museum and/or historical society that features Native American culture.
- Check the local library for books on Native Americans, and then select one to read together.

Linking Up:

Ask students to write sentences, draw pictures, and/or list words related to their prior knowledge of Native Americans. Use the student-generated information as a diagnostic tool. What valid facts do they have? What stereotypes do they possess? If possible, invite a Native American to school to share his or her traditions and to dispel stereotypes by talking about the lifestyles of present-day Native Americans.

Social Studies

1. How Did the First Americans Get Here?

Brief Background. Although some research hints at an earlier and different arrival, traditional scholarship holds that, during the last Ice Age, the ancestors of all Native Americans probably migrated across a Bering Sea land bridge from Asia to North America, as shown in Figure 32-1. As the ice melted, the land bridge was covered by water.

Ask students how they think the first Americans got here. Explain that they are going to trace one possible route. Provide students with globes. Have them find the continents of North America and Asia, and a place where these two continents almost meet. With their fingers, have students point to the Bering Strait on the globe, and from there, let them trace the path of these early human migrations southward. With the globe's scale, students can use string to measure the distances involved in these ancient migrations, from Alaska in the North to various regions in the Americas all the way to the tip of South America.

2. Native American Diversity

Brief Background. Thinking that he had reached the Indies in Asia, Christopher Columbus mistakenly called the Caribbean island natives he met "Indians." It is estimated that at the time of Columbus's journeys there were a total of 15 million native people living in what is now the United States and Canada (compared to a total of about 2.3 million in the mid-1990s). Today, many of the descendants of the first people to live in America prefer to refer to themselves as "Native Americans," and/or associate themselves with particular na-

tions, confederacies, and/or tribes. Today, the United States Government recognizes 547 tribal groups in America.

Provide illustrated books on Native Americans, and challenge students to identify different groups. Native American groups have been divided into cultural areas. Six cultural areas, along with some of their major groups, are listed below. Assign each of the cultural areas to a small group of students to investigate. Each student can research a different group within the cultural area. After students complete their research, help them make a chart that compares and contrasts the clothing, buildings and shelters, and crafts and tools of groups within and across the six cultural areas. Students can also present skits depicting some important characteristics of the Native American cultural areas. (Note: see Instructional Bulletin Board for a map of the cultural areas.)

Far North	Eastern Woodlands	Plains
Chippewa	Fox	Arapaho
Cree	Iroquois	Comanche
Algonquin	Sauks	Crow
Ottawa	Wampanoag	Kiowa
	Cherokee	Mandan
	Choctak	Pawnee
	Creek	Sioux (Dakota)
	Seminole	Blackfeet

Northwest Coast	California-Intermountain	Southwest
Chinook	Flathead	Apache
Klikitat	Yakima	Navajo
Quinault	Nez Perce	Pima
	Shoshoni	Hopi
	Ute	Taos
	Mohave	Zuni

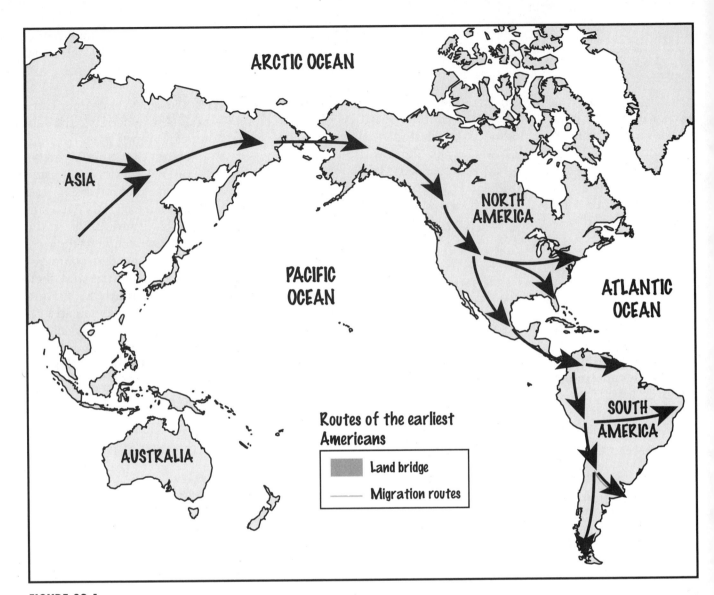

FIGURE 32-1

3. Native American Contributions

Brief Background. Native Americans made many cultural contributions to the American way of life. Before contact with Native Americans, the items listed below were unknown to Europeans.

Have students enumerate all of the foods they eat containing any of the Native American ingredients listed. Let interested students research the importance of the snowshoes, toboggan, and canoe for transportation.

Materials	Foods	Game
snowshoes	corn	lacrosse
toboggan	peanut	

canoe

squash

tomato

potato

pumpkin

4. Before and After

Brief Background. Native American cultures were changed forever by European contact. Most Native Americans who survived the onslaught of white settlers and the destruction of their hunting grounds were forced westward and onto inferior land. Even peaceful contact with Europeans often resulted in negative consequences for Native Americans. Before European contact, for example, Native Americans of the Far North lived entirely off the land by hunting, fishing, and gathering seeds and berries. After the arrival of European fur traders, many Far North groups began to focus their time and energy on trapping beaver and other fur-bearing animals for exchange with whites for food, weapons, and other desired items. As a result, over time these traditionally self-sufficient Native Americans became increasingly dependent on Europeans for their basic needs.

Have students investigate the history and present-day conditions of Native Americans in the local area or region. As students study this local or regional Native American group, help them develop a large, illustrated wall chart that describes and shows the group's way of life before and after contact with outsiders. How did the changes make the Native American group's life better, or worse?

5. Thanksgiving: The Complete (and Sometimes Untold) Story

Brief Background. Although it is true that Native Americans helped the Pilgrims and that they both joined together for a Thanksgiving ceremony in 1621, it is also true that this early friendship was soon replaced by fighting between the two groups. When presenting the story of the first Thanksgiving in Plymouth Colony, it is important that students are provided with a balanced account of what happened. They need to know the reasons for conflict as well as for cooperation.

The concept of land ownership was incomprehensible and unacceptable to Native Americans, while the European settlers took the land for their own. To help students understand Native American perspectives, share selections from *Dancing Moons* by Nancy Wood (Doubleday/BDD, 1995), or another appropriate children's book, that reveals Native American wisdom and insights about their environment. *Dancing Moons* uses painting and poetry to capture Native Americans' close and respectful relationship with nature. Have students research how different Native American groups used the land. Students can also create paintings and poems to show their own personal feelings about nature.

6. Roles of Native American Males and Females

Brief Background. The traditional roles of male and female Native Americans differed greatly. For example, most Eastern Woodland native American groups engaged in some farming. They had gardens and cornfields, and some groups also raised tobacco. The women did all of the farm work. In addition, women cared for the children, gathered wild berries and nuts, prepared and cooked the food, and made clothing and most tools. Males, in contrast, were warriors and hunters and did little other work.

For a vivid picture of Native American women's roles within their cultures, read aloud selections from *The Tried and the True: Native American Women Confronting Colonization* by John Demos (Oxford, 1995), or another appropriate children's book. Have students research the traditional roles of males and females in different Native American groups.

Science:

1. Native Americans and the Land

Brief Background. Traditional Native American tribal groups lived in harmony with the plants and animals in their environment. They saw themselves as part of nature. They believed that if they took care of nature, then nature would take care of them. White frontiersmen, on the other hand, often acted as if the environment did not matter. The destruction of the buffalo is a case study in social irresponsibility. Millions of these mighty animals once roamed across America, and the tribes of the Plains depended on them for all of the necessities of life. But because of relentless and senseless slaughter by whites, the buffalo population was reduced almost to the point of extinction. Today, waste of natural resources continues and social irresponsibility remains.

Have students investigate their own natural environment. What type(s) of habitat(s)—such as forest, desert, grassland, and wetland—is (are) nearby? Do plants and animals in the surrounding natural environment face problems related to pollution and habitat destruction? If possible, invite a Native American to your classroom to talk about traditional and current Native American lifestyles and values. Probe to see if students understand how they are connected to their environment.

Language Arts:

1. Native American Legends and Myths

Brief Background. Every Native American group has legends and myths that explain why and how they and the Earth—including all of its features—were created. These stories were handed down from one generation to the next by storytellers, and through dance, chants, and art.

To give students some examples of these stories, read selections of *The Navajos, The Hopis* and *The Iroquois*, all by Virginia Driving Hawk Sneve (Holiday House, 1993, 1995, respectively), Joseph Bruchac's *Native American Stories* (Fulcrum, 1991), or other appropriate children's books. Encourage students to learn about Native American myths and legends and report their findings to the class. Students can also create myths and legends to describe their own lives, and/or make up Native American myths based upon what they have learned about Native American cultures.

2. Sign Language

Because Native American tribes of the Plains spoke different languages, they developed a sign language to communicate with one another. The hand positions and movements were intended to convey a "picture" of the object or action being communicated. For example, the sign for "buffalo" was a hand positioned on each side of the head with the thumbs and forefingers extended to symbolize the horns of the buffalo. Challenge students to create their own sign language for common classroom objects and actions. What sign would they create for "table" "book," "write," or "test"?

3. Native American Words and Places

Many places in America reflect our Native American heritage. Over half of the 50 states have Native American names. For example, the state of Illinois is named after the Illinois tribe. Provide pairs of students with maps of the United States, and challenge them to find the following places named for Native American groups: Erie, Lake Huron, Illinois, Massachusetts, Miami, Natchez, Cheyenne, Iowa, Kansas, Omaha, Teton, Wichita, Yakima, and Taos. Do place names in the local region reflect our Native American heritage?

4. Who Was Pocahontas?

Brief Background. Perhaps no historical Native American figure has received more attention than Pocahontas, the daughter of Chief Powhatan. She befriended Captain John Smith, leader of America's first permanent English colony at Jamestown in Virginia. Together, they helped establish good relations between the Native Americans and the settlers. In his book about the history of Jamestown, Captain Smith claimed that Pocahontas saved his life. He wrote that Chief Powhatan took him captive and intended to kill him. As Powhatan raised his war club above Smith's head, Pocahontas threw herself between them and begged her father to spare him. Although historians question Smith's account of his rescue, there is agreement about some facts. Pocahontas did help the English settlers, and in 1614 she married John Rolfe, one of the more prominent of them. Their son, Thomas, was born the next year. In 1616 she went with her husband to England, where she was treated like the princess she was. Pocahontas died of smallpox in 1617, just as she was about to return to America. John Rolfe did return to Jamestown, and was killed by Native Americans in 1624. Thomas was educated in England and also returned to America. Many people today claim to be his descendants. John Rolfe's successful cultivation of tobacco ensured the economic future of Jamestown. Until it was replaced by Williamsburg in 1699, Jamestown was the capital of the expanding and prosperous colony of Virginia.

Provide students with a variety of books about Pocahontas and Jamestown. Help students distinguish between factual accounts about Pocahontas and the events at Jamestown found in history books and fictional accounts found in other sources, such as legends, myths, and historical fiction novels, or Disney's movie, *Pocahontas*. Other notable Native American figures that students can investigate include Sitting Bull, Sacajawea, Chief Joseph, Geronomo, Sequoyah, Jim Thorpe, Black Hawk, Cochise, and Squanto.

5. Native American Symbols

Brief Background. Native Americans used picture symbols to communicate words, feelings, and ideas. Have students guess the meanings of the Indian symbols in Figure 32-2, and then challenge them to write messages and stories using their own picture symbols that they have created.

Math:

1. Constructing Native American Shelters

Brief Background. Each Native American cultural area had its own unique type of shelter. Groups of the Far North made bark lodges, groups of the Northwest Coast constructed plank houses, and those of the Southwest fashioned pueblos (villages) of adobe. One very ingenious design was the tepee constructed by the Sioux and other Native American groups of the Plains. The tepee was light, portable, and sturdy. It consisted of wooden poles arranged in the shape of a cone. The crossed poles were tied together near the top. A typical Sioux tepee measured 15 feet across. Buffalo skins sewed together with sinew were then stretched over the poles to form the tent. A flap at the top of the tepee let smoke out, and a flap at the bottom served as a door cover. Inside the tepee, an altar and fire area were located at the center, and beds and a woodpile area were located around the perimeter.

Have students research the form and function of Native American shelters, including tepees, longhouses, adobes, and wigwams. Then, help students make one or more Native American shelters. To make a classroom-sized model of a Sioux tepee like the one shown in Figure 32-3. Provide the following materials: 7 eight-foot-long wooden poles (to start the tepee, tie three poles together to form a tripod), white sheet material dyed brown to represent buffalo skins, rope, scissors, a large needle and brown yarn (to represent sinew). As they plan and construct

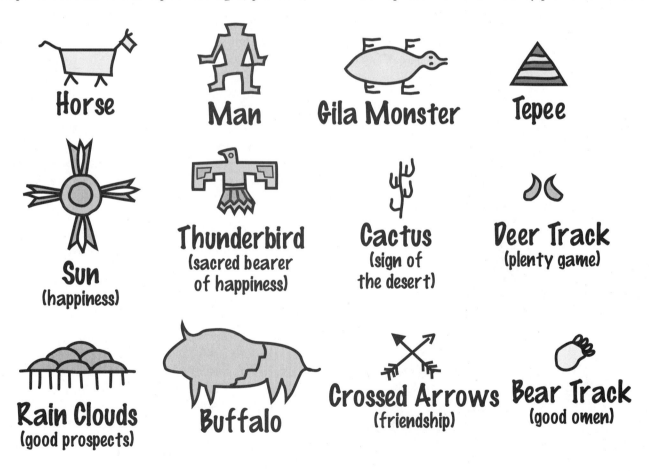

Horse

Man

Gila Monster

Tepee

Sun
(happiness)

Thunderbird
(sacred bearer
of happiness)

Cactus
(sign of
the desert)

Deer Track
(plenty game)

Rain Clouds
(good prospects)

Buffalo

Crossed Arrows
(friendship)

Bear Track
(good omen)

Native American Symbols

FIGURE 32-2

their tepee, students will apply the following math skills: (1) measuring the space to be used and how large to make it; (2) estimating the amount of materials needed; and (3) deciding how many rest areas will fit inside their tepee. A fabric pen can be used to decorate the tepee with Native American symbols.

Art:

1. Native American Designs

Brief Background. Native Americans decorated many of their possessions with intricate and colorful designs like those shown in Figure 32-4. Some designs were woven into blankets and robes, others were painted on animal skins and pottery, and still others were carved on canoes, masks, pipes, and other items.

Show students examples of Native American art contained in library books and other sources. Provide students with art materials, and let them carefully produce authentic-looking Native American designs. They also can create their own designs, just as modern Native American artists do today.

Plains Indian Tepee

FIGURE 32-3

2. Sand Painting

Sand painting (Figure 32-5) is an art form practiced by Native Americans of the Southwest. Show students pictures of Native American sand paintings. Then provide students with colored sand (available at pet shops), pencils, cardboard, and glue, and have them follow these directions: (1) make a sketch of the design on a 10-inch-square piece of cardboard; (2) decide on the colors for the design; (3) spread a thin coat of glue on the portion of the design that is to be of the same color; (4) pour sand of one color on the wet glue, tap excess sand into container, let glue dry; and (5) repeat steps 3 and 4 for each remaining color of sand to be used in the painting. Display the finished sand paintings in the classroom.

Music:

1. Powwows

Brief Background. Native American powwows are held throughout America annually. These festive occasions provide Native Americans with an opportunity to come together for a few days to renew acquaintances and participate in ancient traditions. During powwows, Native Americans, dressed in tribal costumes, dance to the beat of drums and enact tribal legends. Powwows serve an important educational function. They are an authoritative way for young Native Americans to learn about their heritage.

As a culminating activity to their study of Native Americans, let students plan and stage a powwow. Small groups can reenact dances and legends that are representative of the six different Native American cultural areas. To add realism, students can design and wear Native American costumes, make and play drums, and simulate other aspects of Native American culture. If possible, solicit the help of a Native American to advise you on planning and staging the powwow. The following resources can also serve as a guide for authenticity and accuracy. Legends and dances reenacted by Native Americans are available on video from Films for the Humanities and Science, PO Box 2053, Princeton, NJ 08543. For a well-illustrated description of a modern Native American powwow, consult *Powwow* by George Ancona (Harcourt Brace Jovanovich, 1993).

Native American Designs

FIGURE 32-4

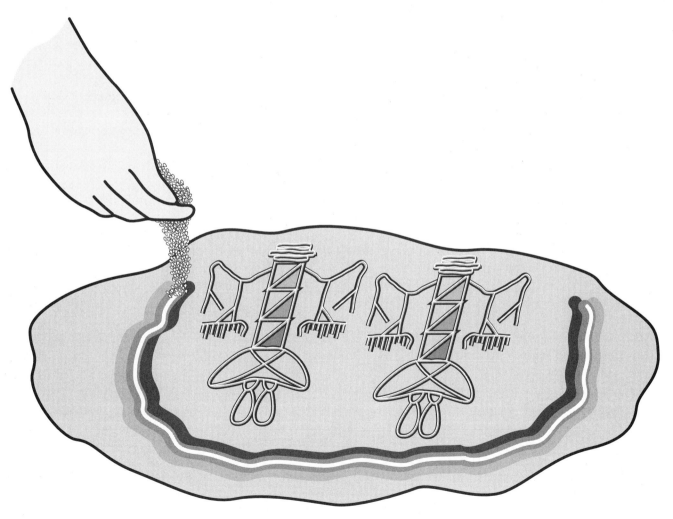

Sand Painting

FIGURE 32-5

343

Books:

1. Lepthien, Emilie U. (1985). *The Cherokee*. Chicago: Children's Press. Primary.

2. Warren, Scott. (1992). *Cities in the Sand: The Ancient Civilizations of the Southwest*. San Francisco: Chronicle Books. Intermediate, Advanced.

3. McGovern, Ann. (1972). *. . . if You Lived with the Sioux Indians*. New York: Four Winds Press. Intermediate, Advanced.

4. Rivinus, Edward. (1990). *Jim Thorpe*. Milwaukee: Raintree Publishers. Intermediate.

5. Wilson, James. (1992). *Native Americans*. New York: Thomson Learning. Advanced.

6. Sneve, Virginia Driving Hawk. (1993). *The Navajos*. New York: Holiday House. Intermediate.

7. Sneve, Virginia Driving Hawk. (1995). *The Iroquois*. New York: Holiday House. Intermediate.

8. Sneve, Virginia Driving Hawk. (1995). *The Hopis*. New York: Holiday House. Intermediate.

9. Sewall, Marcia. (1990). *People of the Breaking Day*. New York: Macmillan Publishing Company. Intermediate.

10. King, Sandra. (1993). *Shannon: An Ojibway Dancer*. Minneapolis: Lerner Publications Company. Intermediate.

11. Stein, R. Conrad. (1993). *The Trail of Tears*. Chicago: Children's Press. Intermediate, Advanced.

12. Ancona, George. (1993). *Powwow*. New York: Harcout Brace Jovanovich. Intermediate, Advanced.

13. Wood, Nancy. (1995). *Dancing Moons*. New York: Doubleday/BDD. Intermediate, Advanced.

14. Demos, John. (1995). *The Tried and the True: Native American Women Confronting Colonization*. New York: Oxford. Intermediate, Advanced.

15. Bruchac, Joseph. *Native American Stories*. (1991). Golden, CO: Fulcrum.

Software:

1. *GTV: A Geographic Perspective on American History*. [GS Mac IBM Laserdisc]. Washington, DC: National Geographic. Advanced.

2. *Had You Lived Then Series: Life in the Woodlands Before the White Man Came*. [Laserdisc VHS]. Chatsworth, CA: AIMS. Advanced.

3. *500 Nations* [Mac MPC CD-ROM]. Redmond, WA: Microsoft. Intermediate, Advanced.

4. *A Navajo Vacation: Living in Two Worlds* [IBM Mac]. Gainesville, FL: Teacher Support Software. Intermediate, Advanced.

5. *The American Indian—A Multimedia Encyclopedia* [IBM CD-ROM]. New York: Facts on File. Advanced.

6. *Native American Indians* [Laserdisc]. Chicago: Clearvue/eav. Intermediate, Advanced.

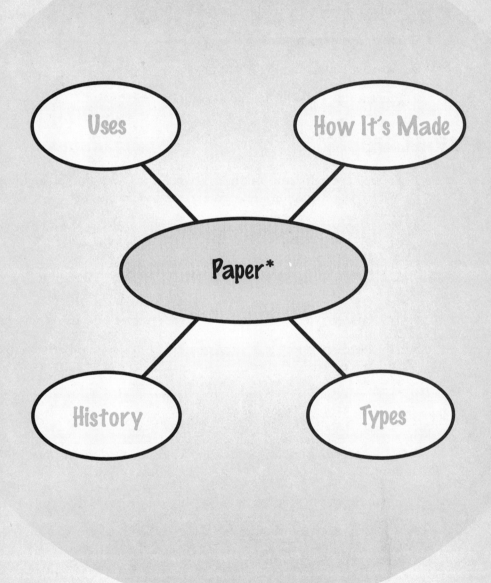

Uses

How It's Made

Paper*

History

Types

Theme Goals:

The student will:

1. identify the many uses of paper.

2. trace the origin and spread of paper.

3. plan and implement a classroom recycling center.

4. identify the parts of a tree.

5. test the effectiveness of different brands of paper towels.

6. study fractions by folding paper.

7. make a papier-mache doll.

8. create a "mind map" for paper.

9. identify the steps in making paper.

Theme Concepts:

1. Paper has many important uses, including writing and reading materials, packaging and containers, and money.

2. Paper was invented in China over 2,000 years ago; knowledge of paper making took 1,000 years to reach Europe.

3. Forest lands throughout the world are threatened with destruction.

4. To conserve trees, we need to recycle paper and use it wisely.

5. The major parts of a tree are roots, trunk, seeds, bark, limbs, and leaves.

6. Paper products can be tested to determine their effectiveness.

7. Many wasps make nests from paper they produce.

8. A piece of paper can be divided in order to demonstrate fractions.

9. Japanese paper folding is called *origami.*

10. A *webbing,* or mind map, for paper can serve as a writing outline.

Vocabulary:

1. recyclying	3. wood pulp
2. social wasps	4. origami

---

*Jill Glover Bauserman contributed many of the activities for this unit.

Instructional Bulletin Board

The purpose of this bulletin board is to display items made of paper that students have gathered. Cover the bulletin board with a large sheet of white paper. Use tape, staples, glue, pins, and wire as needed to attach the paper items to the board.

Parent Letter

Dear Parents:

Paper is everywhere. It is hard to imagine a world without it. Here are just a few of the many interesting facts about paper:

Paper was invented in China over 2,000 years ago.
Many wasps make nests of paper they produce.
For centuries, paper was made from rags.
It takes around 17 trees to make one ton of paper.

As you probably have already guessed, paper is the theme of our upcoming theme of study.

At School:

We have a variety of activities planned, including the following:

- Searching for products made from paper
- Setting up a classroom recycling center
- Learning how paper is made
- Testing paper products
- Using paper to learn about fractions
- Making a papier-mache international doll

At Home:

To stimulate interest in the theme, participate with your child in one or more of the following activities:

- Track down products made of paper in your home.
- Read aloud selections of the newspaper and discuss them with your child.
- Take a walk in the park and identify the trees.

Linking Up:

Show students examples of corrugated cardboard boxes, paper boxes, and paper bags commonly used as containers. Probe to see if students are aware of the extensive use of paper for packaging and containers. Have students search for objects made of paper in the classroom and school. Help them list on the chalkboard as many items as they can find. Then, ask them to help you identify other products made of paper typically found in the home and community, and list those on the board. The list might include products like the following:

filters	books	posters	stamps
cups	magazines	pictures	toys
plates	folders	encyclo-pedias	board games
bags	wrappers	globes	patterns
boxes	cases	binders	cards
envelopes	note paper	money	photo-graphs
paper for writing and printing	comics	tickets	checks
	newspapers	coupons	forms
	maps	labels	flags

Social Studies:

1. Tracing the Origins of Paper

Brief Background. The first writing was done on clay tablets over 5,000 years ago. Ancient peoples also wrote on tree bark and animal skins. The ancient Egyptians used the flattened reeds of the papyrus plant to make writing material. The first real paper was invented in China more than 2,000 years ago. The Chinese used it initially for wrapping presents and for paper money, but not for writing. The Chinese made paper from plant fibers that had been pounded, mixed with water, formed into thin sheets, and then dried, which is basically the same process that is used today. It took more than a thousand years for the formula for making paper

to travel overland from China to Europe. For centuries, paper was made out of cotton and linen rags—not wood.

On a globe and wall map of the world, help students trace the spread of knowledge of paper making westward from China to Samarkand (present-day Uzbekstan), Baghdad (Iraq), Cairo (Egypt), Constantinople (now called Istanbul, in Turkey), Morocco, Spain, and Italy. (The Asian portion of the route is shown in Figure 34-1.)

2. Recycling Paper

Write "waste paper" on the chalkboard, and ask students what this term means. Pose this question for the students' consideration: Should people waste paper? Help students realize that high consumer demand for paper products combined with wasteful habits contributes to the destruction of millions of acres of trees worldwide. Can students identify wasteful habits at home and school? The world's tropical rain forests, which contain millions of species of living things, are especially at risk. Show the class pictures of endangered rain-forest wildlife, such as the orangutan, gorilla, and giant otter. Since it takes 17 trees to make a ton of paper, the more paper we recycle, the better. To show students they can make a difference, involve them in one or more of the following activities: plan and create a classroom paper recycling center; conserve paper (try to write more on less paper); participate in schoolwide and community drives to collect and recycle paper; plant trees in the community; and investigate local and global environmental issues.

Science:

1. The Science of Trees

Pass around different kinds of tree seeds (apple, oak, maple, pine, magnolia, etc.) and display pictures of what those seeds look like when they grow up. Take students on a walking tour of an area with numerous trees. Help them identify different kinds of trees and their basic parts (i.e., roots, trunk, bark, limbs, seeds, and leaves). Back in the classroom, provide students with large sheets of white paper, glue, scissors, real leaves, brown construction paper, and brown yarn. Direct students to use the brown construction paper to make cutouts of

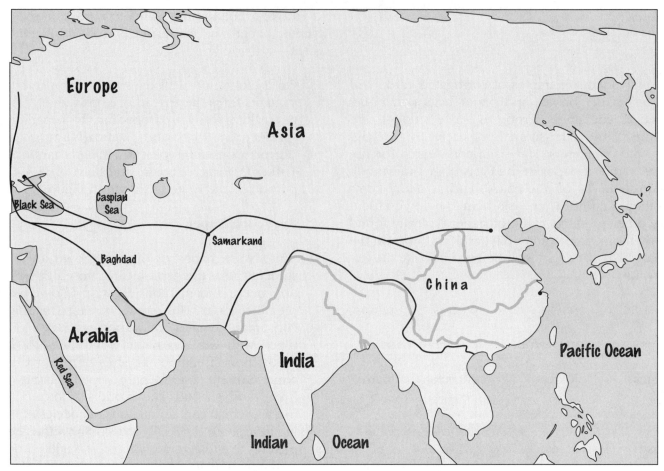

Map of Ancient East-West Routes

FIGURE 34-1

tree trunks and limbs. The cutouts can be glued on the paper. Have them glue strands of yarn on the paper to form the roots. After they attach some real leaves to complete their trees, they can label the parts as shown in Figure 34-2. Display their tree diagrams on the wall.

2. From Trees to Paper

Paper is made from wood pulp. Using an encyclopedia or other source as a guide, help students make a large diagram illustrating the steps in making paper from wood. The process, from start to finish, is as follows. Logs are hauled by trucks and trains to the paper mill, stripped of their bark, and cut into chips. Then, the chips are washed, treated with chemicals, and broken down into fibers. Once the chemicals are washed off, the pulp is sent through screens that remove debris. The pulp is then spread across a moving screen where water is sucked off and a mat

is formed. After more water is pressed out, the paper is dried, rolled, and smoothed. Finally, the finished paper is fed onto a big roll. To help students visualize the paper-making process, assemble the whole class in a line around the classroom and assign small groups of students to "act out" each of the steps in the process.

3. Paper Helicopters

Provide each student with a 4" × 6" blank index card, scissors, and paper clips. Challenge students to create a helicopter that will spin to the ground when dropped. Let students test their designs and discuss their observations. They can use stop watches to measure the amount of time it takes the helicopters to reach the ground after being dropped from the same height. One design for a spinning helicopter is shown in Figure 34-3.

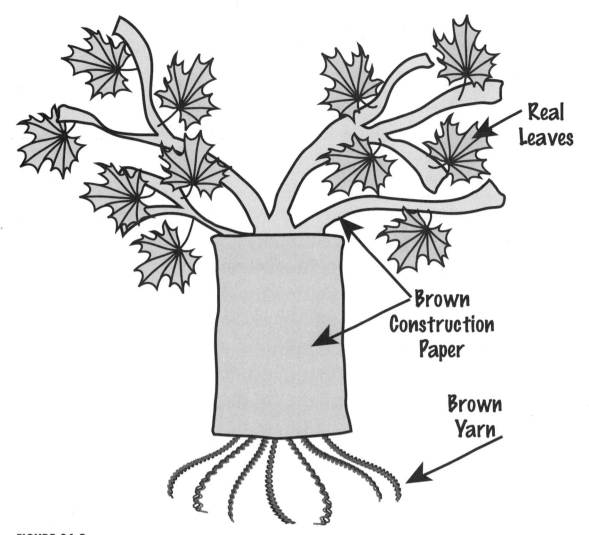

Real Leaves

Brown Construction Paper

Brown Yarn

FIGURE 34-2

4. Paper Towel Testing

Provide pairs of students with sheets of three different brands of paper towels. Explain to the pairs that their job is to determine which of the three brands is the best. They will need to identify qualities that "good" paper towels should possess, such as the ability to absorb liquids, wipe up messes, and resist tearing. Challenge students to design tests to measure those and other factors. The students can make charts and graphs (Figure 34-4) to display and report on test results.

5. Paper-Making Wasps

Brief Background. Some species of wasps can make paper, and they were doing so long before people could. These wasps make their nests out of paper they produce (the female wasp chews up wood to make the paper). Observations of paper-making wasps led one alert scientist to conclude that people could make paper from wood pulp, too.

If one is available, let students examine an empty hornet or yellow jacket nest. Encourage interested students to investigate and report on the characteristics and life cycle of paper-making social wasps, which live in organized communities.

6. Make Your Own Paper

For directions on making new paper from old, download free instructions by using the Internet to gopher to: ericir.syr.edu . . . New Lesson/Science/paper.

Math:

1. Folding Fractions

Provide students with sheets of plain white paper. Demonstrate paper folding and how it relates to fractions: One whole piece of pa-

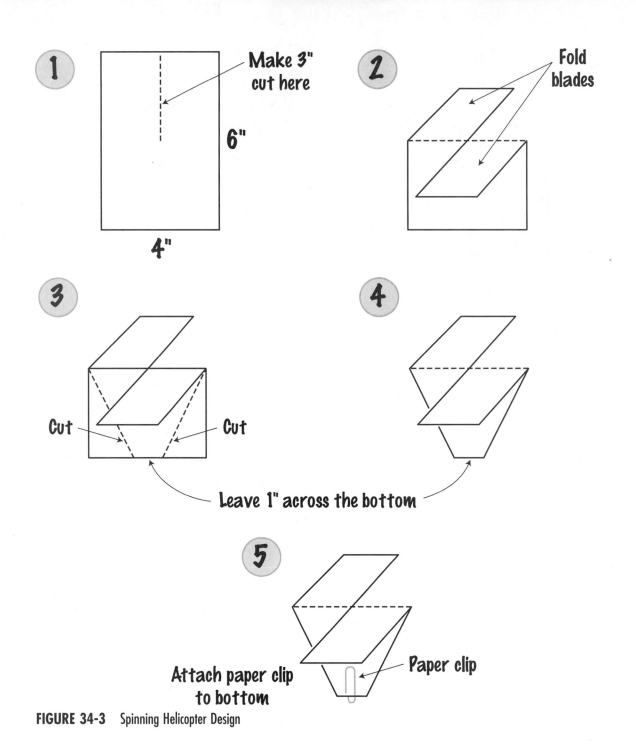

1 Make 3" cut here

6"

4"

2 Fold blades

3 Cut — Cut

Leave 1" across the bottom

4

5 Attach paper clip to bottom — Paper clip

FIGURE 34-3 Spinning Helicopter Design

per can be divided into halves, quarters, eighths, sixteenths, and so on, simply by folding the halves over on themselves. Before each fold, ask students to predict what fraction will result in the next folding. To check for understanding, assign each student the task of folding and labeling a sheet of paper to show one of the fractions. Students can also fold paper into different geometric shapes and label them.

2. Weighing Paper

Related to Social Studies Activity #2, students can weigh and then record the amount of waste paper collected at the classroom recycling center. Help students make a chart that shows the amount, in pounds, of paper collected daily. Periodically, direct students' attention to the chart, and help them discern and analyze any emerging trends or patterns.

PAPER TOWEL TESTING CHART TESTS

Brand	Absorb Liquids	Wipe Up Messes	Strength
A			
B			
C			

FIGURE 34-4

Art:

1. It's in the Bag

Brief Background. The paper bag is one of the world's most successful inventions. After machines were invented to mass-produce them in the 1870s, these handy containers were an instant hit with the public.

Arrange empty paper bags (enough for one for each student) in a line on a table in front of the class. Point out that all the bags look exactly the same. Give each student one of the bags along with crayons, magic markers, scraps of colored paper, and other art materials. Then, challenge students to decorate their bags so that each one has a "personality" all its own. Arrange the decorated bags on the table again, and then have each student, in turn, find her bag and tell why it's unique.

2. Origami

The Japanese have elevated paper folding to an art form called *origami*. Provide students with origami paper (available in art supply

Papier-Mache Doll

FIGURE 34-5

stores) and, using a book on origami as a guide, demonstrate how to fold the paper to create an object such as a bird or fish. Students can use straws, thread, scissors, and tape to make mobiles to display their origami (hang four origami objects on each mobile).

3. Papier-Mache Dolls from Around the World

Assign each student the task of gathering information about, and illustrations of, the traditional or national dress of a country or culture. Then, following the instructions below, let each student make a papier-mache doll and then decorate it in the traditional costume of the particular nation or culture chosen as shown in Figure 34-5. Each student will need an empty one-liter plastic bottle covered with plastic wrap. Provide each student with a wrapped bottle, newspaper strips, paste, pieces of fabric, tape, scissors, yarn, construction paper, and a brush and water colors. Direct them to paste the newspaper strips to the bottle to form the doll's body, and to use the construction paper to make the doll's head. When the papier-mache is dry, the bottles can be removed. Use pieces of fabric for the costume and yarn for the hair. Have each student make a small flag and a label with the name of the nation or culture to place alongside the doll. After the dolls are completed, display them in the classroom.

Language Arts:

1. Reading the Newspaper

Provide students with individual copies of the same newspaper. Show students how to use the index to find information about the following: local, state, national, and international news, sports, obituaries, comics, classifieds, weather, television scheduling, movies, editorials, and letters to the editor.

2. Webbing Paper

Help students create a webbing, or a mind map, for paper (Figure 34-6). They can use the webbing to research and organize a short written report on paper.

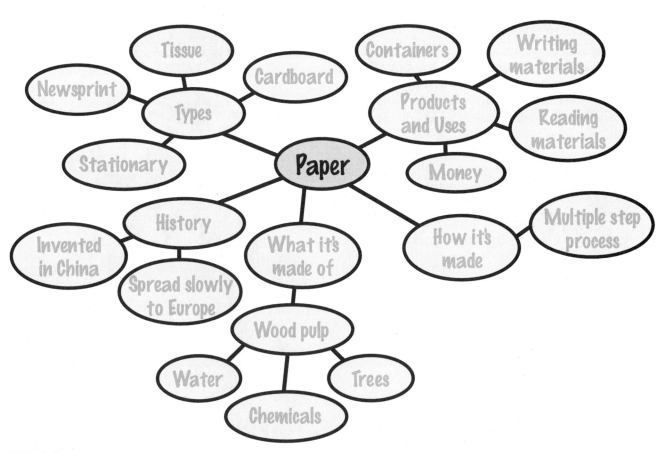

FIGURE 34-6

Books:

1. Bulla, Clyde R. (1960). *A Tree Is a Plant*. New York: Crowell. Primary, Intermediate.

2. Cobb, Vicki. (1981). *The Secret Life of School Supplies*. New York: Lippincott. Advanced.

3. Goerl, Stephen. (1945). *A Pictorial History of Paper*. New York: Bulkey, Dunton Pulp Co. Advanced.

4. Pine, Tillie S., and Levine, Joseph. (1969). *Trees and How We Use Them*. New York: McGraw-Hill. Intermediate, Advanced.

5. Flischman, Paul. (1979). *The Birthday Tree*. New York: Harper and Row. Intermediate, Advanced.

6. Smith, Elizabeth S. (1984). *Paper*. New York: Walker. Intermediate, Advanced.

7. Tofts, Helen. (1990). *The Paper Book*. New York: Simon and Schuster. Intermediate, Advanced.

8. Cosner, Shaaron. (1984). *"Paper" Through the Ages*. Minneapolis: Carolrhoda Books. Primary, Intermediate.

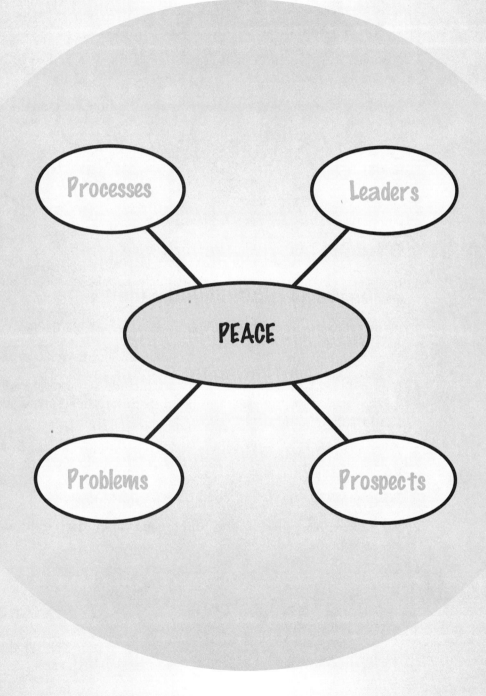

Processes

Leaders

PEACE

Problems

Prospects

Theme Goals

Students will:

1. practice a problem-solving strategy to resolve interpersonal conflicts.

2. explore the multicultural composition of the local community.

3. identify the purpose and activities of the United Nations.

4. identify important leaders in the quest for peace.

5. distinguish between technology designed for war and technology designed for peace.

6. explore environmental conditions that contribute to global violence.

7. express in speaking and writing their feeling and ideas about peace.

8. create symbols of peace.

Theme Concepts:

1. Interpersonal and international conflicts can be resolved successfully by talking and working together.

2. People throughout the world yearn for peace on Earth.

3. The United Nations was formed to maintain international peace.

4. Important leaders in the quest for peace include Mahatma Gandhi, Jane Addams, Elie Wiesel, Desmond Tutu, Mother Teresa, and Martin Luther King, Jr.

5. How technology is used depends on people and the decisions they make.

6. Environmental factors can contribute to global violence.

7. We can express our thoughts and feelings about peace through stories, poems, and symbols.

Vocabulary:

1. interpersonal

2. international

3. conflict

4. compromise

5. mediator

6. United Nations

Instructional Bulletin Board

The purpose of this bulletin board is to help students identify some important leaders in the quest for peace. Gather pictures and information about peace leaders in Social Studies Activity #5 and attach them to the bulletin board. On 3" × 5" cards print the names of the peace leaders. Place the cards in the pocket. Students can take turns pinning the names next to the appropriate persons. Provide an answer key.

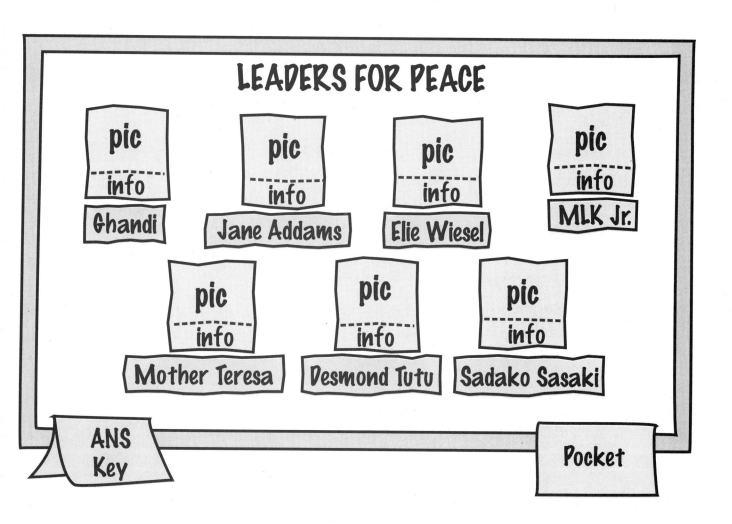

Parent Letter

Dear Parents:

Interpersonal conflicts are a natural part of everyday life. An important part of growing up is learning how to resolve them constructively. International conflicts are also common occurrences. For the future of the world, it is vital that conflicts among nations be resolved peacefully. In this theme, students will practice rational ways to solve their own problems. They will also learn about people and institutions that work for peace worldwide.

At School:

In this theme, students will be doing the following:

* Practicing a problem-solving approach for dealing with interpersonal conflicts
* Participating in "international awareness day" activities
* Role-playing members of the United Nations
* Learning about important peace seekers
* Writing stories and poems about peace
* Creating peace symbols

At Home:

People throughout the world are struggling to stop violence and bring peace to the world. Examples of their activities are sometimes highlighted on television news. To help your child become aware of international efforts for peace, draw attention to these stories and answer your child's questions about them.

Thank you for your continued support.

Linking Up:

Brief Background. Interpersonal conflicts are a natural part of everyday life. Every school-age child has had direct experience with interpersonal conflicts. They are usually in the form of verbal disagreements and arguments, but they can escalate rapidly into physical confrontations, especially for children who lack self-discipline. An important part of growing up is learning how to resolve interpersonal conflicts constructively. International conflicts also commonly occur, and for the future of the world, it is vital that conflicts among nations be resolved peacefully. To encourage students to think constructively about conflict, use hand puppets or a skit format to stage a disagreement or argument between two students. Then, have the students generate as many solutions to this interpersonal problem as possible. Finally, after the process is completed, help students visualize and evaluate some of their potential solutions by recreating them in the classroom, using the same puppet or skit format. Do the solutions seem to treat both parties in the conflict fairly? Ask students to imagine that they are one of the two parties in the conflict. Which solution seems best from each party's point of view?

Social Studies:

1. Working for Peace

Peace will not happen magically. People will have to work hard to make it happen. To teach students peaceful ways to deal successfully with everyday conflicts, use positive reinforcement to "catch" students being peaceful. Any time a student engages in a behavior that supports or encourages peace, such as sharing, cooperating, forgiving, or resolving, verbally acknowledge that student's contribution. Make a class chart that highlights individuals' peaceful behaviors; create "peace" awards for students and tangible rewards for peaceful group behavior, such as a popcorn and movie party or playing an "extra" fun game outdoors.

2. A Problem-Solving Model

Teach students a problem-solving model for dealing with conflict. Use role-playing and other involvement strategies to take students through the following steps of the problem-solving model:

1. Identify the problem—Do both parties agree upon the problem? Have both parties had an opportunity to describe the problem?
2. Identify the cause or causes of the problem—Are the causes of the conflict identified and agreed upon by both parties? Have students focus on describing actions that contributed to the problem, and steer students away from blaming and name calling, which will only make the problem worse.
3. Identify possible solutions to the problem—Since the next solution to come to mind may be the best one, encourage students to identify as many possible solutions as they can. What must each party do to solve the problem?
4. Select an acceptable solution to the problem—What solution meets the needs of both parties? What compromises must both parties make to reach an acceptable solution?
5. Try the solution out—What must each party do to make the solution work? Give the solution adequate time to work. Meet with students periodically to offer encouragement and advise if needed.
6. Evaluate the solution—Did the solution work? If so, great! If not, what needs to be changed to make it work?

3. Students as Mediators

Use role-playing and skits to teach students to help mediate interpersonal conflicts between themselves. A mediator tries to resolve differences between two parties. While the teacher is of course responsible for maintaining a peaceful classroom, research tells us that positive results can be achieved through peer mediation. To be a successful peer mediator, a student needs to have good communications skills, a sense of fairness, and a thorough understanding of the problem-solving steps described above. Role-playing and skits dealing with name calling, arguing, bullying, taking materials, hoarding materials, and other commonly occurring classroom events can be developed for students to practice their mediating skills.

4. International Awareness

Because of modern technology, transportation, and communications, the people of the world are all interconnected. What happens on the other side of the Earth can, only moments later, affect us on this side, and vice versa. To help bring the world's people closer together in your school, hold an "international awareness day." Survey the community to identify individuals from other countries who would be willing to come to your school to share their countries and cultures with your students. International students at local colleges are often more than willing to showcase their countries and cultures. In your search for participants, don't overlook Americans who have had substantial cross-cultural experiences, such as former Peace Corps Volunteers, current and former members of other U.S. government agencies, nongovernmental service organizations, and international businesses. Encourage participants to include one or more of the following in their presentations: pictures, costumes, artifacts, music, dances, and foods. (Note: If you can't find international participants, don't give up on "international awareness day." You can substitute or augment live presentations with illustrations, video, audiotapes, and other media on countries and cultures.)

5. Model United Nations

Brief Background. The United Nations was organized in 1945, when the delegates from 51 nations signed the United Nations Charter in San Francisco. Today, representatives from most of the world's nations meet at the United Nations Building in New York City. The purposes of the United Nations are to maintain international peace, develop friendly relations among countries, cooperate to solve international problems, and promote respect for human rights.

Have students look for examples in the news of work the United Nations is currently doing to help achieve its goals. Divide students into small groups, and assign each group the task of learning about a specific nation. Gather and make available in the classroom children's books and reference books about the nations selected for study. Each student in each group can select one or more of the following questions to answer: Where is the country located? What is its climate like? What are some important natural features of the country? What are the people like? What are the main occupations of the people? and What are the nation's biggest

problems? To create a model United Nations in the classroom, let groups make place cards, flags, and costumes that identify their nations. After students have answered the questions, groups can take turns describing the nations' characteristics and problems. Are some problems shared by more than one country? Pose this question to the groups: How might their nations work together to solve problems that affect the whole Earth?

6. Leaders in the Struggle for Peace

Some important leaders who have worked for peace whom students can investigate are: Mahatma Gandhi, Jane Addams, Elie Wiesel, Desmond Tutu, Mother Teresa, and Martin Luther King, Jr.

Science:

1. Technology: For What Purpose?

Brief Background. Technological advances can be used for different purposes. They can be used to bring the world closer together or drive it farther apart. How technology is used depends on people and the decisions they make.

Help students identify technology designed to cause or promote violence (e.g., missiles and other weapons, armored vehicles, military equipment, violent computer games, violent cartoons and films) and technology designed for peaceful uses (e.g., cars, trucks, sports equipment, nonviolent computer games).

2. Environmental Connections

Brief Background. Mass hunger worldwide contributes to global instability, violence, and war.

Have students examine the connection between the world's unequally distributed food resources and the following:

Cutting down forests
Overuse of farmland
Soil erosion
Population growth
Climate changes

Math:

1. Counting Current Events

Let students cut out newspaper and magazine articles that focus on peace and articles that focus on conflict. They can count and record on a chart the number of articles found in each category. Are there more articles about peace or conflict?

Language Arts:

1. Reaching Out

Have students stand up (and you join them), form a circle, and link hands. Explain to the class that you are going to gently squeeze the hand of the student to your right, and that you then want that person to gently squeeze the hand of the person to his right and so on until the squeeze travels completely around the circle to your left hand. Do this exercise two or three times. Ask children how the activity made them feel. Have they ever had their hands squeezed gently as an expression of love, friendship, and peace? Have students speculate about what the activity has to do with peace on Earth. Explain that peace is about communicating. That means, of course, that people must talk to one another. But just as important as talking to one another is having positive feelings toward one another. Encourage students to share positive qualities they recognize in the words and actions of their friends. List these qualities on the chalkboard.

2. Speaking Out for Peace

Read aloud selections from *On the Wings of Peace* compiled by Sheila Hamanaka (Clarion Books, 1995) and *The Big Book for Peace* by Lloyd Alexander and others (Dutton Children's Books, 1990). Based on the age and maturity of your students, you can choose from international stories, poems, and illustrations on peace by over 70 outstanding writers and artists.

3. Looking for Peace

Have students keep a journal of actions and events in and around the school that are evidence of peaceful student conduct and behavior. Encourage students to report orally on their findings.

4. Peace Poems

Encourage students to write poems that express their feelings about peace.

Art:

1. Folding Paper Cranes for Peace

Read aloud *Sadako* by Eleanor Coerr (Putnam, 1993), the story of a courageous little girl named Sadako Sasaki who survives the atomic bomb dropped on Hiroshima but gets leukemia. Sadako believes that if she folds a thousand tiny paper cranes (the crane is Japan's symbol for long life), her wish to live might be granted. Although she lost her struggle with death, people throughout the world have been inspired by the example of her courage and hope. A peace statue in her memory at Hiroshima Peace Park was built with funds raised by the children of Japan. Today, children throughout the world fold paper cranes to symbolize their desire for peace. While the paper crane is not a simple origami design, it can be mastered by middle- and late-elementary-school-aged students. For illustrated instructions for folding a paper crane consult a book on origami, or for live action video instructions call (800) 827-0949.

Books:

1. Alexander, Lloyd, et al. (1990). *The Big Book for Peace*. New York: Dutton Children's Books. Primary, Intermediate.

2. Greene, Carol. (1991). *Caring for Our People*. Hillside, NJ: Enslow Publishers. Primary, Intermediate.

3. Fisher, Leonard Everett. (1995). *Gandhi*. New York: Atheneum Books for Young Readers. Intermediate.

4. Hamanaka, Sheila, Compiler. (1995). *On the Wings of Peace: In Memory of Hiroshima and Nagasaki*. New York: Clarion Books. Intermediate, Advanced.

5. Hamanaka, Sheila. (1995). *Peace Crane*. New York: Morrow Junior Books. Intermediate.

6. Lucas, Eileen. (1991). *Peace on the Playground*. New York: Franklin Watts. Intermediate.

7. Aaseng, Nathan. (1987). *The Peace Seekers*. Minneapolis: Lerner Publications Company. Advanced.

8. Schraff, Anne. (1994). *Women of Peace: Nobel Peace Prize Winners*. Hillside, NJ: Enslow Publishers, Inc. Advanced.

9. Coerr, Eleanor. (1993). *Sadako*. NY: Putnam. Intermediate.

Software:

1. *Kids on the Block* [Laserdisc]. Columbus, OH: Coronet/MTI (Simon & Schuster). Primary, Intermediate, Advanced.

2. *The Wizard of NO* [Laserdisc]. Columbus, OH: Coronet/MTI (Simon & Schuster). Primary, Intermediate, Advanced.

3. *Choices, Choices* [AppleII Mac IBM]. Watertown, MA: Tom Synder Productions. Primary, Intermediate, Advanced.

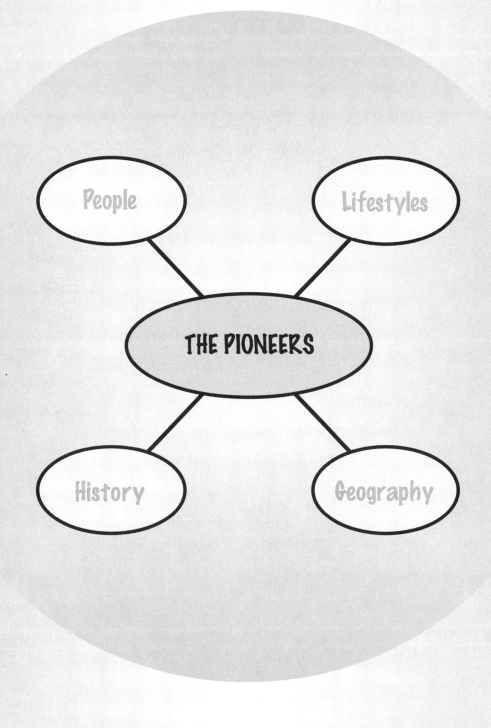

People

Lifestyles

THE PIONEERS

History

Geography

Theme Goals:

Students will:

1. state reasons why pioneers went west.

2. trace the three major trails west.

3. analyze things pioneers wanted and needed.

4. describe things pioneers took west.

5. investigate Native American cultures.

6. keep a frontier diary.

7. decide what to load in a pioneer wagon for a journey west.

8. describe the climates and regions of the Western United States.

Theme Concepts:

1. Pioneers went west in search of a better life. (Specifically, most pioneers wanted to farm their own land; others hoped to find gold; and still others went to escape religious persecution.)

2. The three major trails west were the Oregon Trail, the California Trail, and the Mormon Trail.

3. In preparation for their trip west, pioneers packed many necessities, along with a few luxuries.

4. Many pioneers recorded information about their trips in diaries.

5. A pioneer family usually carried all of its possessions west in a covered wagon.

6. Pioneer homes were constructed from available resources (e.g., log cabins in the Pacific Coast, sod houses in the Great Plains).

7. The climate of the western United States is strongly influenced by westerly wind that blows across the Pacific Ocean and by western mountain ranges.

8. The major geographic regions of the western United States are the Great Plains, Rocky Mountains, Intermountain Region, and Pacific Coast.

Vocabulary:

1. region	5. treaty	9. aspen
2. gold rush	6. necessity	10. sagebrush
3. scythe	7. luxury	11. scorpion
4. hardtack	8. pronghorn	

Instructional Bulletin Board

The purpose of this bulletin board is to help students visualize the locations of various places along the Oregon, California, and Mormon Trails. Display a large blank map of the western United States on the bulletin board. Attach different colored yarn to show the routes followed by the pioneers. Assign pairs of students the task of creating and attaching a small symbol or picture and label for each of the following places: Independence, Council Bluffs, North Platte River, Fort Kearney, Scotts Bluff, Chimney Rock, Fort Laramie, Fort Bridger, Snake River, The Dalles, Oregon City, Great Salt Lake, and Sacramento. Also have students make pictures and labels to show the approximate locations on the map of the following Indian tribes: Wasco, Paiute, Ute, Cheyenne, Arapaho, Shoshone, Pawnee, Kickapoo, Potawatomie, Crow, and Sioux.

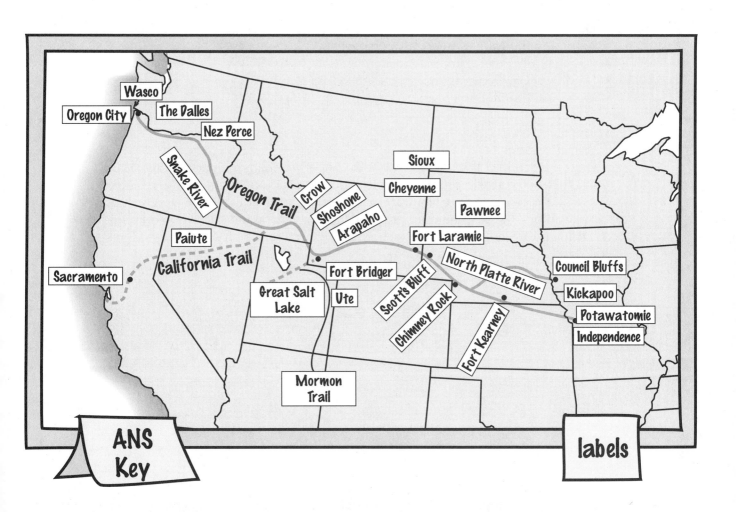

Parent Letter

Dear Parents:

The class is beginning its study of the pioneers. The pioneering spirit of our nation is epitomized by the courageous people who journeyed thousands of miles across the North American continent in search of a better life. They were lured west by stories of fertile farmland and mineral riches. They saw America as a land of opportunity—from sea to shining sea. Far less fortunate were the land's earliest inhabitants, the Native Americans, who gazed in awe and despair at the endless stream of wagon trains heading toward them. They were witnessing the disappearance of their tribal lands and the destruction of their traditional way of life.

At School:

Some of the activities planned for this theme include:

- Mapping the trails west
- Deciding what to take on the trail west
- Assuming the Native American perspective
- Keeping a frontier diary
- Loading a covered wagon
- Exploring the different western regions

At Home:

Help your child collect facts about the pioneers to share with classmates. Have your child tell you where information about this subject might be found. Take your child to a place that has information, such as a library, museum, or historical exhibit, and help him or her record some facts on index cards. Your child will bring the completed cards to school and share them with the other students.

Linking Up:

Have students imagine they are going to start a six-month bike trek across the western United States. They will be traveling on little-used roads in remote areas. Show students pictures of the grueling terrain of this region, including deserts, mountains, and endless prairie. Challenge students to list geographic and survival skills they would need to complete the trip successfully. Write their responses on the chalkboard.

Social Studies:

1. Why Go West?

Brief Background. Between 1840 and 1860, nearly 300,000 pioneers headed west. It was a long, hard trip, and many of them died along the way. Why did they go? The main reason was the hope of a better life. Eastern newspapers sketched an alluring picture of the west, with rich farmland and gold by the handfuls. Most pioneers, like those traveling to Oregon, wanted to farm their own land. Others, like the "Forty-Niners" of California gold rush fame, hoped to strike it rich. One group, the Mormons who settled in Utah, journeyed west to escape religious persecution.

To stimulate students' thinking about moving to unknown places, ask them to tell you why they live where they do. Make a list of their responses, which might include "jobs," "homes," "recreation," "friends," and so on. Next, ask them to think about why people might pack their bags and move somewhere else. Do students feel that people today might move to another place in search of a better life?

2. Mapping the Trails West

Brief Background. The three main trails west crossed a rough and dangerous wilderness. Both the Oregon Trail and California Trail started from Independence, Missouri, and covered over 2,000 miles. The Mormon Trail began at Council Bluffs, Iowa, and ended in the valley of the Great Salt Lake in what is now Utah. All three trails closely paralleled one another until they reached Wyoming.

Provide students with historical maps of the trails. Help students locate important places along the routes, such as the North Platte River, Fort Kearney, Scotts Bluff, Chimney Rock, Fort Laramie, Fort Bridger, Snake River, The Dalles, Oregon City, Great Salt Lake, and Sacramento. After weeks of travel across Nebraska country, pioneers would eagerly search the flat, barren horizon for Chimney Rock, a solitary stone spire that rises spectacularly from the ground. Provide illustrations of places on the trails. Encourage students to draw their own maps of the trails, and have them include rivers, mountains, forts, and landmarks like Chimney Rock.

3. What Should You Take on the Trail West?

Tell students to imagine they are getting ready to move to a new land. Explain that this new land may not have many of things they now have. On a piece of paper, have them each list ten things they would want to take with them to the new land. List the students' items on the chalkboard, and discuss them. Do certain things appear on most of the students' lists? What kinds of things predominate? Have students compare their own lists with the following one, which lists things pioneers actually took with them. How are they similar? How are they different?

Things Pioneers Took with Them on the Journey West

barrels	hardtack	dried fruit	compasses
rope	bacon	baking soda	sewing kits
iron pots	flour		
		vinegar	clothing
iron skillets	beans		
		pens	trunks
tin plates	cornmeal		
		ink bottles	chairs
tin cups	rice		
			coffee grinders
nails	sugar	blankets	
rifles	coffee	pillows	coffee pots
scythes	boots	lanterns	
			pistols
hoes	tools	fishing gear	
			shaving kits
books	knives		
		bullets	

candles	bottles	fiddles	writing books
iron wood-burning stoves	cloth	irons	medicines
			axes

4. Native Americans

Brief Background. Native Americans were the earliest inhabitants of the West. As pioneers moved westward and established settlements (first on the Pacific coast, and then on the Great Plains), tribal lands vanished rapidly. Disappearing, too, were the buffalo and other animals upon which the Indian nations depended for survival. The history of Native American–U.S. Government relations is filled with stories of broken treaties, unkept promises, and inhumane treatment. By the 1890s, the destruction of the Native Americans' traditional way of life was complete.

Read aloud to the class the following quote by Sitting Bull, and then have students discuss what it means: "What treaty that the white man ever made with us have they kept? Not one." Provide students with various resources on Native Americans. Assign pairs of students the task of investigating one of the following Indian nations (that inhabited the lands over which the pioneer trails crossed): Sioux, Cheyenne, Kickapoo, Ute, Arapaho, Shoshone, Nez Perce, Walla Walla, Wasco, and Paiute. Students can draw pictures of the Indian tribe's clothing, shelter, tools, and weapons, and make maps showing the location of the group along the trail. After students have finished their investigations, invite them to step into a pair of Indian moccasins (that you provide), and then tell about their (the Native Americans') feelings about the pioneers and their settlement of the land.

Language Arts:

1. Frontier Diary

Brief Background. Some pioneers kept diaries. They would include entries about such things as illnesses battled, mishaps survived, loved ones lost, distances traveled, destinations reached, landmarks seen, supplies maintained, hunting expeditions taken, rivers crossed, plants and animals seen, and Indians encountered.

Read aloud selections from *A Pioneer Woman's Memoir* by Judith E. Greenberg and Helen Carey McKeever (Watts, 1995), or another appropriate children's book that describes the challenges and struggles of life on the frontier. To give students a vivid picture of life along the Oregon Trail, show video segments from *The Oregon Trail* (available from Films for the Humanities, P.O. Box 2053, Princeton, NJ 08543). Tell students to imagine they are pioneers traveling the Oregon Trail, and have them make entries in their diaries of what happened each day. Encourage students to use words from the list of pioneer things (Social Studies Activity #3) in their diary entries.

2. Awesome Adjectives

Many of the sights on the trails west were quite spectacular. There were beautiful sunsets, towering mountains, noble Indians, huge buffalo, wily coyotes, fierce bears, majestic waterfalls, and many other scenes. Provide the class with illustrations of people, wildlife, and landscapes found on the trails. Then, challenge students to come up with awesome adjectives to describe the things they see such as shown in Figure 36-1.

Math:

1. Load Up the Wagon

Brief Background. Huge covered wagons, called "Prairie Schooners," were the main form of transportation for pioneers journeying west. Traveling in wagon trains, the Prairie Schooners, with their large white canvas tops, looked in the distance like a fleet of sailing ships. The wooden body of the wagons measured 4 feet wide by 4 feet high (wooden sides) by 10 feet long. It took three or four yoke of oxen (1 yoke = 2 oxen) to pull a loaded (about 2,000 pounds) covered wagon. On a good day, an oxen-pulled covered wagon could make about 15 miles. The trip to Oregon took four or five months to complete.

Review the list of things pioneers took west with them (Social Studies Activity #3). Tell students that all of a pioneer family's possessions would have to fit inside the wagon. Provide students

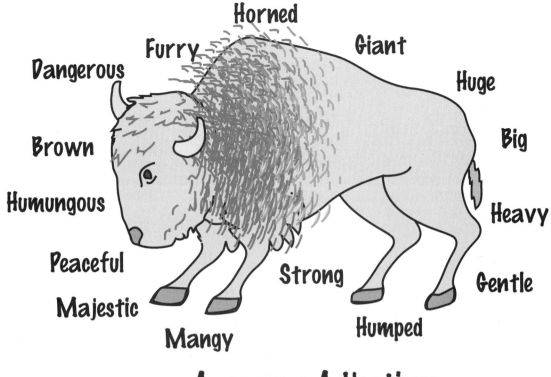

Awesome Adjectives

Horned
Furry
Giant
Dangerous
Huge
Brown
Big
Humungous
Heavy
Peaceful
Strong
Gentle
Majestic
Mangy
Humped

FIGURE 36-1

with construction materials (extra-large card-board applicance and furniture boxes, white sheets, heavy wire, duct tape, scissors) and measuring instruments, and help them them make a replica of a full-sized covered wagon. Have students estimate the amount of food, clothing, tools, and other necessities to load into their "wagon." They can select boxes and other objects to represent the pioneer things they plan to take. Each item should be clearly labeled. For example, if they were to use a broom to represent a pioneer's rifle, they would need to tie a tag labeled "rifle" on the broom. Have students measure objects to obtain correct lengths, widths, and heights. As students make their selections, check to see if the boxes and objects used are close approximations of the real sizes of the actual things. After students fit their things into their wagon, discuss the choices they made and review the loading operation. Did they encounter any difficulties in loading the wagon?

2. On the Trail

Provide highway maps of the western United States, and have students measure distances between various points on the Oregon, California, and Mormon Trails and estimate how many days a wagon would spend traveling from one location to another.

3. Pioneer Homes

Brief Background. Once pioneers finally arrived at their destinations, they used the resources that were available to them. Pioneers who settled on the barren Great Plains—which includes present-day Nebraska, Kansas, and North and South Dakota—built sod houses. They used their plows to cut strips of sod, which were then stacked one on top of the other to form the walls of the house. For the roof, a thick layer of hay was spread over poles and covered with a layer of dirt. In comparison, settlers who journeyed to Oregon constructed log cabins using readily available trees from surrounding forests. A pioneer family's first house was usually cramped and crude. It typically consisted of just one small room (frequently no more than 12 by 14 feet in area), a dirt floor, and a few tiny holes for windows.

Have students measure the area for their pioneer home on the classroom floor. Mark the cabin's dimensions with masking tape. Students can take their supplies from the wagon (the list of supplies was generated in Math Activity #1) and put them in the cabin. Let a "family" of five or six students pretend they have moved into the cabin. Do the family members have enough elbow room? How does their living space in the cabin compare to actual conditions in their own homes?

Science:

1. Climate Causes

Brief Background. As shown in Figure 36-2, the climate of the western United States is strongly influenced by the northwesterly wind that flows across the Pacific Ocean and western mountain ranges. The wind picks up mosiure over the Pacific and forms clouds. When the clouds reach land, the water in them starts to fall to Earth in the form of rain or snow. When the clouds rise over the coast mountain ranges and over the Cascade and Sierra Nevada mountain ranges, almost all of the water drops to Earth. On the eastern side of the mountains, the wind is dry. As the wind continues east, it again picks up moisture, but the Rocky Mountains block moisture from reaching further east. The Great Plains begin on the dry, eastern side of the Rocky Mountains. The western part of the Great Plains is extremely dry and barren.

Provide physical and rainfall maps of the United States. Have students trace the trails west on their maps. Help students find the Great Plains, Rocky Mountains, coast mountain ranges, Cascade Range, Sierra Nevada Range, Great Basin, and various desert areas. Students can make papier-mache, clay, and/or salt and flour relief maps of the western United States.

2. Pioneer Discoveries

Brief Background. Pioneers traveling west found all sorts of new plants and animals. Plant and animal life depends on the climate factors described in Science Activity #1. Assign small groups of students one of the four geographic regions—Great Plains, Rocky Mountains, Intermountain Region, and Pacific Coast—to research. Provide students with various sources of information, including atlases, photographs, illustrated books, and videos on the regions.

Great Plains: The pioneers had never seen anything like the dry, treeless Great Plains, with its big sky and strange dunes, buttes and badlands. In the Great Plains, grasses are the dominant plant. Have students identify and report on the following animals encountered by pioneers on the Great Plains: bison, pronghorn antelope, jackrabbits, ground squirrels, grasshoppers, wolves, coyotes, rattlesnakes, badgers, meadowlarks, hawks, and owls. What animals of the Great Plains feed on vegetation? Which animals are predators? Which domesticated animals have now replaced the bison and pronghorns on the Great Plains? (cattle and sheep) What is the main crop of the Great Plains today? (wheat)

Rocky Mountains: The towering Rocky Mountains were an awesome sight for the pioneers to behold and a rugged obstacle for them to overcome. These mountains stretch south from Canada to New Mexico; they are a dominant part of the geography of Idaho, Montana, Wyoming, Utah, and Colorado. Have students investigate Rocky Mountain plants such as aspen, spruce, and fir, and animals such as red squirrel, elk, whitetail deer, porcupine, mountain lion, and bear. What kind of leaves do

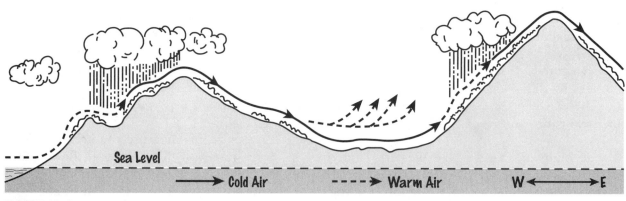

FIGURE 36-2

Sea Level

⟶ Cold Air   ----▸ Warm Air   W ⟵⟶ E

spruce and fir have? What animals are predators? What are some important human uses of this region today? (mining, skiing, and recreation)

Intermountain Region: The area between the Rocky Mountains and the Sierra Nevada and Cascade ranges is called the intermountain region. The region includes most of the present-day states of Arizona, Nevada, and Utah, and parts of Colorado, New Mexico, Washington, Oregon, and California. For the pioneers, travel through the intermountain region was one of the most dangerous parts of the whole journey. This region includes deserts in the southern part and dry, short grassland in the northern part. The Mormon Trail led to the valley of the Great Salt Lake, which is located in this region. Have students research the following plants and animals: cacti, sagebrush, pocket mice, lizards, scorpions, coyotes, hawks, and rattlesnakes. How have desert animals adapted to their environment? What animals are predators? What are the sources of water for present-day cities in this region? (mountain reservoirs)

Pacific Coast: This area extends westward from the Cascade and Sierra Nevada Ranges to the Pacific Ocean. It includes most of the present-day states of Washington, Oregon, and California and was the final destination of most pioneers. The California Trail stopped in Sacramento, the center of the California Gold Rush of the late 1840s. The Oregon Trail ended in the rich farming region of the Willamette Valley of Oregon. The pioneers found a great variety of plants and animals living in this diverse region. Forests cover many parts of the northern Pacific Coast. Have students research plants such as aspen, Douglas fir, sequoia, and redwood, and animals, such as spotted owls, moose, otter, beaver, and elk. What is the land in this region used for today? (farming, lumbering, mining) What animals are endangered today? (spotted owls, beaver, white-tailed deer)

Books:

1. Pelz, Ruth. (1990). *Black Heroes of the Wild West.* Seattle: Open Hand Publishing. Intermediate, Advanced.

2. Erickson, Paul (1994). *Daily Life in a Covered Wagon.* London: Brelish & Foss. Intermediate, Advanced.

3. Cobb, Mary. (1995). *The Quiltblock History of Pioneer Days.* Brookfield, CT: The Millbrook Press. Intermediate.

4. Gintzler, A. S. (1994). *Rough and Ready Homesteaders.* Santa Fe: John Muir Publications. Advanced.

5. Rounds, Glen. (1995). *Sod Houses on the Great Plains.* New York: Holiday House. Primary.

6. Fox, Mary Virginia. (1991). *The Story of Women Who Shaped the West.* Chicago: Children's Press. Intermediate, Advanced.

7. Patent, Dorothy Hinshap. (1995). *West by Covered Wagon: Retracing the Pioneer Trails.* New York: Walker & Company, Inc. Intermediate.

8. Greenwood, Barbara. (1995). *A Pioneer Sampler: The Daily Life of a Pioneer Family in 1840.* New York: Ticknor/Houghton Mifflin. Intermediate, Advanced.

9. Greenberg, Judith E., and McKeever, Helen Carey. (1995). *A Pioneer Woman's Memoir.* New York: Watts. Intermediate, Advanced.

Software:

1. *Writing Along The Oregon Trail* [Mac Windows CD-ROM]. Minneapolis: MECC/Humanities. Intermediate, Advanced.

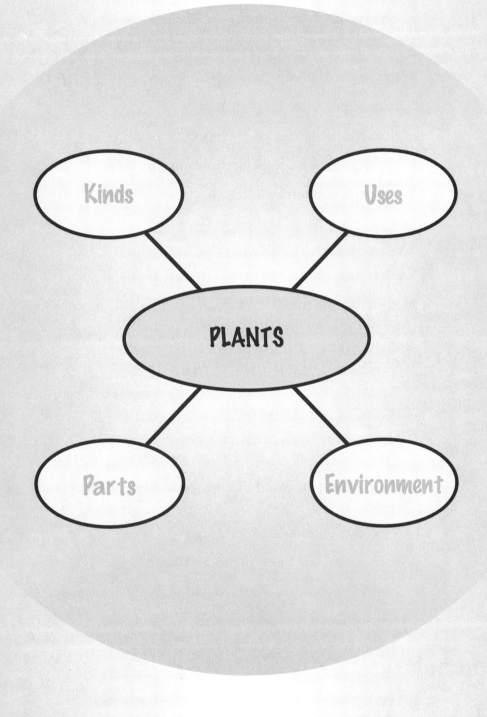

Theme Goals:

Students will:

1. identify ways people use plants.

2. analyze the effects of light on plants.

3. categorize parts of plants they eat.

4. observe plants in their natural habitat.

5. grow plants and observe their development.

6. investigate the importance of rain forests.

7. participate in tree conservation.

8. research the history of an important plant.

9. apply math skills to plant problems and data.

10. make plant prints.

Theme Concepts:

1. Plants are affected by environmental conditions.

2. Roots, leaves, seeds, and stems have specific functions.

3. Plants are used for food, raw materials, and medicine.

4. Plants receive their energy from the sun.

5. People eat the following parts of plants: seeds, roots, leaves, stems, flowers, and fruits.

6. There are many uses for the following plants or substances derived from plants: cotton, wood, rubber, coal, and oil.

7. For plants to grow to full form, certain conditions must be present.

8. Tropical rain forests are endangered.

9. Some plants are more nutritious than others.

10. People can take an active role in saving the world's trees.

11. Plants have played an important part in history.

Vocabulary:

1. endangered

2. extinction

3. xylem

4. phloem

5. global warming

Instructional Bulletin Board

The purpose of this bulletin board is to provide students with an opportunity to categorize leaves. Collect a variety of different kinds of leaves. Put each kind of leaf specimen in its own plastic bag, and then attach the bags to the bulletin board. Place a pushpin near each bag. Make leaf label cards. Punch a small hole at the top center of each label card. Let students match the leaf specimen with the correct name, by hanging a label card on the appropriate pushpin. Attach an envelope for the label cards and an answer key to the bottom of the bulletin board.

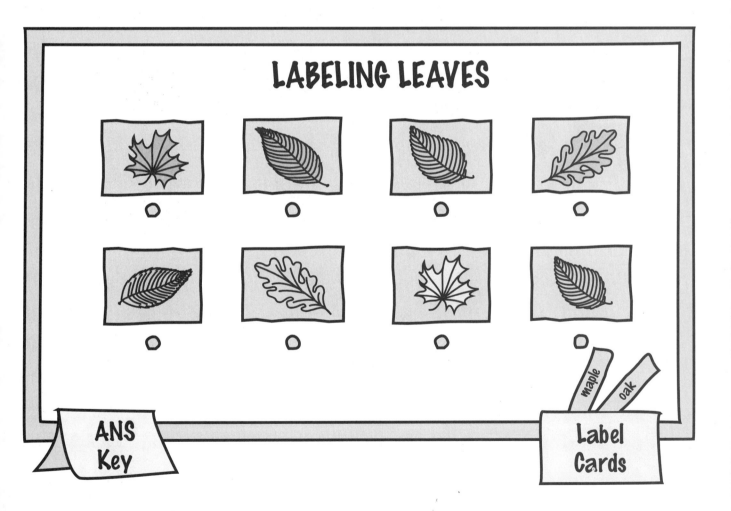

Parent Letter

Dear Parents:

Children are familiar with a variety of plants. They see plants in yards, gardens, parks, and forests; alongside roads; and in homes and shops. In this unit, students will build on their knowledge of plants. Like good biologists, they will use all of their senses—eyes, nose, ears, and hands—to answer questions about plants.

At School:

Students will be engaged in the following activities:

- Tracking down the many important uses of plants
- Investigating the relationship between light and plant growth
- Identifying the parts of plants
- Taking a field trip to observe plants
- Growing plants
- Analyzing the structure and function of plant stems
- Making vegetable soup
- Reporting on plant symbols
- Writing about a favorite plant
- Doing popcorn math

At Home:

To help us reinforce concepts about plants, please consider doing one or more of the following:

- Take your child on a plant-finding expedition around your home and neighborhood.
- See how many different kinds of plants you both can identify.
- Make a favorite vegetable or fruit dish for you both to enjoy.
- Read aloud (or listen to your child read) a book about plants from the community library.

Linking Up:

Provide students with an assortment of real plants and pictures of plants. Encourage students to describe how they use plants. Help students sort and label their "uses." Make certain that they have identified the following categories: food, raw materials, and medicines.

Science:

1. Plant Energy

Ask students where their energy comes from. Have them list the foods they eat. Identify some vegetables on their food list, such as corn, beans, potatoes, and carrots, and ask them where plants' energy comes from. (Students may or may not be aware that plants need the sun's energy to grow and produce food.) Tell students they are going to perform an experiment to help answer the question, "Where does plants' energy come from?"

To prepare the experiment, plant a bean seed in each of 10 plastic or Styrofoam containers filled with potting soil. Place five of the containers at various distances from a light source (but not in direct sunlight). Cover the other five containers so that they are in complete darkness. Except for the presence or absence of light, keep conditions for the 10 plants constant. The soil in all of the containers needs to be kept slightly moist. Give the plants the same amount of water periodically, but don't overwater. Check the plants in the dark condition once a week and compare them with the other five plants that are growing in light. Students can observe and record the effects of the two conditions on the plants. At the conclusion of the experiment, discuss the relationship between light and plant growth.

2. The Food We Eat

Help students categorize the parts of plants they eat. Bring a variety of foods to class. Make label cards for each of the following categories: seeds, roots, leaves, stems, flowers, and fruits. Put each of the label cards on an empty table or desk. As you display the edible part of a plant, ask students to tell the name of the plant and what the part is called. After the part is correctly categorized, let a student place the plant on the desk or table near the appropriate label card. Help students make a chart of the parts and plants. The organization of their chart should be similar to the one below.

3. Mystery Plants

See if students can identify five (or more) plants by using only their sense of smell. Choose flowers, fruits, and other parts from aromatic plants for this activity. Secure five (or more) paper bags. Poke some small holes in the sides of each bag. Place each plant in a separate bag and fasten it shut. Code each bag with a letter or number. Let each student, in turn, smell the bag and predict the name of the plant. After all of the children have made their predictions, open the bags and let them check their answers.

4. Twenty Questions

Put a fruit or vegetable in a box. Let students try to identify the hidden plant by asking up to 20 "yes" or "no" questions. Select one student to answer the students' questions. Position that student so she can see the fruit or vegetable inside the box. Encourage students to ask questions that divide plants into increasingly smaller groups. For example, the following sequence of questions would help identify a tomato.

Seeds	Roots	Leaves	Stems	Flowers	Fruits
corn	carrots	lettuce	celery	broccoli	apple
beans	beets	spinach	asparagus	cauliflower	pear
rice	sweet potato	cabbage	rhubarb		banana

1. Is it round? (Yes)
2. Is it green? (no)
3. Is it red? (Yes)
4. Is it hard? (No)
5. Is it soft? (Yes)
6. Is it a tomato? (Yes)

5. Plant Products

Many materials used by people come from plants. What materials in the classroom can students identify that come from plants? Assign small groups of students the task of brainstorming all of the uses of one or more of the following materials: wood, cotton, rubber, soybeans, maple syrup, turpentine, cork, coal, hemp, and oil.

6. Field Trip

Take students on a field trip to a park or nursery where they can observe a variety of plants up close. Direct students to carefully observe each plant. How many trees, shrubs, flowers, herbs, grasses, and other types of plants can they identify? Let students sketch plants using pencils or charcoal. If possible, take photographs of the different plants observed. Which appear to have been planted by people? What plants appear to be growing wild? If your school happens to be surrounded by streets and buildings, see if students can still find evidence of plant life among the concrete and asphalt. Why do plants sometimes pop up through cracks in concrete? How did the plants get there?

7. Growing Plants

Students can grow their own herbs, vegetables, and flowers from seeds and watch them develop to full form. Consult a florist for suggestions about the best plants to grow, or simply get some packets of seeds and follow the directions provided. Besides seeds, each student will need a small plastic flower pot, potting soil, and a place (near the window but not in direct sun) to grow the plant. Let the children put their names on their pots.

8. Endangered Plants

Brief Background. Some plants are endangered because of habitat destruction and pollution. Overcutting, or using up trees faster than they can be replaced, is causing environmental problems in some parts of the world, including the United States. In the state of Washington, for example, overcutting by loggers is destroying large tracts of forest, including 600-year-old Douglas firs. The possibility of plant extinction is greatest in tropical rain forests. Currently, tropical rain forests are being destroyed at the rate of 49 million acres a year (Figure 37-1). If the tropical rain forests disappear, the natural conditions needed for many kinds of animals and groups of native peoples to survive would not exist.

Have students find the locations of the world's major tropical rain forests (which are found in Central and South America, equatorial Africa, Southeast Asia, and northeastern Australia). Students can develop a list of rain forest animals, and make in-depth studies of particular ones. To spark interest, show them pictures of a few of the more unusual rain forest creatures, such as Indonesia's orangutan, Africa's indri, and Latin America's woolly monkey. Encourage interested students to debate the trade-offs associated with cutting down trees and preserving logging jobs versus protecting endangered species and preserving the environment.

Tropical Rain Forest

FIGURE 37-1

9. Nutrition and Plants

Many plants are chock-full of important nutrients. Potatoes, for example, are one of the world's most nutritious foods. They contain carbohydrates and protein, as well as a wide assortment of vitamins and minerals.

Assign each student the task of researching the nutritional value of a favorite vegetable or fruit. Let students made brief oral reports to the class on their findings.

10. Celery Stems

Brief Background. The plant stem is the connection between the leaves and the roots (Figure 37-2). Most of the stem consists of xylem. *Xylem* cells carry water up the stem from the roots to the leaves. Other stem cells, called *phloem*, move food down the stem.

To examine the structure and function of plant stems up close, provide each student with a stalk of celery, a paper cup of colored water, a measuring instrument, and scissors. Have students place their celery stalks in cups and leave overnight. Then, let students remove the celery and cut the stalk at 1" intervals with the scissors. They can measure and chart how far the colored water moved up the stem.

11. Plants and the Food Chain

Brief Background. Plants are at the beginning of food chains (Figure 37-3). They are the primary nutrient producers. For example, grass collects light energy, transfers it into chemical energy through the process of *photosynthesis*, and stores the energy in its tissues. If a steer eats grass, it consumes the plant's energy and stores it in its tissue. If the steer is eaten by a human in the form of a hamburger, then the human consumes the energy that originally came from the grass.

Help students make food chains that show how nutrients move from plants into the bodies of a succession of living things.

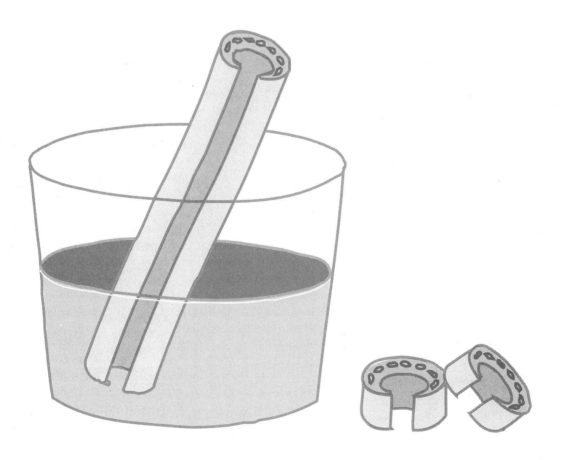

Celery Stem

FIGURE 37-2

Food Chain

FIGURE 37-3

Social Studies:

1. Vegetable Survey

Conduct a survey to determine students' vegetable preferences. Help students compile and graph the data.

2. Conserving Trees

Students can take an active role in saving the world's trees. Encourage students to do the following:

- Recycle newspaper.
- Create classroom recycling center.
- Avoid wasting paper; write more on less paper.
- Plant a tree for Arbor Day.
- Help collect and recycle waste paper.
- Prepare cutting for plant propagation.

3. Causes of Deforestation

Deforestation, or the destruction of forests, is a serious environmental problem. On the chalk-board, help students list causes and consequences of deforestation. "Causes" to consider include cutting down trees for firewood, lumber, plywood, paper, and other wood products, and clearing land for crops and livestock. "Consequences" include plant and animal extinction, soil erosion, increased global warming, loss of ozone layer, loss of living space for native people, loss of groundwater, and reduced precipitation.

4. Plant Economics

Assign individual students the task of researching one of the following careers/occupations associated with plants: farming, florist, botanist, gardener, ecologist, lawn care service, landscape design, forestry, and conservation.

5. Plant Symbols

Brief Background. Each of the nation's fifty states has an official flower. Some states also have an official tree, or are famous for a particular plant. For example, Arizona is well known for the saguaro cactus, Kentucky for bluegrass, South Carolina for the palmetto palm, Vermont for the maple tree, and Kansas for the sunflower.

Let interested students report on the famous plants of selected states. They can illustrate their reports with maps of the states and pictures of the plants.

6. The History of. . . .

Brief Background. Many plants have played a prominent role in trade. Merchants and nations became rich buying and selling spices, sugarcane, cocoa, and other exotic plants. Tobacco was the cash crop of Jamestown, America's first permanent and successful colony. In the South, cotton was king—and the dependence on slavery for its production helped lead to the Civil War. Another plant that had a great impact on history was the potato. The potato plant originated in South America and was the staple food of the Incas. Spaniards brought potatoes to Europe in the middle of the sixteenth century. After the potato was introduced to Ireland, it became that country's most important food, and when Ireland's potato crop failed in the 1840s, almost a million Irish died and hundreds of thousands immigrated to America.

Here is a list of some of history's most important plants for students to investigate: rice, rubber tree, coffee, potato, apple, orange, corn, cotton, sugarcane, pepper, tobacco, soybean, and wheat. Have students create a "plant poster" that includes a written report on the plant, a map that shows where the plant originated, and a real sample or a picture of the plant.

Math:

1. Popcorn Math

Students can practice math skills as they do the following: Estimate the number of popcorn kernels in a jar, then count them; compare estimates with the actual number; predict how much time it will take for the kernels to pop, then measure the actual time; predict the number of popcorn kernels that will pop when heated, then heat them and compare predictions with the actual number; and count popcorn on a string.

2. Buying Produce

Provide students with scales and a variety of vegetables and fruits, together with their per package prices. Students can weigh bags of produce and calculate their costs per unit.

3. Graphing Plant Data

The study of plants offers many opportunities for students to process and display data. They can record and graph plant growth, comparative prices of vegetables and fruits, leading plant-growing states and countries, nutritional values, and average sizes of plants, to name a few.

4. Vegetable Soup

Read *Stone Soup*, then help students prepare and serve a tasty vegetable soup, using a favorite recipe.

Language Arts:

1. Favorite Plants

Flowers and plants are often given as gifts for Mother's Day, birthdays, weddings, and other occasions. Have students write about "My Favorite Flower or Plant . . . ," describing why they would like to receive or give it as a gift.

2. Guess My Plant

Provide each student with an index card. Have each student choose a plant to research, then have them write detailed description of their plants on the cards. Invite a student to read his description, and let the other students try to guess the name of the plant being described. Repeat until all of the students have had an opportunity to read their cards.

3. Vegetable Fairy Tales

Magic beans played a big part in the fairy tale *Jack and the Beanstalk*, and a pumpkin was transformed magically into a royal carriage in *Cinderella*. Read *Jack and the Beanstalk* aloud to the students, then ask them to imagine what might have happened in the story if Jack had traded the cow for some other vegetable seed, such as spinach, carrots, or onions. Pair up students, and let them revise the story by replacing beans with a different vegetable.

Art:

1. Plant Prints

Let students make prints of leaves. They can brush their leaves with paint, then stamp prints on white paper. After the paint dries, have students add other features with Magic Markers.

2. Drawing Plants

Provide plants and drawing materials, and let students draw scientific illustrations of plants. Stress that scientific drawings must be accurate in every detail.

Books:

1. Goldenberg, Janet. (1994). *Weird Things You Can Grow*. New York: Random House. Intermediate, Advanced.

2. Bush-Brown, Louise. (1962). *Young America's Garden Book*. New York: Charles Scribner's Sons. Advanced.

3. Selsam, Millicent. (1981). *The Plants We Eat*. New York: William Morrow and Company. Intermediate.

4. Brown, Marc. (1981). *Your First Garden Book*. Boston: Little, Brown, and Company. Intermediate.

5. Coldrey, Jennifer. (1987). *Discovering Flowering Plants*. New York: The Bookwright Press. Primary, Intermediate.

6. Kramer, Jack. (1978). *Plant Hobbies*. Cleveland: William Collins and World Publishing Co., Inc. Primary, Intermediate.

7. Dowden, Anne. (1990). *The Clover and the Bee: A Book of Pollination*. New York: Thomas Y. Crowell. Intermediate.

8. Challand, Helen J. (1986). *Plants Without Seeds*. Chicago: Children's Press. Primary.

9. Coil, Suzanne M. (1991). *Poisonous Plants*. New York: Franklin Watts. Intermediate.

10. Kavaler, Lucy. (1983). *Green Magic: Algae Rediscovered*. New York: Thomas Y. Crowell. Intermediate, Advanced.

11. McGovern, Ann. *Stone Soup*. (1986). New York: Scholastic.

12. Perrault, Charles. (1994). *Cinderella*. Retold by Christine San Jose. Honesdale, PA: Boyds Mill Press.

13. Alan, Garner. (1992). *Jack and the Beanstalk*. New York: Doubleday Books for Young Readers.

Software:

1. *Wonders of Science CD-ROM Library: A World of Plants* [Mac MPC CD-ROM]. Washington, DC: National Geographic. Primary, Intermediate.

2. *What Is an Ecosystem?/What Is a Food Chain?* [Laserdisc]. Columbus, OH: Coronet/MTI (Simon & Schuster). Primary, Intermediate, Advanced.

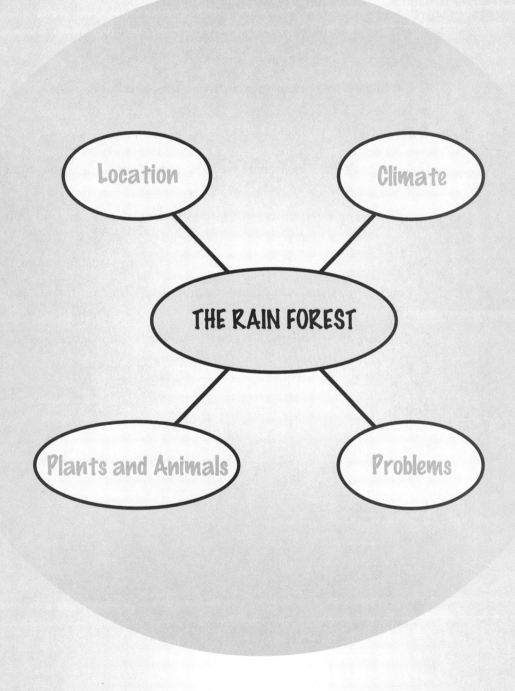

Theme Goals:

Students will:

1. name and locate rain forests on a map.

2. describe characteristics of the rain forest climate.

3. list names of rain forest animals and plants.

4. describe characteristics of rain forest people.

5. identify reasons why rain forests are important.

6. identify reasons why rain forests are threatened.

7. investigate ways rain forests can be protected.

Theme Concepts:

1. Rain forests are located at various places on or near the equator.

2. Rain forests need constant high temperature and plentiful rainfall.

3. Rain forests contain a tremendous variety of plants and animals.

4. People are discovering many valuable uses for rain forest products.

5. Rain forests are being threatened by people and development.

6. People can save the rain forests if they act now.

Vocabulary:

1. ecotourism

2. sustainable agriculture

3. transpiration

4. emergents

5. canopy

6. understory

7. photosynthesis

8. conservation

9. recycle

Instructional Bulletin Board

Cover the bulletin board area with a large sheet of white paper. Make a transparency of the rain forest scene below, project it on the paper, and pencil in the outline. Then, use a black Magic Marker to trace the rain forest scene on the paper. Green tempera paint can be used to color the rain forest plants. Students can fill the rain forest with appropriate animal cutouts they have created. (Note: The size of the animals should be scaled to the dimensions of the background scene.) An excellent source for information about and pictures of rain forest animals is *The Grolier World Encyclopedia of Endangered Species* (Grolier Educational Corporation, 1993). Use pins to attach the animal cutouts to the rain forest scene. (Note: To avoid an overly cluttered look, first display some of the animals, then remove and display a different set.) Challenge students to correctly identify and label the animals displayed.

Parent Letter

Dear Parents:

We are beginning our study of one of nature's grandest spectacles—the rain forest. The world's greatest variety of living things is found there. But tropical rain forests are endangered. Past and current human actions have harmed rain forest plants and animals and their environment.

People cannot save the rain forests, however, if they don't know or care about them. In this theme, the children will be introduced to the rain forests. The children will find out where they are located, what they look like, who lives in them, why they are threatened, and how they can be protected.

At School:

Some of the special activities for your child include:

- Making a rain forest in a jar
- Baking rain forest cookies
- Creating rain forest animals
- Figuring out how big the rain forest is
- Researching how much paper we use
- Recycling paper
- Designing a rain forest advertisement

At Home:

You can help us at home by talking with your child about the rain forests. Stories about the rain forest are frequently in the news. Take a few minutes to explain one of these stories to your child. Please encourage your child to share at school any knowledge he or she has about the rain forests. If your child has questions about the rain forests that you would like us to address at school, jot them down and send them in.

Your support is very much appreciated.

Linking Up:

To help students gain a greater appreciation of natural environments like the rain forest, take them on a field trip to the woods or park. Students can develop ecological concepts through this outdoor experience that cannot be accomplished in the classroom. By closely observing the variety of plants and animals, as well as the interdependent relationships that exist among them, students will have a concrete point of reference when discussing rain forest plant and animal life found in remote environments.

Science:

1. Life in the Layers of the Rain Forest

Brief Background. The rain forest is divided into three layers as shown in Figure 38-1. The three are: (1) *canopy*, or cover, which is formed by the spreading branches of the forest; (2) *emergents*, which consist of the tallest trees that rise above the canopy, some to a height of 200 feet or more; and (3) *understory*, which is made up of the smallest trees and plants. Different types of plants and animals can be found at different vertical levels in the rain forest. Most live in the canopy. In the Amazon rain forest, a variety of plants and wildlife, including flowering plants, monkeys, bats, squirrels, parrots, and other birds, occupy the tree tops. Vines, orchids, snakes, lizards, opossums, and porcupines can be found on tree branches. Among the relatively few living things found on the dark, damp floor of the rain forest are ferns, mosses, rodents, tapirs, antelope, and deer. Insects are the most abundant animals in the rain forest. A tremendous variety of ants, termites, beetles, bees, butterflies, and moths can be found at all levels.

Challenge students to investigate plants and animals found in the rain forest. As students identify rain forest plants and animals, ask them also to try to determine where they live. (Note: This information will be useful to students as they decide where on the rain forest bulletin board scene to place their animal cutouts.) Provide students with a variety of construction materials, including paper tubes, construction and tissue paper of different colors, scissors, pipe cleaners, tape, glue, and modeling clay, and let them make rain forest dioramas.

2. Making a Miniature Rain Forest

To make individual rain forests in a bottle (see Figure 38-2) for the children to take home, each student will need:

1 extra-large, clear glass pickle jar (opening must be wide enough for hand to pass through it)
3 cups fine gravel
1 1/2 cups washed horticultural charcoal
4–5 cups mixed potting soil (premixed with peat moss and perlite)
1 piece of old nylon stocking (large enough to cover bottom of bottle)
an assortment of 3–4 small tropical plants (such as Madagascar palm, tropical foliage, pteris fern, silver tree plant, aluminum plant, and rain tree plant), which can be purchased in flower shops and plant nurseries.

Directions: Wash jar. Place a 1/2-inch layer of gravel on bottom. Cover with 1 cup of charcoal. Cover charcoal with nylon material. Put 1/2 cup of charcoal in potting soil and mix together. Spread potting soil over nylon cover. The potting soil should be deep enough to cover the roots of the plants. Make a small hole and put roots of each tropical plant in soil mixture. Gently press soil around plant until firm. Spoon water around plant, but do not overwater. Fasten lid to jar. Place jar near sunlight, but do not expose to direct sunlight. If the amount of water and distance from sunlight are correct, water droplets should appear on the inside walls of the jar. Add water (and/or place farther from sunlight) if few or no water droplets appear. Remove lid for a few hours if too many water droplets appear. Once all necessary adjustments are made, the plants in the jar will probably not need any further attention.

2. Observing the Minature Rain Forests

Brief Background. Through a process called *respiration*, plants use oxygen and give off carbon dioxide. Decaying matter in soil also gives off carbon dioxide. Through a process called *photosynthesis*, green plants also use carbon dioxide and give off oxygen. Thus, plants continuously recycle oxygen and carbon dioxide. In another process, called *transpiration*, plants give off water vapor through the pores of their leaves. This water vapor in the air changes to water droplets when it is cooled, causing rain. It is estimated that about half of the rain in the rain forest is caused by tran-

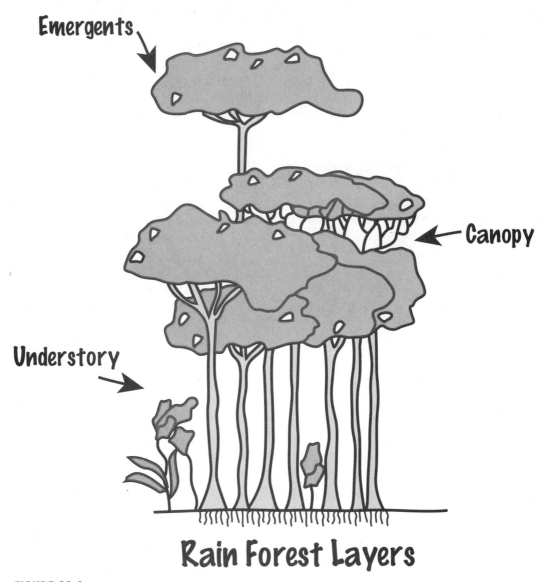

Emergents

Canopy

Understory

Rain Forest Layers

FIGURE 38-1

spiration. By taking in carbon dioxide, giving off oxygen, and returning water to the atmosphere, rain forests help keep the earth's gases in proper balance and help recycle the earth's water.

Ask students to observe their rain forest in a bottle daily and record their observations. Their observations should stimulate critical thinking, and perhaps generate questions like: How can the plants live in the enclosed jar? Where does the water on the inside walls of the jar come from? What is the temperature inside the jar? How is the miniature rain forest in a jar similar to a real rain forest? The preceding background information should be helpful as you respond to the students' questions.

3. Where Are the Rain Forests?

Brief Background. The world's tropical rain forests are located near the equator as shown in Figure 38-3. The world's largest rain forest is located in the Amazon basin of South America. The second largest rain forest is centered in Indonesia, in Southeast Asia. The third largest rain forest is found in East Central Africa.

Assign students to small groups of three or four and let them use atlases and globes to locate the major rain forests. They will discover that tropical rain forests are near the equator and receive heavy rainfall. Have students identify continents and countries that have rain forests.

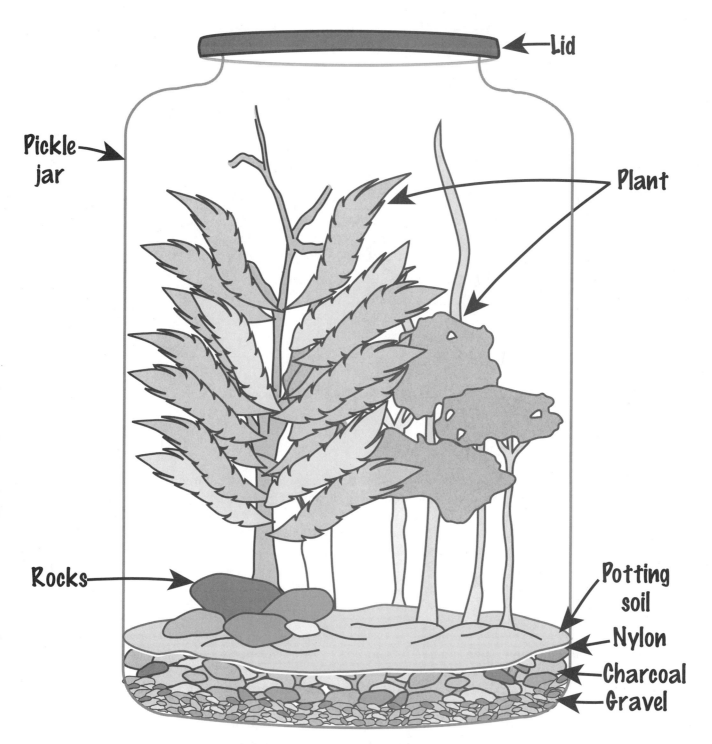

Lid

Plant

Pickle
jar

Rocks

Potting
soil

Nylon

Charcoal

Gravel

Minature Rain Forest

FIGURE 38-2

As a point of reference, students can compare the local annual rainfall with the annual rainfall in rain forests (the wettest rain forest, located in Hawaii, averages 480 inches of rain annually). Use a rain gauge to keep track of the daily rainfall. To find out about weather conditions in rain forest areas worldwide, have students consult the weather section of the daily newspaper.

Math:

1. Saving Trees

One ton of recycled paper saves 17 trees. To make students more environmentally friendly consumers, have them save, weigh, and recycle paper used at school. For recycling pur-

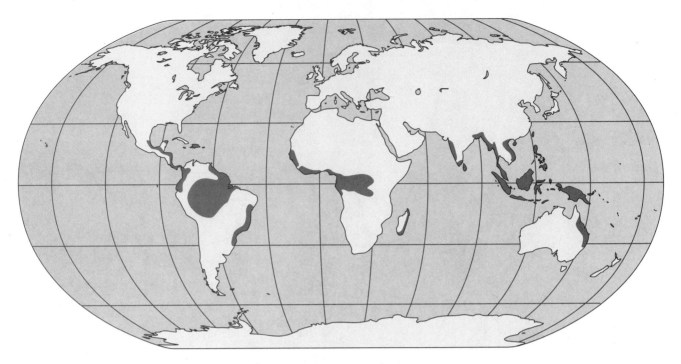

World's Rain Forests

FIGURE 38-3

poses, put white paper in one container and colored paper in another. Students can weigh, record, and graph the amount of paper used each week. Hopefully, the class's paper consumption will decrease as students become more aware of the need to conserve and recycle paper.

2. The Size of Rain Forests

There are approximately 2 billion acres of rain forest in the world. To give students a concrete sense of an area the size of an acre, take them outside and help them mark off one acre (use a yard or meter stick; one acre equals 4,840 square feet, or 4047 square meters; an acre is approximately the same size as a football field). To give students a sense of the magnitude of 2 billion, tell them that if they counted nonstop at the rate of one number per second, it would take them 63.4 years to count to 2 billion. To calculate: 2,000,000,000 ÷ 60 (seconds) ÷ 60 (minutes) ÷ 24 (hours) ÷ 365 (days) = 63.4 (years).

3. Rain Forest Destruction

Brief Background. High estimates of rain forest destroyed annually range from 27 to 40 million acres, while low estimates put the annual loss at around 4 million acres.

Challenge students to figure out how long it would take to destroy all of the world's rain forest if the annual loss was 40 million, the high estimate. To calculate: 2,000,000,000 ÷ 40,000,000 = 50 years. In other words, if the high rate is accurate, rain forest is being destroyed currently at the rate of approximately one acre per second.

4. Rain Forest Cookies

Brief Background. One way to both protect the rain forests and give rain forest people a livelihood is to harvest valuable rain forest products without harming the environment. Harvesting plants without harming them is called *sustainable agriculture*. A great variety of rain forest nuts, fruits, and fibers can be harvested in this way.

Two rain forest nuts—Brazil nuts and cashews—are main ingredients of the cookie recipe below. Together with your students, bake up a batch for a crunchy rain forest snack. Serve with milk. To add another rain forest treat to the menu, include bite-sized pieces of fresh mango fruit (available at many supermarkets).

RAIN FOREST COOKIES

2 cups sifted all-purpose flour
1 teaspoon baking power
3/4 teaspoon salt
1/2 teaspoon nutmeg
3/4 cup butter
1 cup sugar
1 egg
1/4 cup milk
1 teaspoon vanilla extract
1/3 cup chopped Brazil nuts
1/3 cup chopped cashews

Directions: Sift flour with baking powder, salt, and nutmeg. Cream butter in mixing bowl. Add sugar and continue creaming until fluffy. Add egg, milk, and vanilla extract and beat thoroughly. Gradually blend in nuts. Drop rounded teaspoons onto ungreased cookie sheets. Bake at 375° F for 10 to 12 minutes, until golden brown. Makes about 50 cookies.

Social Studies:

1. Why Save the Rain Forests?

Brief Background. Traditional rain forest people lived by hunting and gathering food. Their impact on the environment was minimal. Today, modern agricultural and commercial production is ruining many rain forest environments. Three important reasons why rain forests need to be protected are: (1) Scientists are discovering that extracts from rain forest plants can be used to treat major diseases, such as cancer and high blood pressure; (2) many species of plants and animals that can live only in rain forest environments would be lost forever if the rain forests were destroyed; (3) rain forests help keep the Earth's gasses in proper balance and they help recycle the world's water.

To give students a vivid picture of what is happening, read aloud sections of *People of the Rain Forest* by Lynn Stone (Rouke, 1994) and *Why Save the Rain Forest?* by Donald Silver (Julian Messner, 1993). What special and valuable knowledge of the rain forest do rain forest people possess? Have students study and report on rain forest plants currently being used to treat diseases—such as extract of the rosy periwinkle, which is used to treat cancer. Try to locate a local expert on tropical medicines and invite him or her to visit class to discuss plant-based medicines (Check with the local university or hospital for names of possible speakers.)

2. Conservation Efforts

Invite a conservationist or environmentalist to the classroom to discuss the conserving and protecting of fragile environments, including rain forests. For possible speakers, contact a local chapter of the Sierra Club or some other environmental group. Encourage students to contact organizations concerned about the rain forests, such as the following:

The Nature Conservancy
P.O. Box 17056
Baltimore, MD 21298

RainForest Action Network
300 Broadway Suite 28
San Francisco, CA 94133

Art:

1. Tourism and the Rain Forest

Many rain forest countries are encouraging tourism. If tourists spend lots of money to see them, the rain forests will probably be protected and preserved for future generations—for economic if no other reasons. One important way to attract large numbers of tourists is to advertise. Have students create colorful, well-designed, informative travel advertisements on large sheets of paper that promote the rain forest as an ideal vacation spot.

Language Arts:

1. A Classroom Inquiry Center

Introduce students to the term, *biodiversity*, which refers to the total variety of different species of plants and animals located within a particular place. Of all the Earth's environments, the rain forest environment has the greatest biodiversity. To help students sample some of this biodiversity, create a "Rain Forest Inquiry Center" in the classroom. Decorate the center with travel posters and brochures showing tropical rain forest scenes. Place pictures, maps, books, and articles about rain forest plants and animals at the center. Some excellent books to include are: *At Home in the Rain Forest* by Diane Willow and Laura Jacques (Charlesbridge, 1991); *Vanishing Rain Forest* by Lynn Stone (Rouke, 1994); *The Rainforest* by Billy Goodman (Tern Enterprise, 1991); *What's in the Rainforest?* by Suzanne Ross (Enchanted Rainforest Press,

1991); and *Earth's Vanishing Forests* by Roy Gallant (Macmillan, 1991). At appropriate times during the day, give students an opportunity to browse and read at the center (a couple of comfortable chairs or big pillows would be an added enticement.

2. Rain Forest Countries Pen and Key Pals

Provide students with pen or E-mail pals from rain forest countries, such as Brazil, Costa Rica, Cameroon, and Indonesia. Questions to ask: Have you visited a rain forest? What does your country's rain forests look like? What kinds of plants and animals are found in your country's rain forests? How important is the rain forest to your country's economy? Are you worried about the destruction of rain forests? Should people in the United States try to help save the rain forests?

3. Letters from the Rain Forest

Ask students to think about what it would be like to be a person living in a rain forest. Then have them, as that person, write a letter home to a friend telling about what was happening there. Make certain they have ample factual information about the rain forest as a basis for the development of their fictional accounts.

Books:

1. Stone, Lynn. (1994). *Vanishing Rain Forest.* Vero Beach, FL: The Rourke Corporation. Primary.

2. Gallant, Roy A. (1991). *Earth's Vanishing Forests.* New York: Macmillan. Advanced.

3. Stone, Lynn. (1994). *People of the Rain Forest.* Vero Beach, FL: The Rourke Corporation. Primary.

4. Willow, Diane, and Jacques, Laura. (1991). *At Home in the Rain Forest.* Charlesbridge Publishing. Primary.

5. Stone, Lynn. (1989). *Rain Forests.* Vero Beach, FL: The Rourke Corporation. Primary, Intermediate.

6. Silver, Donald. (1993). *Why Save the Rain Forest?* New York: Julian Messner. Intermediate.

7. Ross, Suzanne. (1991). *What's in the Rainforest? 106 Answers From A to Z.* Enchanted Rainforest Press. Intermediate.

8. Mitel, Cornelia, and Rodgers, Mary. (1991). *Our Endangered Planet: Tropical Rainforests.* Minneapolis: Lerner Publications. Intermediate.

9. Goodman, Billy. (1991). *The Rainforest.* New York: Tern Enterprise. Intermediate.

10. *The Grolier World Encyclopedia of Endangered Species.* (1993). Danbury, CT: Grolier Educational Corporation). Intermediate, Advanced.

Software:

1. *Eco-Adventures in the Rainforest* [Mac IBM]. San Diego: Chariot Software Group. Intermediate, Advanced.

2. *Rain Forest: Imagination Express* [Mac MPC CD-ROM]. Redmond, WA: Edmark. Primary, Intermediate, Advanced.

3. *Tropical Rainforest* [Laserdisc]. Denver: Lumivision. Intermediate, Advanced.

4. *The Amazon Trail* [Mac IBM Windows MPC CD-ROM]. Minneapolis: MECC. Intermediate, Advanced.

39

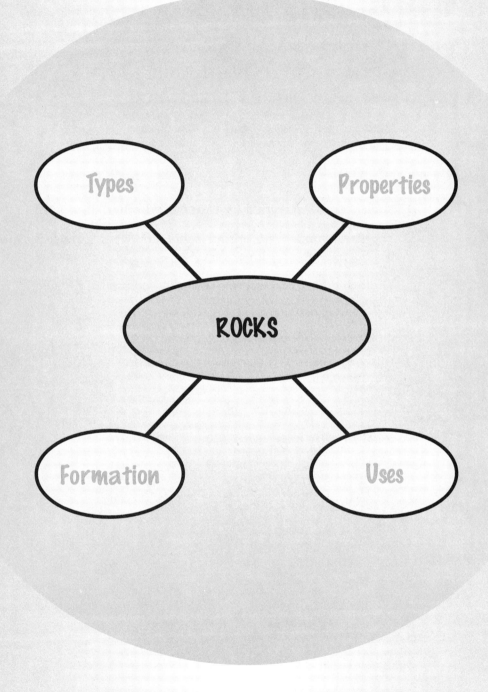

Types

Properties

ROCKS

Formation

Uses

Theme Goals:

Students will:

1. investigate the properties of rocks.

2. identify different layers of the Earth.

3. identify how rocks are used.

4. plot the locations of rock, mineral, and ore raw materials.

5. use metal artifacts to make inferences.

6. compare the prices of different precious minerals.

7. write stories with fortune-hunting themes.

8. create rocks, mosaics, and fossils.

Theme Concepts:

1. Rocks can be classified by texture and other attributes.

2. The Earth is made up of four concentric layers: the crust, mantle, outer core, and inner core.

3. There are three major forms of rocks: sedimentary, igneous, and metamorphic.

4. Rocks are used in many important ways.

5. Different kinds of rocks, minerals, and ores are found throughout the world.

6. Ancient people learned how to make metal tools.

7. Artists use rocks to make mosaics and statues.

8. Rock fossils can tell us about the past.

Vocabulary:

1. weathering
2. crust
3. mantle
4. core
5. minerals
6. sedimentary
7. igneous
8. metamorphic
9. karat
10. fossils

Instructional Bulletin Board

The purpose of this bulletin board is to help students develop classification skills. To prepare the bulletin board, place eight or more different types of rocks in separate, small, heavy-duty plastic bags. Use a permanent marker to put an identification number on each bag and each rock specimen. Staple the bags to the bulletin board as shown below. Attach a Velcro patch under each bag. Print the names of the rocks together with a list of some of their distinguishing characteristics on separate cards. Glue a Velcro patch on the back side of each card. Put the rock name cards in a large envelope attached to the lower right corner of the board. Attach a covered answer key to the lower left corner.

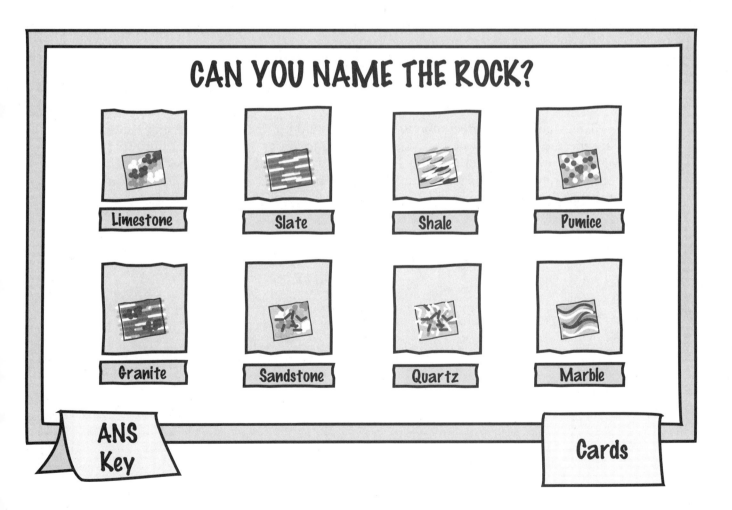

Parent Letter

Dear Parents:

Children are constantly seeking explanations and understandings of the natural world. One substance that is easily accessible to children's investigation can be found almost anywhere—rocks. The Earth is composed mainly of rock. In this unit, children will be analyzing the attributes of rocks and exploring how rocks are used.

At School:

Some of the activities planned for this theme include:

• Going on a rock-hunting expedition
• Making soil from rocks
• Molding a model of the inside of the Earth
• Classifying rocks by texture, shape, and color
• Identifying products that contain rocks
• Reading and writing about fortune-hunting adventures

At Home:

This would be an ideal time to take your child on a rock-hunting expedition around the home and neighborhood. As you travel in the car, point out buildings and other structures made from stone, brick, and glass. At home and in stores, point out items that contain rocks, minerals, or ore. Make a list of all of the items found by you and your child, and let him or her take the list to school to share with the class.

Linking Up:

Let students play the role of rock detective and search for ways rocks are used. Ask students: What rocks are used to build things? What rocks are used to make jewelry? and What rocks are used to make heat? Have them look for and list products that contain rocks, minerals, and ore. They can use the headings below to organize their list. A few examples are given. To determine the kinds of raw materials contained in various products, let students study information in library references and other sources, or provide them with information gathered by you.

Product	Rock/Mineral/Ore
wire	copper
aluminum can	bauxite
ring	diamond and gold
pottery	clay

Science:

1. Rock-Hunting Expedition

Find out about the rocks and minerals that are common in your area. If possible, take students on a field trip to a rock quarry or some other area where rocks are plentiful. Invite a geologist, or some other rock hunter, to accompany you and the class. Make a rough map of the site. Bring a camera along and take photographs of rocks and rock formations. If a field trip is not an option, take students on a rock-hunting trip around the school or let them bring in rocks they have found at home. Back in the classroom, let students handle and sort the rocks. What similarities and differences about the rocks do students observe? Did students use any of the following labels as a basis for grouping their rocks: *smooth rocks*, *rough rocks*, *dull rocks*, and *shiny/sparkling rocks*. Some rocks are harder than others. To check for hardness, students can rub two chunks of the same rock together over a sheet of white paper. Then, with a hand lens, they can look at the pieces of rock on the paper. How many pieces of rock are on the paper? Have students repeat this process for each type of rock specimen. Do some rocks fail to break into tiny pieces? Based on their testing, have students list categories of hardness, such as: *does not break*, *breaks into smaller pieces*, *breaks into tiny grains of sand*, and *rock breaks into fine powder*.

2. Making Soil

Brief Background. The natural breakdown of rocks is called *weathering*. Weathering takes place on Earth constantly. Some of the natural causes of weathering are temperature changes and the actions of ice, wind, water, and chemicals.

Take the class outside. Show students some large rocks, and then ask them to speculate about how the rocks could be broken. Put some of the rocks in a heavy burlap bag, place the closed bag on the schoolyard pavement or another hard surface, and hit the bag with a hammer until the rocks break into smaller rocks, grains of sand, or powder. (You may want to let students take turns hitting the bag under your supervision.) Probe to see if students are aware that it takes a lot of energy to break the rocks. Relate the demonstration to the concept of weathering. Put some rock powder in a jar. To make soil, add some humus (which can be purchased at a nursery) and mix. Will plants grow in the soil? To investigate this question, perform an experiment. Let students put the soil in cups, add seeds, provide sunlight and water according to directions on the seed package, and then check periodically to see what happens.

3. Inside the Earth

Brief Background. The following four concentric spheres of matter make up the Earth's interior: an *inner core* of solid metal; an *outer core* of molten iron and nickel; a *mantle* of dense rock some 1800 miles thick; and an outer *crust* of less dense rock about 25 miles thick on land (Figure 39-1).

To help students learn some essential points about the Earth's geology, have them make a model of the Earth's interior. Cut Styrofoam balls (3–4" diameter) in half. Give pairs of students a half sphere and red, blue, yellow, and green playdough. To make a cross-section of the earth, have pairs use the playdough to make concentric circles of different colors on the flat surface of the half sphere. Direct students to do the following: For the inner core, mold a circle of blue playdough in the center of the flat surface of the half sphere; for the outer core, mold a ring of yellow playdough around the blue circle; for the mantle, mold a thick ring of red playdough around the yellow ring; and for the crust, mold a very thin green ring of playdough around the edge of the half sphere.

4. The Three Forms of Rocks

Brief Background. There are three major forms of rocks: sedimentary, igneous, and metamorphic. Sedimentary rock is formed by sediments or particles that are deposited at the mouths of rivers and are then compressed by the weight of water and top layers of sediment. Igneous rock is formed by volcanic activity. Metamorphic rock is formed as a result of great pressure on igneous or sedimentary rocks deep within the Earth.

Provide pairs of students with hand lenses and one or more examples of each of the three rock forms. (Note: For help securing different kinds of rocks, check with a geologist at a nearby government agency, business, or college. After you gather the rock specimens, put a coded identification number on each one with a permanent marker.) Encourage students to devise

their own tests for the rocks. For example, hardness might be checked by whether or not the rock leaves a scratch mark on glass. They should also come up with their own terms (glassy, bright, dull, layered, polished, rough, sharp, smooth, etc.) to describe the rocks. Make certain that students take careful notes and make detailed drawings of the rock specimens. Can students sort each rock specimen into one of three groups—sedimentary, igneous, or metamorphic—based on their observations? Characteristics of some common kinds of sedimentary, igneous, and metamorphic rocks are listed at the bottom of the facing page.

5. Make a Rock

Students can make their own rocks. This is a great activity for outdoors. Each student will need a shallow 6-inch-square cardboard box lined with aluminum foil in which to make the rock. Help each student do the following: (1) fill the box half full of water; (2) mix three parts of sand with one part of builder's cement (limestone) in a tray; (3) add mixture to water and stir; (4) let mixture harden slightly; (5) add pieces of various rocks and shells; (6) let the mixture harden completely (one or two days); and (7) cut away the box.

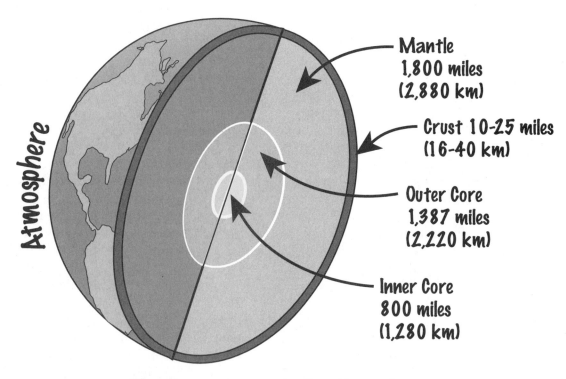

The Interior of the Earth

FIGURE 39-1

Social Studies:

1. Global Rock Hound

Have students use reference books and maps to identify and locate countries that are major producers/exporters of rock, mineral, and ore raw materials. Let students create a map legend and symbols for these raw materials and plot their locations on a blank outline map of the world. For example, students could place a symbol for copper on major copper-producing countries, such as Zambia, Chile, Australia, and the United States.

2. The Rocks-Manufacturing Connection

Brief Background. Pittsburgh, Pennsylvania, is an example of how an abundance of the right kinds of rocks helped turn a trading town into a large urban manufacturing center. As the Industrial Revolution began to develop, it became obvious that the mineral resources needed to manufacture many products were located near Pittsburgh. These resources included coal and iron ore to produce nails, axes, and other tools, as well as sand and limestone to produce glass.

Have students investigate manufacturing companies in the local area or region. What kinds of mineral resources are needed to produce their products? From where do these resources come?

3. Archaeology

Brief Background. Slowly but surely, ancient people learned how to use rocks to make tools and weapons. The first tools were handheld stones. They were followed by stone axes and clubs. Much later, people learned to how to forge tin and copper alloys into bronze. The Hittites were among the first civilizations to make iron tools and weapons. Their iron-tipped lances and iron axes helped them defeat their less technologically advanced enemies.

Rock and metal remains of early cultures help archaeologists reconstruct the daily life and customs of ancient peoples. Provide students with some rock or metal artifacts, such as an assortment of arrowheads or old coins—and let them role-play archaeologists and make inferences about the "ancient" people who used them.

4. Digging for Treasure

Decorate a tiny cardboard box and fill it with some costume jewelry to create a "treasure chest." Have students make their own maps of the classroom or playground that show the lo-

ROCK CHARACTERISTICS

Sedimentary Rocks

Rock	Composition	Shape	Texture	Hardness	Color
limestone	calcite	varied	rough	soft	varied
sandstone	sand	varied	smooth	soft/hard	varied
shale	clay/mud	flat	smooth	soft/hard	gray

Igneous Rocks

Rock	Composition	Shape	Texture	Hardness	Color
granite	feldspar/quartz	varied	coarse	hard	varied
quartz	quartz	crystal	smooth	hard	varied
basalt	lava	varied	smooth	hard	varied
pumice	lava	varied	porous	soft	varied
obsidian lava	varied	smooth	hard	glassy	black

Metamorphic Rocks

Rock	Composition	Shape	Texture	Hardness	Color
marble	limestone	varied	varied	hard	varied
slate	shale	flat	smooth	hard	black
gneiss	granite	varied	coarse	hard	varied

cation of the "buried" treasure chest. Collect and duplicate the maps. Using the information contained on the maps, students can take turns hiding and finding the treasure chest.

Math:

1. A Gem of a Buy

Provide students with a variety of store catalogues featuring gems and fine jewelry. Have students compare the prices for different gem stones, such as diamonds, rubies, sapphires, topaz, jade, and opal. Make certain that students compare different kinds of gems of the same weight (*carat* is the unit of weight for precious stones; one carat = 200 milligrams). What is the most expensive gem? What is the least expensive gem?

2. Precious Metals

Brief Background. Gold, silver, and platinum are three of the world's most valuable substances. The value of an ounce of each of these precious metals varies from day to day.

Many newspapers list the daily price of precious metals in the business section. Have students compare the value of an ounce of gold, silver, and platinum with an ounce of other substances, such as perfume, coffee, milk, pepper, sugar, or breakfast cereal. They can make a bar graph to display their findings. Students can also track the daily price of precious metals over an extended period. Before they start, have students predict whether the price of the precious metals will go up or down.

Language Arts:

1. Golden Language

References to "gold" and things "golden" frequently appear in conversation and writing. Some golden words and phrases are listed below. Challenge students to track down their origins and meanings. Can students think of other golden words and phrases to add to the list?

golden years	gold medal
The Golden Age	goldbrick
a band of gold	gold digger
golden opportunity	golden rule
all that glitters is not gold	good as gold
pot of gold	go for the gold
fool's gold	golden mean
golden anniversary	gold rush
gold standard	silence is golden

2. Stories About Rocky Riches

The search for precious minerals—gold, silver, and gems—has been a theme of adventure stories down through the ages. For colorful descriptions of the exploits of fortune hunters, read aloud selections from Robert Louis Stevenson's *Treasure Island*, or some other appropriate book. Have students create their own adventure stories about hunting for gold and diamonds. To get them started, let them brainstorm ideas for stories and record their suggestions for characters and plots on the chalkboard.

3. Will It Sell?

Have pairs of students create their own product made of rocks and then make a TV commercial to advertise it. They can make storyboards for their commercials. Storyboards are sketches that show the commercial's actions and dialogue in sequential order. After the storyboards are finished, give the pairs ample time to rehearse the commercials. Videotape the students during the presentation of the commercials.

Art:

1. Mineral Masterpieces

Artists have created beautiful mosaics from small pieces of stone or glass. Instead of using stone or glass, students can made their mosaics from the main ingredient of limestone and marble: calcium carbonate. Calcium carbonate is a white, crystalline mineral which is used in some toothpastes and stomach anti-acid medicines. It is also the main ingredient of eggshells (Figure 39-2). For students to make their own min-

Egg-Shell Mosaic

FIGURE 39-2

eral mosaics, they will need some eggshells, poster paints, cardboard, a pencil, and white glue. Direct them to do the following: Wash the eggshell pieces. After they dry, paint them with different colors of poster paint. Make a pencil sketch of a picture on the cardboard. Spread glue on a small section of the picture. Break off pieces of colored eggshell and push them onto the glue. After the glue has dried, display the students' mosaics on the classroom wall.

2. Fossils

Brief Background. Fossils are stone imprints and images of ancient plants and animals.

Students can make their own fossil imprints of leaves by following these directions: (1) dip a leaf in light oil, (2) put the leaf on a piece of wax paper, (3) press a layer of moist clay on top of the leaf, and (4) after the clay hardens, remove the leaf.

Books:

1. Ferguson, Diana. (1977). *Rocks*. New York: Wonder Books. Primary.

2. Bains, Rae. (1985). *Rocks and Minerals*. Mahwah, NJ: Troll Associates. Primary.

3. Barkan, Joanne. (1990). *Rocks, Rocks Big and Small*. Englewood Cliffs, NJ: Silver Press. Primary.

4. Selsam, Millicent. (1984). *A First Look At Rocks*. New York: Walker and Company. Primary.

5. Jennings, Terry. (1991). *Rocks*. London: A&C Black Pub Limited. Primary.

6. Horenstein, Sidney. (1993). *Rocks Tell Stories*. Brookfield, CT: Millbrook Press. Intermediate.

7. Jennings, Terry. (1982). *Rocks and Soil*. Chicago: Children's Press. Intermediate.

8. Gans, Roma. (1984). *Rock Collecting*. New York: Thomas Y. Crowell. Primary.

9. Shedenhelm, W.R.C. (1978). *The Young Rockhound's Handbook*. New York: G.P. Putnam's Sons. Advanced.

10. Oliver, Ray. (1993). *Rocks and Fossils*. New York: Random House. Intermediate.

11. Stevenson, Robert Louis (1991). *Treasure Island*. adapted by June Edwards. Austin, TX: Steck Vaughn.

Software:

1. *Gems and Minerals: A Closer Look* [Laserdisc]. Van Nuys, CA: Churchill Media. Intermediate, Advanced.

2. *Rocks, Minerals and Fossils* [Laserdisc]. Chicago: Clearvue/eav. Advanced.

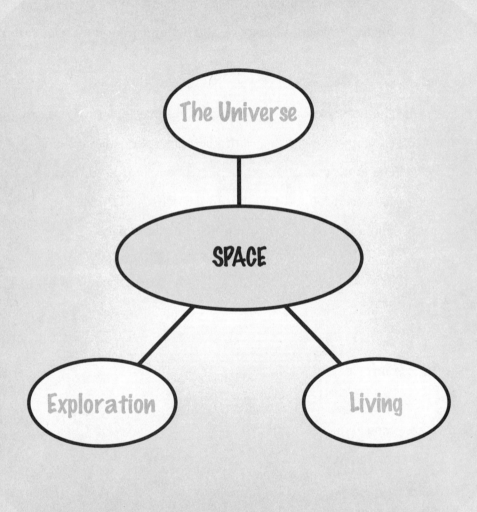

The Universe

SPACE

Exploration

Living

Theme Goals:

Students will:

1. define what space is and identify the planets that are part of the solar system.

2. list some important discoveries in space exploration.

3. examine how people live in space.

4. discuss plans for future space exploration.

5. calculate the effect of gravitational forces on the weight of objects on different planets.

6. create dictionaries depicting and defining important science terms.

Theme Concepts:

1. The universe consists of everything that is known to exist.

2. The Sun is a star that is the center of the solar system.

3. The Earth and eight other planets circle around the Sun.

4. Stars are grouped together in galaxies.

5. Humans have sent many spacecraft into space.

6. Technology makes space exploration possible.

Vocabulary:

1. planets

2. universe

3. galaxies

4. gravitation

5. solar system

Instructional Bulletin Board

The purpose of this bulletin board is to help students recall the relative positions of the nine planets that orbit the Sun. Cover the bulletin board with a large piece of white paper. The sun and planets will be represented by circles of different colors and sizes cut from construction paper. Use yellow construction paper to make the biggest circle, which will represent the Sun. The diameter of the circles for the planets should reflect their relative sizes. Draw the orbital paths of the planets around the sun and attach each planet to its orbit with glue. With a felt-tipped pen, neatly draw a line from each planet to a point along the border of the bulletin board. Make certain the lines do not cross one another. Attach a pushpin at the end of each line drawn from the planet. Print the name of each planet on a card and laminate. Punch a hole in the top of the card at the center. The children can match each planet to its orbit by hanging the correct label card on the pushpin. Keep the planet labels in an envelope attached to one side of the bulletin board. On the other side of the bulletin board, place a covered answer key with a labeled diagram of the solar system so students can check their work. Below is what the bulletin board would look like after a student has completed the task correctly.

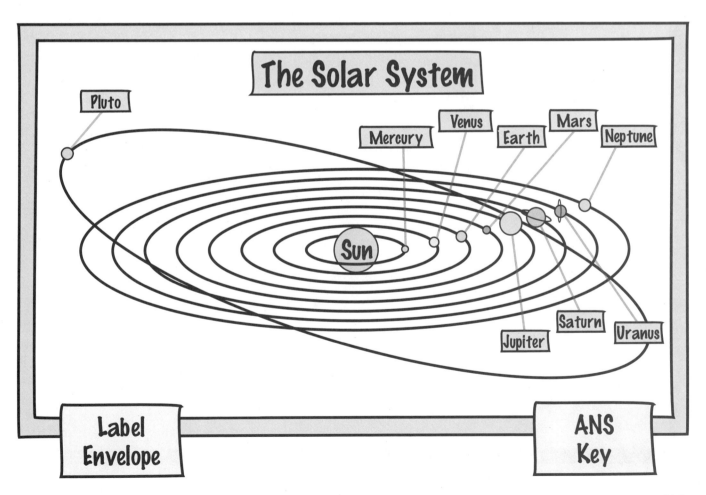

Parent Letter

Dear Parents:

We live in an age of space exploration. Americans have walked on the Moon. Early in the twenty-first century, a permanent, manned space station could be orbiting the Earth. There are also plans to establish a base on the Moon. From that lunar outpost, we might someday send astronauts to Mars and beyond. In this unit the children will be exploring space. They will be involved in a variety of activities that will expand their understanding of space and increase their zest for exploration.

At School:

Some of the activities in this theme include:

- Making balloon rockets
- Constructing miniature solar systems
- Designing space stations
- Examining gravitational force
- Reading myths and legends about the universe

At Home:

This would be a great time to take your child on a stargazing outing. The trip may take you no farther than your own backyard. Pick a clear night, and find an open, unilluminated place to view the sky. Besides stars, you may spot one or more planets. If you are lucky, you may even see a meteor shower.

Linking Up:

You can help children relate some simple, concrete observations in the school yard to the motion of the Earth in space. At different times during the day, have children measure the length of their shadows and note the Sun's position in the sky. Back inside the classroom, let children observe the length of shadows cast on a screen by an object that is rotated in front of a stationary light source. The children will discover that by moving the object, and thereby changing the angle of the object in relation to the light source, they can control the length of the shadow.

Social Studies:

1. Living in Space

Brief Background. Some of the problems with which future crew members of a space station will have to deal are limited living space, boredom, lack of privacy, and separation from family and friends, as well as the constant interaction with other crew members.

Discuss the problems of living in space with the children. Have children imagine that their classroom is a space station and that they are orbiting the Earth. Have them draw pictures showing how they would arrange the living quarters in their space station. If possible, rearrange the room to reflect a consensus of the students' ideas, which might include the following: a quiet spot for quiet reading and reflection, a place to exercise, and a space to grow vegetables and fruit so the crew would have fresh food to eat.

2. Space Baggage

What would children want to take with them on a long space trip? Let them draw and cut out pictures of things that they would take. Have students talk about their choices. The pictures can be pasted to large sheet of white paper to create a collage of "Space Baggage."

3. Naming the Planets

The planets in the solar system are named after Roman gods. Let students research one of the following Roman gods: Mercury (winged messenger of the gods); Venus (goddess of love), Earth (called Gaia, the mother of all gods); Mars (god of war); Jupiter (king of the gods); Saturn (god of harvest); Uranus (god of the heavens); Neptune (god of the sea); and Pluto (god of the dead).

4. Space "Firsts"

Jumble the important historical space "firsts" listed below and write them on the chalkboard. Ask students to use library resources to find the year each event occurred. Then, have them make a time line by putting the events in chronological order. The events are:

- The Soviet Union launched "Sputnik," world's first artificial satellite (1957).
- Yuri Gagarin (Soviet Union) became first person to orbit Earth (1961).
- John Glenn became first American to orbit Earth (1962).
- Neil Armstrong and Edwin Aldrin, Jr., became the first persons to walk on the moon (1969).
- The Soviet Union operated the first manned orbiting space station (1971).
- The United States launched space shuttle *Columbia*, the first reusable manned spacecraft (1981).
- Norm Thagard became the first American to board Russia's *Mir* space station, where he joined the Russian crew for a three-month stay (1995).
- American Shannon Lucid logged the most flight hours in orbit by a woman (1996).

Math:

1. Lose or Gain a Few Pounds

Brief Background. *Weight* is a planet's gravitational force exerted on an object located on that planet. Because the gravitational force exerted by each planet in the solar system varies depending on the planet's and object's mass, a person's weight would differ from planet to planet. The gravitational force of Venus is 88 percent of Earth's. If a person weighed a 100 pounds on Earth, she would weigh 88 pounds on Venus (100 pounds × 88%).

Bring a scale to class so students can weigh themselves. Then provide students with the gravitational forces (relative to Earth) of the planets listed below and let them calculate their weights on each of the planets. The gravitational force of each planet is as follows: Mercury (38%); Venus (88%); Mars (38%); Jupiter (234%); Saturn (92%); Uranus (79%); Neptune (112%); and Pluto (16%).

2. Miles and Miles Away

Let students make accurate scale drawings of the planets in the solar system. The pictures should be scaled based on each planet's diameter relative to Earth. The diameter of the Earth is 7,921 miles. Since Jupiter's diameter is 11 times greater than Earth's, a picture of Jupiter would be 11 inches in diameter if the Earth's picture was one inch in diameter. The diameters in miles of the planets are as follows: Mercury (3,030); Venus (7,520); Mars (4,215); Jupiter (88,700); Saturn (74,975); Uranus (32,200); Neptune (30,800); and Pluto (1,423).

3. Mars

If humans someday reach the surface of Mars, they will behold some spectacular land forms. Although slightly more than half the diameter of Earth, Mars's highest mountain is three times as high as Earth's and it's deepest canyon is four times deeper that the Grand Canyon. Have students make a diagram that compares the following measurements on Earth and Mars: highest mountain, deepest canyon, and average surface temperature.

4. Scale Model Planets

Have students choose a scale (such as one foot equals 30 million miles) to represent the distance from the Sun of each of the nine planets. Take students out to the playground, and help them identify a spot to represent the Sun's location (let one student display a sign on which "Sun" has been printed.) Then, from that spot, use a tape measure to visually display the following distances from the Sun (in millions of miles): Mercury (36), Venus (67), Earth (93), Mars (142), and Jupiter (483), and Saturn (887). Distances can be marked by students holding large cards on which the planets' names have been printed. Students should gain an even greater understanding of the magnitude of these immense distances as they attempt to represent

the outermost planets of the solar system and their distances from the Sun: Uranus (1,782), Neptune (2,793), and Pluto (3,664).

Science:

1. Observing Photographs

The National Aeronautics and Space Administration (NASA) has taken thousands of spectacular photographs documenting America's program of space exploration. They include views of the Earth from outer space, pictures of astronauts working inside and outside their spacecraft and walking on the moon, and images of Mercury, Venus, and Mars, as well as Jupiter and the other gas planets and their moons and rings. Check your school's and/or community's library for picture books, posters, and filmstrips that display NASA photographs. Let children tell you what they see in the photographs. Record their observations on the chalkboard.

2. 3-2-1 Blast Off

Brief Background. Isaac Newton's Third Law of Motion states that for every action there is an opposite and equal reaction. This principle explains how a rocket ship moves.

To demonstrate this principle, have students launch their own rocket ships. For the demonstration, balloons will represent the rockets. Provide each student with a balloon. One student at a time can launch his balloon rocket by doing the following: Blow up the balloon, hold the air in with one hand, and then, on signal, release the balloon. The balloon pushes air backward and the escaping air pushes the balloon forward. Ask students to describe and explain the motion of the balloons. Which balloons traveled higher and farther? Why is it impossible to control the direction of each balloon's movement? How does the balloon rocket differ from a jet plane or real rocket in form and shape? Can students figure out a way to control the balloon-rocket's flight path?

3. What Are the Planets Made Of?

From space, each planet in the solar system has a distinct appearance based on its composition. Mercury, Venus, Earth, and Mars are called terrestrial planets because of their solid, rocky composition. Jupiter, Saturn, Uranus, and Neptune are called the gas planets. These huge planets are composed mainly of hydrogen and other gases. The smallest and outermost planet, Pluto, is possibly composed of frozen gases. Mars's reddish color comes from the iron oxide in its soil. Earth's blue and white color comes from water and clouds.

Assign students the task of investigating the particular composition of one of the planets. Their reports can include charts, graphs, and/or pictures displaying the main components of the planet.

Language Arts:

1. Stories About the Stars

Brief Background. The small groups of stars that form many of the constellations are very important in Greek mythology (Figure 40-1). The Greeks created stories to explain the formation of the constellation shapes.

Assign students the task of researching and writing about the story of one of the following constellations' formation: Andromeda, Centaurus, Pegasus, Perseus, Hercules, Hydra, Cepheus, and Casssiopeia.

2. Visitors From Afar

Brief Background. Science fiction writers have speculated about life on other worlds in the universe. Early astronomers erroneously thought they could see canals on Mars, which led to the widespread belief that life existed there. One science fiction story by H. G. Wells, *War of the Worlds*, which described a Martian invasion of Earth, was so believable that it caused radio listeners to panic when it was broadcast in the 1930s. Today, radio telescopes are used to try to detect messages from outer space but, so far, no extraterrestrial beings have been discovered.

Read aloud, or have students read, short stories by Ray Bradbury, H. G. Wells, Isaac Asimov, and other science fiction writers. Have students create their own science fiction stories about what life might be like on imaginary worlds.

3. Space Dictionaries

Have students make illustrated space dictionaries that define and depict the following terms: *big bang* (explosion that began expansion of universe), *stars* (gas bodies that produce energy by fusion), *binary stars* (pairs of stars that orbit each other), *black holes* (stars so massive that light cannot escape their gravitational force), *galaxies* (systems of billions of stars separated from one another by empty space), *milky way* (the galaxy to which the Earth and Sun belong), *Nebulae* (patches of gas and dust), *pulsars* (stars that emit electromagnetic signals), *quasars* (distant sources of great energy), and *red giants* (dying stars that have used up their hydrogen fuel).

4. Future Space Missions

Assign cooperative groups of three or four students the task of researching one of the planets of the solar system. Each group can gather basic information about their planet. After groups have completed their investigations, let them decide which planet would make the most feasible destination for a future manned space mission. Each group can create a short oral report on the reasons to visit its planet.

5. Space Personalities

Have students research and report on the lives of notable space personalities, such as Christa McAuliffe, Norman Thagard, Sally Ride, Neil Armstrong, John Glenn, Alan Sheppard, and Yuri Gagarin.

Art:

1. Model Planets

Students can make papier-mache models of the planets.

2. An Imaginary Planet

Have students draw a picture showing what they imagine they might find on a planet in another galaxy.

3. Constellations

Students can use black construction paper and silver stars to make constellations. See Figure

Constellations of the Northern Sky

FIGURE 40-1

40-1 for "pictures" of some constellations in the northern sky. Consult a constellation map for locations of stars in constellations.

4. What Shall I Wear?

Let students create "space suits" from things they have brought from home, such as large brown paper bags, cardboard boxes, aluminum foil, wires, plastic tubing, and other materials.

Music:

1. "The Sun and the Planets" Song

(Sing to the tune "Mary Had a Little Lamb")
I'm the Sun, yellow and round,
Yellow and round, yellow and round.
I'm the Sun, yellow and round,
In the center I'm found.
I'm Mercury, cratered and small,

Cratered and small, cratered and small.
I'm Mercury, cratered and small,
With no water at all.
I'm Venus, mysterious and bright,
Mysterious and bright, mysterious and bright.
I'm Venus, mysterious and bright,
So easy to see at night.
I'm Earth, a blue-and-white sphere,
A blue-and-white sphere, a blue-and-white
    sphere.
I'm Earth, a blue-and-white sphere,
Oceans, air, and life are here.
I'm Mars, red and cold,
Red and cold, red and cold.
I'm Mars, red and cold,
Visit me if you're bold.
I'm Jupiter, gigantic and hot,
Gigantic and hot, gigantic and hot.

I'm Jupiter, gigantic and hot,
With the Great Red Spot.
I'm Saturn, surrounded by rings,
Surrounded by rings, surrounded by rings.
I'm Saturn, surrounded by rings—
Hundreds of the icy things.
I'm Uranus, tipped on my side,
Tipped on my side, tipped on my side.
I'm Uranus, tipped on my side,
And 32,000 miles wide.
I'm Neptune, big and blue,
Big and blue, big and blue.
I'm Neptune, big and blue,
And cold and icy, too.
I'm Pluto, little and far,
Little and far, little and far.
I'm Pluto, little and far,
You can't reach me by car!

Books:

1. Ride, Sally, and Okie, Susan. (1986). *To Space and Back*. Studio City, CA: Dovel W. Morrow Books on tape. Intermediate.

2. Branley, Franklyn. (1985). *Mysteries of Outer Space*. New York: Dutton. Advanced.

3. Hansen, Rosanna. (1985). *My First Book of Space*. New York: Little Simon Books. Primary, Intermediate.

4. Krupp, E.C. (1985). *The Comet and You*. New York: Macmillan Publishing Co. Primary, Intermediate.

5. Simon, Seymour. (1988). *Galaxies*. New York: Morrow Junior Books. Intermediate, Advanced.

6. Simon, Seymour. (1986). *Stars*. New York: Morrow. Intermediate, Advanced.

7. Branley, Franklyn. (1986). *Journey into a Black Hole*. New York: T.Y. Crowell. Primary.

8. Wells, H.G. (1995). *War of the Worlds*. Thorndike, ME: G.K. Hall.

Software:

1. *Stars and Planets* [GS IBM]. Mill Valley, CA: Advanced Ideas. Primary.

2. *Exploring Our Solar System* [Mac Windows CD-ROM]. Chatsworth, CA: AIMS. Advanced.

3. *Space Shuttle* {mac MPC CD-ROM]. Novato, CA: Mindscape Educational Software. Intermediate, Advanced.

4. *Issac Asimov's Library of the Universe* [Mac MPC CD-ROM]. Chicago: Clearvue/eav. Advanced.

5. *The View from Earth* [Mac MPC CD-ROM]. New York: Time Warner Interactive. Advanced.

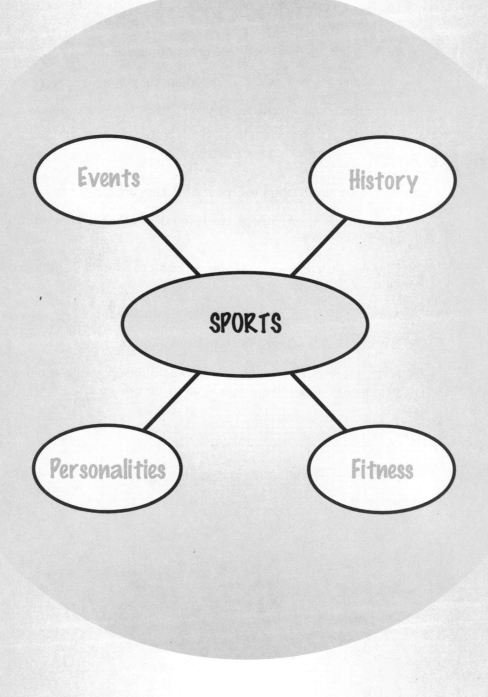

Theme Goals:

Students will:

1. learn names and locations of various sports teams.

2. study how sports have changed over time.

3. examine characteristics of a healthful diet.

4. conduct a survey to determine students' sports and exercise preferences.

5. apply math skills to analyze sports numerical data.

6. analyze characteristics of selected sports personalities.

7. use writing skills to develop sports stories.

Theme Concepts:

1. Sports are an important aspect of American life.

2. Professional sports teams are located in urban centers throughout the country.

3. High-level performance requires practice, exercise, and a proper diet.

4. Mathematics skills are used in sports analysis.

5. Writing skills are used in developing sports stories.

6. Some sports personalities, like Jackie Robinson, demonstrate great personal courage that inspires us to do our best.

Vocabulary:

1. supply and demand

2. muscles

3. league

4. physiologist

5. box score

6. standings

Instructional Bulletin Board

Place the word "Sports" in large letters at the top center of the bulletin board. Use a 2-inch-wide strip of colorful paper to divide the bulletin board into two equal left and right sides. Label the left side "The Way It Used to Be" and the right side "The Way It Is Now." Have students find pictures of sports figures, equipment, and events. They can attach them to one side of the board or the other. Make certain that students can give logical reasons for their choices. Have students use the pictorial data to write or tape-record a brief story entitled "Sports: Then and Now." The students' written and transcribed stories can be displayed around the border of the board.

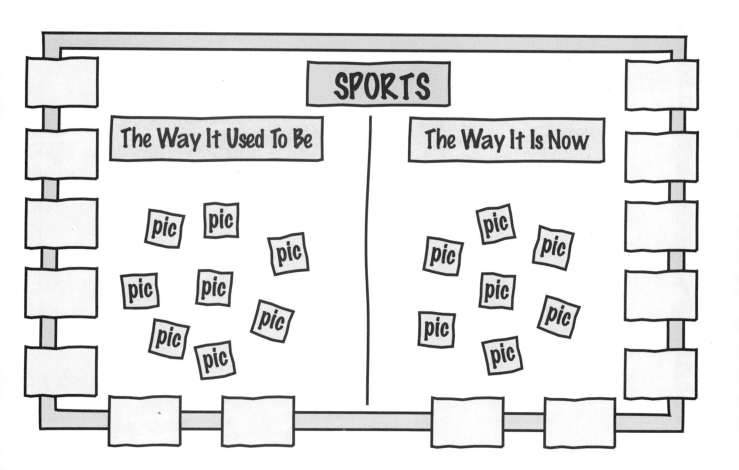

Parent Letter

Dear Parents:

We will be studying a topic that many children already know a lot about—sports. Keeping that it mind, we will try to build on the children's prior knowledge as we explore the many ways that sports connect to reading, writing, science, language arts, social studies, physical education, and other areas of the curriculum.

At School:

We will be involved in a variety of interesting activities in our study of sports. They include the following:

* Mapping the locations of major league teams
* Investigating the Olympic Games of Ancient Greece
* Celebrating our own Olympic Games, complete with a parade and Olympic flags and gold medals
* Measuring world records
* Learning about sports personalities
* Writing real sports stories

At Home:

Now would be a good time to talk to your child about your and his or her favorite sports personalities. Find out why he or she enjoys watching and playing particular sports. Do you share the same sports interests? If you or your child collects sports cards or memorabilia, discuss the collection. You can also help your child select a couple of sports books from the community library.

Linking Up:

Ask students to tell you about their favorite athletes and sports. List them on the chalkboard. What do they like about particular sports? What skills do different sports require? What games and activities promote competition? Which sports promote cooperation and team building? Which sports promote both competition and cooperation?

Social Studies:

1. Gathering Data

Have students interview elderly persons to find out what types of games and sports were popular when they were the children's age.

2. Mapping Sports Team Locations

Give students blank outline maps of the United States (Figure 41-1), including southern Canada, and have each of them plot the locations of teams that are members of one of the major baseball, hockey, or football leagues or the National

Basketball Association. Sites of American and National League baseball teams are listed below.

American League:

Baltimore, MD	Kansas City, MO	Minneapolis, MN
Detroit, MI	Seattle, WA	Toronto, Canada
Oakland, CA	Dallas, TX	Cleveland, OH
Boston, MA	Chicago, IL	New York, NY
Anaheim, CA	Milwaukee, WI	

National League:

Chicago, IL	Cincinnati, OH	New York, NY
Atlanta, GA	St. Louis, MO	San Diego, CA
Denver, CO	Miami, FL	Montreal, Canada
Philadelphia, PA	Pittsburgh, PA	Houston, TX
San Francisco, CA	Los Angeles, CA	

CITIES WITH MAJOR LEAGUE BASEBALL TEAMS

FIGURE 41-1

3. Changes in Sports Attire and Equipment

Brief Background. Changes in sports clothing and equipment have occurred over time. For example, a few years ago, professional tennis players were expected to wear all-white tennis outfits only, and they all used wooden tennis rackets. In contrast, today's players wear a variety of colorful outfits, and they use an assortment of metal rackets.

Let each student gather information and illustrations on clothing and equipment changes for a particular sport of her choice. Are changes in sports related to technological changes?

4. Olympic Games

Brief Background. Sports played an important role in Ancient Greece. The first Olympic Games originated in Greece over 2,000 years ago. Some sports included in the ancient Olympics were running races, discus throw, javelin throw, and long jump. The modern Olympic Games were first held in Athens, Greece, in 1896. With a few exceptions, they have been held every four years since. The Winter Olympic Games, which are also held every four years, began in 1924.

After students have gathered background information on the ancient and modern Olympic Games, they can plan and stage their own Olympic Games. Encourage students to select games and activities for their Olympics. (Note: Discuss the Special Olympics, and provide appropriate games and activities for physically challenged students.) If you hold the Olympics outside, then you can include foot races and field activities. For indoors, games like a bean-bag toss, hopscotch (using masking tape to form the grid), and bowling (using a plastic ball and pins) would be appropriate. To open the Olympic Games with fanfare, have students march around the playground dressed in sports outfits and carrying Olympic flags (which can be made by using fabric pens to decorate old sheets with sports scenes and symbols). Each student can make his own Olympic medal (see Figure 41-2) by following these steps: Cut out a cardboard circle (three inches in diameter), cover by gluing on silver- or gold-colored foil, punch one small (1/4 inch) hole along the edge, push a 14-inch-long ribbon through the hole, and tie the ends (to allow the child to wear the medal around the neck). Once the medals have

been constructed, students can embellish them with personal designs etched on the foil using light pressure with a blunt-tipped instrument.

5. Sports Histories

Brief Background. Every sport has its own interesting history. In 1891, when physical education teacher James Naismith was asked by his boss to create a team sport that could be played indoors in winter, the result was the invention of basketball, a game first played with a soccer ball and two peach baskets as goals.

Assign students the task of researching the history of a sport of their choice. Invite students to report their findings orally to the class.

6. Sports Card Collections

Let students bring in some of their sports trading cards and talk to the class about their hobby. Why do they like to collect sports trading cards? How much are some of the cards worth? How is the value of a particular card determined? Do collectors barter with one another to get the cards they want? Introduce the concept of "supply and demand." Does a card's supply and demand affect its fair market price?

Science:

1. Sports and Health

To perform a sport well takes practice, conditioning, and a healthy body. People who want to perform at a high level need to adopt good health habits and avoid unhealthy ones. Some unhealthy habits that students can investigate include the following: smoking, drinking alcohol, using illegal drugs, and eating poorly or overeating. Let students create posters that are designed to dissuade people from engaging in unhealthy habits.

2. You Are What You Eat

To make students more aware of their own eating habits, let them keep a food diary for a week or longer. Have students list the foods they eat for breakfast, lunch, dinner, and snacks each day. If necessary, parents can help monitor this activity.

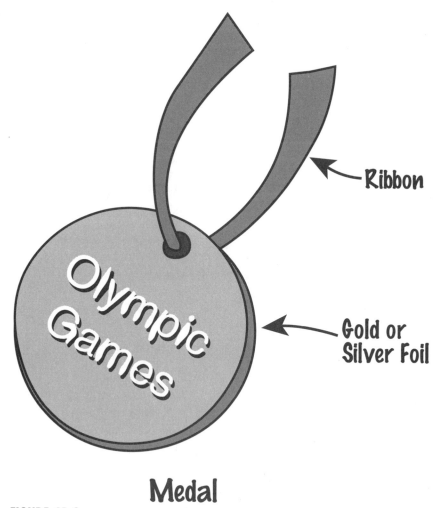

Ribbon

Gold or
Silver Foil

Medal

FIGURE 41-2

3. The Food Pyramid

Provide individual copies of the Food Guide Pyramid (found on most packaged foods). Discuss the six food groups and the recommended daily food choices. Give each student a white paper plate and let her use crayons to draw foods on the plate that reflect smart food choices. (Note: Instead of drawing the foods, some students might prefer to paste cutout pictures of foods on the plate.)

4. Careers in Sports Medicine

Let interested students investigate and report on one or more of the following careers in sports medicine: physician, athletic trainer, physiologist, physical therapist, nutritionist, and physical educator.

5. Insect Record Holders

Brief Background. For their modest size and weight, most insects are amazing jumpers, flyers, runners, swimmers, and weightlifters. For example, some ants can lift 50 times their body weight, and the 1/8-inch-long common flea can jump 13 inches!

Challenge students to track down the world-record performances of different insects, as well as other animals. After they gather information about them, they can report their findings to the class.

Math:

1. Classroom Surveys

Students can conduct a survey to identify student sports preferences and exercise habits. Help students develop a survey sheet that asks questions like these: What is your favorite sport to watch? What is your favorite sport to play? and How many minutes do you exercise each day? Have students compile and graph the survey responses.

2. World Record Distances

Provide, or have students gather, information in current almanacs on Olympic records in the following field events: pole vault, high jump, long jump, triple jump, shot put, discus throw, hammer throw, and javelin throw. Provide tape measures and challenge small groups of students to devise a unique way to visually represent one of the records. For example, strips of colored construction paper could be taped together and then attached to the wall to represent the high jump record. Because of the distances involved, most of the records will need to be displayed in the hallway, gymnasium, or outdoors. Other sports records in the *Guiness Book of World Records* and other sources can also be displayed by the students.

3. Box Scores

Have student use their math skills to analyze sports data found in the daily newspaper. Give students baseball box scores with totals deleted and let them use their addition skills to calculate total at bats, runs, hits, and runs-batted-in for each team (Figure 41-3). Similar calculations can be performed using basketball box scores. Students can solve math problems like the following using professional baseball, basketball, hockey, and football league and division standings data: If a football team has played five games and lost two, how many games has it won? How many more games has the first-place basketball team won than the third-place team? and What percentage of games has the fifth-place hockey team won?

4. Creating Word Problems

Invent math problems that also test students' knowledge of sports. Invite sports-minded students to create their own sports math problems for the class to solve. To get students started, give them this math problem: Add together the numbers of players on a basketball team and the number of players on a football team. Then, divide by the number of players in a singles tennis match. Next, multiply by the number of holes in a game of golf. Finally, subtract from this total the number of innings in a regular baseball game. (Answer: $5 + 11 = 16 \div 2 = 8 \times 18 = 144 - 9 = 135$)

Language Arts:

1. Sports Categories

Have students give examples of sports that can be placed in one or more of the following categories: (1) ball games; (2) ice and snow sports; (3) water sports; (4) team sports; (5) individual sports; (6) contact sports; (7) noncontact sports; and (8) dangerous sports.

2. The Sports Page

Let students play the role of sports journalist for a newspaper. Show students a videotape of a short segment of a sports event. Have them take careful notes of their observations. If the students request, play the video segment over again. Have students write a paragraph that accurately describes what they have seen. Tell the students that the readers of the newspaper—their imaginary audience—did not see the game, but they are very interested in what happened. Encourage students to come up with catchy headlines for their sports news reports.

3. Letters About Historic Sports Events

Brief Background. History has recorded the exploits of outstanding sports figures. For example, Jackie Robinson changed the game of baseball for all time—and the example of his life inspired millions to carry on the fight for equality and justice. In 1947, Robinson became the major league's first black baseball player. At that time, fear and intimidation were being used to keep blacks "in their place," and the law of the land allowed African Americans to be segregated into inferior schools.

Inning	1	2	3	4	5	6	7	8	9	H	R	E
Yankees	0	1	1	0	0	0	0	3	0	12	5	1
Braves	0	0	0	1	0	1	0	0	0	7	2	2

FIGURE 41-3

Read sections of Barbara Cohen's *Thank You, Jackie Robinson* (Lothrop, Lee & Shepard, Co., 1974) or another biography of Robinson to the class. Ask them to think about how Jackie Robinson might have felt the day he played in his first major league game. Encourage students to imagine that they are Jackie Robinson. With that image in mind, have them write a letter to a friend in which they describe their thoughts and feelings about that historic day in 1947. Other notable sports figures from the past for students to research include Jim Thorpe, Jesse Owens, Lou Gerig, Babe Ruth, Bill Russell, Ted Williams, Muhammed Ali, Jack Nicklaus, Arthur Ashe, Chris Evert Lloyd, Wilma Rudolph, Babe Zaharias, and Peggy Fleming.

4. Sports Favorites

Invite students to share the names of their sports heroes. Write the names on the chalkboard. Identify and discuss the types of people who are on their lists. What special talents do these people have? What have they accomplished? Let students read and write about one of their own sports heroes. Students can dress in the sports costume of their hero and give a brief oral report to the class.

5. Lessons from the Coach

Let students be the coach. Challenge students to develop a set of clear, step-by-step directions for performing actions like the following: serving a tennis ball, rowing a boat, hitting a baseball, passing a football, shooting a free throw, and kicking a soccer ball. Invite volunteers to try to perform the actions as the directions are read aloud to them. Let students revise their directions if necessary based on the results of the performances.

Dramatic Play:

1. Guess the Sport

Print the name of each of the sports listed below on an index card. Put the cards in a box.

Students take turns drawing a card from the box. Each student pantomimes the actions of a person engaged in the particular sport printed on the card. The other students try to guess the sport being pantomimed.

baseball	tennis	skiing
basketball	soccer	swimming
bowling	table tennis	roller skating
football	volleyball	surfing
golf	hockey	wrestling
biking	running	boxing

Music:

1. Famous Sports Songs

Play songs associated with popular sports or teams, such as "Take Me Out to the Ball Game," or the Michigan or Notre Dame "Fight Song."

2. School Cheers

Let small teams of students create and demonstrate a school cheer.

Art:

1. Student Athletes

Provide large sheets of paper, Magic Markers, crayons, paint, and brushes, and have students make pictures of themselves engaged in sports activities. Display their work on the wall.

Books:

1. Howard, Dak. (1994). *Soccer Around the World*. Chicago: Children's Press. Advanced.

2. Ritter, Lawrence. (1983). *The Story of Baseball*. New York: William Morrow. Advanced.

3. Frommer, Harvey. (1987). *Olympic Controversies*. New York: Franklin Watts. Advanced.

4. Olney, Ross. (1982). *Super Champions of Ice Hockey*. New York: Clarion Books. Intermediate.

5. Gutman, Dan. (1993). *Baseball's Biggest Bloopers: The Games That Got Away*. New York: Viking. Intermediate.

6. Sullivan, George. (1987). *All About Football*. New York: Dodd, Mead. Intermediate.

7. Broekel, Ray. (1983). *Football*. Chicago: Children's Press. Primary.

8. Anderson, Dave. (1988). *The Story of Basketball*. New York: William Morrow. Advanced.

9. Glubok, Shirley, and Tamarin, Alfred. (1976). *Olympic Games in Ancient Greece*. New York: Harper and Row. Advanced.

10. Harris, Jack. (1990). *The Winter Olympics*. Mankato, MN: Creative Education. Intermediate.

11. Cohen, Barbara. (1974). *Thank You, Jackie Robinson*. New York: Lothrop, Lee & Shepard, Co.

12. *Guiness Book of World Records*. (1990). eds. Donald McFarlan et al. New York: Bantam Books.

Software:

1. *NFL Math* [Mac MPC CD-ROM]. San Mateo, CA: Sanctury Woods. Intermediate, Advanced.

2. *Touchdown Math* [Mac]. Big Springs, TX: Gamco. Primary, Intermediate, Advanced.

3. *Sports in Action* [Mac MPC CD-ROM]. Torrance, CA: Davidson/Jasmine. Advanced.

4. *Sports Problems 1,2,3* [AppleII Mac IBM]. Fairfield, CT: Intellectual Software Queue. Intermediate, Advanced.

5. *Sports Reporter* [Mac IBM]. Fairfield, CT: Toucan Queue. Intermediate, Advanced.

6. *Microsoft Complete Basketball* [MPC CD-ROM]. Redmond, WA: Microsoft. Intermediate, Advanced.

7. *Microsoft Complete Baseball* [MPC CD-ROM]. Redmond, WA: Microsoft. Intermediate, Advanced.

8. *Sports Illustrated for Kids: Awesome Athletes* [MPC CD-ROM]. Portland, OR: Creative Multimedia. Intermediate, Advanced.

9. *Baseball's Greatest Hits* [Mac MPC CD-ROM]. New York: Voyager. Intermediate, Advanced.

42

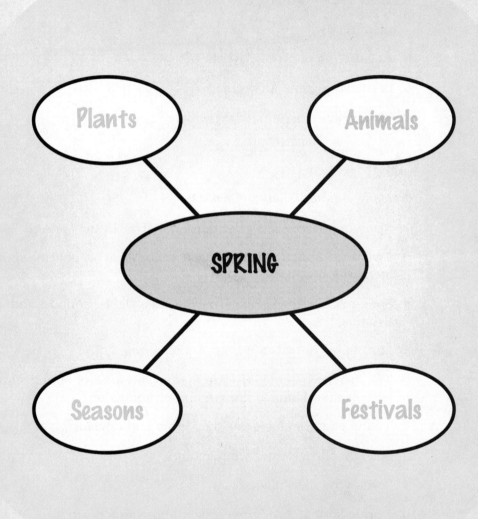

Theme Goals:

Students will:

1. describe special spring days.

2. write (or dictate) a story about springtime.

3. identify the names of baby animals.

4. observe changes in the environment during spring.

5. observe animals.

6. analyze the warming effects of sunlight.

7. plant seeds.

8. calculate amounts of daylight.

9. create springtime art work.

10. participate in a springtime picnic.

Theme Concepts:

1. Many cultures celebrate May Day.

2. Many northern states celebrate Arbor Day in the spring.

3. Two very important religious celebrations that occur in the spring are Easter and Passover.

4. Spring is filled with many new smells, sights, sounds, and activities.

5. Most baby animals are born in the spring.

6. The increased sunlight, warmth, and mositure of spring stimulate plant and animal growth and reproduction.

7. Young animals change as they grow and develop.

8. Sunlight affects water temperature.

9. Seeds grow into plants.

10. During spring, days grow longer and warmer.

Vocabulary:

1. Passover

2. Arbor Day

3. May Day

4. Cinco de Mayo

Instructional Bulletin Board

The purpose of this bulletin board is to provide students with an opportunity to identify the parts of a plant and create a unique spring flower. Each student can make his own plant by correctly arranging the roots, stem, and leaves of the plant on the bulletin board (as shown below). To make the flower, provide students with paper plates, scissors, different colored tissue paper and glue, and let them create their own unique flowers to attach to the top of their plants.

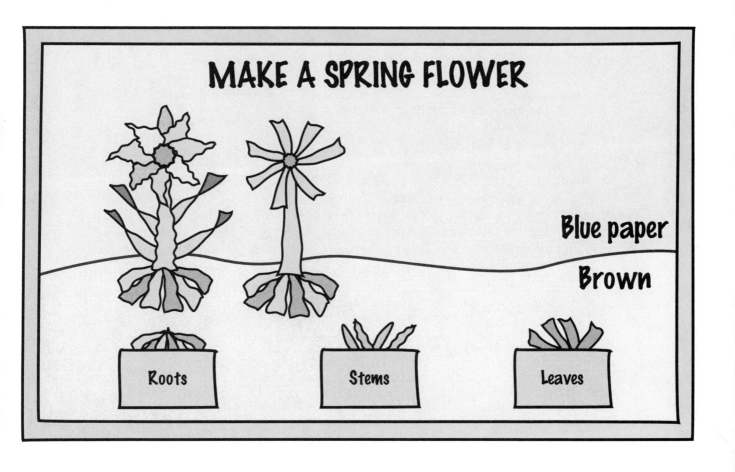

Parent Letter

Dear Parents:

Spring is the time for new life. Sunlight warms the earth. Gentle rains fall. Baby animals are born. Leaves reappear on the trees. Grass grows green again. Birds sing. As we celebrate the return of spring, your child will be involved in many interesting activities.

At School:

During our study of spring, we will be involved in the following activities:

- Celebrating some special spring days
- Creating stories about springtime
- Learning the names of baby animals
- Observing changes in the environment
- Experimenting with sunlight
- Planting seeds
- Measuring amounts of daylight
- Painting a springtime mural
- Participating in a springtime picnic

At Home:

How can you help your child learn more about spring? That's easy! Just select a springtime outdoor activity that you and your child enjoy doing together, and then do it. Back in the classroom, your child can report on what you both did.

Linking Up:

Write the word "spring" on the chalkboard. Have students think of all of the things they like about spring (the smell of the air, the warm sunshine, the pretty flowers, the beginning of baseball season, etc.). List their responses on the chalkboard. Have each student write or dictate a short paragraph about what she likes best about spring.

Social Studies:

1. May Day

Brief Background. Many cultures and countries have a long tradition of celebrating the arrival of spring on May Day. The ancient Egyptians held a spring festival. The Romans called their spring festival *Floralia*, in honor of the goddess of springtime. The Celts incorporated traditions learned from the Romans into their own May Day celebration. May Day became very popular during the Middle Ages.

Involve students in planning their own May Day festival. Make paper flowers to decorate the classroom. A popular English May Day custom was dancing around the maypole. To construct a maypole, use an 8-foot-long 2 × 2 piece of lumber. Screw a 4-inch-long wood screw into the center of one end of the Maypole, leaving 2 inches of the screw exposed. Attach several streamers of crepe paper to the screw. Use a large Christmas tree stand to secure the base of the Maypole. Wrap the Maypole with alternating colors of crepe paper. Play and sing some springtime songs, and let children take turns holding the ends of the streamers as they dance around the Maypole.

2. Arbor Day

Brief Background. Arbor Day is a day designated for planting trees. The day is celebrated in many northern states in the spring.

Help the class celebrate by planting a tree on the school grounds or someplace else in the community. This would also be a good time to involve the class in one or more of the following projects: observing trees on the school grounds, recycling paper, collecting waste paper, and conserving school paper and wood products.

3. Easter

Brief Background. The religious observance of Easter celebrates the Christian belief in the Resurrection, or return to life, of Jesus Christ, the founder of Christianity. The story of Jesus' death and resurrection is told in the New Testament of the Bible.

You may want to explain the meaning of the following Easter symbols: cross (symbolizes Jesus' victory over death); Sunday (associated with the day of Resurrection); the light of candles (symbolizes Jesus' return to earth); and Easter lilies (these flowers represent the purity of Jesus' life). Two familiar symbols associated with Easter in America are "Easter" eggs and the "Easter" rabbit.

4. Passover

Brief Background. The Jewish religious observance of Passover celebrates the flight of the Israelites from Egyptian bondage. At a special feast, called a *Seder*, the story of the Jewish exodus from Egypt is read, and unleavened (flat) bread called *matzo* is served.

You may want explain the meaning of the Passover celebration.

5. Cinco de Mayo

Brief Background. Cinco de Mayo, which means "Fifth of May," commemorates an important military victory that occurred during a war between Mexico and France. On May 5, 1862, a greatly outnumbered Mexican army defeated French troops at the Battle of Puebla.

Have students decorate the classroom with paper Mexican flags and red, green, and white banners they have made. Play a videotape or audiocassette that includes Mexican songs, such as "La Cucaracha" and "Cielito Lindo," and dances, such as the Mexican Hat Dance. Encourage students to sing the songs and even learn them in Spanish. Cinco de Mayo is like the United States's Fourth of July. Ask students what Independence Day means to them. Invite a Mexican or Mexican American to class to talk about the significance of Cinco de Mayo.

Language Arts:

1. Baby Animals

Most baby animals are born in spring. Provide pictures of the following baby animals and introduce or review their names. Have each student choose a young animal to investigate. After students learn about how their animals develop, they can report their findings to the class.

fawn (baby deer)	duckling (baby duck)
cub (baby bear)	piglet (baby hog)
kitten (baby cat)	lamb (baby sheep)
puppy (baby dog)	joey (baby kangaroo)
chick (baby chicken)	cygnet (baby swan)
kid (baby goat)	poult (baby turkey)
calf (baby cattle)	pup (baby seal)

Science:

1. Spring Changes

In temperate zones of the Northern Hemisphere, the transition between the colder weather of winter and the warmer weather of spring occurs gradually. Have students make daily observations of the local environment and record their observations in individual notebooks. They should be on the lookout for buds, blossoms, blooming flowers, grass growing green, and new leaves on bushes and trees, as well as for the first appearance of insects, birds, and animals that have roused themselves from winter hibernation. Students can illustrate their notebooks with drawings of the plants and animals observed.

2. Observing Tadpoles

One sure sign of spring is the sound of frogs croaking from a pond. Put water, aquarium gravel, and a water plant in a large glass jar. Let the water stand 24 hours. Gather some tadpoles and put them in the jar, as shown in Figure 42-1. Let students take turns observing the tadpoles. They can make drawings of the tadpoles, noting any changes in their appearance.

3. Raising Chicks

Spring is the time for new life. Plants bloom and many animals reproduce. Students will enjoy waiting and watching for their own chicks to hatch. If you have access to an incubator, get some fertilized eggs from a hatchery. Follow the guidelines that come with the incubator. Instead of hatching the chicks in the classroom, you might want to simply purchase a few chicks from a hatchery or farm supply or pet store. A large wood box is ideal for raising the chicks (allow one square foot per chick). Place wood shavings or straw 2"–5" deep in the bottom of the box. Place a heat lamp or light bulb approximately 20" above the chicks. Put a thermometer at chick level. The temperature should be 90°–95° F for day-old chicks. Reduce temperature 5°F each week until a minimum of 65° F is reached. Purchase a feeder, a waterer, and food from a feed store. Keep waterer filled with fresh, clean water daily. You might have to dip chicks' beaks in the water to induce drinking. Elevate the waterer after the first week to reduce contamination from litter. Clean and disinfect the bedding, feeder, and waterer weekly (disinfectant can be purchased at a farm supply or pet store). Have students make observations of the chicks daily.

4. Warming Up

During springtime, increased amounts of sunlight warm the water and ground. Have pairs of students perform an experiment to measure the sun's warming effects. Have them follow these directions: (1) place cold water in two glasses; (2) label one "sun" and the other "no sun;" (3) place a thermometer in each glass (use only alcohol thermometers); (4) record the temperatures on a chart; (5) place the glass of water labeled "sun" in sunlight, and the other glass in the shade; (6) wait three or four hours and record the temperatures again; (7) record the results on the chart (see Figure 42-2); and (8) compare the two sets of temperatures. What do the results tell the students about the warming effect of the sun?

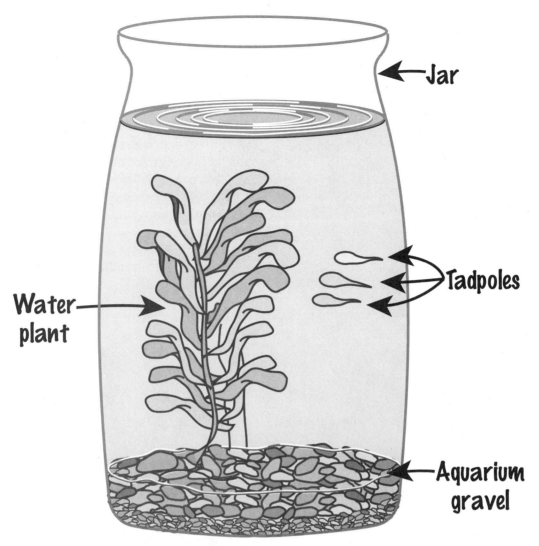

Tadpole Aquarium

FIGURE 42-1

5. From Seed to Plant

Provide each student with a plastic cup filled with potting soil and either a bean or corn seed. Label each cup with the child's name and "bean" or "corn" (depending on which kind of seed the child has). Have students plant their seeds in the soil. Have each student predict how many days will elapse before the seeds sprout. Record their observations on a chart. Place the cups in a location that gets a lot of indirect sunlight. Provide a plant watering can, and let each student water his cup when necessary, but make sure students don't overwater. Have students observe their cups daily. Each student can record the date when her seed sprouts. Are the students' predictions accurate? Which kind of seed (corn or bean) sprouts first?

Condition	After 3 hours	After 6 hours
Sun	_____°F	_____°F
No Sun	_____°F	_____°F

FIGURE 42-2 Temperatures of water

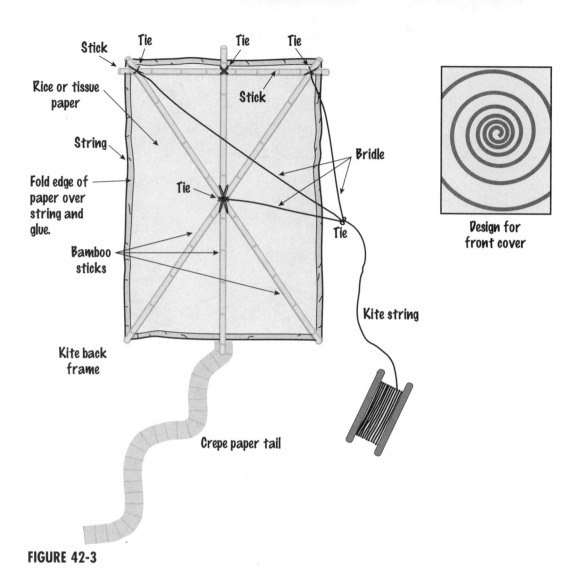

Stick
Tie
Tie
Tie
Rice or tissue paper
Stick
String
Bridle
Fold edge of paper over string and glue.
Tie
Bamboo sticks
Tie
Kite string
Kite back frame
Crepe paper tail

Design for front cover

FIGURE 42-3

Math:

1. Measuring Days and Nights

Spring begins on the day of the March equinox, which occurs on either March 20 or 21, depending on the year. On the equinox, the Sun is directly above the equator, and day and night are of equal length. As spring approaches, have students check the local times for sunrise and sunset in the daily newspaper. Up to the March equinox, nights are getting shorter, but they are still longer than days. After the March equinox, days get increasingly longer than nights up through June 20 or 21. Let students keep a record of sunrises and sunsets and temperature during the spring season. They can calculate the hours and minutes of daylight each day and record the daily temperature, and then plot the increasing length of daylight and temperatures on graphs.

Art:

1. Spring Greenery

Show students pictures of trees or take the class outside to observe them. Back inside the classroom, let students recreate the trees with paper and paint. Provide each student with large sheets of white paper, brown construction paper, green paint, a small piece of sponge, scissors, and paste. Each student can follow these directions: Use the brown construction paper to make a trunk and branches for the tree; paste the trunk and branches on the white paper; let the paste dry; add leaves by dabbing the sponge in the green paint and then pressing the sponge gently on and about the tree branches.

2. Springtime Mural

Take students on a springtime nature walk. When you return to the classroom, provide pairs of students with crayons and large sheets of white paper, and let them create springtime murals. The murals should include scenes showing plants and animals that were observed on the walk. When they are finished, each pair of students can show the class its mural and talk briefly about it.

Crafts:

1. Japanese Kites

Spring is the perfect time to fly kites. To make Japanese kites, use thin (about 1/4") sticks of split bamboo for the kite frame and rice or tissue paper for the cover. For each kite, you will need three 24" bamboo sticks, one 15" bamboo stick, a rectangular piece of paper large enough to cover the frame, and glue, heavy thread, and string. Arrange the bamboo sticks as shown in Figure 42-3. Use heavy thread to tie sticks at center and top crossings and glue. Run string around the kite and secure. Cover with paper, fold edge of paper over string, and glue. Decorate kite face with painted design. Attach strings to the two top corners and to the center crossing and tie the three loose ends together to form the bridle. Tie the kite string to bridle. To add a tail to the kite, attach a 15- to 20-foot-long streamer of crepe paper to the bottom of the center stick.

Food:

1. Spring Picnic

Spring is a great time for a picnic. Students can help you plan the menu. Include some spring vegetables fresh from the garden.

Books:

1. Michels, Tilde. (1989). *At the Frog Pond*. New York: Lippincott. Primary.

2. Gibbons, Gail. (1991). *From Seed to Plant*. New York: Holiday House. Primary, Intermediate.

3. Cross, Diana Harding. (1983). *Some Plants Have Funny Names*. New York: Crown Publishers. Primary.

4. Hirschi, Ron. (1990). *Spring*. New York: Cobblehill Books. Primary.

5. Stone, Lynn M. (1994). *Spring as the Earth Turns*. Vero Beach, FL: The Rourke Book Company, Inc. Primary.

6. Rosen, Mike. (1991). *Spring Festivals*. New York: Bookwright Press. Intermediate.

7. Schweninger, Ann. (1993). *Springtime*. New York: Penguin Books. Primary.

8. Landau, Elaine. (1992). *State Flowers*. New York: Franklin Watts. Advanced.

9. Wilson, Ron. (1986). *Things to See and Do in Spring*. London: Young Library Ltd. Intermediate.

Software:

1. *Spring Brings Changes* [Laserdisc]. Van Nuys, CA: Churchill Media. Primary, Intermediate.

2. *Children's Songs Around the World* [Laserdisc VHS]. Baldwin, NY: Educational Activities. Primary, Intermediate.

3. *Ballet Folklorico Nacional de Mexico* [VHS]. Roanoke, VA: Gessler Publishing. Intermediate, Advanced.

43

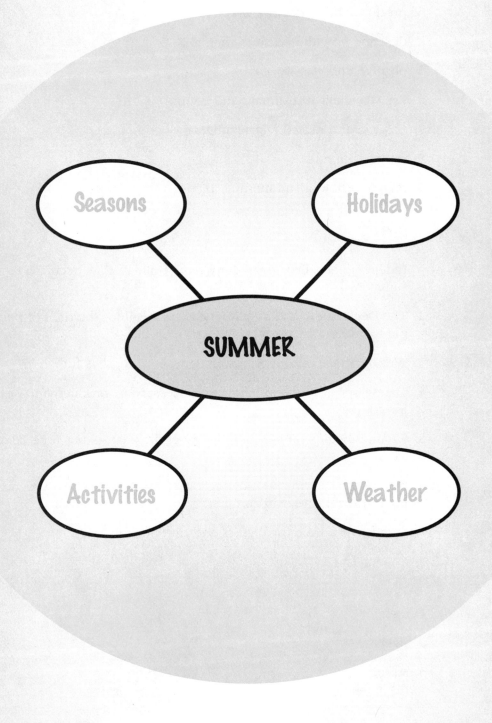

Theme Goals:

Students will:

1. explain the meanings of quotations from the Declaration of Independence.

2. write about summertime activities.

3. produce and perform a play.

4. describe how the seasons change.

5. observe and classify leaves.

6. use sea shells to estimate and count.

7. observe and record temperatures.

8. create a mural.

9. plan and hold a summertime picnic.

Theme Concepts:

1. Independence Day is an important holiday that occurs in the summer.

2. The Declaration of Independence was a call for the right of people to govern themselves.

3. Writing about our favorite summertime "things" is fun.

4. Teamwork and cooperation are necessary to produce and perform a play.

5. Summer begins on the longest day of the year, either June 20 or 21.

6. In most places in the United States, average temperatures are highest for the year in summer.

7. Summer is a time for picnics and outdoor fun.

Vocabulary:

1. equal

2. rights

3. solstice

Instructional Bulletin Board

The purpose of this bulletin board is to provide opportunities for students to sort pictures of summertime topics. Use strips of construction paper to divide the bulletin board into vertical columns, and label each column with one of the following summertime topics: sports, foods, vacations, flowers, indoor activities, and outdoor activities. Have students bring in appropriate pictures and pin or staple them in the various columns.

Parent Letter

Dear Parents:

Most children look forward to summer. It is a time for outdoor activities, family vacations, and just plain fun. Some of the fun activities planned for our theme on summer are listed below.

At School:

During their study of summer, students will be doing the following activities.

- Recreating the adoption of the Declaration of Independence on July 4, 1776
- Writing about summertime activities
- Producing and performing a play
- Gathering and sorting leaves
- Doing math with sea shells
- Recording temperatures
- Creating a mural
- Holding a summertime picnic

At Home:

To get your child thinking about summer, ask him or her to draw a picture of a favorite summertime activity. Your child can bring the picture to school to share with the class.

Thank you for your continued cooperation.

Linking Up:

Most children look forward to summer. It is a time for outdoor activities, family vacations, and just plain fun. Because of students' positive past associations with summertime, interest and motivation to talk about and anticipate summer should be high. Tell the class about some of the fun activities you have planned for yourself for the summer. Invite students to tell you about the summertime activities they most enjoy. Make a list of the activities. Do students like some of the same activities? Are most of the activities done indoors or outdoors?

Social Studies:

1. Independence Day Recreation

Brief Background. The Fourth of July commemorates the day when delegates to the Second Continental Congress adopted the Declaration of Independence at Philadelphia on July 4, 1776. Among the participants at that historic event were Thomas Jefferson (who also wrote the document), Benjamin Franklin, John Adams, Samuel Adams, Robert Morris, and John Hancock.

Unfortunately, since Independence Day occurs during summer, this important event in our nation's history sometimes doesn't receive as much attention at school as other holidays. To give the Fourth of July the recognition it deserves, recreate the historical event, which is depicted in Figure 43-1, in the classroom. Students can design and wear colonial costumes and decorate the room so that it resembles the scene at Independence Hall. To prepare students for the reenactment, read aloud selections from children's books that focus on that historic event, such as *In 1776*, by Jean Marzollo (Scholastic, 1994), which explains the meaning of the creation of the Declaration of Independence through rhyme and illustrations, and *If You Were There in 1776*, by Barbara Brenner (Bradbury, 1994), which describes the work, dress, home life, and recreation of the colonial period. The Declaration of Independence was a call for the right of a people to govern themselves. Read selections of the document and discuss its meaning. Below are some of the powerful statements contained in the document, together with interpretations of their meaning.

"When in the course of human events it becomes necessary for one people to dissolve the political bands which have connected them with another. . ." (the Declaration is addressed to the whole world; it states that one group can separate from another group for good causes).

What are some important messages that students would like to send to the whole world today? Would any of the following be part of their message: friendship, peace, safety, eliminating hunger, or correcting injustice?

"We hold these truths to be self-evident, that all men [people] are created equal, . . [and have the rights of] "Life, Liberty and the pursuit of Happiness. . ." (all humans everywhere in the world have these same three natural rights).

Have students draw and cut out pictures that illustrate activities in life that people value doing, ways that liberty, or freedom, is expressed and protected, and ways that people find happiness in life.

"The history of the present King of Great Britain is a history of repeated injuries and usurpations, all having in direct object the establishment of an absolute Tyranny over these States. . ." (Britain's King George is blamed for violating the colonists' natural rights; the violations justify America's separation from Great Britain).

Discuss characters in fairy tales and other familiar stories who were denied certain freedoms and opportunities to lead full and happy lives, but managed to overcome their difficult circumstances by the end of the stories.

2. Birthday Celebration

Conclude Social Studies Activity #1 with a "Happy Birthday America" party complete with songs, flags, banners, bunting, and cake.

Language Arts:

1. Writing About Summer

Since summer is the favorite season of the year for many children, motivation to talk about summer activities and fun ought to be high. To

Event Card 1776

FIGURE 43-1

enhance interest, bring to class a bag filled with "summer things," such as swimwear, summer sports equipment, sunblock lotion, travel brochures, and yard and garden tools. Take each item out of the bag one at a time and discuss its connection to your summer plans. Students can bring their own summer things to share with the class, and then write or dictate a paragraph or short story about a how a personal summer item is used.

2. Shakespeare on the Green

Take the class outside on a warm, sunny day and read aloud William Shakespeare's *A Midsummer Night's Dream* as retold by Bruce Corville (Dial, 1996). This adaptation of William Shakespeare's delightful play about how fairies transform the fate of two young couples will enthrall children. With its 34 full-color illustrations and accessible prose, this dramatic picture book gives students everything they need to produce their own version of the play. They can write scripts, create simple costumes, and then perform the play for another class. Be sure to videotape the play so all of the students can watch themselves perform.

Science:

1. Summer Solstice

Brief Background. The length of days changes as the Earth revolves around the Sun because the earth is tilted. The Earth is always tilted the same way as it revolves around the Sun. When the North Pole is tilted toward the Sun, the northern half of the Earth has longer days and shorter nights. On the summer solstice in the Northern Hemisphere, June 20 or 21, the Sun is directly over the Tropic of Cancer. This is the longest day of the year, after which days gradually begin to grow shorter.

To introduce or review the changing seasons, demonstrate the journey of the Earth around the sun using a globe and a bright spotlight; the person holding the spotlight should keep the light beam trained on the globe; remember to keep the tilted position of the Earth constant as you make your way around the spotlight). Let students make their own globes out of oranges, Styrofoam, or balls of modeling clay. They can stick a pencil or other thin stick through the center of their sphere to represent the imaginary axis of the tilted earth. Put the students in small groups, give each group a spotlight, and then let group members take turns moving their "earths" around the "sun."

2. Summer Plants

Summer is usually the best time to observe the greatest variety of plant and animal life. Take students on a walking tour of a nearby park or nature trail. Provide them with sandwich bags to collect leaves. Back in the classroom, have pairs of students sort the leaves into groups according to an identified characteristic. (Note: Let students decide on the bases for grouping the leaves; any of the following characteristics could be used: big or small, smooth or jagged, and narrow or wide.) Explain to students that leaves are food factories. Tiny openings in the leaves take in carbon dioxide. The leaves' veins supply water. Chloroplast (which give leaves their green color) absorb the sun's energy. Through the process of photosynthesis, which is diagrammed in Figure 43-2, the water, carbon dioxide, and light energy are transformed into food.

3. Summer Gardening

Let students grow plants in containers on the windowsill, or another suitable place. By following the directions on the seed packages, they can learn to plant and watch marigolds, pansies, carrots, lettuce, and various other flowers and vegetables come out.

4. Nature Photography

Photography is a way for children to capture summertime nature scenes forever. You will need a camera (you can use an inexpensive, disposable one). Provide students with a simple workshop on the use of a camera. Have students look for things in the classroom to photograph. Anything, no matter how commonplace or obvious, can be the subject of a photograph. In the classroom, the subject might be a pencil, a clock face, a desk, or a student. Show students how to engage in "photographic seeing" by framing their hands around their eyes (as shown in Figure 43-3) to capture the picture as it would appear if taken by a camera. When students think they have the best possible pic-

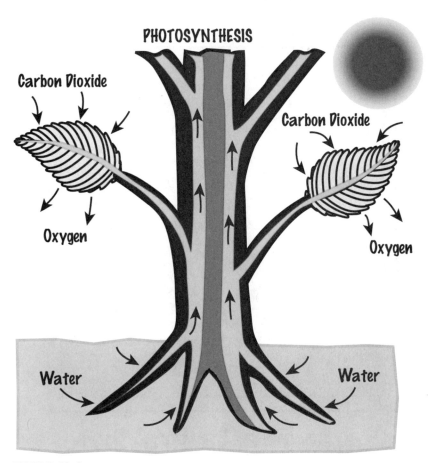

PHOTOSYNTHESIS

Carbon Dioxide

Oxygen

Carbon Dioxide

Oxygen

Water

Water

FIGURE 43-2

ture, they can indicate this by saying "click!" Take students on a photographic safari of a nearby nature area. Let students practice photographic seeing. What do they want to capture on film? It might be a flower, a blade of grass, leaves, a squirrel, or a shadow. After students have identified their subjects, they can take turns taking real photographs. After students write or dictate captions for their developed photographs, display them on the wall.

Math:

1. Estimating and Counting Shells

Give each student a sandwich bag filled with tiny sea shells. Tell students to imagine that they have just returned from a trip to the beach. Have students estimate how many shells are in their bags. Then, let students count the shells in their bags and compare their estimates with the actual numbers.

2. Summer Weather

Average temperatures are highest for the year in summer. Have students check an outdoor thermometer daily and record the temperature. Students can make a graph to display the temperatures. They can also check the temperatures for other nearby and faraway places in the local newspaper.

Art:

1. Summer Mural

Provide students with an assortment of art materials and have them make a mural of summertime scenes.

Cooking:

1. Summertime Picnic

Help the class plan and hold an outdoor summertime picnic. What are some of their favorite summertime foods? You might want to consider traditional American favorites like the following: hot dogs, fried or baked chicken, baked beans, potato chips, lemonade, and watermelon. After the meal, play a few games, such as a relay, beanbag toss or softball, to make the picnic even more enjoyable.

Framing a "Camera" Shot

FIGURE 43-3

Books:

1. Markle, Sandra. (1987). *Exploring Summer.* New York: Atheneum. Advanced.

2. Jeunesse, Gallimard, and Cohat, Elisabeth. (1995). *The Seashore.* New York: Scholastic Inc. Primary.

3. Yolen, Jan. (1993). *Songs of Summer.* Honesdale, PA: Caroline House/Boyds Mill Press. Primary, Intermediate.

4. Thomson, Ruth. (1990). *Summer.* New York: Franklin Watts. Primary, Intermediate.

5. Rosen, Mike. (1991). *Summer Festivals.* New York: The Bookwright Press. Intermediate.

6. Boelts, Maribeth. (1995). *Summer's End.* Boston: Houghton Mifflin Company. Primary.

7. Schweninger, Ann. (1993). *Summertime.* New York: Penguin Books. Primary.

8. Branley, Franklyn M. (1985). *Sunshine Makes the Seasons.* New York: Thomas Y. Crowell. Primary, Intermediate.

9. Prelutsky, Jack. (1984). *What I Did Last Summer.* New York: Greenwillow Books. Primary, Intermediate.

10. Shakespeare, William. *A Midsummer Night's Dream.* (1996). retold by Bruce Corville. Pittsburgh, PA: Dial Publishing. Advanced.

Software:

1. *Summertime on Cherry Street* [Mac]. Dimondale, MI: Hartley/Jostens. Primary.

2. *Changing Seasons/Children & Seasons* [Laserdisc]. Chicago: Encyclopaedia Britannica. Primary.

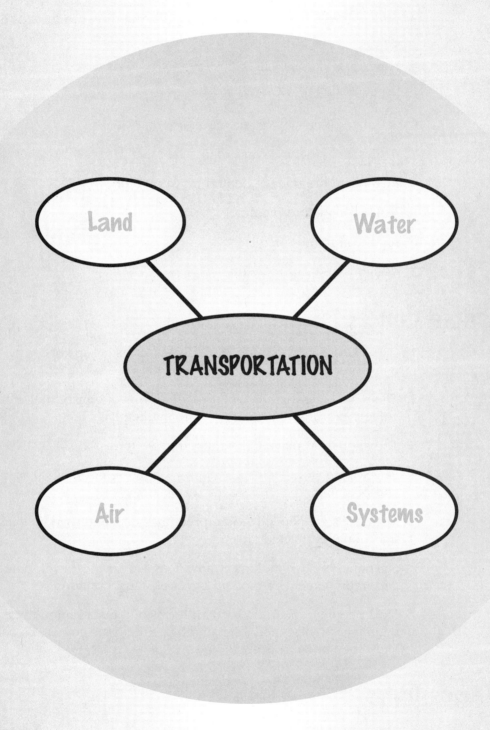

Theme Goals:

Students will:

1. identify the different types of transportation.

2. identify roles of workers in the transportation industry.

3. trace the role transportation plays in bringing a product to the marketplace.

4. conduct a transportation survey.

5. examine how forms of transportation have changed over time.

6. calculate distances and travel times.

7. read travel itineraries and train schedules.

8. investigate the science behind transportation.

9. make a miniature pipeline.

10. report on traffic safety.

11. design a new car model.

Theme Concepts:

1. Cars, buses, trucks, ships, trains, and planes are major forms of transportation.

2. There are many different people and forms of transportation involved in bringing products to the marketplace.

3. Transportation played an important role in history.

4. Developing good transportation systems requires much study and planning.

5. Math skills are needed to interpret travel data and work in many transportation-related areas.

6. Scientific and technological advances led to the development and improvement of modern types of transportation.

7. Most people depend on modern forms of transportation to take them where they need to go and bring them the goods and services they need to live.

Vocabulary:

1. transportation	4. dugout	7. prairie schooner
2. sled	5. chariot	8. iron horse
3. travois	6. Conestoga wagon	9. air cushion vehicle

Instructional Bulletin Board

The purpose of this bulletin board is to help students develop classification skills. Divide the bulletin board into categories of transportation as shown (or let students suggest the categories). Have students gather pictures and photographs of vehicles and other movers of people and things, and then attach them with push-pins under the appropriate categories.

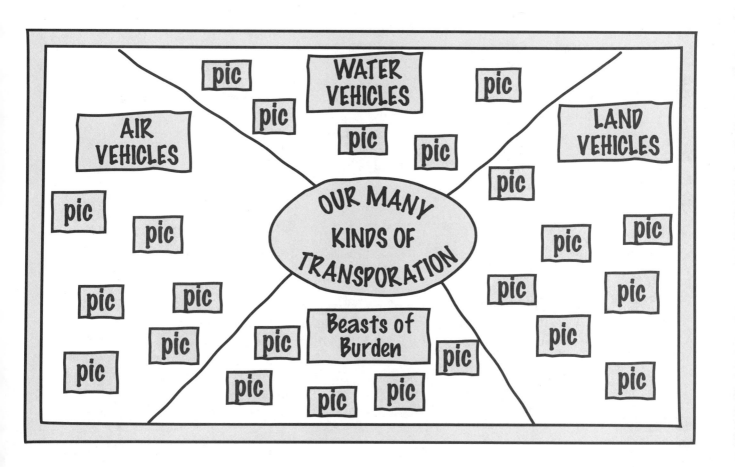

Parent Letter

Dear Parents:

We are beginning a theme of study on transportation. We will be exploring all of the different ways of moving people and goods from one place to another. Children will be asked to examine the important part transportation plays in their own lives.

At School:

Much of our study of transportation will center on a simulated jet trip that the class will be taking. To familiarize children with the dynamics of the real world, they will have to plan the itinerary for the trip, and as they travel from their community to a foreign destination, then role-play airline passengers and transportation workers. Here are some of the other activities planned:

- Tracing how the transportation system brings products to the marketplace
- Conducting a transportation survey
- Examining how transportation has changed over time
- Calculating distances and travel times
- Looking at the science behind transportation
- Reporting on traffic safety

At Home:

This would be a good time to try any of the following activities with your child.

- Allow your child to help you plan a short car trip to a local attraction.
- Discuss how transportation has changed since you were your child's age.
- Help your child make a model boat, car, train, truck, or plane.

Linking Up:

Ask children to bring to class toy/model cars, trucks, buses, planes, ships, space craft, and specialized vehicles. Let students talk about their toys. Why do they like to play with them? Would they like to operate the "real thing" someday?

Social Studies:

1. Transportation Survey

Have students do a class survey to determine the forms of transportation used. Help students design the survey question-and-response format. Students can make bar graphs to display the results of their survey. What does the graph tell the class about their transportation usage? Here are some possible questions? Have you ever traveled on a(n). . .

1. bicycle?	Yes	No
2. truck?	Yes	No
3. boat?	Yes	No
4. train?	Yes	No
5. ocean liner?	Yes	No
6. bus?	Yes	No
7. car?	Yes	No
8. airplane?	Yes	No
9. horse?	Yes	No
10. elevator or escalator?	Yes	No

2. Transportation Through Time

Brief Background. Each type of transportation has its own interesting history. Two kinds of vehicles that made an important contribution to the settlement of America were covered wagons and trains. In the mid-eighteenth century, teams of Conestoga wagons traveled down the National Road, America's first highway to the interior of the continent. By the mid-nineteenth century, caravans of hundreds of covered wagons, called "Prairie Schooners," were transporting Mormons, California gold seekers, and Oregon-bound pioneers across the Great Plains and Rockies. During the 1870s and 1880s, the construction of four transcontinental railways allowed hordes of land-hungry settlers to reach America's rapidly disappearing last frontier cheaply and quickly.

Gather books dealing with the history of transportation and make them available in the classroom. Assign students the task of researching different types of transportation, such as the following: sled, travois, dugout, chariot, cart, stagecoach, sailing ship, steamboat, buggy, horse-drawn streetcar, steam locomotive, covered wagon, horseless carriage, airship, steamship, propeller-driven airplane, diesel train, and jet plane. Provide students with pieces of wood, small boxes, tape, scissors, paper, cardboard, poster paint, Styrofoam, glue, and other materials, and let them make miniature models of the different vehicles. (Note: You may need to make some cuts for the students with a sharp knife and/or small saw.)

3. What's Wrong with Our Transportation System?

Create a simple map of a town that depicts a variety of transportation problems. For example, the map might show streets too close together, main roads located too far from the business district, industries located too far from railway lines and harbors, and residential areas located too close to an airport. After students have identified problems on the map, assign small groups the task of planning a new, improved transportation system for the town. Spread large pieces of butcher paper on the classroom floor. The paper can represent the land area for the town. Provide blocks and other materials, and let each group make a model of the town. After the model is finished, students can use the paper to draw a map of the town with its new transportation system.

4. Beasts of Burden

Brief Background. For thousands of years, humans have used animals to transport themselves and their goods. The horse played an important role in the way of life of the Sioux Indian. Oxen pulled the great prairie schooners west to California and Oregon. Camels still carry people and goods across the sands of the Sahara, as they have for centuries.

Assign students the task of researching one of the following beasts of burden: camel, ox, horse, llama, dog, elephant, donkey, yak, reindeer, mule, and water buffalo.

5. Let's Take a Trip

Help students take off on a simulated jet airliner trip from your nearest jet airport to a foreign city. Correlate this jet plane simulation with the study of a particular foreign country or culture. Write to the country's embassy for free information and/or contact a travel agency for travel brochures, posters, and maps. Here is a list of things the class will need to do for the trip:

1. Give students globes and world maps to study. Have them trace possible air routes from the local airport to their destination. Over what land areas and/or bodies of water will they fly? Let them use the map scale to calculate approximate trip mileage. What is the average speed of a jet plane? If the speed averages 550 mph, how much flight time will be required?

2. Since students will role-play airline passengers and different transportation workers, they will need to identify and gather background information on all of the people it takes to get airline passengers to a destination and back again, such as baggage handlers, bus drivers, ticket agents, flight attendants, pilots, and so forth. Assign each student a specific role to research and play.

3. Have students make a time line of the events that they anticipate will take place on the trip. Then let them consider questions like the following: What time should they leave for the airport? Who will take them from their homes to the airport? What baggage will they take with them on the trip? What types of items cannot be taken on board a plane for security reasons? What snacks will be served on the plane? and How long will the trip take?

4. If possible, invite a travel agent to share some travel tips and answer students' questions.

5. Have students create their own passports. What information will they need?

6. Prepare copies of the itinerary and boarding passes. A travel agent can help you prepare an itinerary for the trip. The itinerary will list the following information: name of passenger; date of ticket purchase; dates and places of departure and return; airline; times of departure and arrival; and seat number. You can also prepare a boarding pass for each student, complete with seat number. Give students their itinerary and ask them questions about it, such as On what airline are you flying? How long does the flight last between _____ and _____? and When does the flight arrive?

7. Rearrange the classroom to look like the rows of seats in the cabin of a jet airliner. Form an aisle down the center of your cabin. Put three seats (chairs or desks) on each side of the aisle to form each row. Display seat numbers prominently (rows are numbered consecutively from front to back, and each seat is identified by a letter; seats in the first row would be identified as 1A, 1B, 1C, 1D, 1E, and 1F).

8. After passengers take their assigned seats, flight attendants can review safety information and procedures. Once the plane is airborne, flight attendants can also serve refreshments to the passengers. During the flight, show a short video about attractions at the destination site. On a poster meant to look like a videoscreen, draw a map of the route to be covered on the trip. Flight attendants can update passengers on the flight's progress by using a magic marker to show the area that has been flown over. The pilot can make an announcement about weather conditions, based on international weather news from a newspaper.

9. When the passengers reach their foreign destination, the plane's cabin can become a tour bus. Students can travel on the bus to historic and cultural attractions. Help students plan an itinerary for the bus tour. Let students take turns being tour guides. Each guide can talk about a particular attraction in the foreign city/country. For example, if the country visited is Britain, students might develop an itinerary that would require them to gather information about Hadrian's Wall, Stonehenge, Buckingham Palace, and Westminster Abbey. This would also be a good time to bring nationals of the country and/or other knowledgeable speakers into the classroom as "guest" tour guides. They could talk about and demonstrate the traditions, customs, and language of the country. To give students the sense of "being there," each guided tour of an attraction should be profusely illustrated.

Math:

1. Graphing Speeds

Let the class record the time it takes each student in the class to walk 50 feet. Help students graph the results, and then calculate the class's average walking speeed for 50 feet. Graph the average speeds or miles per hour (mph) for the following kinds of transportation: *walking*, 4 mph; *bicycle*, 10 mph; *ocean liner*, 33 mph; *bus*, 54 mph; *air cushion vehicle*, 69 mph; *electric train*, 85 mph; and *jet airliner*, 550 mph.

2. How Long Does It Take?

Have students solve the following problems (rounded to the nearest hour): How long will it take to travel 1,650 miles by jet airliner traveling at 550 miles per hour? (3 hours); How long will it take to travel 3,000 miles by ocean liner at 33 miles per hour? (91 hours); and How long will it take to travel 180 miles by bicycle at 10 miles per hour? (18 hours). Encourage students to make up their own "How long does it take?" problems.

3. Reading Train Schedules

Provide students with multiple copies of an Amtrak schedule. (Note: Available free at Amtrak ticket offices, the schedules show train names and numbers, days of operation, stops, arrival and departure times, and special services.) Challenge students to use the Amtrak schedule to answer questions like the following: What time will you depart from _____ on Train #__? How many stops will Train #__ make between _____ and _____? and How long will it take to travel from _____ to _____ on Train #__?

4. Walking Near and Far

Walking is the oldest form of human transportation. Students can calculate the approximate distance they travel inside the school on a typical day. Provide measurement instruments. Let students measure the various routes they travel, and then calculate the total for a day. Some routes students might measure include the following:

- From the entrance of the school to their classroom

- From the classroom to the water fountain, restroom, library, gym, playground, cafeteria, etc.
- From the student's desk to various places in the classroom, such as the pencil sharpener, teacher's desk, etc.

5. Getting Around the School and Town

Provide students with classroom, school, playground, or community maps. Challenge students to use their map skills to find the shortest route between different points on the map.

6. Counting Trucks

Show students pictures of the following kinds of trucks (found in an encyclopedia or other library resource): pickup, small van, large van, dump truck, tow truck, garbage truck, ready-mix concrete truck, tractor-semitrailer, tank truck, and log carrier. After students have studied the different kinds of trucks, have them predict the three kinds that would most frequently be seen on the road. Take the class on a field trip to a major street or highway used by trucks. Assign pairs of students the task of counting one of the kinds of trucks. Back in the classroom, have students make a large bar graph that shows the results of their talleys.

Science:

1. The Science Behind Transportation

Read selections from Robin Kerrod's *Let's Investigate Science: Transportation* (Marshall Cavendish, 1994), or another appropriate children's book, that explains the scientific principles behind cars, trains, airplanes, boats, and other vehicles.

2. The Inside Picture

The most important form of transportation to most Americans is the car. Provide students with diagrams of cars that show the major systems (power, fuel, exhaust, cooling, and lubrication). Obtain an assortment of used engine parts from an auto repair garage or car salvage yard. Clean the parts and display them in the classroom. Let students examine the parts and try to pinpoint their location on the car diagrams. Invite an auto mechanic to class to demonstrate the use of certain tools in the repair of a car. (Note: Diagrams that illustrate the major systems of a car are often available free from car dealerships.)

3. Market Research

Have students interview their parents and other adults to determine what drivers like and dislike about their cars. To help students compile the data, make a list on the chalkboard of the likes and dislikes. Help students sort the items into major categories, such as *safety*, *comfort*, and *performance*.

4. Pipeline Contest

Brief Background. Pipelines crisscross the United States. They use extreme pressure to move substances, including oil, natural gas, and sewage, great distances. In the United States, natural gas is transported through over two million miles of pipeline.

Challenge students to build their own minature pipelines (Figure 44-1). Provide pairs of students with the following materials: a ruler, 10 rigid plastic straws, a small funnel (to make funnel, cut the tip of a small cone-shaped paper cup), two flex straws, two one-quart containers (one filled with water and one empty), electrical tape, and scissors. Take the class outdoors. Challenge the pairs to use the materials to build a leakproof pipeline. Give teams the following directions: use one flex straw for the beginning of the pipeline and the other for the end; use six rigid straws to form the rest of the pipeline; use four rigid straws (which can be cut) to build a platform as needed to support the pipeline; and use the force of gravity to move the water (thus, the beginning of the pipeline will need to higher than the end of the pipeline). Tell the pairs that their objective is to transport one quart of water (students can pretend that the liquid is oil) through the pipeline safely (i.e.,

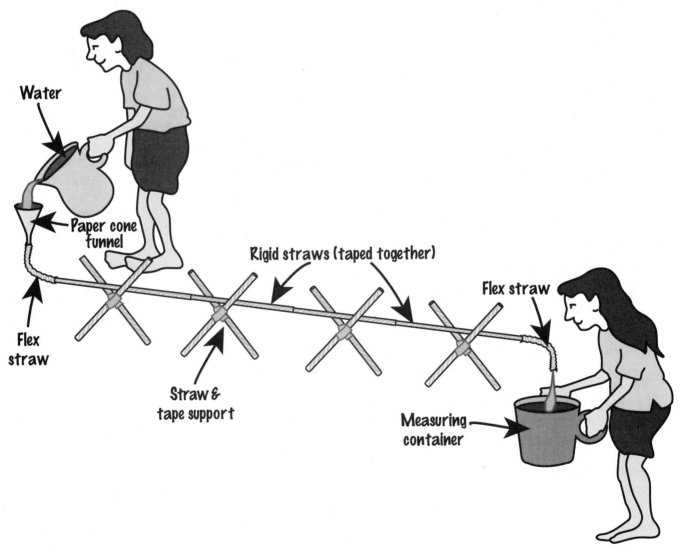

Water

Paper cone funnel

Flex straw

Straw & tape support

Rigid straws (taped together)

Flex straw

Measuring container

FIGURE 44-1

with no leaking or loss of liquid). They can use the funnel to get the water from the container into the opening of the flex straw. At the other end of the pipeline, position the flex straw so that the water flows into the empty container. Debriefing should include a discussion of the important role pipelines play in oil transport. Because of the often fragile natural habitats they cross, it is vital that pipelines be soundly constructed and safe for the environment.

Language Arts:

1. From There to Here

Assign small groups of students the task of researching and telling the story of one of their favorite foods—meat, fruit, grain, dairy product, or vegetable. The story should focus on all of the forms of transportation and drivers of vehicles involved in producing and distributing the food. For example, for "beef," the story, from ranch to table, might include cowboys and their horses, farmers and their tractors, railroad workers and their cattle cars, and truck drivers and their refrigerated trucks, to name a few of the people and types of transportation. Let each group share the story of its food with the class. Encourage groups to incorporate illustrations, maps, and diagrams into their presentations.

2. Travel Safety Tips

On a walking trip in the community, have students look for examples of travel safety concerns and traffic signs and symbols. Take photographs of traffic signs and safety problems the students spot. Back in the classroom, create an enticing "Travel Safety" learning center complete with displays of appropriate books and the photographs taken during the trip. Also discuss safety do's and don'ts related to travel in cars and on the school bus. Assign students the task of developing a brief oral report on tips for a particular safety topic. For example, one student might focus on the safety tips related to stop signs and traffic lights, another student on tips for using seat belts correctly, and another on bicycle safety tips. Each student's oral report to the class should include pictures, diagrams, and other appropriate visuals.

3. Travel Poster

Students can create colorful travel posters. Each poster should incorporate facts about a particular vacation spot and promote one of the following modes of travel: bicycle, car, boat or ship, bus, train, or airplane.

4. Vacation Postcard

Provide students with plain index cards. Have each student imagine that she has just arrived at a favorite vacation spot and decided to send a postcard to a friend. They can draw a scene from the vacation spot on one side of the card and write a brief message about the trip on the other side.

5. Transportation Booklet

Have students research and write illustrated booklets about the following types of transportation: bicycles, cars, buses, trucks, boats/ships, trains, and planes. Each booklet should include a title page, table of contents, chapters (one for each type of transportation), and a bibliography.

Art:

1. New Car Design

After the class's research has identified drivers' likes and dislikes, let students create designs for new, improved car models. They can make pencil sketches of their designs, and then fashion three-dimensional models of the cars from clay.

Books:

1. (1981). *Let's Discover Land Travel.* eds: Patricia Daniels et al. Milwaukee: Raintree Publishers. Primary.

2. (1981). *Let's Discover Ships and Boats.* eds: Patricia Daniels et al. Milwaukee: Raintree Publishers. Primary.

3. Lasky, Kathryn, and Knight, Christopher. (1978). *Tall Ships*. New York: Charles Scribner's Sons. Intermediae, Advanced.

4. Davies, Eryl. (1992). *Timelines: Transport On Land, Road, and Rail*. New York: Franklin Watts. Intermediate.

5. McNeese, Tim. (1993). *Conestogas and Stagecoaches*. New York: Crestwood House. Intermediate.

6. Hastings, Paul. (1972). *Railroads, An International History*. New York: Praeger Publishers. Advanced.

7. Long, Kim. (1990). *The Astronaut Training Book for Kids*. New York: Lodestar Books. Intermediate, Advanced.

8. Ross, Frank, Jr. (1973). *Historic Plane Models*. New York: Lothrop, Lee, and Shepard Co. Intermediate, Advanced.

9. Sandak, Cass. (1984). *Tunnels*. New York: Franklin Watts. Primary.

10. Kerrod, Robin. (1994). *Let's Investigate Science: Transportation*. New York: Marshall Cavendish. Intermediate.

Software:

1. *Transportation Transformation* [AppleII IBM]. Fairfield, CT: Toucan/Queue. Primary, Intermediate, Advanced.

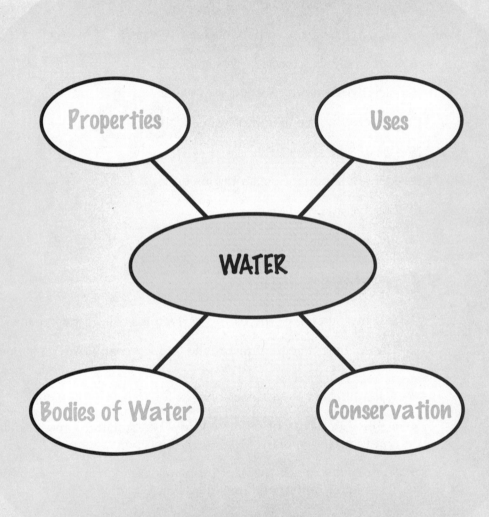

Theme Goals:

The students will:

1. locate major bodies of water on a globe and map.

2. examine the relationship between human settlements and water.

3. locate areas of low and high precipitation.

4. identify water problems.

5. list ways to conserve water.

6. study ocean currents.

7. identify the many important uses of water.

8. participate in scientific investigations.

9. identify the three properties of water.

10. analyze the interaction of water with other substances.

11. discuss the water cycle.

12. identify important ocean resources.

13. observe aquatic life.

14. measure liquids.

Theme Concepts:

1. Seventy percent of the earth's surface is covered by oceans.

2. The Atlantic, Pacific, Indian, and Arctic oceans are major bodies of water.

3. Water affected the choices of sites for human settlement.

4. Deserts are areas of extremely low precipitation, and tropical rain forests are areas of extremely high precipitation.

5. Some of the causes of water problems are industrial discharges, agricultural runoff, and untreated waste.

6. Water is used in the home as well as for irrigation, industry, power, transportation, and recreation.

7. Water interacts with other substances in predictable ways.

8. Water can be a solid, a liquid, or a gas.

9. Water is a powerful force that can cut through the Earth's surface.

10. Because of the water cycle, the Earth's water can be used over and over again.

11. Many important resources come from the oceans.

12. If people are aware of their water consumption habits, they will be more likely to conserve water.

Vocabulary:

1. precipitation

2. evaporation

3. water cycle

4. currents

5. liquid

6. solid

7. vapor/gas

Instructional Bulletin Board

The purpose of this bulletin board is to let students showcase efforts that they have made to improve a waterway in their community. (Note: You might want to substitute another type of problem involving water for the focus of the class's investigation. Other possibilities include the scarcity of water for drinking, farming, recreation, and other uses.) Take students to various waterways in the community. Have children identify and investigate water pollution at one particular site. The pollution might be found in a creek, stream, pond, lake, river, or any other body of water. Divide the bulletin board into the following sections: (1) statement of the pollution problem, (2) photos of students gathering evidence, (3) pictures of physical evidence, (4) graphs and charts displaying evidence, (5) letters to the newspaper and local officials, (6) posters highlighting the problem, and (7) examples of responses and solutions to the problem, such as letters from public officials or articles in newspapers. After the waterway project is completed, students can develop written reports structured on the bulletin board format.

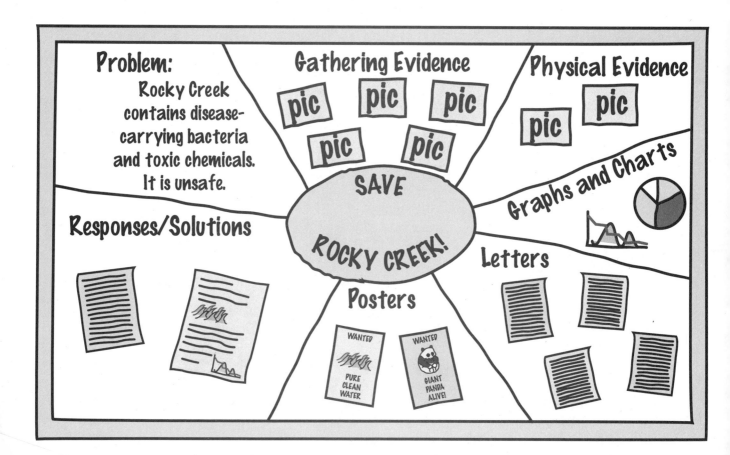

Parent Letter

Dear Parents:

Without water, life as we know it on Earth would be impossible. Yet, despite the important role it plays, it is easy to take water for granted. We turn the faucet handle and out it flows. This unit focuses on water. Students will learn about the water cycle and how water gets to homes and businesses. They will also learn that, although water is abundant on Earth, there are still plenty of water pollution and supply problems to be solved. The children will explore ways to protect and conserve water.

At School

Some of the interesting projects on water include:

- Analyzing the three properties of water
- Finding bodies of water near and far
- Creating three-dimensional models of the ocean
- Observing aquatic life close up
- Measuring liquids
- Sampling watery fruits and vegetables
- Experimenting with water

At Home

Together with your child, investigate ways you might conserve water in the home. Possibilities include using special shower heads that conserve water, reducing the amount of water required to flush toilets, running the dishwasher and washing machine as efficiently and infrequently as possible, and repairing leaky water pipes and faucets.

If you and your child are interested in doing some experiments with water at home, contact us for more information.

Linking Up:

To activate students' prior knowledge, pour a glass of water from one container to another. Ask students to help you compile a list of all of the uses of water in their daily lives. After the list has been compiled, discuss ways of categorizing the uses of water. Ask: Which uses of water on our list seem to go together? What might we call the ones that go together? For example, both "brushing teeth" and "cooking" can be categorized under "water in our homes." Other categories that might be used to help organize the students' thinking are "water in our bodies," "water for irrigation," "water for industry," "water for power," "water for transportation," and "water for recreation." On the chalkboard, make columns for each of the categories. Write the items from the students' list under the appropriate categories. After students have organized their ideas about the uses of water, they should be able to write or dictate a detailed paragraph that begins with the topic sentence, "Water has many important uses."

Social Studies:

1. Water: Where Is It?

Put students in a circle and let them take turns holding a globe. As each child holds the globe, ask him/her whether the hands are covering mostly land or mostly water. This exercise should help the children realize that most (70%) of the earth's surface is covered by water. Provide students with globes and world maps. Have them locate bodies of water. Make certain they can locate the oceans (Atlantic, Pacific, Indian, and Arctic), Mediterranean Sea, Caribbean Sea, and Gulf of Mexico. In addition, help students identify the Great Lakes as well as the Mississippi, Missouri, and Colorado rivers. Also, identify regional and local bodies of water on appropriate maps. Let students identify bodies of water on individual blank maps and/or have them make salt and flour relief maps that highlight the Earth's major bodies of water.

2. Settlements and Water

Have students imagine they are early settlers choosing a place to live. What would they care the most about? Would water affect their choice of a site? What might be the advantages and disadvantages of being near a river? Provide maps of the world, the United States, and your state. Let students observe the location of major cities on the maps. How many of the cities are located on or near bodies of water? On the chalkboard make two columns, one labeled *cities on or near bodies of water* and the other *cities not on or near bodies of water*. After students review the lists, ask: Which column has the longest list? Why?

3. Water Extremes

Brief Background. Although the world has plenty of water, it is not distributed equally across the globe. Because of climate and other factors, some areas receive a lot of precipitation or rainfall and others receive very little.

On the chalkboard make two columns, one labeled *very little rain* and the other *plenty of rain*. Have students locate major deserts and rain forest regions on a map that shows the world's biomes or plant regions. Help students list the desert areas under the appropriate column heading (they are found in the Southwestern United States, North and South Africa, Central Australia, Central Asia, and the Middle East). Have students locate the world's three major tropical rain forests (they are the Amazon Basin in South America, Indonesia in Southeast Asia, and Central West Africa). Have students check average annual precipitation for locations within the two regions. (The average annual precipitation of some desert areas is near zero; Nevada averages 9 inches; the average for some rain forest areas is over 400 inches.)

4. Water Problems

Water pollution is a worldwide problem. Have students identify some of the sources of water pollution nationally and locally (such as industrial chemical discharges, agricultural runoff, and untreated waste as shown in Figure 46-1). If possible, take students on a field trip to the local water purification plant. Help them create a diagram that traces the flow of water through the treatment plant and underground mains to their homes.

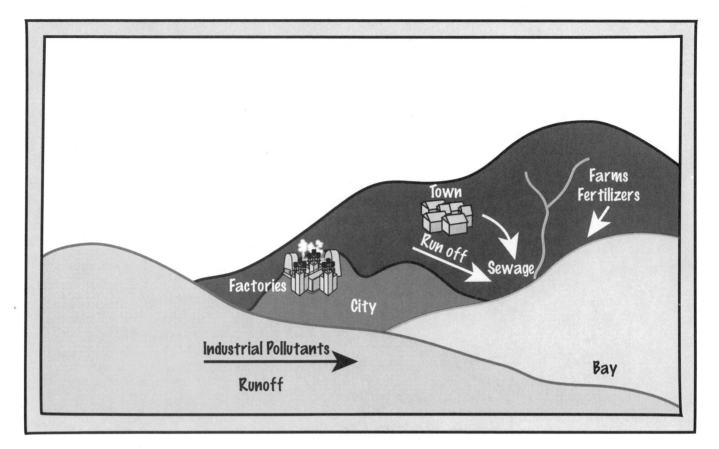

Pollution Runoff Affects Larger Environment

FIGURE 46-1

5. Water Conservation

Much water is wasted every day. Have students make a checklist of things that they can do at home to conserve water. To make them more aware of water in their lives, they can keep a daily log of each time they use it.

6. Ocean "Rivers"

Brief Background. Winds blowing across the surface of the ocean create currents. These currents are "rivers" of water that flow in circular paths. Early sailors used the winds and ocean currents to help them reach their destinations.

Have students compare the route of Columbus's voyage in 1492 with a map that shows Atlantic wind and current systems like the one in Figure 46-2. After looking at the maps, can students give reasons why Columbus reached the West Indies instead of Canada?

Language Arts:

1. On the Edge of the Sea

Have students read, or read aloud, sections of *Island of the Blue Dolphins* by Scott O'Dell. This fiction adventure story should help students visualize the natural environment and climatic conditions of islands and their relationship with the ocean. Among the topics treated in the book are seasonal storms; resources from the sea, including abalones, scallops, sealskins, and seashells; and emotional conflict that develops over the destruction of animals, including seals and sea otters. Have students connect their own experiences with storms and water to the events in the book.

2. Ocean Scientist

To give students some fascinating insights into what scientists really do, read selections from Seymour Simon's *How to Be an Ocean Scien-*

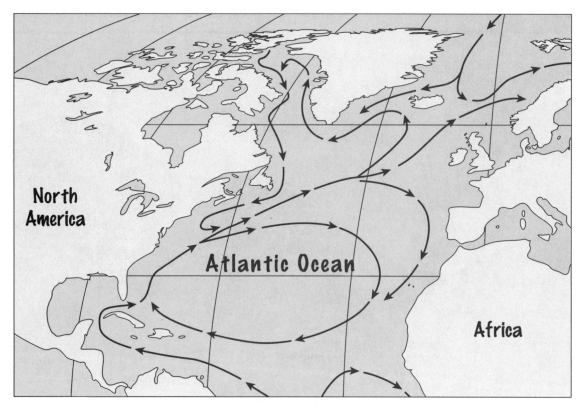

Ocean Currents

FIGURE 46-2

tist in Your Own Home (Lippincott, 1988), or another appropriate children's book. Simon's book provides detailed directions for setting up simple experiments to answer a variety of scientific questions about the ocean, such as "How can you make fresh water from seawater?"

Science:

1. Water and "Things"

Provide each pair of students with a clear plastic cup of water and a small bag containing an assortment of small objects (such as a toothpick, piece of sponge, rubber ball or eraser, paper clip, aluminum foil, and marble). Have the pairs predict which objects will float and which will sink. To test their predictions, let them put one object at a time in the water and then record the results. As you observe students working with the materials, note individual student actions and discoveries. When the pairs are finished, ask students to tell you about their discoveries. Can they describe what happened to the materials in the water? What concepts are students developing to explain the interactions

of the materials in the water? Follow up by having students make a chart of their results under the headings "Things That Float" and "Things That Sink."

2. Aluminum Boats

Give each student a container of water, pieces of aluminum foil, and a uniform set of small weights (such as a bunch of paper clips, pins, or tiny washers). Provide a scale so students can weigh their weights. Challenge students to make aluminum foil boats that can float. After they have made the boats, they can load them with cargo. Have them gently put one weight at a time in their boats. How many weights can each boat hold before it sinks? Does changing the design of the boats affect the amount of cargo they can carry? Which boat can hold the most weight?

3. Surface Tension

Brief Background. Molecules of water pack more tightly together (increase in density) when they come into contact with air or other substances. This phenomenon is called *surface tension*. Surface tension allows water to support objects heavier than itself. For example, if a metal pin is dropped in a glass of water it will sink. However, if the same pin is placed gently enough on the still surface of the water, it can float.

Have students try to make heavier-than-water objects float. (Note: For these objects to float, the surface of the water must be absolutely still.) Students can observe the effects of different substances on surface tension by doing the following: Provide eye-droppers and let students put droplets of water on an assortment of substances, such as wax paper, writing paper, and plastic. Do the water molecules in the drops appear to cling tightly together? What shape does the water take on the different substances? Next, place the wax paper and other substances on an inclined surface and have students make observations of water dropped under these conditions.

4. The Properties of Water

Water can be a liquid, a solid, or a gas. To demonstrate the three properties of water, involve students in the following hands-on activities.

Liquid: Students should be able to cite numerous examples of water in liquid form. Make a list of their examples. Does the class's list include particular examples related to water for drinking, washing, bathing, boating, swimming, cleaning, cooling machines, and raising crops? Provide each child with two small plastic cups, one cup filled with six ounces of water and the other empty. One important attribute of liquid water is that it moves freely. That is because molecules of liquid water are close together and move about freely. Students can observe this characteristic as they carefully pour the water from one container to another.

Solid: Have each student use a marking pen to write his name on the side of the cup and to also mark the water level. Note the temperature of the classroom as indicated on a thermometer. Then, put the students' cups of water along with a refrigerator thermometer in a freezer overnight. When students examine their containers the next day, let them note any changes observed. Encourage students to answer these questions: Why did the water change form? (ice forms at 32° F); and why has the ice in the containers risen above the pen marks? (Unlike most substances that contract as they become colder,

water expands when it becomes colder than 39° F.) The molecules in solid water (ice) are far apart and almost motionless. Put some ice in containers of liquid water. Have students discuss what might cause ice to float (air fills the space around the molecules of ice; air is lighter than water). Have students list examples of solid water on their retrieval chart (ice cubes, ice cones, icebergs, etc.)

Gas: Place the students' cups of ice on a table. Have students offer predictions about what will happen to the ice next (the ice will melt at room temperature and the volume of liquid water will be less that the volume of solid water). Have students record how long it takes the ice to melt after it is removed from the freezer. Once the ice has melted, have students make predictions about what will happen next (the water will eventually "disappear," i.e., the water molecules will enter the air as vapor). Have students record how long it takes all of the water in their glasses to turn to vapor. Can students name the process by which water changes from liquid to vapor or gas? (*evaporation*)

5. Water: A Powerful Force

Hold a glass of water in one hand and a rock in the other. Ask students: Which one of these is the more powerful force? Show students pictures of the Grand Canyon. Ask them to speculate about how it was formed. Explain that water is constantly at work changing the Earth's surface. Moving water can wear away the land. Over time, it can cut through solid rock. It took two billion years for the Colorado River to carve the one-mile-deep Grand Canyon. To observe firsthand how water causes erosion, help students create a miniature river in the classroom. Cover a table with a plastic tablecloth. Prop a large-sized, aluminum baking pan up with two or more books so that the lower end is hanging over the edge of the table. Punch a hole in the middle of the lower end of the pan so that water from it can drain into a large container. Place sand in the upper half of the pan and smooth it out. Carve a shallow channel in the sand with your finger. Pour a gallon of water from a pitcher so that it will slowly, but continuously, drain into the top of the channel. Let the water flow down the channel until the pitcher is empty. Have students draw a diagram of the effects of the water on the "land," and then describe the effects orally and in writing.

6. The Water Cycle

Brief Background. Water covers 70 percent of the Earth's surface, and 97 percent of the Earth's water is contained in the oceans. All of the world's water eventually enters the atmosphere as water vapor, most of this as a result of the process of *evaporation*, and some as the result of *transpiration*, which is the process whereby water vapor is emitted from the surface of plants. It returns to earth as *precipitation*. Most of the rain that falls on land ends up in rivers that eventually flow into the oceans. The continuous movement of the Earth's water from oceans, to air, to land, and back to oceans is called *the water cycle* which is shown in Figure 46-3. Because of the water cycle, the earth's water can be used over and over again.

On a map, let students locate all of the places on earth where water is found. Have them estimate how much of the earth's surface is covered by water. Remind students that water enters the atmosphere as a gas. Review with students the three properties of water. Use the chalkboard to diagram the water cycle. Then, let students draw and label the parts.

7. The Oceans

Have students list important resources that come from the ocean. Probe to see if students are aware that the ocean is a source of food (fish, shellfish, and plants), energy (oil and natural gas), minerals (sand, gravel), medicines (from marine plants and animals), transportation (passenger ships, oil tankers, freighters), and recreation (swimming, boating, surfing). Provide crayons, paint, paper, and brushes, and let students illustrate important ocean resources.

8. Classroom Aquarium

A classroom aquarium will provide students with countless opportunities to observe aquatic life close up. Some activities that can be developed around the aquarium include:

1. Observe the behavior of the aquatic animals and plants.
2. Record data on feeding, water temperature, ph level, and clearness.
3. Care for aquatic animals and plants.
4. Clean and maintain the aquarium.

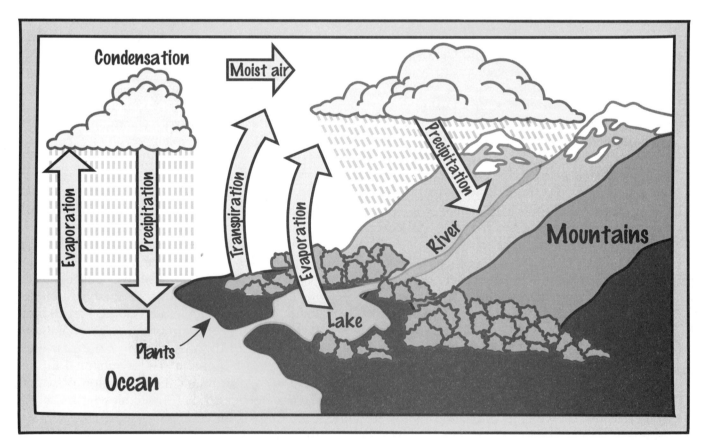

Water Cycle

FIGURE 46-3

5. Keep a journal or log of observations and thoughts.
6. Imagine you are one of the animals in the aquarium and write a diary from the animal's point of view.
7. Investigate questions that arise as a consequence of observations, such as "How can fish live in water?"
8. Draw and paint detailed pictures of fish and other animals.

Brief Background. All living things need water. The human body consists of 65 percent water. Inside the body, watery solutions dissolve and transport nutrients, allow chemical reactions to occur, and carry away wastes.

Discuss with children the critical function water plays in their bodies. Remind students of the importance of water in their diet. Every person needs about 2 1/2 quarts of water every day. Provide each student with a paper plate of freshly cut, bite-sized pieces of fruits and vegetables, such as celery, tomato, corn, carrot, pineapple, watermelon, orange, potato, and apple. Based on the students' visual observations of their water content, have students rank-order the plants from "very watery" to "*not* very watery." After they have finished their visual observations, invite students to taste each plant. Does the taste test support their visual observations of each plant's water content?

Math:

1. How Much Does It Take?

We use a lot of water, but much of this consumption goes unnoticed. To help students appreciate the magnitude of the large quantities of water consumed daily, hold a gallon container filled with water and ask the class to predict how many gallons of water are needed to do each of the following. After students make each prediction, show them the amount, which is stated in gallons in parentheses.

To flush a toilet (7 gallons)
To shower for one minute (5 gallons)
To run the washing machine (40 gallons)
To make a ton of steel (38,000 gallons)
To grow enough wheat to make a loaf of bread (115 gallons)
To make a gallon of gasoline (7 gallons)

To make the paper for one Sunday newspaper (80 gallons)

2. Finding the Volume

Provide measuring containers and access to water. Let students measure the volume of an assortment of empty containers of different sizes by filling them up with water.

3. How Much Does Water Weigh?

How much does the water in the aquarium weigh? Provide a scale and empty containers of various sizes and shapes. Have students predict how much water would weigh in the various containers. They can fill and weigh the containers to check their predictions.

4. Measuring Leaks

Leaky faucets waste water. To make students aware of water waste, show them how much can be wasted. Find an accessible leaky faucet in the school, or open a faucet slightly so that it slowly drips water. Have students place a measuring cup under the leaky faucet and measure the amount of water that drips into the cup over a quater-of-an-hour period. Then, let the class multiply the amount collected by 96 to determine the amount of water wasted over a 24-hour period. For the loss over a year, multiply the resultant figure by 365. Encourage students to spot leaks and measure the amount of water wasted at home.

Art:

1. Ocean Diorama

Show students underwater photographs of sealife for ideas for their dioramas. Have each child bring to class a small empty box for her diorama. Then, give them colored paper, tagboard, scissors, paint, crayons, string or thread, pipe cleaners, foil, cloth, glue, and other materials. Encourage students to create a colorful background for their underwater scenes. Students can cut out fish and other aquatic animals and suspend them in the "water" with thread. Before displaying the dioramas, protect the front of each one with a covering of plastic wrap.

2. Watercolors

Have children make charcoal or pencil-and-ink sketches outlining underwater scenes. After the outlines are completed, watercolor can be applied.

Music:

1. Nautical Music

Select a few nautical songs for the children's listening pleasure.

Books:

1. Branley, Franklyn. (1982). *Water for the World*. New York: T.Y. Crowell. Intermediate.

2. Pringle, Laurence. (1982). *Water: The Next Great Resource Battle*. New York: Macmillan Pub. Co., Inc. Advanced.

3. Tesar, Jenny. (1991). *Threatened Oceans*. New York: Facts On File. Intermediate.

4. Bailey, Donna. (1991). *Wasting Water*. New York: Franklin Watts. Primary.

5. Lefkowitz, R.J. (1973). *Water for Today and Tommorow*. New York: Parent's Magazine Press. Primary.

6. Johnston, Tom. (1988). *Water! Water!* Milwaukee: Gareth Stevens Publishing. Primary.

7. Cooper, Jason. (1992). *Science Secretes: Water*. Vero Beach, FL: The Rourke Corp., Inc. Primary.

8. Rauzon, Mark, and Bix, Cynthia Overbeck. (1994). *Water, Water Everywhere*. San Fransico: Sierra Club Books for Children. Primary.

9. Leutscher, Alfred. (1993). *Water*. New York: The Dial Press. Primary.

10. (1993). *Do Fish Drink? First Questions and Answers About Water*. Alexandria, VA: Time Life for Children. Primary.

11. Simon, Seymore. (1988). *How to Be an Ocean Scientist in Your Own Home*. New York: J.B. Lippincott. Intermediate.

12. Kovacs, Deborah. (1987). *A Day Under Water*. New York: Scholastic, Inc. Primary.

13. O'Dell, Scott. (1960 & 1990). *Island of the Blue Dolphins*. Boston: Houghton Mifflin.

Software:

1. *Freshwater/Freshwater Wetlands* [Laserdisc]. Columbus, OH: Coronet/MTI (Simon & Schuster). Intermediate, Advanced.

2. *National Geographic's STV Series: Water* [Mac Laserdisc]. Washington, DC: National Geographic. Primary, Intermediate, Advanced.

3. *GTV: Planetary Manager* [GS Mac IBM Laserdisc]. Washington, DC: National Geographic. Advanced.

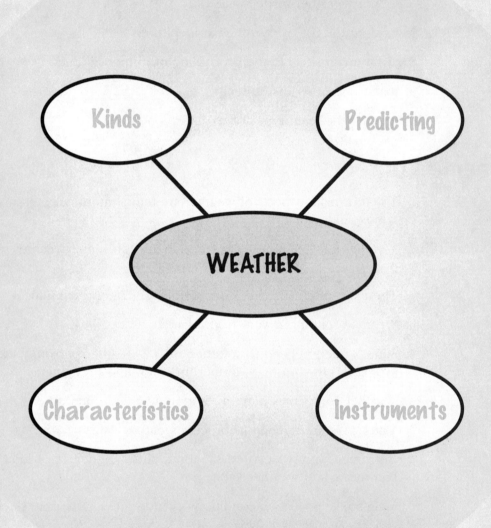

Kinds

Predicting

WEATHER

Characteristics

Instruments

Theme Goals:

Students will:

1. identify the four characteristics of weather.

2. collect weather data.

3. plan and present a weather report.

4. identify kinds of clouds.

5. match clothing and weather conditions.

6. identify weather-related careers.

7. explore the role of weather in literature.

8. apply math skills in the processing of numerical data.

9. make a weather instrument.

10. identify the main types of weather conditions.

Theme Concepts:

1. The four main aspects of weather are temperature, air pressure, winds, and moisture.

2. Weather information is used to plan and present a weather report.

3. The main kinds of clouds are stratus, cirrus, and cumulus.

4. Weather conditions vary from place to place.

5. Some careers related to weather are TV weather person, meteorologist, airplane pilot, farmer, mariner, and firefighter.

6. Weather sometimes plays an important role in literature.

7. Math skills are needed to process weather data.

9. Instruments to observe data about the weather include the barometer and weather vane.

10. Main types of weather conditions include snow, rain, clear skies, cloudy, and partly cloudy.

Vocabulary:

1. air pressure

2. barometer

3. precipitation

4. cirrus clouds

5. stratus clouds

6. cumulus clouds

7. climate

8. weather vane

Instructional Bulletin Board

The purpose of this bulletin board is to provide students with opportunities to compare and contrast local and distant weather conditions. Assign small groups of students the task of recording daily weather data for the local area and selected foreign cities, (see the weather section of the newspaper). Daily temperature, precipitation, and general weather conditions can be recorded on cards and pinned in the spaces provided. Students can decorate the bulletin board with maps showing the locations or the chosen cities. The example below focuses on Paris (France), Rio de Janeiro (Brazil), Nairobi (Kenya), and Sydney (Australia).

WEATHER AROUND THE WORLD ON MAY 10, 19--

U.S.A Local City	FRANCE Paris	BRAZIL Rio de Janeiro	KENYA Nairobi	AUSTRALIA Sydney
Temperature 70°	**Temperature**	**Temperature**	**Temperature**	**Temperature**
Precipitation $\frac{1"}{2}$	**Precipitation**	**Precipitation**	**Precipitation**	**Precipitation**
Conditions Partly Cloudy	**Conditions**	**Conditions**	**Conditions**	**Conditions**

Parent Letter

Dear Parents:

Wind, rain, sleet, hail, snow, sunshine—we are affected by weather all of the time. Weather is something people are always talking—and sometimes complaining—about. During our study of the weather, not only will the class be talking about the weather, they will be investigating its characeristics and effects as well.

At School:

Here are some of the weather-related activities planned for the theme:

- Using weather instruments to measure the four main aspects of weather: temperature, air pressure, winds, and moisture
- Planning and presenting a TV-style weather report
- Making predictions about the weather
- Observing and learning about the different kinds of clouds
- Recreating scenes from children's literature in which weather plays an important role
- Using math to understand the weather
- Making our own weather instruments

At Home:

There are many things you and your child can do at home together to reinforce concepts learned at school. Please consider one or more of the following:

- Watch the TV weather report.
- Discuss how weather conditions have affected you personally.
- Talk about weather-related current news events.
- Read and discuss the weather section of the daily newspaper.
- Spend time outdoors experiencing the weather up close.

Linking Up:

Take students outside (or tell students to look out the classroom window). Ask: What's the weather like today? How does the weather look? How does it feel? How does it smell? What words can be used to describe it? Does everyone agree on the description? Which types of weather do students enjoy the most, and the least?

Science:

1. Weather: What Is It?

Brief Background. Weather refers to the atmospheric condition of the air on a day-to-day basis. There are four aspects of weather: temperature, air pressure, wind, and mositure.

To demonstrate each aspect, involve students in the following activities:

Temperature: Have students check the temperature on an outside thermometer located within view of the classroom window. Students can use one of the following descriptors for each day's temperature: hot, warm, cool, and cold. Both the temperature (in degrees) and the descriptor can be recorded on a weather-chart calendar. Can students "feel" the temperature?

Air pressure: The force of the air pushing down on the Earth is called *air pressure*. To show students the effects of air pressure, provide them with straws and cups of water. The students can manipulate air pressure by sucking the straws. The sucking causes a vacuum (or a condition of absence of air) within the straw, which allows the higher air pressure outside the straw to push the water up the straw. Show students a *barometer*, which is a device that measures air pressure. The barometer gauge shows that as air pressure goes from very low to very high, weather changes from stormy to rain to fair to very dry. Have students check the barometer daily and record the air pressure on the weather chart.

Wind: The movement of air from areas of high pressure to areas of low pressure is called *wind*. Wind is often whipped up in places where land and water meet. This is because the temperature of the air over water is generally different than the temperature of the air over land. The cooling sea breeze that is often experienced by people at the beach is an example of the flow of air from areas of high to low pressure. Students can observe the flag in front of the school daily to determine whether or not a strong wind is blowing. Set up a weather vane in the school yard to determine from which direction the wind blows. Have students check the weather vane daily and record the wind direction on the weather chart.

Moisture: Moisture enters the air as a vapor. When water vapor condenses, it returns to Earth as precipitation in the forms of rain, snow, sleet, and hail. Place a rain gauge outside, and have students note and record the type and amount of precipitation daily on the weather chart.

2. Weather Report

Using information collected in Science Activity #1, let students take turns planning and presenting the daily weather report. The reports should include a weather map. Show students weather maps that appear in local daily newspapers. For their maps, have students create their own symbols for the following weather conditions: high (pressure), low (pressure), rain, thunderstorms, snow, fog, windy, clear or sunny skies, cloudy, and partly cloudy. Arrows can indicate wind direction.

Barometer

FIGURE 47-1

3. Predicting the Weather

Have students predict the next day's weather. They can compare their daily weather predictions with the actual conditions.

4. Clouds and the Weather

Brief Background. Clouds are masses of droplets of water or ice crystals floating in the air that affect the weather. Clouds close to the ground that are layered or sheetlike are called *stratus* clouds. Clouds higher from the ground that are wispy looking are called *cirrus* clouds. Piles of puffy clouds that extend from high to low altitudes are called *cumulus* clouds.

Have students check the sky daily for the presence or absence of clouds. If clouds are in the sky, students can practice identifying them according to their appearance. Have students note the relationship between kinds of clouds observed and the occurrence of rain, sleet, or snow.

5. Making Rain

Brief Background. Clouds are formed by the process of *condensation*. Condensation occurs when warm, moist air cools. To demonstrate condensation, put ice cubes in a jar of water and fasten the lid on the jar. Wait a few minutes for water droplets to form on the outside of the jar. Challenge students to explain how the water droplets got there. Probe to determine if students understand that condensation occurred when the warm, moist air in the classroom came in contact with the cold surface of the jar.

6. Weather and the Environment

Brief Background. Plants, wildlife, and people are affected by the weather. For example, desert plants and animals can spring magically to life after a rare rain, a heavy frost can wipe out all of the adult mosquitoes in a given area, or a deep snowfall can cover the plants that deer eat. Hurricanes, tornados, thunderstorms, and flash floods can cause death and destruction.

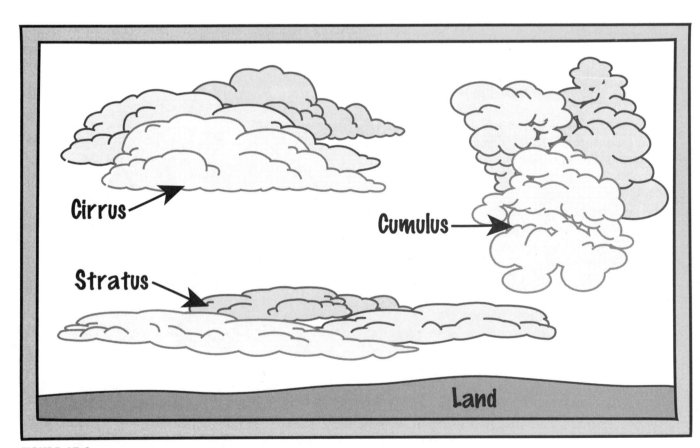

FIGURE 47-2

Ask students to look for examples of weather's effects on the environment. How do different weather conditions affect the following people: a city dweller, a farmer, an airplane pilot, and a ship captain.

Social Studies:

1. Adopt a City

Assign each student the task of keeping track of the weather in a foreign city of her choice. Most daily newspapers list temperature and weather conditions for major cities of the world. Students can also research geographic and climate factors that would affect their cities' weather. Provide globes and maps that show different latitudes and climate zones. Students can discuss how climate relates to weather, and how climate affects foods grown, life in cities, and economic conditions.

2. Weather Gear

Let students draw pictures of people dressed in clothing that would be appropriate for different weather conditions.

3. Weather–Career Connections

Let interested students investigate the connections between weather and the following careers: TV weather persons, meteorologists, farmers, airplane pilots, mariners, firefighters, truckers, postal employees, and forest rangers.

Language Arts:

1. Doing Something About the Weather

Mark Twain once said that everybody complains about the weather, but nobody does anything about it. Have small groups of students create brief skits in which the characters are complaining about and/or doing something about the weather. After groups have had an opportunity to develop and practice their skits, they can take turns presenting them to the class.

2. Starring "The Weather"

Students can recreate scenes from children's literature in which weather—thunderstorms, lightning, tornadoes, hurricanes, blizzards, typhoons, drought, and the like—plays a prominent role. To stimulate creative thinking, read selections from appropriate children's books, such as the passages in *The Wizard of Oz* about the tornado that transports Dorothy and Toto to Oz, or the hurricane that capsizes Mafuta's canoe, in Armstrong Sperry's *Call It Courage* (Macmillan, 1941).

3. Weather Words

Challenge students to think of words and phrases that help readers visualize weather and sense the moods that different types of weather evoke. To help set the tone, give students a few examples of weather words, such as "wailing wind," "thunder that roared and howled like demons," and "covered with a fuzzy blanket of fog."

4. What Do You Do on a _____ Day?

Have students write a paragraph in which they describe what they like to do on one or more of the following days: sunny, rainy, windy, hot, cold, damp, foggy, cloudy, snowy, and stormy.

5. What's Next?

Let students imagine and describe in writing a realistic and exciting situation in which one of the following weather conditions is present: a blizzard, a thunderstorm, dark clouds, lightening, a twister, and sunshine.

Math:

1. Weather Numbers

Weather is all about numbers. Students can compare today's temperature with yesterday's or last week's. They can calculate how many degrees warmer, hotter, colder, or cooler the same place is at different points in time, or different places are at the same point in time. Addition can be used to calculate total inches of precipitation over days, weeks, months, and years. Subtraction can be used to calculate in-

495

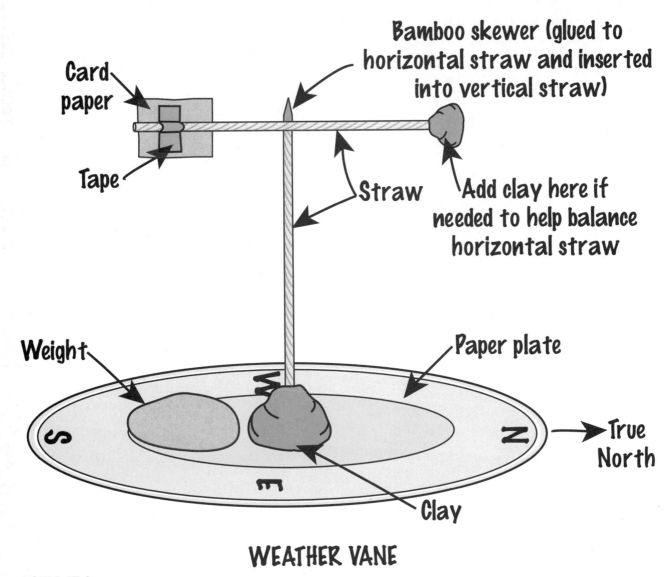

Card paper

Tape

Bamboo skewer (glued to horizontal straw and inserted into vertical straw)

Straw

Add clay here if needed to help balance horizontal straw

Weight

Paper plate

True North

Clay

WEATHER VANE

FIGURE 47-3

creases and decreases in precipitation over time. Both addition and division can be used to calculate average temperatures and average precipitation over different time periods.

Art:

1. Weather Express

Provide students with an assortment of art materials, and let them use art to express different weather conditions. For example, cotton balls can be used to depict snow or clouds, swirls of blue and black finger paint can bring to mind a thunderstorm, and pieces of yellow yarn radiating from a painting of the Sun can suggest the brilliance and warmth of a clear summer's day.

2. What Do You See?

Because of the action of wind, clouds are constantly moving and changing shape. On a cloudy day, provide students with drawing materials, take them outside, and let them pick out clouds to draw. Challenge them to find clouds shaped like people, animals, plants, and objects. Have students draw the shapes, and then display their art work on the wall.

3. Weather Crafters

Have students make portable weather vanes to show the wind's direction. To make a weather vane, each student will need one 8" bamboo skewer, one plastic plate, two plastic straws, a 3" × 4" rectangle of card paper, tape, modeling clay, and glue. Follow these directions: (1) using a permanent marker, write the cardinal directions—N, S, W, and E—on the plastic plate to form a compass rose; (2) mold a piece of clay (clay needs to be large enough to support the straw in vertical position) to the center of the plate; (3) stick one end of one of the straws into clay; (4) tape the 3" × 4" piece of card paper to one end of the other straw to form the shape of a paddle; (5) push the bamboo skewer through the middle of the straw (make certain that the bamboo skewer and card paper are parallel to one another); (6) use glue to firmly attach the straw to the bamboo skewer; and (7) put the long end of the bamboo skewer into the end of the other straw. When completed, the straw attached to the skewer should turn when the card paper paddle catches a breeze. When both sides of the paddle catch the wind equally, the other end of the straw will point in the direction from which the wind blows. To use the weather vane, take it outside and position it so that the N on the plate points north (you may need to place a rock or other heavy object on the plate to keep it from moving in the wind).

Books:

1. Peters, Lisa. (1988). *The Sun, the Wind, and the Rain.* New York: Henry Holt & Co. Primary.

2. Ruckman, Ivy. (1984). *Night of the Twisters.* New York: Crowell. Advanced.

3. Simon, Seymour. (1989). *Storms.* New York: Morrow Junior Books. Advanced.

4. Briggs, Carol. (1988). *Research Balloons: Exploring Hidden Worlds.* Minneapolis: Lerner Publications Co. Intermediate.

5. Merk, Ann. (1994). *Weather Signs.* Vero Beach, FL.: Rourke Corp. Primary.

6. Sperry, Armstrong. (1941). *Call it Courage.* New York: Macmillan.

Software:

1. *Atmospheric Science* [Laserdisc]. Columbus, OH: Coronet/MTI (Simon & Schuster). Intermediate, Advanced.

2. *Weather: Air in Action Series* [Mac Windows CD-ROM]. Chatsworth, CA: AIMS. Advanced.

3. *Everything Weather* [Mac MPC CD-ROM]. Princeton, NJ: Bureau of Electronic Publishing (Thynx). Intermediate, Advanced.

4. *Weather Dynamics* [Laserdisc]. Chicago: Clearvue/eav. Advanced.

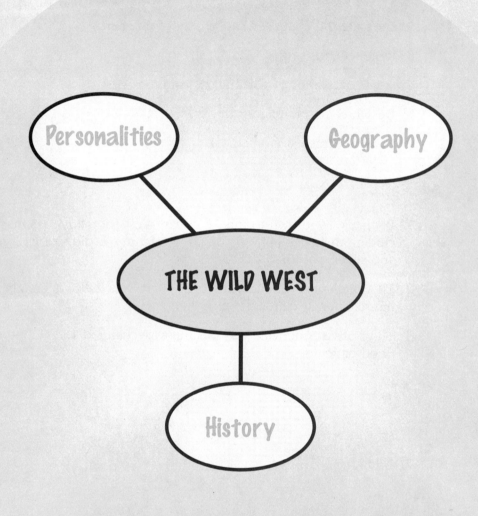

Personalities

Geography

THE WILD WEST

History

Theme Goals:

Students will:

1. discuss the contributions of African Americans and women to the settling of the West.

2. examine the Native American perspective of expansion

3. identify the different routes traveled to the West.

4. create a Plains Indian village and compare their way of life with that of settlers.

5. calculate the expenses and profits of ranchers.

6. write legends of the Wild West.

7. create glossaries of vocabulary from the West.

8. Design cattle brands.

9. Cook a "chuck wagon" meal.

Theme Concepts:

1. People were drawn to the American West for many reasons, including the availability of cheap farmland, the discovery of gold and silver, and the cattle business.

2. The settlement of the American West was helped greatly by transcontiental railroads.

3. The Native American way of life was changed forever by the flood of settlers.

Vocabulary:

1. six-shooter

2. wild

3. sinew

4. longhorn

5. dogies

6. cowpuncher

7. chaps

8. stampede

9. chuck wagon

Instructional Bulletin Board

The purpose of this bulletin board is to display the students' own research of the Wild West. Encourage each student to furnish a report and illustration (either hand drawn or gathered from another source) for one of the personalities, events, or terms treated in the unit. Display five students' reports and illustrations at a time on the bulletin board for a few days, then replace them with another set of five. Repeat the process until all of the students' work has been displayed.

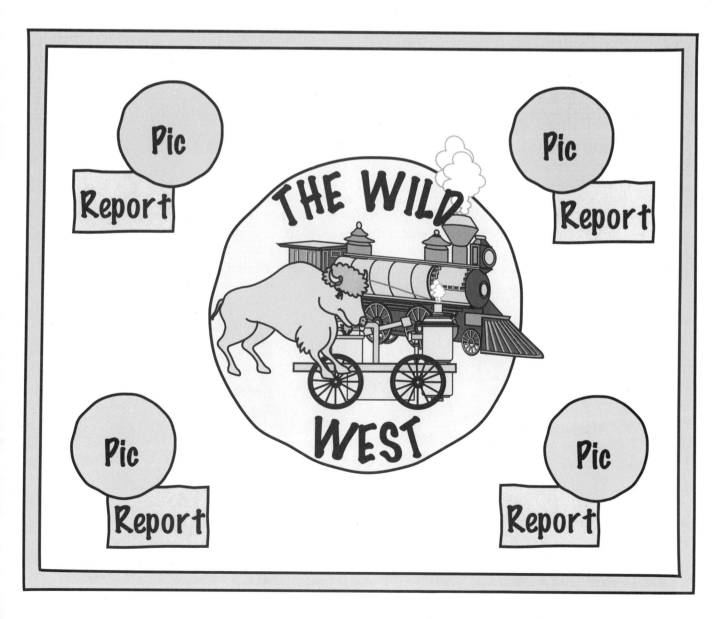

Parent Letter

Dear Parents:

The Wild West was America's last frontier. Explorers, trappers, and scouts were the first to come. By the 1840s, wagon trains were traveling along the Oregon Trail and other paths westward. This region became the center of the range-cattle industry and the home of cowpunchers. By the 1890s, cities and farms with barbed-wire fences had replaced the open range, and the Wild West was gone. We are beginning our study of the Wild West, one of the most colorful chapters in our nation's history.

At School:

Among the activities planned are the following:

- Creating our own cattle brands
- Calculating cattle drive profits
- Cooking and sampling frontier food
- Singing western songs
- Considering the winning of the West from the Native American perspective

At Home:

You can reinforce the concepts of this theme by doing one or more of the following: Check out a library book on the Wild West for your child to read, or for you to read aloud; watch a TV documentary about the Wild West with your child; take your child to a museum that includes exhibits on the Wild West; and explain to your child how your own image of the Wild West was formed (include information about any favorite western personalities, songs, books, TV shows, films, etc.).

Linking Up:

This unit deals with events that occurred long ago. The notion of historical time is very difficult for young learners to grasp. One way to help them gain a time perspective is to *show* them the order in which events happened with a time line. To make a classroom-size time line, divide a 20-foot clothesline rope into one-foot sections and let each foot equal 10 years. The rope can cover the time period from 1800 to the present. Clothspins can be used to attach on the rope event cards that indicate the precise points of the events' occurrence. Each event card should include the name of the event as well as the date when it occurred. Have students attach cards on the rope to mark their birth years, as well as those of parents, grandparents, and even great-grandparents.

Social Studies:

1. Pictures of the Past

Brief Background. Frederic Remington and George Catlin were two talented artists who saw the nineteenth-century American West firsthand. In their art, they tried to show life on the western frontier as it really was. Remington is known for his action paintings of cowpunchers and Native Americans that capture the spirit and vitality of the West, while Catlin is famous for his realistic paintings of the culture of the Plains Indian.

Show students pictures of Remington's and Catlin's western art (which can be found in large-page illustrated art books from the school or community library). Explain to students that these artists—along with a few others—give us a rare glimpse of many Native American customs and traditions—and of a way of life that is gone. As the students observe the pictures, let them describe their feelings and impressions.

2. African American Cow Punchers and Settlers

An overlooked aspect of history is the role of blacks in the settlement of the Wild West. There were over 5,000 African Americans who lived on the range and herded cattle. Two of the most famous were Nat Love and Jim Beckwourth. Love worked on cattle drives for 20 years. He was expert at riding, roping, branding, and shooting. Beckwourth lived for a time with the Crow Indians, served as an Army scout, and participated in the Colorado Gold Rush of 1859. Read aloud sections of *The Story of Nat Love* by Robert Miller (Silver Press, 1995) and *Black Frontiers: A History of African American Heroes in the Old West* by Lillian Schlissel (Simon and Schuster, 1995), and other appropriate children's books. Encourage students to report on the lives of different African Americans who contributed to the settlement of the West.

3. Native American Perspectives

Brief Background. Native Americans did not give up their traditional hunting lands to the white settlers without a fight. The most famous conflict between Native Americans and the U.S. Army occurred in what is now Montana. On June 25, 1876, Sitting Bull, a great Sioux chief and medicine man, and Crazy Horse led an attack against U.S. Army forces that were under the command of General George Custer. Custer and his entire command were killed. Other famous Native Americans who fought courageously to protect their land were Apache leader Geronimo and his warriors in the Southwest, and Nez Perce Chief Joseph in present-day Idaho. The Indians were ultimately overcome by superior numbers and weapons, and by 1890, the survivors had been moved to reservations.

In the past, the media have often presented the Indian as villains rather than victim. To help students gain a different, and more accurate, perspective, read aloud slections from *A Multicultural Portrait of the Move West* by Petra Press (Marshall Cavendish, 1994), which looks at westward expansion from the Native American viewpoint. Assign students the task of reading different parts of the book and retelling their section to the class (you may want to read aloud to the class as an alternative). Have students discuss the challenges faced by the Native Americans, the responses tribes made to Westward expansion, and their own feelings about the plight of Native Americans today.

4. Frontier Women

Brief Background. Women played import roles on the frontier. They farmed, raised the children, and taught school, among other things. A few, like Calamity Jane and Annie Oakley, gained fame for their expert sharpshooting and toured in Wild West shows. One woman, Helen Hunt Jackson, who lived in Colorado, wrote movingly about the mistreatment of the Indians.

To give students an account of the role of women in the American West, read aloud *Buffalo Gals: Women of the Old West* by Brandon Marie Miller (Lerner, 1995), or another appropriate children's book. For the story of African American women on the western frontier, read aloud selections from *Black Women of the Old West* by William Loren Katz (Atheneum, 1995). Assign interested students the task of reporting on the life of a frontier woman. They can illustrate their presentation with pictures and maps.

5. Outlaws & Law Enforcers

Brief Background. A main reason the Wild West was called "wild" was because of its reputation for lawlessness: It was a place where justice was dispensed from the barrel of a six-shooter. The Wild West covered a vast, untamed country. There were simply too few law officers for too much territory. For example, from 1875 to 1896, one judge had sole responsibility for over 74,000 square miles and 60,000 people in Arkansas and Indian Territory. Among the criminal characters who gave the Wild West its infamous reputation, were Jesse James, Billy the Kid, Belle Starr, Charles Quantrell, the Dalton gang, and Cole Younger.

Have interested students gather information about these colorful outlaws, as well as about the following equally colorful enforcers of western law: "Wild Bill" Hickok, Wyatt Earp, "Bat" Masterson, and "Hanging Judge" Isaac Parker. Students can create brief scripts and skits that depict life in a frontier town inhabited by some of these colorful characters.

6. Routes West

Brief Background. The major pioneer routes to the West were the Mormon Trail, Santa Fe Trail, Oregon Trail, and California Trail as shown in Figure 48-1. A pioneer family traveling on one of these trails carried everything it owned in a covered wagon. The 2,000-mile Oregon Trail was the longest and most dangerous. Cattle were driven over several trails, including the Chisholm Trail, which led from San Antonio, Texas, to Abilene, Kansas. After the completion of the first continental railroad in 1869, it became a lot safer, easier,

and faster for people and goods to move across the country.

Discuss how the railroads affected the lives of the following frontier groups: Indians, miners, ranchers, shop owners, and farmers. To reinforce geographic concepts, make a large map of the western region (use an overhead projector to project an outline map of the western states on a white sheet and use a fabric pen to trace the outline of the region), place the map on the wall, and let students take turns finding different locations along the routes, using a reference map to guide them.

Science

1. The Environment of the Great Plains

Brief Background. Before the onrush of white settlers, the Great Plains was the habitat of the buffalo. These magnificent creatures once roamed the open plains in herds of ten thousand to ten million. Almost all of the Plains Indians' culture centered around the buffalo. From the buffalo's hide, muscle, bones, sinews, and hair came the Indians' food, clothing, shelter, tools, ornaments, and toys. The nomadic Plains Indians believed the land was precious, and they lived in harmony with the natural environment. In contrast, white settlers, as they pushed West, showed little concern for the natural environment, and they participated, directly and indirectly, in the destruction of the Indians' culture. The Indians were either killed or forcibly removed from their traditional hunting grounds, and the enormous herds of buffalo were slaughtered, almost to the point of extinction. Famous Wild West showman "Buffalo Bill" Cody gained his nickname by killing plenty of buffalo, including over 4,000 during an 18-month period.

Let students observe pictures and maps of the natural environment of the Great Plains. Point out the vast amount of territory that comprises the region, from Canada in the North to the Red River in the South. Almost every variety of climate, terrain, and soil can be found there. Although mostly treeless and bitterly cold in winter, the northern area populated by the Plains Indian was especially rich in animals and fish, and the river valleys were very fertile. Ask students to speculate about how Native Americans adapted to that environment. Discuss how the

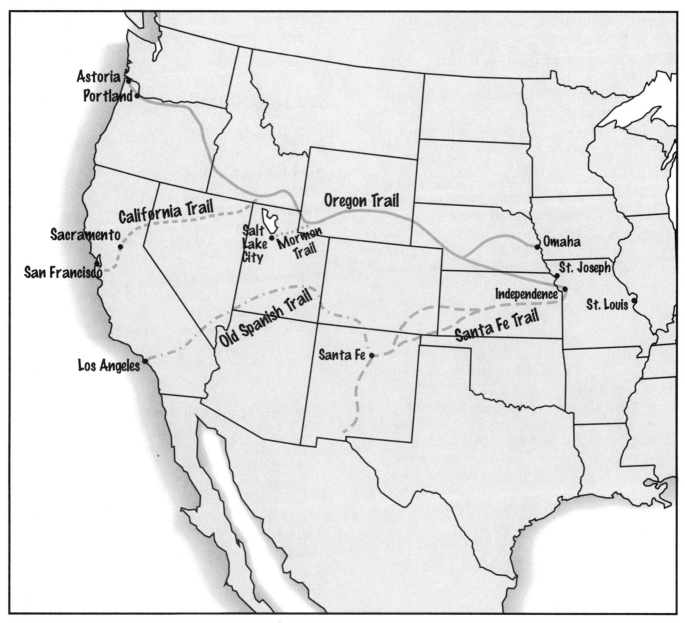

Routes West

FIGURE 48-1

geography of the region relates to the Indians' customs and lifestyle. Have students make a model of a Plains Indian settlement, complete with miniature tepees and tools. After students create their models, they can hypothesize about the Indians' impact on the environment, and compare it to the settlers'. What are the students' attitudes and ideas about saving the environment for future generations?

2. Saving the Buffalo From Extinction

Brief Background. Thanks to conservationists and other concerned Americans, efforts have been made to increase the buffalo population in the western United States. By the 1880s, there were only around 200 buffalo left in America. Today, they number in thousands and are protected in national parks and preserves and on private land.

Have students study the buffalo. They can read (or be told) about the buffalo, its habitat, and efforts to save it from extinction. Let interested students make illustrated drawings of the animal and its habitat. What can students do to help preserve and conserve natural environments in the local area?

Math:

1. The Business of Herding Cattle

Brief Background. Ranchers could make a tremendous profit driving Texas longhorns north to railway points in Kansas and Nebraska, such as Dodge City, Abilene and Ogallala, known as "cow towns."

Put your students in the boots of a western rancher. Tell them to imagine they are ranchers whose job is to organize a crew of cowpunchers to drive a big herd of cattle up north. Have students use their subtraction and multiplication skills to calculate the profit on the sale of the cattle. Give them the following information:

- There are 3,000 cattle in the herd.
- The rancher paid $4 for each cow.
- Each cow sold for $35.
- The crew consisted of ten cowhands.
- Each cowhand was paid $40 a month.
- The cattle drive took three months.
- The cattle fed on the free range grass.

Music:

1. Sing a Cowhand Song

Brief Background. A cowpuncher's life was often hard and lonely. To calm the cattle at night, some cowhands would sing as they guarded the herd, and they also sang while sitting around the campfire in the evening.

Let students sing along with audiotapes of traditional cowboy folk songs, such as "Home on the Range" and "Doney Gal." Possible sources for audiocassettes are the school media center, music teacher, teacher resource store, and community library.

2. Square Dance

Two square-dance tunes the children would enjoy are "Red River Valley" and "Skip To My Lou." The music teacher, parents, or other teachers, might be able to provide music tapes and dancing instructions, if needed.

Language Arts:

1. Tall Tales

Brief Background. The greatest cowboy of them all was the legendary Pecos Bill. He rode cyclones, dug the Rio Grande River, and tied rattlesnakes together to make a lasso, to name just a few of his mythical exploits.

Introduce your students to a tall tale about Pecos Bill (some elementary-level reading programs include a Pecos Bill story, or check your school's media center for one). After students hear about Pecos Bill, encourage them to create their own legends about the Wild West.

2. Words of the Old West

The Wild West contributed many words to America's vocabulary. Some of the words were either Spanish, such as "amigo," or came from Spanish, such as "rodeo." Have students create a Wild West glossary of frontier words. To get them started, have them check and report on the meaning of the following words:

ranch	chile	taco
lasso	dogies (calves)	puncher (driver of a herd of cattle)
fiesta		
	rodeo	
ten-gallon hat	sombrero	chaps
		stampede
forty-niner	maverick	

3. Cattle Brands

Brief Background. Branding irons were used to show who owned western cattle. The design of a particular brand was determined by the creativity and imagination of the owner of the cattle. Draw the brands below on the chalkboard and challenge students to "read" them aloud. (The way to say the name each brand is in parentheses.)

(Double H) (Running W) (Lazy Nine) (Box T)

Ask students to create their own designs for brands and decide how the brands should be pronounced. Then, have students take turns displaying their brands, and let the class try to guess how they are pronounced.

Cooking:

1. Chuck Wagon Meal

Brief Background. An important part of the cattle drives were the cook and his chuck wagon.

(*Chuck* was a western expression for food.) The chuck wagon contained all of the food, cooking equipment, and eating utensils for the cowhands. Chuck wagon cooks came up with some interesting dishes, like son-of-a-gun stew and frying-pan bread.

Your students should enjoy the following simple, yet tasty, cowhand-style meal. To the extent possible, let students prepare and serve the meal.

CHUCK WAGON BISCUITS AND BEANS

Biscuits:

2 cups all-purpose flour
3 tsp baking powder
1/4 cup margarine
2/3 cup milk
2 tbsp confectioner sugar

Directions: Put flour in a large bowl and stir in baking powder. Blend in margarine. Stir in sugar, then stir in milk. Knead dough into a ball. With a rolling pin, roll dough until 3/4 inches thick. Use 2-inch round cookie cutter to form 12 biscuits. Place on greased cookie sheet and bake in preheated (425° F) oven for 7–10 minutes, or until done.

Beans:

1 16 oz. can of baked beans
1 small onion, finely chopped
1 tbsp honey
1/2 tsp of chili powder
1 tbsp cooking oil
3 oz. grated cheese (optional)

Directions: Heat oil in skillet and cook chopped onions until they are translucent. Add beans, chili powder, and honey, and heat thoroughly. Serve the biscuits and beans open-faced sandwich style. Cut the biscuits in half, and place a small amount of beans on top of each half. Sprinkle grated cheese on top if desired. Serves 24.

Books:

1. Collins, James L. (1990). *Lawmen of the Old West*. New York: Franklin Watts. Intermediate.

2. Stein, R. Conrad. (1978). *The Story of the Homestead Act*. Chicago: Children's Press. Primary, Intermediate.

3. Press, Petra. (1994). *A Multicultural Portrait of the Move West*. New York: Marshall Cavendish. Advanced.

4. Matthews, Leonard J. (1989). *The Wild West in American History: Cowboys*. Vero Beach, FL: Rourke Publications. Intermediate.

5. May, Robin. (1978). *The Wild West*. London: Macdonald Educational Ltd. Intermediate.

6. Lyons, Grant. (1981). *Mustangs, Six-Shooters and Barbed Wire: How the West Was Really Won*. New York: Julian Messner. Intermediate, Advanced .

7. Alter, Judith. (1989). *Growing Up in the Old West*. New York: Franklin Watts. Primary, Intermediate.

8. Freedman, Russell. (1985). *Cowboys of the Wild West*. New York: Clarion Books. Intermediate.

9. Freedman, Russell. (1983). *Children of the Wild West*. New York: Clarion Books. Intermediate.

10. Berry, Erick. (1966). *When Wagon Trains Rolled to Santa Fe*. Champaign, IL: Ganard Publishing Co. Intermediate.

11. Katz, William Loren. (1995). *Black Women of the Old West*. New York: Atheneum. Intermediate, Advanced.

12. Schlissel, Lillian. (1995). *Black Frontiers: A History of African American Heroes in the Old West*. New York: Simon and Schuster. Intermediate, Advanced.

13. Miller, Robert. (1995). *The Story Nat Love*. Englewood Cliffs, NJ: Silver Press.

14. Miller, Brandon Marie. (1995). *Buffalo Gals: Women of the Old West*. Minneapolis: Lerner Publications.

Software:

1. *Oregon Trail* [AppleII Mac IBM Windows]. Minneapolis: MECC. Advanced.

2. *Wyatt Earp's Old West* [Mac MPC CD-ROM]. Danbury, CT: Crolier Electronic Publishing. Advanced.

3. *Apple Pie Music: Music of American History* [Mac MPC CD-ROM]. Fairfield, CT: Queue. Intermediate, Advanced.

49

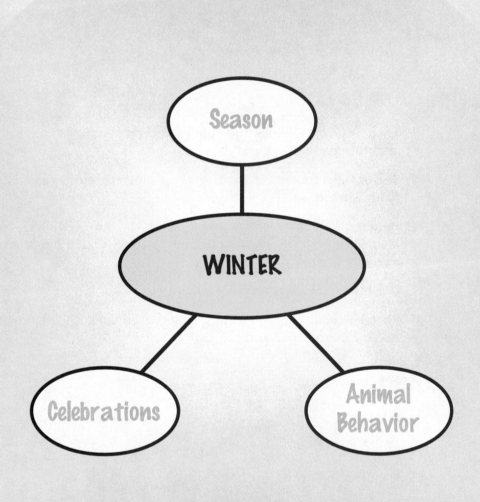

Theme Goals:

Students will:

1. compare and contrast wintertime celebrations in the United States and around the world.

2. understand why there are four seasons.

3. explain what selected animals do in winter.

4. observe characteristics of a winter environment.

5. gather and record weather data.

6. compose a book about winter.

7. create winter scenes.

Theme Concepts:

1. There is great religious and cultural diversity in the United States and throughout the word.

2. Seasons change as the Earth goes around the sun because the Earth is tilted.

3. Because the Earth receives less solar energy during winter, some plants and animals die or become inactive, and some animals travel to warmer places.

4. During winter, days are shorter and nights are longer.

5. There are many sights, feelings, sounds, activities, and places that make winter a special time.

Vocabulary:

1. solstice

2. Christmas

3. Hanukkah

4. Kwanzaa

5. piñata

6. menorah

7. hibernate

Instructional Bulletin Board

The purpose of this bulletin board is to help students learn about the many special things that happen in wintertime. Encourage students to find appropriate pictures in magazines to add to the bulletin board.

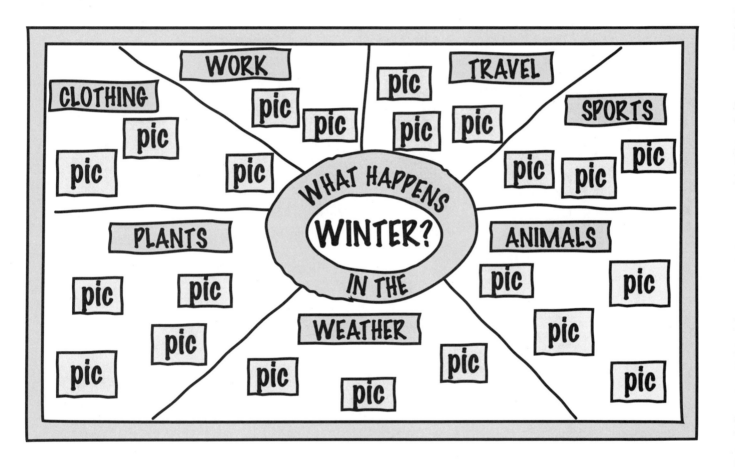

Parent Letter

Dear Parents:

We our beginning our study of winter. In many parts of the United States winter means frosty mornings, chilly days, and landscapes transformed into white-carpeted wonderlands. Winter is also a time when most Americans celebrate some of their most cherished holidays. Some of the questions students will be examining in school include:

At School:

- Why is it so dark and cold in many parts of the United States the wintertime?
- Why are there different seasons?
- What do animals do in the winter?
- What can we observe outside on a winter day?
- How can we compose a book about wintertime?

At Home:

Spend some time outdoors enjoying the winter weather with your child. Have him or her draw a picture of some activity you did together. Your child can bring the picture to school and share it with the class.

Linking Up:

Ask students to discuss their favorite wintertime activities. What do they like to do best? Are most of the items on the students' lists outdoor or indoor activities?

Social Studies:

1. Wintertime Celebrations

Brief Background. Winter is a time when many religions and cultural groups participate in special celebrations. Many ancient peoples who lived in the higher latitudes celebrated winter solstice: It marked the end of longer nights and the return of longer days. Our modern-day practice of burning a Yule log at Christmas time is derived from the ancient pagan custom of burning a large log to honor the sun.

To expose students to information about the religious and cultural diversity present in the United States and throughout the world, compare and contrast selected aspects of the celebrations described below. (Note: Remember that the purpose of the following activities is to teach about holidays rather than celebrate holidays. Before implementing any of the activities, check your school's policy regarding the teaching of the wintertime holidays.) To provide students with interesting background information, read aloud selections from *Winter Festivals* by Mike Rosen (Bookwright Press, 1990) and other appropriate children's books that show some of the fascinating customs exhibited in these winter celebrations. Assign small groups of students the task of researching one of the winter celebrations in depth. Gather library books and other reference media on wintertime holidays around the world and place them in a learning center located in a special area of the classroom. Decorate the center with wintertime scenes. If possible, invite parent volunteers to supervise the center. They can read stories, explain directions for activities, and provide individual guidance.

2. Christmas Around the World

Brief Background. Christmas (December 25) commemorates the birth of Jesus Christ, founder of Christianity. The word *Christmas* means *Christ's Mass.* For Christians around the world, Christmas is a time of worship and great joy. Churches are decorated with manger scenes that show the baby Jesus, Christmas carols are sung, and the story of Christ's birth is retold. Different countries and cultures have established their own unique Christmas-season symbols and traditions. In the United States, Christmas cards are exchanged, Christmas trees are decorated with colorful ornaments, families have a traditional Christmas dinner, gifts are exchanged, and according to legend, on Christmas Eve, Santa Claus brings gifts to the homes of children who have been good throughout the previous year. Some Christmas customs practiced in the United States come from Britain. They include exchanging Christmas cards, hanging mistletoe, caroling, and lighting candles in the windows. Father Christmas is the British counterpart of our Santa Claus. The custom of decorating Christmas trees with cookies and cakes probably originated in Germany. From Saint Nicholas, German children receive gifts of sweets, which they open on St. Nicholas Day, December 6. In Mexico, a traditional custom at Christmas is breaking the *piñata*, a papier-mache or clay figure filled with treats.

3. Hanukkah (Note: Although technically Hanukkah usually falls in late autumn, it is included here as a "wintertime" celebration.)

Hanukkah, which means "dedication," is an important Jewish festival that usually is celebrated in December. It commemorates the Jews' defeat of the Syrians in 165 B.C. The Syrians had tried to force the Jews to give up their religion. After their victory, the Jews cast the Syrian idols out of the Temple in Jerusalem and held a feast there in celebration to God for their newly regained religious freedom. Another name for Hanukkah is the Feast of Lights. Each evening during the eight days of celebration, a candle is lighted on a special eight-branched candleholder, called a *menorah*.

4. Kwanzaa

Brief Background. *Kwanzaa* is a winter season holiday celebrated by African Americans. It begins on December 26 and lasts seven days. Kwanzaa, which means "first fruits," is based upon traditional African harvest festivals. Each day of the festival is devoted to one of the following principles of black culture: *Umoja* (unity); *Kujichagulia* (self-determination); *Ujima* (collective work and responsibility); *Ujamaa* (cooperative economics); *Nia* (purpose); *Kuumba* (creativity), and *Imani* (faith). Read aloud selections from *Seven Candles for Kwanzaa* by Andrea Davis Pinkney (Dial, 1996), or another appropriate children's book, that describes the Kwanzaa celebration in detail.

5. Chinese New Year

Brief Background. Chinese New Year occurs sometime between January 21 and February 20. Traditional Chinese New Year rituals are performed in honor of family gods. One of them, the god of the kitchen, is described in Mike Rosen's excellent book, *Winter Festivals* (The Bookwright Press, 1990). One week before the new year, members of the household conduct a ceremony that releases the god of the kitchen so it can journey to the Emperor of Heaven. On New Year's Eve a feast and other ceremonies are held to welcome the god back to the house. Also on New Year's Eve, money and gifts are exchanged. On New Year's Day everyone goes outside to watch a procession that features dancers holding a giant paper dragon. The dragon twists and turns its way through the street to the musical accompaniment of drums.

Have students make their own dragons. They can form the body and tail from a section of cardboard or Styrofoam egg carton and make the dragon's head from a Styrofoam ball as shown.

Science:

1. Winter Solstice

The length of days changes as the Earth goes around the Sun because the Earth is tilted. The Earth is always tilted the same way as it revolves around the Sun (see diagram). When the North Pole is tilted away from the Sun, the northern half of the Earth has short days and long nights. During this time of the year, it is winter in the Northern Hemisphere. On the winter solstice in the Northern Hemisphere, December 21 or 22, the sun is directly over the Tropic of Capricorn. This is the shortest day of the year. To introduce or review the changing seasons, demonstrate the journey of the Earth around the Sun diagrammed in Figure 49-2 (use a globe and a bright spotlight; the person holding the spotlight should keep the light beam trained on the globe; remember to keep the tilted position of the Earth constant as you make your way around the spotlight). Let students make their own globes out of oranges or balls of modeling clay. They can stick a pencil all the way through the center of the orange or ball of clay to represent the imaginary axis of the tilted earth. A line to represent the equator can be drawn (with a Magic Marker) around the orange or etched with a stick around the clay. When the globes are made, put students in small groups, give each group a flashlight, and let group members take turns moving their "earths" around the "sun."

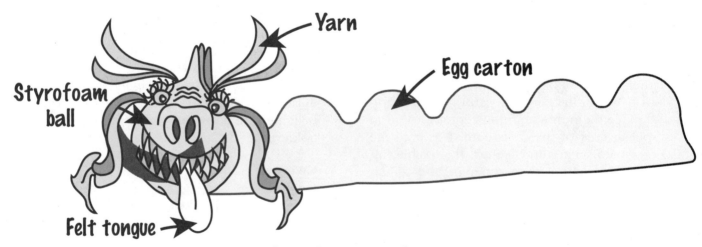

Egg-Carton Dragon

FIGURE 49-1

514

2. What Do Animals Do in the Winter?

Because the Earth receives less solar energy during winter, some plants and animals die or become inactive, and some animals travel to warmer places. To help students learn what happens to animals in winter, provide an assortment of books and other resources on animals. Ask students to name various animals. List them on the chalkboard, and then ask students what the animals do to survive the winter. Some animals, such as cardinals, deer, and wolves, remain active in winter. Many animals hibernate, or pass the winter in a resting state that protects them from the cold. The body temperature of hibernating animals drops considerably, which reduces the amount of energy they need to stay alive. Among the hibernators are the following animals: nighthawks, bats, chipmunks, ground squirrels, hamsters, frogs, toads, lizards, snakes, and turtles. Some animals migrate to warmer places (including many songbirds, whales, ducks, geese, terns, as well as some insects). Monarch butterflies can fly thousands of miles to reach their winter homes in the southern United States and central Mexico. To help students learn what happens to summer insects, read aloud selections from *Where Do They Go? Insects in Winter* by Millicent E. Selsam (Four Winds Press, 1982), or some other appropriate children's book that describes insect behavior. Students will probably

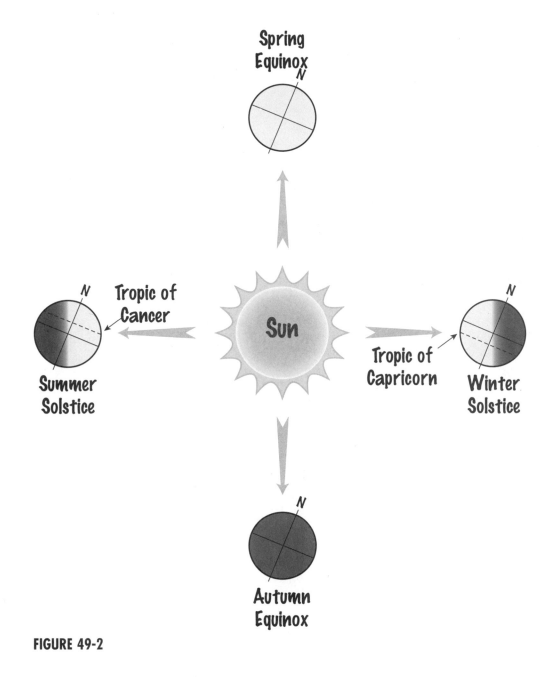

FIGURE 49-2

be surprised to learn that although they are out of sight, many kinds of insects are still nearby, hidden under bark and stones, or burrowed in the ground.

3. Winter Walk

Take the class on a winter walk. Have students observe the condition of trees and other plants, while looking for signs of animal life. When students return to the classroom, let them draw pictures of their observations.

Math:

1. Winter Weather Report

During winter, days are becoming increasingly longer, but they are still shorter than nights. Have students check daily newspapers to find out the time of sunrise and sunset. They can calculate the length (in hours and minutes) of each day and record the amount of daylight on a chart. They can also check a thermometer mounted outside the classroom window and record the daily temperature on another chart. What changes in amount of daylight and temperature occur over time? What do the results of their analysis tell them about seasonal changes?

Language Arts:

1. A Winter Book

Have the class compose a book about winter. Make each child responsible for one page in the book. Each page of the book should include a few facts or feelings about winter and a colorful illustration. Have students consider developing pages on winter that answer these questions: When is the first day of winter? What are winter days and nights like? How does my neighborhood change in winter? What happens to animals in winter? What happens to plants in winter? What holidays are held in winter? What is the best thing about winter? What is the worst thing about winter? What does a maple tree (or some other kind) look like in winter? What is the temperature like in winter? What is the weather like in winter? What is the best winter sport? Where is the best place to visit in the winter? What food tastes best in the winter?

2. Winter Words

Have students generate a list of winter words that fall under the following categories. To get them thinking, give students the words listed here.

Weather	Activities	Places	Sounds
frosty	skiing	ice rink	whine
blustery	skating	North Pole	howl
freezing	shoveling	slopes	crunch

Art:

1. Winter Wonderland

Give students a piece of poster board and an assortment of art materials (Magic Markers, crayons, paints, brushes, glue, different colored construction paper, cotton balls, yard, pieces of cloth, etc.), and let them create winter scenes to display on the wall.

Books:

1. Sanders, John. (1984). *All About Animal Migrations.* Mahwah, NJ: Troll Associates. Intermediate.

2. Gundersheimer, Karen. (1982). *Happy Winter.* Harper & Row Publishers. Primary.

3. Prelutsky, Jack. (1984). *It's Snowing! It's Snowing!* New York: Greenwillow Books. Primary, Intermediate.

4. Cole, Joanna. (1973). *Plants in Winter.* New York: Thomas Y. Crowell Company. Primary, Intermediate.

5. Gibbons, Gail. (1995). *The Reasons for the Seasons*. New York: Holiday House. Primary, Intermediate.

6. Selsam, Millicent E. (1982). *Where Do They Go? Insects in Winter*. New York: Four Winds Press. Intermediate, Advanced.

7. Hirschi, Ron. (1990). *Winter*. New York: Cobblehill Books. Primary.

8. Davis, Bette J. (1973). *Winter Buds*. New York: Lothrop, Lee, & Shepard Co. Intermediate, Advanced.

9. Rosen, Mike. (1990). *Winter Festivals*. New York: The Bookwright Press. Intermediate.

10. Jackson, Ellen. (1994). *The Winter Solstice*. Brookfield, CT: The Millbrook Press. Primary.

11. Kleven, Elisa. (1996). *¡Viva! . . . ¡Una Piñata!*. New York: Dutton. Primary.

12. Jaffe, Nina, and August, Louise. (1996). *In the Month of Kislev*. New York: Viking. Intermediate.

13. Pinkney, Andrea Davis. (1996). *Seven Candles for Kwanzaa*. New York: Dial. Intermediate, Advanced.

Software:

1. *Changing Seasons/Children & Seasons* [Laserdisc]. Chicago: Encyclopaedia Britannica. Primary, Intermediate.

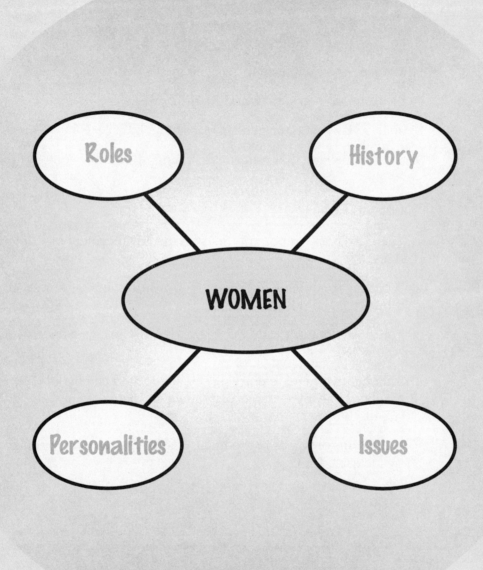

Theme Goals:

Students will:

1. identify important "firsts" in the advancement of women's rights.

2. identify women from different backgrounds and cultures who have made contributions to the development of America.

3. describe experiences of ordinary women in American history.

4. appreciate the point of view of women as they struggled for equal rights.

5. analyze their attitudes and preferences.

6. examine the qualifications for different science-related jobs.

7. measure women's track and field records.

8. analyze language for gender bias

9. create a collage that reflects the changing role of women.

Theme Concepts:

1. There are many important "firsts" in the advancement of women's rights.

2. Women from many different backgrounds and cultures contributed to the development of America.

3. The first women's rights convention was held at Seneca Falls, NY, in 1848.

4. Although women are entering science-related careers in growing numbers, the percentage of women in many of these fields is still quite low.

5. Male forms of words in the English language have been replaced by inclusive forms.

Vocabulary:

1. equality

2. gender

Instructional Bulletin Board

The purpose of this bulletin board is to let students match the names of famous women with their contributions to the development of America. On the left side of the board, use Velcro patches to attach name cards for eight women. Next to the names, attach the pictures of the women, if available. On the right side of the bulletin board attach a flip chart for each woman. Use manila folders for the flip charts. On the outside cover of the flip chart, write the contribution, and inside, write the name of the woman who made it. Attach a Velcro patch at the bottom of each flip chart. Students can remove the name cards from the left side and try to match them with the correct contributions by attaching the name cards to the Velcro patches under the flip charts. After a student tries to match names and contributions, he can check answers by flipping the covers up to reveal the correct names.

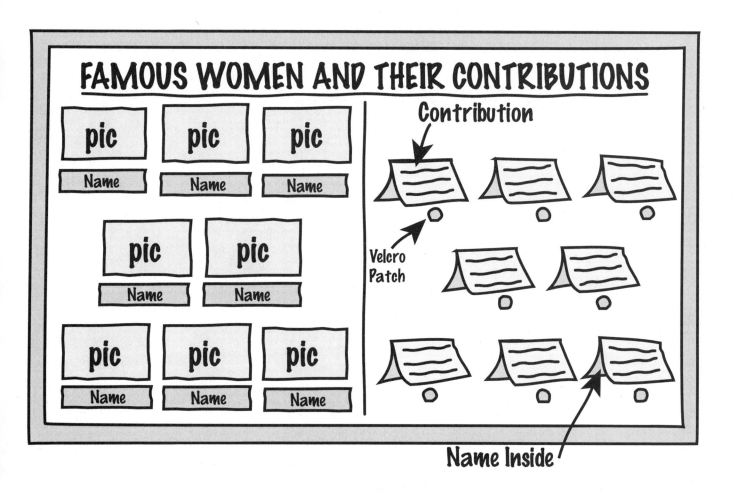

Parent Letter

Dear Parents:

We are beginning the study of a theme that focuses on the contributions of women to the development of America. Some are famous Americans, such as Sacajawea (Native American member of the Lewis and Clark Expedition), Deborah Sampson (Revolutionary War soldier), and Rosa Parks (civil rights activist). Others are unsung heroes whose accomplishments are only just beginning to receive the attention they deserve.

At School:

During our study of women, students will be engaged in the following activities:

* Making a time line of women's "firsts"
* Studying the lives of ordinary women
* Exploring science-related career opportunities
* Identifying women inventors and their inventions
* Analyzing changes in attitudes and expectations

At Home:

Select a biography of an important woman in American history to read aloud to your child.

Linking Up:

Ask students to name women who have made important contributions to history and modern society. What names appear on the students' list?

Social Studies:

1. Famous "Firsts" for Women

Brief Background. Throughout history and across different societies, there has been a pattern of inequality in male and female roles. In general, men have dominated women, and women have been restricted to lower-status positions in society, compared to men. Slowly but surely, these inequities are being eliminated.

To help students recognize some of the important positive changes that have occurred, have them make a large, illustrated time line that shows the following historic "firsts" in the advancement of women's social, economic, and political rights. Display the completed time line on the wall of the classroom. The first:

- woman to receive a U.S. patent (Mary Kies, 1809)
- college to accept women students (Oberlin, 1833)
- women's rights convention was held (Seneca Falls, NY, 1848)
- woman to receive a medical degree (Elizabeth Blackwell, 1849)
- woman to be ordained a minister (Antoinette Brown, 1852)
- four-year college for women (Vassar, 1865)
- labor union to admit women (Cigar-makers, 1867)
- woman to be admitted to a state bar to practice law (Arbella Mansfield, 1869)
- state to grant women the right to vote (Wyoming, 1890)
- nation to grant women full voting rights (New Zealand, 1893)
- U.S. military service for women (Army Nurse Corps, 1901)
- woman elected to the U.S. House of Representatives (Jeanette Rankin of Montana, 1916)
- time women could vote in every state (1920)

- woman elected governor (Nellie Ross of Wyoming, 1924)
- woman to fly solo across the Atlantic Ocean (Amelia Earhart, 1932)
- woman elected to the U.S. Senate (Hattie Caraway of Arkansas, 1932).
- woman appointed to the president's cabinet (Frances Perkins, Secretary of Labor, 1932)
- woman justice of U.S. Supreme Court (Sandra Day O'Connor, 1981)
- American woman in space (Sally Ride, 1983)
- woman vice-presidential nominee (Geraldine Ferraro, 1984)

2. Black Women Who Made a Difference

Brief Background. The struggle for equality by black women in American society has been extra difficult. They have had to deal with the barriers of both gender *and* racism.

Read aloud selections about the lives of black women—some famous, but others unsung heroes—who have made a difference in *Famous Firsts of Black Women* by Martha Ward Plowden (Pelican Publishing, 1993), or another appropriate book for young readers. Among the profiles included are: Mary McLeod Bethune, the first black women to head a federal office; Marian Anderson, the first African American women to sing, as a regular cast member, an important role at the famous Metropolitan Opera Company; Wilma Rudolph, the first black woman to win three gold medals in track and field in a single Olympics; Hattie McDaniel, the first back woman to win an Oscar; and Maggie Walker, the first African American woman bank president. Include famous firsts by black women in the time line activity (Social Studies Activity #1). Encourage interested students to do research and then present oral reports on these inspiring trailblazers. As a follow-up project, have a panel of distinguished black women from the community speak to the class about their accomplishments, as well as about any barriers they have had to overcome.

3. Women in American History Learning Center

Many women from different backgrounds and cultures have made and are making contributions to the development of America. They include names like Pocahontas, Sacajawea, Deborah Sampson, Elizabeth Blackwell, Jane Addams, Harriet Beecher Stowe, Harriet Tubman, Eleanor Roosevelt, Rosa Parks, Barbara Jordan, and Sandra Day O'Connor. Transform a section of the classroom into a center for the study of women in American history. A small area with a bookshelf and a couple of chairs will do nicely. Decorate the area with a colorful sign that identifies the center and with pictures of two or three prominent women from American history. Gather biographies of important American women and put them on the bookshelf. To enhance motivation, generate a list of interesting and researchable questions pertaining to the biographies. Then, challenge students to use the biographies to find the answers.

4. Ordinary Women

To bring the experiences of ordinary American women into the classroom, use background information from *The Young Oxford History of Women in the United States: Volumes 1–10*, edited by Nancy F. Cott (Oxford University Press, 1994). This unique series is the first history of the public and private lives of American women from colonial times to the present. The first volume deals with Native American women confronting colonialism, while the last volume, entitled "The Road to Equality," examines American women since 1962. Although the text is too difficult for most young readers, the books are profusely illustrated, and the period paintings, engravings, and photographs will give students a vivid image of women's struggles, contributions, and changing roles over the past four centuries.

5. Women's Movement

Brief Background. In 1848, the first women's rights convention was held at Seneca Falls, NY. The delegates to the convention called for women to be accorded all the rights and privileges of American citizenship. Yet, despite the subsequent efforts of women like Susan B. Anthony, Lucy Stone, and others, women were not granted the right to vote until 1920.

Pocahontas

Harriet Tubman

Sandra Day O'Connor

Eleanor Roosevelt

Rosa Parks

Beverly Sills

Sketches of Famous Women

FIGURE 50-1

To help students appreciate how women back then might have felt about their unequal treatment, stage a mock election in which only females can be nominated and only females can vote. Since all of the students are "citizens" of the classroom, a lively discussion should ensue regarding the unfairness of excluding males from participation in the election process. Relate the unfair classroom election to the unfair political conditions that American women once faced: Prior to 1920, although women were citizens, they did not have the right to vote.

6. "Gender Gap"

Social scientists tell us that attitudes and values of male and female voters differ on some issues. For example, female voters seem to favor social programs, while male voters tend to favor military spending. Help students develop and administer a simple questionnaire designed to analyze students' attitudes. Would you predict a "gender gap" in the way male and female students would respond to these questions?

1. Do you like school?
   Yes   No
2. What school subject do you like best?
   _____
3. What is your favorite TV program?
   _____
4. What is your favorite sport? _____
5. What is your favorite hobby? _____

Science:

1. Breaking Down Barriers

Help students list science-related jobs that have traditionally been held by men, such as commercial airline pilot, astronaut, physician, physicist, chemist, pharmacist, military pilot, college science professor, engineer, dentist, forest ranger, naturalist, astronomer, computer scientist, and high school science teacher. Although more and more women are entering science-related occupations, the percentage of women in many of these fields is still quite low. For example, only around 10 percent of dentists are female. Provide students with information about different science-related jobs, and help them answer the following questions for each one:

What are the qualifications for the job? What do people do in this job? and, Can males and females do the job equally well? Invite women who hold science-related positions to class to talk about their careers.

2. Women Inventors

For most of America's history, women were expected to stay home and raise children while men went on to college and careers. Some women, however, refused to let society's expectations for them inhibit their inventive genius. To introduce students to some of these creative and resourceful women, read aloud selections from *Feminine Ingenuity: Women and Invention in America* by Anne L. Macdonald (Ballantine Books, 1992), or other appropriate books for younger readers. Included among the women your students should meet are: Mary Kies, who was the first woman to be granted a U.S. patent; Catherine Greene, who helped Eli Whitney perfect the cotton gin; Sybilla Masters, whose machine pounded corn into cornmeal; and Margaret Knight, who was called the "Woman Edison." Assign each student a woman inventor to investigate. Students can present oral reports to the class. Included with each report should be an accurate drawing of the invention.

Math:

1. Women Record Holders

Provide small groups of students with women's world and Olympic track and field records (records are listed in world almanacs), and have them use instruments to measure the records in the hallway, gym, or outdoors on the playground. Include current records for the following field events: high jump, shot put, long jump, triple jump, discus, and javelin.

2. Women in the News

Have students record the number of times women are mentioned in the following sections of the daily newspapers: front page, sports, business, film and entertainment, and editorial. Are women mentioned more often or less often than men in each of the sections? What might account for any differences noted?

Language Arts:

1. Changing Words for Changing Times

Words in the English language are changing to reflect changing attitudes and values about women's and men's traditional roles in society. Male forms of words for occupations and positions are seen and heard less and less. They have been replaced by inclusive forms, represented by the words in the column to the right below. Discuss the changes. Have students ever heard or seen the old male forms of the words? Do students favor inclusive forms? Why, or why not?

Male Forms	Inclusive Forms
policeman	police officer
fireman	firefighter
postman	letter carrier
fisherman	angler
sportsman	sports person
workman	worker
chairman	chair
headman	head

Art:

1. Expanding Opportunities Collage

Let students make a collage that shows women's expanding opportunities in various sectors of society. Provide students with an assortment of profusely illustrated magazines, scissors, and glue. Then, let them cut out pictures of women engaged in various activities that represent their expanding role. Finally, students can glue their pictures on a large sheet of white paper to create the collage.

Books:

1. Kirby, Mona. (1989). *Beverly Sills, America's Own Opera Star*. New York: Penguin Group. Advanced.

2. Jacobs, William Jay. (1991). *Eleanor Roosevelt: A Life of Happiness and Tears*. Lakeville, CT: Grey Castle Press. Advanced.

3. Rosen, Dorothy Schack. (1995). *A Fire in Her Bones: The Story of Mary Lyon*. Minneapolis: Carolrodha Books. Intermediate.

4. Greene, Carol. (1991). *Elizabeth Blackwell, First Woman Doctor*. Chicago: Children's Press. Primary.

5. Adler, David. (1992). *A Picture Book of Harriet Tubman*. New York: Holiday House. Primary, Intermediate.

6. Adler, David. (1992). *A Picture Book of Sojourner Truth*. New York: Holiday House. Primary, Intermediate.

7. Gherman, Beverly. (1991). *Sandra Day O'Connor*. New York: Viking Penguin. Advanced.

8. Glassman, Bruce. (1992). *Wilma Mankiller: Chief of the Cherokee Nation*. New York: Blackbirch Press. Advanced.

9. Pelz, Ruth. (1995). *Women of the Wild West*. Seattle: Open Hand Publishing. Advanced.

10. McKissack, Patrician, and McKissack, Frederick. (1992). *Zora Neale Hurston: Writer and Storyteller*. Hillside, NJ: Enslow Publishers Inc. Intermediate.

11. Macdonald, Anne L. (1992). *Feminine Ingenuity: Women and Invention in America*. New York: Ballantine Books. Advanced.

12. Plowden, Martha Ward. (1993). *Famous Firsts of Black Women*. Gretna, LA: Pelican Publishing Company.

13. *The Young Oxford History of Women in the United States: Volumes 1–10*. (1994). ed. Nancy F. Cott. NY: Oxford University Press.

Software:

1. *TimeLiner 4.0: Women in History* [AppleII Mac Windows]. Watertown, MA: Tom Synder Productions. Primary, Intermediate, Advanced.

2. *Her Heritage* [Mac MPC CD-ROM]. Cambrix Publishing. Advanced.

3. *A Women's Place* [VHS]. View Video. Advanced.